To my children, Mira Linda and Ira Jay, with whom I grew up and regained my lost childhood. And because I wanted to set a good example, I strived to grow in mind. I thank them for the privilege of becoming a grandmother to three handsome and upstanding young men—Aylon, Michael Drake, Brian Harris.

To my mother and father, who died much too young. To my sister Fraida, who never lived to see her children become adults and her two children who hadn't been given a chance to grow up. To my little sister Edzia, who's soul wouldn't allow me to die with typhus and knocked the fever out of me with a broom. To my aunts Pearl, Hudesa, and Hanna. And to all my cousins and marters who died by the hands of hate and ignorance.

I especially dedicate this book to my beloved sister, Bela, herself a child, given the role of mother and died, though in freedom, but much too young, and I will never stop grieving for her.

Acknowledgement:

Thank you, Adele Engel. After telling the surface of my story to colleges, high schools, and universities, and some small parts of my story to friends, everyone encouraged me to write my story. Only you took precious time to help me with proofreading. You and your husband, Lou, are real friends indeed.

Chapter One: Returning to Memories of Horror

Los Angeles International Airport was a busy place today, July 1985. Parents attempted to calm restless children in the long lines at the check-in counters. Others strained their necks to read the bulletins for arrivals and departures. A tall man pulling two large, bulging suitcases on wheels and a carry-on on each shoulder rushed through the double doors to stand in line behind my friend, Carla Stevenson. I judged him to be in his early thirties. A petite brunette with wavy hair bouncing on her shoulders followed the man in quick short steps and stopped in front of him. I guessed her to be in her mid twenties. The man pushed the suitcases aside and gently took his wife's left hand and kissed the finger with the large diamond and matching wedding band. I looked on with a little bit of envy and wondered how different my life would have been, had my childhood and teenage life not been destroyed? How it would feel to go out on a first date, or go to prom, fall in love, and marry the man of my dreams.

"Newlyweds?" I asked.

A tress of brown hair covered the man's right eye as he looked lovingly at his bride and nodded.

"We are going to New York on our honeymoon," he said, still holding his bride's small hand in his large hand.

I congratulated the young couple and sincerely wished them a long happy life together.

After checking in our luggage, we stood facing the large windows and watched the comings and goings of the planes.

"Are you sure you are going to Poland with me because you think you'll enjoy the country, not because you know I would be too chicken to go alone?" I asked Carla.

Carla Stevenson is five feet ten inches tall, to my five feet. She placed both hands on my shoulders and towered over me. Her blue eyes sparkled on my green. "Come on, Yaja. How many times must I tell you, I always wanted to visit Poland? With your knowledge of the Polish language, it will make my trip so much more interesting," she smiled, straightened to her full height, and ran her fingers through short strawberry blond hair.

"Thank you Carla, you're a good friend. If I were to go alone, I'm not sure I would have had the courage to carry out my mission.

I was concerned that the people living in the cull-de-sac would see strangers asking questions. Someone might remember that Jews once lived on Plac Stare Miasto six, and I didn't want Carla to get hurt because of me, for that's the way it was during the German occupation. A bearded man with stooped shoulders wearing the black garb was an easy target. Otherwise, the Germans didn't know the difference between a Polish Jew and a Polish Catholic until the white armbands with the Star of David insignia were enforced. The main fear was that a Polish neighbor would point him or her out to a German, which was a frequent occurrence.

We sat down on the blue plastic airport chairs, and Carla began a conversation with a woman sitting next to her. Suddenly, I became anxious. What if I was unable to protect my friend? What if the Polish Police found out that I was Jewish and arrested me for escaping from Poland at the end of 1945? What if I could never see my children again? I unzipped my purse and removed my passport. I was anxious to see where it read that I was a United States Citizen. In large letters I read, "United States Of America." I still didn't see where it said that I was a citizen of the United States of America. As I silently began to panic, I saw it "The Secretary of the United States Of America hereby requests all whom it may concern to permit the citizen, national of the United States, named herein to pass without delay or hindrance, and in case of need, to give all lawful aid and protection." I proudly clutched the passport to my chest and closed my eyes. I visualized the cull-de-sac where I played as a child, and my mind went back to May 1945. Six years of war against innocent Jewish people had come to an end much too late. I survived five concentration camps. If there is such a thing as hell, then I had been there. I had returned to Poland. The name of the town where I was born is called Radom. The only home I knew before everyone in it that I loved had vanished.

Radom lies in the very heart of Poland, eighty kilometers south of Warsaw. Before World War II, the population in Radom had been one hundred thousand, thirty thousand of which were Jews. The Jews played a vital part in the economic development. Radom was the center of the leather industry. Seventy percent were Jewish-owned, creating employment for over one hundred tanneries and shoe factories.

Jews pioneered in developing iron works, lumber mills, furniture factories, chemical plants, soap and candle factories, brick and ceramic factories, and much more. The products were exported to many European countries, and thousands of people enjoyed secure employment.

I was only a teenager when I returned from the camps, and at a glance, I could see that nothing had changed. The very moment I had stepped foot on Polish soil, I was afraid of falling prey into the hands of anti Semites.

Every survivor heard the angry question, "You're still alive?" The truculent scowls warned all who returned to be wary of our neighbors, for they were not happy to see the handful of Jews returning to their rightful homeland. The killings had begun with the first group of Jews returning to Poland.

My only reason for returning to Radom had been that of a child's dream. I thought that if I had the courage to open the door to my home, a miracle would happen, and my family would be waiting for me inside with open arms, but I was too frightened to press down the door handle.

I never again climbed the same three flights of the gray, marble-stairs to the home of my childhood, but I often wished I had the courage to open the door.

Living in America forty years and not having to fear my neighbors, it had become easy for me to be bold. I was still haunted by the door I so desperately needed to open.

The thought of returning to the scene of the most heinous crimes the world has ever known brought a chill down my spine, and I wished my sister Bela hadn't died in 1976 of colon cancer and was traveling with me. Though she was only three years older than I was, she had been my rock throughout the entire war. I could never have survived had she not been with me.

Two-months before Bela died in June 1976, she gave me a little gold heart on a thin gold chain to wear around my neck. She gave the same gold heart to her two sons, Eli and Jerry. Before I had begun to pack my bag for my trip to Poland, I touched the little heart. "You are coming with me," I whispered.

I can't imagine living in any other country except the United States of America. I'm grateful to my America for lifting me from the ashes and giving me a future. I was going back to Poland not to stay, but only to step inside the home where I was showered with hugs and kisses by my Mama, my Tata (Father), three sisters, and a brother. I was hoping that whoever lived in my home wouldn't mind opening the door and allowing me one last look, to stand quietly a few moments and listen to the echoes of my loving family.

My mind was in a far away place and many years in the past when our flight-number was announced. I heard Carla's voice, "Come on, Yaja, it's time to get in line."

We sat strapped in our seats waiting for the plane to take off for New York, and there we would be changing planes for Warsaw. Forty-five minutes later, the captain apologized for the delay and asked everyone to vacate the plane and wait until the mechanical problem was resolved.

At three o'clock in the afternoon, we boarded a different plane. Now, our first stop was Frankfurt, Germany, instead of New York.

Without delay, the jet was beginning to inch up towards the runway and picked up speed. Gracefully and effortlessly as an eagle, the large body lifted and began climbing.

I listened to the rhythmic sound of the engine and relaxed, never giving another thought to the delay. My eyes hung on blue sky, and my mind on the wonders of modern technology. Suddenly, a curtain of clouds rolled in, and slowly an enormous sunset appeared and scattered the clouds into puffs of dark gray. The sunset took on the shape of a fireball and painted the sky orange. Though my mouth was dry, I was unable to turn away, even for a moment to accept refreshments the flight attendant was now serving. Suddenly, the beauty I saw amidst the orange blanket and gray clouds was my beloved family and all my relatives that were torn from me when I was only a child. I felt a warm glow, and all of my fears had washed away. I felt as if I were sheltered with the wings of at least forty relatives, my guardian angels. Their love penetrated and melted my heart. They smiled and waved me on. Maybe I didn't really see them, and it was only a strong wish, but I was grateful for the gift and didn't question the phenomena. I saw my little sister Edzia clinging to Mama, and I silently thanked her for knocking the fever out of me when I had Typhoid fever in The Blizin Concentration Camp. I saw Bela the way she looked when we were children tumbling cartwheels on the grass near the river. She looked healthy with a sun kissed complexion and her straight blond hair bounced on her shoulders as she ran into the arms of one relative to the next. She smiled down at me, showing straight white teeth. When Bela stood up and ran into our Tata's arms, I suddenly felt very lonely. I, too, wanted to be in the arms of my parent. My eyes misted and blurred my vision. I quickly wiped the tears, for I didn't want to loose a single moment of the gift. The sunset had suddenly disappeared, but my relatives continued gliding alongside the jet on a transparent blue sky.

With the rhythmic sound of the engine, I could clearly hear Mama urging me to remember and tell the truth and all nodding in agreement.

"You are the only one left to speak for us," were the soft voices in unison.

Suddenly, my memory of the time when I was a small child had become as clear as if it were only yesterday. I remembered sitting at Mama's feet on the little stool my Tata had made for us. With my head on Mama's lap, I listened to the stories of a time when my parents were themselves children and their struggles until the very end of their lives. I remembered vividly, to the smallest details, the stories I heard Mama tell over and over.

My friends had been urging me to write my story, and now I know that I must, but my story has to begin with Mindala, my mama.

Chapter Two: Mindala's Story

Mindala's parents, Fraida and Lopek Diament, were proud owners of a fine bakery in Radom, Poland. The bakery was situated one flight directly beneath the family's living quarters. Fraida had worked along side her husband and gained the reputation for being the best cheesecake baker in Radom and earned the title, "Fraida the baker."

Mindala, being the youngest of seven children, received the most attention. Every morning, except on the Sabbath, Mindala woke up to the wonderful aroma of freshly baked bread. The breads and pastries that were removed from the oven early in the morning permeated the family's apartment. Every Thursday and Friday morning, the entire Diament family was in the bakery helping their parents prepare bakery goods to satisfy their customers for the Sabbath, with hallah, cookies, and cakes. Mindala loved being in the bakery, especially on cold winter nights. Lopek placed a small basin of water in front of her and washed her hands.

"To be clean, is the first and most important thing to becoming a good baker," he said, then dipped his index finger in flour and touched her thin narrow nose. He sat her down on a high, wooden stool next to the worktable. "Pay special attention to your mama and your sisters, and in no time at all you will be known in Radom as "Mindala the baker," he said lovingly, pinching her pink cheek with flowery fingers.

Mindala's two brothers, Jacob and Charley owned a small leather-shoe factory and only helped out in the bakery on Thursday evenings.

Everyone had a chore. Mindala's mama prepared the cheese filling for the cheesecakes and laid out all the ingredients and supervised her daughters, making sure that nothing had been forgotten, or it would have been disastrous. Hanna, Sophie, and Pearl peeled and grated apples for strudel. Jacob and Charley lifted sacks of flour onto the bread bins or wherever their father needed them to be. Hudesa was the only sister not living at home. She lived and worked as a nurse in the Jewish hospital and seldom had a day off.

Instead of watching her mother and sisters, Mindala was fascinated by her tata's hand movements. With one hand he mixed, and the other added flour, eggs, sugar and raisins. What first looked as if it would never stick together soon became apparent, when the movement of his right hand began slapping the dough until it felt and looked like rubber. After the process of rising and kneading, he cut out strips of rubbery dough. Mindala moved close to her tata and watched as his fingers pinched, rolled, and twisted. With quick movements, he braided and created one perfect hallah after another. As if lifting an infant child, he placed his creations on a large baking pan and brushed them with the rich egg yoke. When the oven's heat began to caress the braids, the hallah began to swell and turn golden. When it looked as if all of the dough had disappeared, Mindala watched her Tata dip his hand into a deep basin and scrape out a chunk of cookie pastry as large as his fist and begin his hand movements all over again. He pulled, twisted, and rolled. A pinch and roll between his fingers created a head and body. Quick movements between his thumb and index finger, and arms and legs appeared. He used a small knife to create stubby toes and fingers. Two raisins made two eyes. A small pinch, and lips appeared. He rolled a very small piece of dough between his fingers and placed it between the eyes.

"It's a tiny nose, just like yours," he chuckled touching the tip of her nose with floury fingers, and Mindala giggled. He flattened the last piece of dough in the palm of his hand and attached it to the doll's waist. "Now, we know it's a girl," he said, kissing her chestnut hair.

Gently, so as not to damage his work of art, he placed the cookie doll on a small cookie sheet and shoveled it into the oven cavity. When the cookie doll turned golden, Lopek removed it from the oven and placed it on the worktable.

"You must wait for your doll to cool before you could eat it, or you'll burn your mouth," he warned.

To Mindala, the wait for her cookie doll to cool seamed longer than the entire process. Five minutes later, her father's, now washed, hands cupped her pink face and looked into her green eyes, a mirror image of his own eyes. "Now, it is ready," he said with so much love it could have melted the ice crystals that hung down from the bakery's roof.

Adoringly, Mindala cradled the cookie doll in both palms as everyone watched to see how long it would take before she took the first bite. She looked mischievously at her family and began with the toes, taking small bites, and only ate one leg. Then, she dug the raisins from the eyes and ate them. She bit off the head and placed the cookie doll back into the cookie sheet and wrapped her arms around her Tata's neck.

"You make the best cookie dolls," she said giggling.

"You always say that," Lopek chuckled, kissing the top of her head.

13

Mindala picked up the cookie doll and handed the one legged, headless body to her Tata.

"Please cut it so everyone could have a taste."

"The generous Mindala," her mother said.

From that moment on, "generous Mindala" had become her nickname. Every Friday morning, the scent of vanilla, cinnamon, and fresh butter coming from the bakery was an invitation for the community to come in to the bakery store where Fraida Diament sat behind the counter, and within hours, there was not a trace of baked goods left.

Every Friday, late afternoon, Mindala waited impatiently for Hudesa to come home. The hospital where she had worked and lived had been Jewish owned, and all the doctors and nurses were Jewish. It was a small hospital with only three nurses and two orderlies. The young unmarried nurses took turns going home for the Sabbath. It had always been a special occasion for Mindala when Hudesa came home, but she was sad when she woke up on Saturday morning, and Hudesa was not in her bed. No one saw her leave, for she had to be back at the hospital at dawn. Friday night the family sat at the large, rectangular, mahogany table covered with a white linen tablecloth. Five candles in the silver candelabra set in the center of the best china and silverware.

Fraida encircled the flickering candles three times, then covered her eyes with warm hands and whispered a prayer to welcome the Sabbath.

Her older daughters served the traditional sweet, boiled fish, with the hallah Lopek had baked only hours before.

On one such occasion when the family was finished with the chicken soup and cooked dry fruit for desert, Fraida sat down close to her husband and looked into his green eyes, the same color as her own, and said, "Lopek, I pray to God for a long life together. I couldn't think of living even one day without you, but just in case God should decide that you should go before me, I'm asking him, now, to take us both together."

Lopek bent over and kissed his wife on the cheek, looked proudly at his children, and

asked Mindala to come and sit in his lap. He kissed her chestnut hair and turned to his wife.

"Fraidala, how can we think of dying before we have grandchildren, and do we have a

dowry for our beautiful Mindala?"

Seeing Mindala's large green eyes fill with tears, Hudesa told her parents to stop talking about dying. "You are both still too young to think about such a thing."

It never occurred to the Diament children that Fraida's wish would one day come true. Most of all, Mindala never expected to be orphaned at the age of twelve.

Poland's climate is drastic. Long, bitter, cold winters and short hot summers. In 1912, most homes in Radom had no plumbing. When the snow melted, the flies buzzed around the outhouses, bringing such epidemics as cholera, typhoid, scarlet fever, and quite frequently dysentery.

On a torrid mid July day, the weathered Jewish cemetery, marked by tall headstones, inscribed in Hebrew scroll, separated only by patches of grass, had been filled to capacity with mourners for Fraida and Lopek Diament, who died on the same day of dysentery.

Though her brothers and sisters stood protectively on each side of her, twelve year old Mindala stood shivering in the blistering sun, convinced that her mother's wish had been granted. She knelt between two freshly dug, adjoining, open graves, heaps of soil alongside each grave. As the caretakers began lowering Fraida and Lopek Diament, enshrouded in white cotton, Mindala's chin began to quiver. As the shovels of soil had begun to cover her parents, Mindala fell to the ground and sobbed.

After the last shovels of soil covered Fraida and Lopek Diament, Jacob wiped his eyes with the handkerchief his mother had embroidered for him. He helped his youngest sister to her feet, dusted the sand from her clothes, then wiped her tears with the same handkerchief. He cupped her face with both hands and said, "Look into my eyes and remember that we all love you, and we won't abandon you. We only have each other now." Jacob kissed his sister on the forehead covered with sand and led the family away from the graves.

Jacob was the oldest brother and cherished by his entire family. He held Mindala's hand and said, "Soon, I will go to America. I'll work hard, and one by one, I will send you all tickets. Everyone knows that the streets in America are paved with gold, so it shouldn't take me too long before the entire family will leave Poland."

Leaving the black wrought-iron gate, friends and neighbors ranging from the elderly to infants in their mother's arms and bare footed children followed the grieving Diament family on sun-baked cobblestones.

Mindala's many friends, always animated and garrulous, were now taciturn as they followed their friend.

Fearing the same fate, children held on tight to his or her parent's hand as they watched the Diament family climb the stairs to get ready for the seven-day mourning (Shiva).

Mindala didn't follow her brothers and sisters up the stairs. She ran to the bakery store and looked through the locked glass door. It was still early enough, and her Mama would be sitting behind the counter selling the bread and pastries. She saw the shiny copper scale Fraida often polished until she could see her face in it. The only time Mindala remembered the store looking so clean, devoid of crumbs, was before Passover, when everything had to be scrubbed clean to get ready for the matzos. Mindala's eyes rested on the padlock, and she ran from the store to her Tata's bakery. Tata would now be standing at the worktable, preparing the sour for the bread. It was Thursday, and the tables would be loaded with rising dough. Enormous basins would be filled with farmers-cheese, raisins, sugar, butter, and apples, graded or just pealed. The bulging dough would be filled with all the goodness the Diaments were famous for. All of Mindala's sisters and brothers were now married. The last six months, before her parents' fatal illness, Mindala was standing next to her mama rolling out the dough for the strudel and cheesecake. Now, she stood in the eerie bakery and didn't hear her friends called her name.

The apprentice, fourteen-year old Jeremy Sztraiman, would be standing next to her Tata, learning to be a baker. Mindala liked the short boy with the big muscles. Jeremy worked six days a week and walked many kilometers from the nearby farm to learn the bakery business. Mindala loved watching him flex his muscles as he stood in the oven pit, throwing large chunks of wood into the oven cavity. A warning look with his almond shaped green eyes and hand movement cautioned her not stay too close to flying sparks from the oven cavity. Mindala loved observing the camaraderie between employer and his employees. Most of all, she enjoyed seeing her Tata's belly shake with laughter.

Now, there was only darkness and silence. No sparks were coming from the oven cavity, no sound of laughter. The tables, rolling pins, basins, and knives were all scrubbed clean, and the oven cavity was dark as a tomb. Mindala's eyes were fixed on the wall between the two worktables, where her Tata's white apron, encrusted with dough, hung on a nail outlining his round belly. Any minute now, my Tata will come down and put it on, she mused. Suddenly, she realized that her Tata was never going to wear that apron again. "I'm an orphan!" she sobbed.

16

Jeremy arrived to work, unaware that his beloved boss and mentor and his smiling wife with the rosy cheeks had been buried today. Before entering the building, he was met by the neighborhood children and learned of the tragedy that had befallen the Diament family. As he rushed inside the building, he saw that the door to the bakery was open and was startled to see Mindala standing in the middle of the room, her eyes fixed on her Tata's white apron. He picked up a towel from the hook and wiped her tears.

"Lets go upstairs. I want to pay my condolences to your family," he cajoled, but Mindala didn't respond. He took her hand with a gentle tug, and she followed him up the stairs

During the seven days of mourning, Mindala's sisters and brothers had decided that since Jacob and Charley were leaving Poland and Pearl, being the oldest, knew most everything about the bakery business, she and her husband, Medel, were to take over the bakery. They were to live in the family apartment, and Mindala was to live with them and not be uprooted.

On the seventh day, the last day of the daily mourners prayers, Mendel took charge of the bakery even though he had never stepped foot in a bakery before, for he had been a shoe repairman. Thus, Mendel the shoe repairman had suddenly become Mendel the baker. It didn't take him long to learn how to be a boss without working. He wore a long black coat and a round hat with a narrow visor. The traditional garb gave him a priestly look.

In Radom almost everyone had a nickname. People were known by their trades, deeds, disfigurements, habits, and the way he or she looked in general. Medel had two nicknames. He was known as Mendel the Shoemaker; although, he was now the proud owner of a fine bakery. He was also known as Mendel the Goat, because of the wispy brown beard that was divided in two sections, pointed at the end.

Although the Diament bakery was now Medel's bakery, Jeremy worked hard. The same as if it had still belonged to Lopek, and he was soon known as the best bread baker in town.

Pearl took her mother's place behind the counter, and Mindala took over the household, and on Thursdays and Fridays, she also help out in the bakery. She never complained. She patiently waited for her two brothers to immigrate to America. She held on to the promise her oldest brother Jacob made to her and cherished the words, "America is lined with gold. As soon as I'm able, I'll send for you."

By the end of 1913, all of Mindala's sisters and sister-in-laws had given birth, and Jacob and Charley sailed to America, leaving their wives and children, promising to send for them as soon as they were able.

Several months had passed before the first letter had arrived. The return envelope was marked Brooklyn, New York, USA. The Diament family had declared that day a holiday. Soon, packages with pretty jars of jam, cans of sardines, and American chocolates were beginning to arrive, and Mindala was hopeful.

Chapter Three: World War One

The hope of leaving Poland was soon interrupted and turned to tears and hopelessness. July 28, 1914 World War One broke out, and correspondence from America came to a halt.

Each time Mama Mindala told us her story, she would stop at the part when the family had lost contact with Jacob and Charley and became blinded with tears. But she had the need to tell us about her experiences, for she craved for a better life.

The seatbelt sign lit up for descend toward the Frankfurt airport, and my thoughts had returned to the present time.

Carla and I were shuttled for overnight stay in a hotel before continuing to Warsaw. The sun in Frankfurt was still strong. We placed our bags on our beds and went for a walk. We strolled on side streets alongside small, white wooden houses, nestled in lush gardens. Heavy branches laden with red, juicy, sour cherries, my favorite, were hanging over tall white picket fences. I was never able to pass a fruit tree without picking a fruit. As careful as I always am about washing the fruits, this time I ate the cherries as I picked them and enjoyed each sour mouthful. Carla, too, enjoyed picking and eating. Only, she had no trouble reaching for the branches and reached handfuls for me too. Our only concern was not to get caught. I felt like a kid and enjoyed every moment.

Our hotel room hadn't been more than a non-descriptive motel in California. Two single beds on each side of the only window that was facing an alley. A long, narrow, brown table stood between our single beds. A small colorless lamp stood on each side of the table. I was too tired to give the room much thought. As I lay in bed on a well-used mattress, in the land where evil was born, I prayed, as I had many times before, for my heart to be big enough to forgive. My mind is forever annexed with memories of horror that will stay with me for the rest of my life, but I believe that to be able to forgive is the greatest gift I could give to myself.

I closed my eyes and went back to the time before I was born and to the time of Mindala, my mama. The Cossacks galloped into Radom, and all the Diament family dreams of leaving Poland were what they had always been, just dreams.

Mindala had the same empty feeling in her gut as when she had finally accepted the fact that she would never see her tata braiding hallah or listen to the song her mama sang to her. She remembered that when the Germans marched into Poland, they were mostly polite and said thank you when the hot bread was put into sacks and taken for their soldiers, and the town was left without, but Jews were not singled out. She also remembered with horror when the Cossacks galloped through town on their large horses with sabers hanging from their hips. A young girl wasn't safe in or outside her home. They savagely looted and destroyed without mercy. Each time they stormed into the bakery, they gathered up all the bread and never paid for it. The bakers had to work harder and bake twice as many loaves of bread in order to feed their families and the hungry people in town. The bakers laughed when Mendel put on an apron and stood at the board kneading dough. His black coat and beard were white with flour. When he kneaded the bread, he moved rhythmically as if praying. "He probably was praying," Mama said, rolling her eyes and making us all laugh.

To keep up with the demands, Jeremy's two older brothers, Mailach and Laizer, both were skilled bakers, agreed to work with Jeremy in Mendel's bakery.

It was too far and dangerous for Jeremy to walk home to the farm and often stayed in town with his two married brothers or slept in the bakery on the loft.

Almost daily, the Cossacks confiscated the food products on his parent's farm, and Jeremy's wages went to feed his family. On the days when he didn't come home, he worried about his parents and his little brother, Gershon.

The first time Jeremy came to work for her tata as an apprentice, Mindala giggled when she saw him stand in the oven pit, his face level with the oven's cavity. Now, she never thought of his height and the fact that at fifteen she was already three inches taller than Jeremy was, and Jeremy was very much aware of the beauty she had become. He was aware of her chiseled facial features and lustrous chestnut hair bouncing on her shoulders. Her ivory complexion sported a pink blush each time she saw him glance at her. Jeremy had been aware of the changes in Mindala, but he had also been aware of her sisters' watchful eyes and kept his distance.

From the beginning, the Cossacks had learned that the bread wouldn't be ready before dawn, but there were nights when a new battalion of Cossacks stormed into the bakery demanding bread. It had not been an easy task to make them understand that the bread wouldn't be ready before dawn.

The bakery was the safest place for Mindala's friends to socialize. Many nights during the week, teenagers gathered in the bakery, and the bakers kept vigilance. Jeremy and his brothers were alert to sounds of galloping horses, and the teenagers felt more secure in the bakery than in their homes. Mindala had been unable to understand why her heart pounded against her ample bosom each time her eyes met with Jeremy's. She only knew that she couldn't stay away from the bakery, knowing that he was inside.

On a cold Thursday night in November, Jeremy heard Mindala's footsteps running down the stairs and dash into the bakery. She never admitted that she wanted to be alone in the bakery with him before her friends arrived and always pretended to be a annoyed for coming down before her friends. Jeremy assured her that her friends would arrive shortly. He invited her to sit on the floor facing the oven while he shoveled out a large thick cracker sprinkled sparsely with sugar and placed it on a plate next to her.

Seeing the thick cracker Mindala's eyes became wet emeralds.

"I didn't know that offering a cookie to a beautiful girl would make her cry? When I bring one to my little brother, Gershon, he smiles and gives me a big hug. It goes to show you how much I know about girls," said Jeremy.

Mindala pulled out an embroidered handkerchief from the pocket of her crocheted sweater her mama had made for her and wiped her eyes. "My tata always made a cookie for me," she whimpered.

"I remember the pretty cookies your tata made for you, but my brother wouldn't like to eat a doll," Jeremy chuckled, as he wiped away a tear from her cheek with his thumb. "At least taste it and tell me if my cookie is as good as your tata's?"

Mindala broke off a very small piece of the warm cracker and put it in her mouth while Jeremy waited for her comment. "It's every bit as good, and it will be better after the war, when we'll have enough butter and sugar," she said, avoiding eye contact.

As the war lingered, so did poverty. Pearl hired a housekeeper to keep up with the cooking, and the young girl was glad to work for just food. Radom's beggars found out about Mindala's kind heart and had become steady visitors. They knew when Mendel wasn't home, Mindala made sure that nobody left the house hungry. Gita, the housekeeper, knew that Mindala saw her putting food in her basket every night before she left to go home. She also knew that Mendel would never approve of Mindala giving away so much food to the beggars. No words were necessary to keep each other's secret from Mendel. The longer the war lasted, the more in love Mindala was with Jeremy, and it kept her awake at night, knowing he was right beneath her window. Every morning at dawn Mindala smelled the freshly baked bread and knew that Jeremy would be removing it from the oven, and she visualized him wearing a sleeveless T-shirt, his broad shoulders and muscular arms exposed.

Chapter Four: Mindala's Engagement to Josef

Pearl was beginning to worry that her youngest sister had been spending too much time in the bakery talking to Jeremy. She told her other sisters, and everyone had decided it was time to find her a suitor. The Radomer matchmaker had been alerted, and Pearl had described the match she wanted for her youngest sister. "Most importantly, he has to be religious," Pearl said running a hand over her sheitel, a wig worn by orthodox Jewish married women in keeping with an old rabbinical precept that forbids a woman from leaving her hair uncovered in sight of a man other than her husband. The sheitel made Pearl look years older, Mindala thought. She wasn't about to let anyone shave off her long hair and cover her head with an ugly sheitel.

When Mindala got wind of it, she was ready to run away and hide. Instead, she ran down to the bakery and told Jeremy of Pearl's plans for her. "Maybe you could become more religious and go to the synagogue on Friday nights and Saturday?" she asked Jeremy.

"And come to the bakery in a long black coat and Yiddish hat and maybe grow a beard like Mendel?" Jeremy and Mindala laughed at the thought of it.

"Be quiet. I think I hear horses," Laizer whispered.

By the time Mindala had a chance to run out of the bakery and run up the stairs, the Cossacks were pushing the hallway door open, giving Mindala enough time to squeeze herself between the two work bins. Though Mindala was slender, there had only been enough space to wiggle in sideways. Jeremy urged her to move all the way to the wall. She crawled on her hands and knees until she reached the wall and remained that way, for there hadn't been enough space to turn around. Jeremy hung two aprons on the wall in front of Mindala just as four Cossacks stormed in.

As she sat sideways on her knees, she turned her head and gazed at the outline of her tata's apron, still caked in flour, and suddenly felt calm. She was glad that she didn't allow anyone to remove her tata's apron from the wall.

The Cossacks raved and ranted, wanting bread, but the bakers showed them that the bread was not ready. "Come back in the morning," Laizer cajoled.

One of the Cassocks stood between the two bins where Mindala was hiding and blocked off her air. "We will wait until the bread is ready," he bellowed, refusing to move.

Jeremy had to think fast, or Mindala would suffocate. He went over to the worktable, elbowed the Cassock until he moved a few inches, and opened the bin where the dough was rising. He scooped out the bread dough, placed it on the next table, and began to knead. He scooped up fistfuls of flour and sprinkled the dough with quick hand movements getting the flour all over the Cossack's uniforms. When his brothers saw what he was doing, they joined in and the bakery became a thick fog.

"What are you doing?" the Cassocks shouted in unison, between coughing and gasping and waving the sabers in the air.

"You wanted us to rush with the bread, but I tell you if we bake it before it has a chance to rise you will break your teeth trying to eat it. If you'll come back at five in the morning, it will be ready," Mailach said, trying to sound Russian, though it was mostly Polish, and he had to repeat several times before the four Cassocks moved towards the door. As they turned to leave, one shouted, "If you give this bread to anybody else, we'll cut your throats!"

Malach and Lazer moved the bins apart as Jeremy lifted Mindala, who was gasping for air, off the floor and carried her out to the hallway. He sat down on the steps, cradling her in his lap. As he held her close to his chest, he knew he could never let her marry anyone else. His lips brushed her forehead, and Mindala opened her eyes. Her long eyelashes were white with flour. She looked into Jeremy's eyes with unwavering gaze and knew she would never want to spend a single day away from him.

When Mama reminisced that moment, she laughed the soft musical laugh from years gone by. Then, tears filled her eyes when she remembered Pearl's anger.

"You will not marry a man who never goes to the synagogue. I found you a man the family will be proud of, and you will do as I say," said Pearl.

As always, Mindala didn't speak in her own defense. Since her brothers had sailed to America, it was always Pearl making all the rules, and her other sisters had no say in her behalf.

While the entire world had been fighting a war, the sisters were busy preparing for Mindala's engagement party, and Mindala prayed that the Cassocks would leave so she could be free to run away from her sister Pearl. But her prayers were unanswered, and preparations for her engagement party to a man she had never met began, with all her sisters cooking and baking for the party which was to take place the next day.

Hudesa had to work and was unable to participate, giving Mindala a place to go and stay away from the house all day. To avoid the Cassocks, she left Pearl and Mendel's house at dawn and ran all the way to the hospital. The large, brown door to the main entrance was always locked. Mindala pulled the cord that sounded like a church bell. The caretaker's one room apartment was only one foot away from the main entrance. After the bell rang three times, he opened the door with a scowl. He was wearing a long flannel nightgown, wool socks, and a wool hat. No matter how many times he had seen Mindala, he never failed to stand hunched at the door waiting to hear her say, "To Hudesa, please."

Hudesa was putting on her uniform when Mindala rushed in breathlessly. "Mindala, what are you doing here? You should be home. Tomorrow is your engagement party."

"I don't want anything to do with that man I'm suppose marry. How could I marry a man I never met? For all I know, he may be another one of Mendel's brothers!"

Hudesa put a finger to her mouth. "You'll wake the baby," her whisper was more of a sigh. She wanted to reach out to her sister and tell her that she didn't have to marry that man, but Hudesa knew that it was the only way. Her marriage, too, had been arranged. She never knew, until her engagement, that she would be marrying Mendel's brother, who later became an orderly at the hospital. "Mendel doesn't have any more brothers," Hudesa smiled and embraced her sister.

"I know I have to obey, but I don't have to help, and as far as I'm concerned, they can have the engagement with only the groom," Mindala whispered, as Hudesa was leaving to start her day at the hospital. While Hudesa was tending to the sick, Mindala cleaned the little apartment that consisted of one long narrow room. A two burner, wood-burning clay stove stood attached to the wall opposite five single metal hospital beds. In front of the window, parallel with the door, stood a small rectangular brown-wooden table and two brown-wooden chairs. All though Hudesa's apartment was one-third the size of the home where Mindala and her sisters and brothers grew up, she wished she could live here and never go back to Pearl and the engagement party. Hudesa returned several times to nurse her baby and urged Mindala to go home. "Harsh Josef will take care of the baby until his night shift begins," she pleaded, but Mindala turned her back towards her sister and cried. She was still in Hudesa's home on her final return for the evening, and Harsh Josef went to work. Hudesa begged her sister not to disgrace the family. "Stay here

tonight, and in the morning, I'll go back with you and help with the party."
After crying all night, the two sisters ran home the next morning, leaving
Harsh Josef to take care of the baby.

While the sisters fussed with her hair and new dress, Mindala stood like
a stone, hoping to be rescued by Jeremy. Pearl had fired Jeremy when she
found out that Mindala had been in the bakery the night the Cassocks had
stormed in.

When Jeremy's brothers found out that Jeremy was fired, they too walked
out of Mendel's Bakery. The Sztraiman boys were known as the best bakers
in Radom and had no problem finding employment with better pay. The only
reason Jeremy worked for Mendel was to be close to Mindala.

Until Jeremy found out that the Diaments' had found a suitor for Mindala,
it had never entered his mind that he would lose her to another man some
day. Words of love were never a part of their nightly conversations, only
touching hands as they sat on the floor, dangled their legs inside the pit, and
gazed at the glow in the oven cavity. Occasionally, Jeremy would slide his
hand over her forehead and brush aside a tendril from her face and gaze into
her eyes for a long time. Now, Jeremy realized that he was jealous of the
suitor.

"I'm going to show up at the engagement party and beat-up the suitor,"
Jeremy told his brothers.

Laizer warned him not to interfere, for he would make their parents very
unhappy.

"They have enough to worry about."

"If it's not the Cassacks, it's the anti-Semites," Mailach added, his hands
in tight fists.

Josef had never met Mindala, although he knew her nickname was "pretty
Mindala." With trepidation, he had been ushered into the house that was still
known as the Diament home. Through sideway glances, he saw that his
betrothed's nickname suited her perfectly. Being orthodox, Josef knew that
it was forbidden to look directly at a woman, but he couldn't help himself.

Each time Mindala saw Josef glance at her, she visualized herself looking
like Pearl, wearing a sheitel.

Josef was a young man, but having a beard and wearing the long black
garb gave him an unapproachable priestly look. In Mindala's eyes, he looked
the same as all the other older men on Synagogue Street did.

Mindala's eyes hung on the door, hoping Jeremy would storm in and
rescue her, as he did the night the Cossacks stormed into the bakery. There

were moments when she thought she had seen him at the door, but she was sure it was only in her imagination or wishful thinking. Mindala's sisters were busy serving and catering to the guests, and the families on both sides enjoyed the celebration, and the wedding was to take place in two months.

Josef asked his tata's permission to stay and talk to his betrothed, but his tata had told him there would be plenty of time for that. "You will see her at the wedding, and you'll have the rest of your lives together." Josef didn't like what his tata had said, but Tata had to be obeyed.

After the guests had left, Mindala sat sobbing at the long, now empty, table. Sophy sat down next to her, put her arm around her youngest sister, and smoothed wet tendrils away from her face. "This should be the happiest day of your life, and all you do is cry your eyes out," Sophy said, as she wiped the tears from her sister's face with the tablecloth.

"When Mama and Tata died, it was the worst day of my life. Today, is the second worst day of my life, even worse than living with Pearl and Mendel!"

"Why, Mindala? You are marrying a wonderful boy, from a very orthodox family, and he's not bad looking. He told us that when the war will be over, he would take you to America. His family is in the leather business. Even if he doesn't go to America, he will make a very good living in Radom."

Mindala turned to her sister, her face wet with tears. "Jeremy may not be Orthodox and doesn't have a beard, but I love him, and Tata liked him too. Sophy, I'd rather be killed by Cossacks, than marry Josef," she wailed.

Sophy turned her head and spat twice. She didn't actually spit, it was more a gesture, "Pooh, pooh, don't say things like that. God will punish you."

"I don't care. It can't be a worse punishment than if I marry a man that looks like Mendel, and I will look like Pearl with the sheitel," she said and began to cry again.

The day after the engagement party, Mindala waited for Jeremy's arrival behind the Friedman building. They fell into each other's arms and didn't separate until Mailach and Laizer arrived and told them it was blasphemy. "She is betrothed to another man, Jeremy. You can't ignore it!" Mailach shouted.

"I will break the engagement and marry Jeremy!" Mindala shouted back.

The Friedman bakery was only on the next street from her home, and Mindala waited every night for Jeremy's arrival, and each time they would hold on to each other until one of the brothers separated them.

Four weeks before the wedding, Mindala decided it was time to tell her sisters that she was breaking off the engagement, and nobody would be able to stop her.

The initial shock of Mindala's news caused Hanna to faint, and Sophy and Pearl's faces turned green as they stood twisting their hands while throwing cold water on Hanna.

Hudesa had to work and had been spared hours of shouting and pleading.

Pearl let Mindala know that she was throwing her life away for a man who would never amount to anything. "If you break off the engagement and marry Jeremy, the little farmer boy, you can never step foot in this house. Even if you starve, I won't help you. He will always be a worker, and you will always be poor!" Pearl bellowed.

"Maybe I'll be poor, but I'll be happy," Mindala retorted.

The sisters saw that her mind was made up, and they would have to stand in front of the Rabbi and break the engagement.

"This will be like a funeral," Pearl cried, but Pearl was wrong. It was worse than a funeral. The air in the synagogue was thick with hate. Josef walked around in circles twisting his hands, and his mother, a big woman, looked as if her black wig had been placed on her head in haste. Her arms flopping in the air, she looked like a turkey trying to take flight. "I curse you Mindala! I wish you misery for the rest of your life, the same misery you have caused my Josef!" she shouted, her big, round face red with fury.

Mindala begged the woman to take back the curse, but she took her son's hand and stormed out from the synagogue.

Chapter Five: The Murder

March 1917, a revolution broke out in Russia. Four days later, the Czar abdicated. The Russian troops on the eastern front retreated, and anti-Semitism was on the rise, and the pogroms began.

Jeremy was just removing the bread from the oven, when his fourteen-year old brother, Gershon, came running in breathless to tell his brothers that their parents had been brutally murdered. Mailach gave him a drink of water and made him sit down and tell them what had happen.

"I was sleeping in the loft and heard a noise," he said between gasps. "I climbed down and opened the door ajar to Tata and Mama's room, thinking maybe they were having an argument. You know? Tata always said that it was Mama's fault for letting our sister, Jadzia, and Natan run away to Argentina."

Jeremy remembered the time before World War One had begun, when his oldest brother and sister pleaded with their parents to help them get out of Poland, and their mother finally gave in and gave them all their savings, and the two teenagers made it to Buenos Aires.

"Mama worried because she didn't hear from them since the war began." Gershon made a sound like a wounded animal. He turned pale and closed his eyes. Jeremy grabbed him, for he was about to fall off the chair. The brothers splashed water on his face, and he opened his eyes.

"What did you see?" Laizer asked, his hands shaking, spilling the water on the bakery floor.

"I listened at the door and heard Mama say, "Janek, what are you doing here in the middle of the night?" Gershon began to sob and between hysterics he said, "Janek took a knife from behind his back and grabbed Tata...a...a...and...c...c...cut his throat." Gershon's eyes rolled into his head again and again. Laizer splashed water on his face until he opened his eyes. When he regained consciousness he muttered, "I was about to open the door and fight him, but...but...but...it took only seconds when he did the same to Mama." Gerhson was gasping for air and vomited all over Malach's apron.

The brothers needed to know the details, in case there would be a glimmer of hope that their parents would still be alive, and continued splashing water on their youngest brother's face.

"How did you get away?" Jeremy asked, unable to control the tears followed by fury, but he restrained himself, for Gershon was struggling to get the words out.

"I saw him looking towards my door, so I opened the window in the loft and ran

out and...a...a...and I ran all the way here," he gasped and collapsed into Jeremy's arms.

After the brothers revived Gershon, Jeremy picked up a knife in one hand and a large stick in the other. His eyes were wild with rage.

"Did you take a good look at the murderer's face?" Lazer asked, his own face was white as the flour sitting on the bin.

"It was Janek, our next door neighbor," Gershon managed before he collapsed again into Jeremy's arms, and again, the brothers splashed water on his face.

"I'm going to kill the basted anti-Semite," Jeremy ranted.

Mailach and Laizer took the knife and stick away from Jeremy. "If you go now, you will not return alive, even if we all go," Mailach, the oldest brother, said.

"We can't let him get away with killing our parents, Mailach," Jeremy shouted, his entire body trembled with rage.

Mailach pinned Jeremy against the work bin. "Now, hear me out. If we go to the farm now, there will be at least ten of them from the nearby farms with knives waiting for us."

"What about the police?" Gershon whimpered.

"Do you think the police will believe a Jew? If they did believe, do you think they would arrest the murderer? They would question him and accept his lies, but we will go to the police in the morning and ask to be escorted to our home so we can bury our parents and tell them what Gershon witnessed. We will never be able to go home again because they won't let us live.

By the time the brothers and a policeman entered the family farmhouse, there was nothing left of the farm. Everything was stripped to the bare walls, including the livestock. There had been no sign of the horse and buggy.

The Sztraiman boy's parents were stretched out on the floor, in a pool of blood.

The brothers knew they would never get over the sight of their once vibrant, productive parents, whose Polish neighbors praised them for their generosity and know-how about farming and always sharing, when one neighbor's crop didn't do as well.

The brothers buried their parents in the Jewish cemetery in Radom and never returned to the family farm. As predicted, nobody was punished for the heinous crime.

Jeremy and Gershon were now orphans and homeless.

Chapter Six: Mindala and Jeremy's Wedding

Two months after the Sztraiman family buried their parents, Mindala and Jeremy were married. Unlike the elaborate wedding Pearl had planned for Mindala to Josef, the wedding to Jeremy was only for the immediate family and mirrored any Friday night celebration of the Sabbath.

Gershon came to live with Mindala and Jeremy on Walowa Street. Mindala loved having Gershon living with them in their tiny one room apartment on the fifth floor. It was like having a little brother, and she was now the big sister.

While Mindala was pregnant with her first child, Jeremy was building his bakery brick by brick. Every morning after only a few hour of sleep, he worked on his bakery until it was time to go to work in the Friedman bakery. One month before Mindala and Jeremy's daughter was born, Jeremy was the proud owner of a bakery.

Like her mother, Mindala worked side by side with her husband until their daughter Fraida was born.

Fraida was a beautiful baby, with big green eyes and blond hair. Each time Mindala's friends admired the child, Mindala was afraid of the evil eye. Even with the red ribbon she had tied on Fraida's wrist to make sure that no harm would come to her, she still "pooh, poohed" when anyone as much as looked at her daughter. She prayed that Josef's mother's curse would not come true.

Two weeks after Fraida was born, Mindala put the infant in a wicker-basket and sat the basket down next to her behind the counter while selling the bakery goods her husband had baked. It was the happiest time in her entire life. Her husband was happy because he didn't have to work for a boss, and she was happy because she had married the man she loved and now had a beautiful baby daughter.

Chapter Seven: World War One Was Over -- Jews Are Scapegoats

November 11, 1918, the Bolsheviks overthrew the Kerensky government and asked Germany for an armistice. They had lost Poland and nearly all the territory bordering the Baltic Sea. The Great War was finally over, and anti-Semitism was on the rise.

Ben, Sophy's husband, left his wife with three children and immigrated to America.

Gershon was now working in a butcher shop, learning the trade.

Each time Jeremy read in the Jewish newspaper about Jews being murdered, he cursed the ground that he walked on. He could think of nothing else except to get his family out of Poland, but not to America.

"Palestine is the only place for Jews," he told Mindala. "And aren't the Goyim always screaming at us, while they are throwing rocks, Zydi do Palestiny? (Jews to Palestine?) Mindala, we must go to Palestine and help build a Jewish Land," he pleaded.

When Fraida was two years old, Jeremy sold everything, including his bakery and the entire household, and took his family on a journey to Palestine. They had reached Cyprus, and the English wouldn't let them go any farther. With money dwindling quickly, Jeremy urged Mindala to take Fraida and return home.

Mindala cried all the way home. Not only because she had been separated from her husband, but she had discovered that she was pregnant with her second child.

When Mindala and Fraida returned, she had no home, no furniture, and no money. All she had left, which were in Sophy's possession, were a naphtha lamp and a large wicker basket, left over from the bakery.

Sophy's husband, Ben was sending money and packages and promised that soon they would all join him.

Sophy took Mindala and the child into her home, but Mindala felt unwelcome by Sophy's oldest son Lopek, now eight years old. He often told her to take her basket and lamp and get out! Mindala was convinced that Josef's mother's curse had come true.

Josef had departed to America, and his mother vowed never to forgive

Mindala for breaking the engagement. Several times Mindala went to see her and begged for forgiveness. She pleaded with her to take back the curse, but the woman slammed the door in her face.

Hanna came to visit Sophy and found Mindala on the floor on a straw mattress, crying. "Did you get bad news from Jeremy?" Hanna asked.

"No, but Lopek is taunting me. He tells me to take my basket and lamp and get out, and when I'm not looking, he hits Fraida. Hanna, I'm doomed. Josef's Mother won't take back the curse and look what happened to me. I don't know if I'll ever see my Jeremy," she sobbed.

Hanna packed up Mindala's meager belongings and told her to come and live with her.

Hanna's husband had left Hanna with three children for another woman. Hanna must fend for herself and her children. Hanna earned her living by baking cheesecake and apple cake. Rain or shine, winter or summer, Hanna stood on Walowa Street, a Jewish market place, and sold her pastries.

Hanna was six years older than Mindala and felt protective of her youngest sister.

Unlike Pearl and Mendel, she had faith in Jeremy and liked him.

Pearl had told everyone in the family, including Jacob and Charley, that Jeremy had abandoned his pregnant wife and daughter, but Hanna told Mindala not to worry. "Jeremy loves you, and he will do everything in his power for you to be together."

Mindala helped Hanna with the baking and the household. She told Hanna that if Jeremy made it to Palestine or returned home, that would be a sign that the curse had been removed from her. Just to be on the safe side, she picked up Fraida and went to see the Rabbi and told him all about the curse. "Many times I went to see Josef's Mother," Mindala cried. "I begged for her forgiveness, but she refuses to remove the curse," she sobbed.

The tall, distinguished looking Rabbi with the long black garb was a compassionate man. He knew of the tragedy the young girl standing in front of him had endured. He remembered the sudden loss of her parents at a young age, and he also remembered her second nickname, "the generous Mindala." He ran his hand over his long brown beard and began moving his body in prayer. When he finished, he said, "Now, take your child home. I promise you, generous Mindala, after I finish praying for you, you will be cleansed of the curse. I will even put in a good word for Jeremy, even though he never comes to the synagogue."

As soon as Mindala left the Rabbi's house, she felt a heavy weight lift from her shoulders and was certain that Jeremy would not forget her.

Three months after Mindala's return, Jeremy arrived into town hitching a ride in the back of a horse and buggy. Mindala wasn't concerned that he looked gaunt, only that he had returned a different man. The man she remembered before he had sold the bakery was vibrant and full of hope for a new life in his homeland. Today, her heart was breaking for the man she loved. He looked as if the lights in his once sparkling green eyes had been turned off. He embraced his wife, who was now showing a small round belly, and was happy his family was all right.

"The English kept me imprisoned in Cyprus. When they released me, they made sure I would not step foot into Palestine. The Goyim scream at us, Jews to Palestine! When we give up all of our possessions and go to Palestine, the English throw us in prison for wanting to live in our homeland. How much can we be asked to endure?" Jeremy said in a helpless tone in his voice.

Mindala smiled wanly trying to hold back the tears, but lost the battle.

After being his own boss, Jeremy had been unable to work for an employer. As soon as an employer asked him to do it his way, Jeremy stepped out of the oven pit and walked off the job. Without a paycheck and a loaf of bread, Jeremy was too ashamed to go home. He would meet with the unemployed Union Members and drink vodka until a friend would find him asleep against the wall of the Union building and bring him home. When he sobered up, he promised Mindala he would try harder. Jeremy kept his promise and tried hard to be more humble and earned a steady job.

Mindala gave birth to a boy and they named him Icek, after Jeremy's father, but his name was immediately changed to Sonny. Soon after Sonny was born, Jeremy moved his family away from Hanna's small one room apartment to a slightly larger one-room apartment on the ground floor. The landlord's name was Penc. Penc was a tall, thin, unfriendly man, of German descent. He lived with his wife, daughter, Ola, and son, Zygmund, in a large, white, wooden, ranch-style house, nestled in a colorful orchard. The house was surrounded with flowers of every kind, apple trees, pears, and cherries. In the winter months when snow covered the trees, it became a beautiful wonderland.

No one would dare trespass or worse, get caught picking a fruit. His trained German shepherd would attack and kill the strongest man. A hundred feet from his private home, Penc owned the entire street, all of which were two story buildings. His tenants were mostly low income. When rent wasn't paid on time, within days of the deadline, the family's few meager belongings would be sitting on the sidewalks.

Penc hated Jews as much as most Polish people did, but he tolerated Jeremy. Jeremy was clean-shaven, not only his face, for in the summer he shaved his hair on his head, too. Jeremy liked living on Penc's property. It reminded him of his parents' farm. He had a stable where he kept his horse and wagon. He had a spits-dog, with hair as white as fresh fallen snowflakes, and a black nose, and he named her Snow. He had a cat named Hanna-Gitala and a rooster named Madia. On the roof of the building, Jeremy built a large cage where he was raising white doves. He would open the cage in the morning, and the doves would fly freely. At dusk all of the doves returned to the cage. When Sonny was old enough to hold the long stick with a rag tied to it, to guide the doves in and out of the cage, Tata taught him to feed and care for the doves. Mindala was never surprised when Jeremy would come home with a stray, and all the creatures followed him around as if he was their Tata, too.

In 1921, Sophy, along with Charley's wife and their children, left to join their husbands in America.

Jacob's wife, Nesza, had fallen in love with another man and refused to leave Poland. She divorced Jacob, but Haskel went to America with his father. Lopek, Sophy's oldest son, had eye allergies. His eyes often itched and were red rimmed. He was not allowed to enter America until his condition improved. His parent's hearts were broken, for they had to leave him behind with relatives for several years. He told his mother that he preferred to stay with Mindala and Jeremy. He was a hyperactive boy and difficult to handle, but he loved Jeremy. Jeremy included him in all his activities, especially with the animals and planting flowers on the patch of land in the back yard. In 1925, Lopek was well enough to join his parents in America.

Mindala and Jeremy had three more daughters. Bela was a beautiful child with straight white hair and green eyes. She was the tomboy and daredevil, and she loved being outside in the sun. I was born three years after Bela. My hair was much darker than Bela's was, but my complexion was very fair, and the sun was my enemy. Edzia was the youngest child. She was a beautiful little girl with large green eyes and straight dark hair. Sonny had become the apple of our parents' eyes. He was a quiet boy whose main interests were his white doves. He had named every one of them, of which there were at least two-dozen.

Our tata was happier, now, since he had a steady job and had been able to save a little money towards building his bakery.

"I'll build our bakery with my own two hands," he often told Mama.

Every morning before leaving the bakery at dawn, Jeremy stuffed warm rolls in his pockets and a large cookie doll for his children the same as Lopek Diament had baked for his youngest daughter, Mindala. On cold winter mornings, he placed the loaf of bread under his arm between the coat and jacket to keep the bread from freezing. The next stop was to the slaughterhouse where Gershon was working. He always gave his brother some rolls, and Gershon gave him some scraps of meat and a juicy bone for Snow, wrapped in newspapers. This had been a daily routine.

On one of those cold winter mornings, Jeremy walked home happily, knowing he had something for everyone. As he turned on Walowa Street towards Stare Miasto Street, two tall men ordered him to stop. Each politely introduced himself as an officer of law. "Where are you going so early in the morning?" one asked.

"I'm a baker. As you gentlemen know, bakers work all night so the people in town could have fresh bread in the morning. May I ask why I was stopped, Officers?"

"Last night a high ranking official had been murdered by communists on this spot, and everyone passing this street is a suspect," one officer said politely and asked Jeremy to unbutton his coat. When he did, the bread fell from under his arm, and the other officer picked it up and handed it back to Tata. After searching his pockets, they didn't remove the rolls and the cookie. When one officer began unwrapping the dog meat, Jeremy said, "Every morning on my may home from work, I stop at the slaughterhouse for bones and scraps of meat for my dog."

The Officer wrapped the meat back in the newspaper, and Jeremy put it back in his pocket.

As one officer waived him on, the other told him to wait a moment, "We need your identification, sir; it's routine."

Jeremy reached in his breast pocket, removed an identification card, and handed it to the officer standing closest to him.

"Is your name Jeremy Sztraiman?"

"Yes," Jeremy replied nervously to the sudden angry tone in the Officer's voice.

Looking closer at the identification card's marked religion, the officer's gloved hands tightened into fists. "So you are a Jew," he growled.

Jeremy's blood turned to ice. He suddenly had the feeling that he would not live to bring the bread home for his children. "Yes…sir…" he said stumbling for words.

"Are you a Jew?" he asked again, as if unable to believe.

Being certain he had nothing to lose, Jeremy lifted his head up high.

"Yes, sir, I'm a Jew," he said with pride.

The first blow to his head knocked him to the ground. Jeremy was a proud man and wanted desperately to defend himself. He knew that in a fair fight, he could have had a chance, but the two officers had clubs.

All he heard between fists to his face and kicks to his stomach was "ty parszywy Zyd, Communist." (You mangy Jew, Communist)

The punching and kicking continued until Jeremy lay unconscious in deep snow, in below 0 degrees temperature.

Snow's devotion to Jeremy knew no boundaries, and Jeremy treated Snow as if she were one of his children. When Jeremy didn't come home at the usual time, Snow had become very nervous. She jumped up on Mindala's bed and began to bark.

During the winter months, Mindala never got out of bed until Jeremy came home and started a fire in the brick oven he built for his family every winter. When the room would be warm, everyone got out of bed, and the day would begin. But this morning, Snow knew that her master was in trouble, and she had to get out to save him. Mindala pulled the quilt over her shoulders and ordered the dog to be quiet. "You'll wake the children," she whispered. Snow bit into the quilt and pulled it off Mindala and her four daughters in bed next to her. When Mindala scolded the dog and took the quilt back and covered the children, Snow leaped through the window shattering the glass. A gust of wind blew in through the broken window, and everyone was now awake and shivering with cold. The two older children helped Mindala carry the younger children to Jeremy's and Sonny's little white bed and covered the younger children with double quilts.

Mindala removed the straw mattress from her bed and pushed it against the broken window.

There were no clocks or watches in the apartment, and the sky that February morning was gray, threatening a snowstorm. Mindala didn't know that Jeremy was late coming home and was angry at the dog for causing such chaos. As she ran across to the stable to gather wood and coal to start a fire in the brick oven, Mindala saw that it was daylight and had begun to worry that Jeremy wasn't home yet. What if he slipped on the ice and is hurt?

"If he isn't home in a few minutes I'm going out to look for your Tata," she told Fraida when she returned with an armful of wood and two pieces of coal.

There were no cars or public transportation in Radom. There were droszki, a horse and coach. The Droszkasz (the Coachman) sat in front, unprotected from the hot sun in summer and freezing cold winters. He wore a hat with a shiny black visor and sat many hours lined up the way taxies are, hoping to have a busy day so his family and horse could eat. Most of the population in Radom traveled by foot through the entire town. It never occurred to anyone, except the wealthy and out of town visitors, that there had been a need for any other way to get around town.

On freezing mornings like today, Mindala wished that there had been transportation, the kind she had experienced in Warsaw. She remembered the time when her beloved brother, Jakob, had arrived from America to take a bride, a distant cousin living with her siblings in an orphanage in Warsaw. During Jacob's two months stay in Warsaw, he had sent Mindala a train ticket to come for a visit. I remember Mama's eyes were as big as green marbles as she described the trolley car ride. I had never seen a trolley car before and asked many questions. Mama tried to describe the trolley, the clanking sound it made, but I could only visualize the carrousel, the one that came to town with the circus every summer. I lifted my head from her lap and saw her high cheekbones taking on a pink blush as she reminisced the time she had enjoyed with her brother and his new wife and the ride on the trolley.

"Some day when your tata has his own bakery, we will take a trip to Warsaw. Did you know that in Warsaw people have toilets inside their apartments?"

"I wouldn't like that, It would stink up the house," I said, pinching my nose.

"No, it doesn't stink. There is a water-tank on the ceiling. You pull a chain, and water comes into the toilet and cleans the bowl," Mama said, and I could see that she liked the idea. As many times as mama was telling that story, I couldn't understand how that worked. All I could envision was a large water tank tipping over a bucket, the same bucket we had to use at night, and each time the chain was pulled, water would spill into the bucket and all over the floor.

Snow didn't need transportation. She knew the route Jeremy took to work, and she also knew all the shortcuts. She often followed him to work, sat down at the bakery door, and would stay all night if Jeremy didn't order her to go home. In the summer, Snow would jump through the open window at dawn, run to wait for Jeremy outside of the bakery, follow him to the slaughterhouse, and then home. Snow loved Jeremy and would gladly give her life for him, and he equally loved Snow. It was easy to see how gentle he had always been with Snow, Hanna the cat, Madia the rooster, the nameless goat, and countless strays he would find that were hurt or sick. He nurtured them all and sent them on their way. Jeremy was a true lover of all living things, and he was loved in return.

Snow ran with the wind until she found Jeremy in a bed of snow. She pulled and tugged at him until he opened his eyes. The dog bit into Jeremy's sleeve and began to pull until, with great effort, Jeremy raised himself off the hardened snow, slipping several times before he stood up. He gathered the bread and rolls that were scattered on the ice and stuffed them in his pockets. He checked his coat pocket and was happy to feel the meat for his beloved Snow.

Holding on to his bruised stomach, he followed his dog home and fell unconscious at the door.

Though the brick oven was lit, the wind was blowing in from the broken window, causing the apartment to be only a little warmer than the entrance hall to the building.

Everyone waited for Jeremy to come home. He would immediately cut some glass and fix the window then bring the oven to a roaring fire. "You have golden hands, Jeremy," Mama would often say.

It was still too early for the two older children to get ready for school, and the three younger children were glad to be in the warm bed with the feather comforters. Snow barked and scratched at the door. Mindala opened the door. She didn't want the dog to jump through the window and knock down the straw mattress. Seeing her strong husband lying limp at the door, Mindala began to scream for help. Within seconds every neighbor in the building was at the Sztraiman door trying to bring Jeremy around. Mindala took her three youngest girls from the warm bed and put them in the cold musical cradle and covered us with the quilt from her bed, and she straightened the little white bed for Jeremy.

Four men lifted Jeremy off the floor and carefully placed him in the white bed. Moshek Altman, the Droszka's oldest son, a shoe repairman, slapped Jeremy's face several times.

Mindala and her two older children rubbed Jeremy's hands and feet to get him warm.

Jeremy opened his eyes, and his teeth began to chatter. Mindala ordered Snow to climb on top of him. Jeremy cried out in pain, but he held on to the dog. After a few minutes, Snow's body heat calmed him, and he relaxed.

The neighbors replaced the glass on the window, and the apartment was once again warm. The next few days, Jeremy's entire body was purple. After two weeks of staying home, the money Jeremy had saved towards a bakery had gone for food and heat.

After Jeremy recovered from the assault, he craved again to leave Poland, but with seven mouths' to feed, he felt hopeless. No matter how hard he worked, he was still only able to put shoes on his children's feet, pay the rent to Penc, and put food on the table. With each passing year, Jeremy had become more disillusioned. Even Mindala's promise that her brothers and sister would get them all out of Poland didn't help anymore.

"Your brother Jacob came back to Warsaw and married Sala. Now, there is a new family, Sala's family in Warsaw. They too are waiting for Jacob to send them visas. Do you think he would bring me to America, before them? Especially after your sister Pearl told him what a bad provider I am?" Jeremy counted.

"Jeremy, he promised me he would. Didn't he help us with packages and a few dollars, while you were recovering? The money you saved for the bakery was gone in one week. We would have starved to death if he hadn't helped us. You'll see, we'll all be in America, one day," Mindala pledged, though she too began to loose faith.

Every day Jeremy read in the Jewish newspaper about pogroms in small towns. Jews were being beaten and murdered. Hardly a day went by that some Jewish boy or old man with a long beard didn't get beaten half to death or murdered. Gradually, Jeremy began neglecting his job and was fired. The children were hungry when he didn't bring home the bread in the morning. When he didn't work, he was too embarrassed to come home. When he did come home, there were always two of his friends with him speaking in whispers.

Fraida was learning to read and write Yiddish, so Mama could correspond with her family in America. When she became proficient, she would often read the Yiddish newspaper out loud. Mindala heard Fraida read that a group of anti-Semites ganged up on an old Jew and beat him half to death. They would have killed him if not for three Jews with sticks. Now, Mindala knew why Jeremy wasn't home at night. She knew that Jeremy and his two friends were the Jews with sticks, roaming the streets at night and saving Jews from being murdered, while neglecting his own family. Soon, Jeremy along with his friends had gained a reputation in the Jewish community of being troublemakers.

"If this continues, we will have a pogrom," the religious cried, but Jeremy couldn't keep his head bent and look frightened as he walked down the street.

I remember when I was five years old, my heart pounded as I watched my tata being carried inside the apartment, his head bandaged, and I heard his friends tell Mama that Jeremy had been ambushed by the anti-Semites who waited for him with knives.

It was several weeks before my tata recovered. During that time, he came to realize that he could lose his life, and his children would be orphans like him. He promised Mama that he would get a steady job, and everything would be all right.

He tried as hard as he could to stay home during the day and work all night. He devoted his time to his family and his animals. We never knew what kind of animal he would bring home next. He walked around in Penc's large backyard and planted flowers and nurtured them. Madia the rooster followed behind. The same was with our cat, Hanna. She could be on the roof trying to steal a dove from the cage; hearing Tata's voice, she dived to his feet, like a little soldier.

One morning, I woke up and found Tata holding two white guinea pigs. At first sight, I thought that they were rats. I had seen rats in our building, though not white ones.

Seeing how frightened I was, my tata laughed, showing an array of straight white teeth. He sat down on my bed and kissed my face. "Open both of your hands, Jadziala." When I hesitated, he looked at Mama and laughed again.

"I don't like mice!" I cried.

"They aren't mice, Jentala; they are guinea pigs," Mama laughed softly. She always called me Jentala, when she was in a loving mood, which was very often, but I hated to be called by my Jewish name. I wanted to be called Jadzia, like my Polish friends. I didn't want to be separated by a name, and so I always corrected her, but she never remembered.

Hesitating, I touched the soft little animal. "They have no bones!" I cried, kneading the little doughy bodies, and my little sister Edzia, immediately began to cradle one of the guinea pigs. Bela ignored the guinea pigs and played with Snow's daughter, Citra, Snow's mirror image, only Citra was smaller. Citra was a beautiful puppy with a black nose and white hair, resembling freshly fallen snowflakes, just like Snow. Citra was Bela's dog, and no one would dare touch her without permission. Except for her green almond eyes, Bela didn't resemble anyone in the family. Her hair was flaxen blond. Every summer her face and body would become brown, and her straight hair would turn from yellow to white. When she laughed, she showed an array of straight white teeth, the same as our tata's. She was the neighborhood tomboy. On cold winter days, Bela would attach a piece of wood to each foot and skid down on a frozen hill or make snow a man or throw snowballs at us all with a perfect pitch. In the summer on warm days, she turned cartwheels on the grass near the river, and Edzia and I would crawl under her, or she would cajole the neighborhood kids to slide down the little waterfall. Bela was beloved by Penc's married daughter, Ola, and her two-year old son, Kaitek. After Ola married, Penc gave her one of the nicer apartments in our building. Ola's husband owned a motorcycle with a passenger seat for two, and Bela was often invited to sit in the passenger seat with Kaitek in her lap, while Ola sat behind her husband holding on to his waist. The motor roared and sped away with Bela's white hair flying with the wind as Edzia and I stood on the sidewalk watching with envious eyes.

Fraida was a very feminine, beautiful teenager. Her alabaster complexion was a perfect contrast to the large green almond eyes. At fifteen, she was as tall as mama with perfect curves. Her chestnut hair shined in the sunlight with copper tones. Joel Altman, the Droszkosz's son, was in love with Fraida, and she with him. At seventeen, Joel lived with his parents, two sisters, and four brothers in a one-room apartment, directly above our apartment. Joel and his older brother, Moszek, were shoe repairman. We could hear them hammer late into the night. I loved watching the brothers sit on little stools, removing one nail at a time from his mouth and hammered it into old shoes. When the brothers carried a conversation, they talked with only one side of the mouth. The nails rested on the other corner between the lower and upper lip. The words were muffled. I never understood a single word and was concerned that they would swallow the nails.

My tata wanted a lot more for his oldest daughter, but departure from Poland was not materializing, and living in such close quarters made it impossible to keep the two teenagers apart.

Sonny resembled our tata, though at thirteen, he was already taller. His main interests were his doves.

I resembled Mama and Fraida, at least everyone said so, and that made me happy, though I hoped to be as tall as them.

Edzia had straight dark brown hair with long bangs. She had a small face and large green eyes. Like Bela, she was a daredevil, and Mama was always chasing after her.

We all loved our animals, but no one could ever love an animal the way Bela loved Citra. When she didn't stop Citra from sniffing the guinea pig, I became concerned. When Citra began playing rough with the little guinea pig, I was afraid she would kill it, and I took the little creature away from the dog. Bela picked up Citra and cradled the pretty little dog lovingly in her arms. "Citra wouldn't hurt your little pig. She was only playing" Bela argued, kissing her dog's black nose.

Snow sniffed at Citra and followed Tata to his bed and stretched out on the floor next to him.

My parents were loving and playful with each other and with us and never spanked us. I grew up without riches. When Tata worked, we had enough food and heating on cold winter nights. The times when he didn't work, Mama had no money to buy food. She would sit at the table next to Fraida and dictate a letter, in Yiddish, to her brother, Jacob or her sister Sophy, in America. As much as she hated asking her brother and sister for help, she looked at her hungry children, and her pride dissipated. Some weeks later, she would receive a five-dollar bill in a letter and paid back the money she owed to the grocer. During the depression, help didn't come often and many nights we went to sleep hungry, but with dignity.

Chapter Eight

After forty years, my American shoes stepped on Polish soil.

I turned to Carla. "Here, I'm not Jewish," I said.

Carla didn't ask for an explanation, she only nodded. When we arrived at the Warsaw hotel, Carla remembered that on her last travel to England, she had met a Polish girl from Warsaw. They had exchanged telephone numbers and hoped to meet again some day.

After we registered, Carla handed me Kazia's phone number. I asked the clerk to dial the number. Kazia's younger sister answered and told me that Kazia was out of town. "My name is Zosia. My tata and I will be at your hotel in twenty minutes," she said excitedly.

As we stepped inside the elevator to take our bags up to our room, we were surprised at the new modern hotel. Our room was spacious. A pleasant landscape hung between the twin beds. Everything was new and modern, with new beige carpet and drapes, brass lamps on each side of our beds, and new beige bedspreads. We placed our bags on the luggage rack and went back down to wait in front of our hotel for Zosia and her father.

Twenty minutes later, the smallest red car I had ever seen stopped in from us.

Zosia, an attractive eighteen-year-old with short blond hair, blue eyes, and fair complexion, stepped out of the little car and held out her hand. Maciek Lesnicki, Zosia's tata stepped out from behind the wheel and stretched his arm to shake our hands. Maciek was a short, middle-aged man, with graying hair and a pleasant smile. He was wearing a white shirt and tie. After we shook hands and said introductions, Maciek pushed the front seat forward and politely asked us to step in the back seat. To my surprise, we all fit in the little red car that resembled a toy car. Maciek was anxious to show us Warsaw, and I translated our conversation to Carla. She smiled gratefully and told me to thank him for her.

Though I had only finished four grades before the German occupation and had been away from Poland since January 3, 1946, I was surprised at how easy it was for me speak and understand the language.

As Maciek graciously showed us parts of Warsaw, I was anxious to see the Warsaw Ghetto, but I didn't want them to figure out that I was Jewish.

After seeing the Warsaw Square and the lavish park, rich with roses of every color, green shrubs, and tall trees, I invited our guides to lunch. During lunch, I found out that Zosia's main interests were blue jeans and pantyhose. After lunch, I told Maciek that I had some Jewish friends in Los Angeles who asked me to take pictures of the Ghetto. Maciek was glad to take us to see the remnants of the Ghetto, which was only part of a wall attached to barbed wires and a monument.

It was three o'clock in the afternoon, and Maciek Lesnicki was anxious for us to meet his wife and show us his home. As he neared the building where the Lesnickis' lived, Maciek complained about the sloppy work of the Polish builders. "Look at this construction. The building is practically new, but it's already falling apart," he laughed and guided us up to the third floor. The apartment was sparsely furnished. The living room consisted of a brown couch, a brown, wooden coffee table, and an overstuffed colorful club chair where Maciek's wife, Wanda, sat. Wanda was a short, obese woman with a pleasant round dimpled face. Like her daughter, she had blond hair and small blue eyes. When she laughed, her entire body shook with pleasure. We soon felt as if we were celebrities in the Lesnickis' home. Pan Lesnicki had the need to point out the rest of the defects in his house. He asked me to look at his little balcony. "It would have been very nice if we could sit out here, but we are afraid to step on it, for fear we'd get killed if the balcony pulled away from the wall," he bantered.

Wanda lifted her ample body from the club chair and disappeared. She returned moments later with a half-full quart bottle of vodka and placed it on the brown, wood coffee table. Maciek filled five water glasses and passed them around.

Though I never drink alcohol because I don't like the smell or taste, I knew I had to keep up the façade. Seeing Maciek lift his glass for a toast, I signaled Carla to follow his lead. I put my left hand behind my head and the glass to my lips and let the liquid burn down my throat in one gulp, and the Lesnicki family was very proud of me. "You're true Polka," Wanda bantered and mother and daughter wrapped their arms around me and Carla took a picture. At that moment, I would have loved to see the expression on their faces had I said, "I am Jewish."

After we all drank the vodka, Zosia had begun to complain about her work place. "The Jews have taken from us the highest positions. They collect the highest wages, and we can't get rid of them because the bosses protect them.

46

My stomach was churning as she was speaking, and I felt the vodka backing up my throat. Though I was still smiling, Carla saw the change in my face and asked what was wrong? "Deja vu. I'll tell you later," I mumbled.

"How do you know that they are Jews? I understand that there may only be a handful of Jews left in all Poland, and they are all very old, too old to work," I said smiling.

"Oh, but we know that they are Jews."

"How do you know? Do they look different from you or me?"

"No, they look like us, but we know."

I was beginning to feel anger building up in me, and I felt my fists tighten, but I knew that I couldn't blow it now. "So tell me, Zosia, I'm curious. How do you know that the people in high positions are Jews?" I asked, sitting between mother and daughter on the brown couch, their arms securely around my shoulders as if we were related or at least old friends.

"It's the way they pronounce the letter "R," and they only mingle with each other," Zosia said with a scowl.

I realized that I'd better stop before the Lesnicki family became suspicious and wonder why I was so interested in Jews. I could never convince them that there were no Jews of working age left in Poland. There was no point in continuing the conversation on the subject. Poland still needed someone to blame. Although, there were only a handful of old Jews left in Poland, the phantom Jews were perfect scapegoats.

The next two days we visited Warsaw on our own. Though Poland had been under the rule of the Soviet Union, Warsaw was a very pretty and well kept city. We walked through the Lazienka park, and we sat down on a bench across from the rose garden. The roses were in full bloom, and all the shrubs and old and young trees were a lush green.

On the left near the entrance, we stopped to look at the monument of the famous pianist, composer, and statesman, Ignace Paderewski. We browsed through the market-square and listened to young Polish singers butchering the English language as they sang "When the Saints come marching in." Carla and I looked at each other trying not to laugh. We had the advantage of long daylight and found ourselves standing in front of the Parliament. I spoke to the young soldier standing guard, and he graciously showed us the interior. The building looked deserted, and the soldier explained that nothing had been scheduled for today. As we climbed up the two flights of curved marble stairs, I was in awe, for I had not expected to see such elegant building in Poland. The high ceilings held up by light color marble walls and the sparsely lit assembly room exuded elegance and comfort with heavily cushioned seats. I was truly grateful to the polite young man. As a child in Radom, I had never known such beautiful building. I sat down in a comfortable cushioned seat and remembered the building where I grew up, the building where my Aunt Hanna lived, and many of my friend's homes in Radom. We never gave a second thought to the old chipped paint on the exterior or the interior of the apartment buildings we lived in or the smelly outhouses. I was happy to see my tata brush white paint and cover the bedbug-infested walls in our apartment every spring. We were happy to have had a roof over our heads. I didn't know better, and I didn't know that elegant places such as the Parliament building in Warsaw existed.

Leaving our hotel room, I had to squint. It was a sunny Friday early afternoon. The sky was aquamarine with only an occasional gray puff. There wasn't a hint of the tragedy that took place from 1939-1945. I knew that today was the day when I was to open the door to the home of my childhood and look into my past. My heart pounded throughout the entire train ride to Radom. Anxiety had begun to build, and fear had weld up in me, but I couldn't let Carla see what I felt, or she might want to leave before I would accomplish what took me forty years to accomplish.

After the train-ride to Radom, we checked into the Europa hotel. Carla announced that she was hungry. I was too distraught to remember that we hadn't eaten since early morning. We put our bags on our beds and went outside looking for a place to buy food.

We had exchanged dollars at the airport in Warsaw, so we had plenty of Polish money.

As we began to walk, every street looked familiar. I spotted a little grocery store on Rinek Street. "Let's check it out," I told Carla.

Seven women were standing in line waiting to be served. I didn't know if ration cards were needed, and I didn't want to seem as if I was trying to take food away from the people standing in line. While Carla automatically took her place in line, I approached the counter. "Can we buy some food?" I asked. All eyes were on our jeans, tennis shoes, and the self-assured look on our faces that said, "We are Americans."

"What would you like?" the woman behind the counter asked.

I saw fresh bread and pint size bottles of sour cream. The sour cream in Poland is liquid and is sold in bottles. "Is the bread and sour cream sold without the ration cards?" I asked.

"Yes," the woman said expressionless.

I thanked her and took my place next to Carla. When it was our turn, I bought two bottles of sour cream and a loaf of bread. The sun was still high up in the sky, and it was quite warm. We sat down on a bench next to a playground. As I took the first bite of bread, my eyes rested on a brick building with a tall brown door.

"I had three friends living in that building," I told Carla. "Dora Friedman, Sala Kaplan, and Jonas Chonikman, a boy I liked. None of them survived the war."

Carla looked thoughtful. "Are you sure you want to go back to your painful past, Yaja?" To make my name less complicated for the American ear I had changed the spelling from Jadzia to Yaja.

"Being here where it had all begun and knowing that I'm free to leave, hopefully, might lessen the nightmares. But if it's too difficult for you to listen, it is perfectly all right. I'll just close my eyes and remember," I said hoping that I didn't upset her.

"It's fine, I would like to know. I only thought that it would be hard for you talk about it. Please continue."

"Thanks Carla, you're a good friend."

I put the bread on my lap and the sour cream bottle on the bench next to me.

"Yes, it is very hard to talk about it, but these memories had never left my mind. Dora Friedman went to school with me. Her parents owned a bakery in that very same building. The family's living quarters were situated directly above the bakery. The kitchen floor of the family's quarters covered only half of the store, causing the counter where Dora's mother was sitting and selling bakery goods to have a very low ceiling. When the curtain that separated the family kitchen from store was not drawn, everyone coming into the store could see the entire kitchen by looking upwards. In June 1939, when school let out for summer vacation, I suggested to Dora that we put on a show in her house. Her kitchen would make a perfect stage. The audience would be standing in the store looking up to the kitchen which would be the stage and watch the show. Dora liked the idea, and we had begun to rehearse. We decided to do the show on Friday late afternoon because the bakery goods would have been sold out, and the store would be closed until Sunday morning. Friday late afternoon was standing room only in Dora's bakery store. I was the producer, director, and the star."

"Were you good?" Carla wanted to know.

"After the show, a man approached me and put five zloty in my hand.

'This is for you, only, because you are the prettiest and the best one,' he said, pinching me lightly on my cheek."

"That wasn't very nice. Why did you let him pinch your cheek?"

"In Poland, a light pinch on the cheek was meant as a compliment and that was a big compliment. The five zloty were more than what we took in from the entire crowd. I handed the five zloty to Dora, and I never told her what the man had said."

"That wasn't very smart," Carla laughed.

After we finished the bread and sour cream, I sauntered towards the building for a closer look. An obese woman wearing a drab, stained apron was standing at the main entrance and eyed us with suspicion.

"Excuse me, Pani," I said. "Many years ago there was a bakery in this building. Is the bakery still there?" I asked her.

"No, there is no bakery here, and there never was a bakery here!" she shouted, a truculent scowl masked her rotund face.

I tried to tell the woman that my friend's parents owned this bakery, but she ran inside slamming the tall wooden door in my face. It occurred to me that the woman was afraid that I might be the owner of the building and returned to claim it. I had heard of such fears from other Jews visiting Poland. I began walking towards Stare Miasto Street, with Carla lagging behind. Though I knew I was walking in the right direction, I saw a trolley car turning the corner, and for a moment, the area didn't look familiar. I noticed that I didn't see the droszki lined up waiting for a fare. Carla reminded me that it's been forty years since I had returned from the camps. I approached two young men, about twenty years old, smoking cigarettes in front of a building, and asked them where Plac Stare Miasto Street was? They pointed in the direction I was heading and began to follow us.

"I'll show you the way," one said, a bright smile revealed gums devoid of teeth.

"Thank you very much, but I need to do it myself," I said.

One of the men continued to follow us, but he soon stopped and turned back. Now that I recognized the entire area, I decided that my first stop should be Penc's house, where I was born and lived until 1935.

I could barely recognize the landmark. There was no sign of Ola and Kaitek or the motorcycle or Penc's house or Zigmund, Ola's brother, who during the German occupation, walked around looking for Jews to maim with the brass knuckles he wore for an easy kill. The entire area looked deserted, only the long block of apartments was recognizable, for they hadn't changed in fifty years. Still the same dingy gray stucco with old red bricks showing through. The cracked brown entry doors fanning back and forth.

The door to the one room apartment on the ground floor where I lived with my family was open. A bucket with white paint stood in the middle of the floor, but no one was on the premises. As I stepped inside, I felt the presence of my entire family, the same presence I had felt on the flight to Poland. I remembered the excitement, when once a year, around the holidays, we received a large carton of used clothing from America to be divided between all of Mama's sisters and their families. I stood in the middle of the small room, my eyes closed, and remembered all my aunts and cousins gathering around the carton, trying to find something that would fit or could be altered. Sometimes there was something for everyone, though not very often, but the anticipation was exciting. I remembered a beautiful pair of children's shiny, black, patent-leather shoes with gold buckles. I sat down on the floor and tried them on, but they were too small. I pushed my feet into them until my toes were red and began to cramp. Once a week for the next three month, I picked up the shoes from under my bed and tried them on, hoping my feet would shrink. Instead, the shoes seemed smaller still. I finally gave up and let Edzia play with them, for they were too large for her.

Each time all the Diament women dipped into the carton, Mama thought of Hudesa's only daughter, Eva. Two years Eva was lying in bed, tuberculosis eating away at her lungs, every day a little more, until there would be nothing left. Often Aunt Hudesa would dip in the box and pick up a colorful dress. Pain ravaged her face as she examined it. As if reading each other's minds, the sisters embraced, soaking each other's shoulders with tears.

One summer day, the hospital grounds were filled with mourners. I looked through the window where I always saw Eva in bed urging me not to come too close to her bed. Now, there was an empty space, for even the bed was gone. I saw my tata lean against the large chestnut tree, banging his head on the bark as if it were a ball. It had been the first time I had seen my tata cry. He loved Hudesa and her children. He also liked Hanna, but Hudesa was his favorite. She never judged him, and he loved her for that.

I had a sudden urge to go to the hospital where my aunt Hudesa lived. I didn't recognize the grounds. There was no long brown door, no doorbell, and no caretaker, only a short fence. A nurse was sitting outside close to the fence. I asked her what had happened to the hospital. She was a young girl and said she didn't know.

"This is a sanitarium for tuberculosis," she said and added that no one was allowed entrance.

I wanted to see if the chestnut tree we had spent many summers under was still there, but I didn't want to intimidate the young nurse. I turned back to Penc's house. There was so much more I needed to remember. Most of all, I remembered Mama's kind heart.

The times when Tata worked, and we had enough money for food, Mama always cooked enough for two more people. "Just in case someone drops in while we are eating," she would say. Whether it was potato soup or just bread, Mama never turned away a hungry beggar. The name "generous Mindala" stayed with her for as long as she lived. She never insulted anyone, not even when her Polish neighbors would patronize her by telling her that they liked her because she was different from other Jews.

"What could I say to someone that doesn't know or doesn't want to know us? Could I tell Pani Franciszkowa that I like her because she doesn't hate the Jews as much as her sister in law does? I like her because she is a nice person, and Pani Antoniowa is an anti-Semite," Mama said, holding little Edzia in her arms and kissed her. "Pani Antoniowa is a very unhappy woman because she never had children, and when she sees my beautiful children, she is angry. She blames the Jews for her infertility."

Chapter Nine: Moving from Penc's Building.

It was 1935, the year I was to start school, but it wasn't for several month, and Tata had already bought me a teczka, leather briefcase. I couldn't wait to start school. I wanted everyone to see my beautiful, shiny, brown leather teczka with a chrome buckle. "Nobody will have such a beautiful teczka," I told my tata.

I twirled myself around with the teczka, and little Edzia tried to take it away from me. Mama laughed while Tata lifted me in midst of a twirl and sat me down on his right shoulder, my teczka dangling in my hand. With his left hand, he scooped up Edzia and sat her down on his left shoulder and danced with us around the rectangular table that stood in the middle of the floor, and Mama chased after us. "Jeremy, be careful, you'll get dizzy and drop the children!"

"Don't worry, Mindala. I won't get dizzy; they're as light as two little ducklings!"

Edzia and I giggled when he eased us down on our bed and began blowing raspberries on our bellies. As they often did, our parents embraced and kissed, while Edzia and I tumbled on our bed until we heard the sound of a bed board dropping onto the floor.

The next day, I came home from playing outside with Hanna, our cat, and was frightened to see Mama standing at the large, round, shallow, wooden washtub called balia. She scrubbed the laundry on a washboard, and her tears were dripping into the soapy water.

Frightened I said, "Mama, what's wrong? Why are you crying?"

She wiped her eyes with her apron and sat down on a straight wooden chair. She lifted me on to her lap and kissed my cheek.

As I was standing in the empty room next to the bucket of white paint in the middle of the floor, I could still feel my mama's arms around me and her lips on my cheek.

"I'm afraid that there will be hard times for Jews, Jentala," Mama said, her large, round, green eyes shined from the tears she had shed only moments ago. This time it didn't bothered me when she called me Jentala again, and I didn't correct her. Other times I would say, "My name is Jadzia, Mama."

"Why are you crying, Mama? You are frightening me. Where is Tata?"

That was the first thing that entered my mind. Whenever Mama cried, it had to be because of Tata. Did the goyim hurt him while trying to protect an old Jew? Did he quit his job? Were people saying bad things about him?

"Don't talk too loud," she whispered. "Tata is sleeping, he needs a good rest. It's Thursday, and he will be working hard tonight, standing at the hot oven shoveling, not just the bread, but pastries for Sabbath.

"But why are you crying, Mama?"

"You are too young to understand," she said.

"Did Tata hit a guy with a stick for trying to kill Jews?"

"No," mama whispered. "Tata didn't hit anyone, but I'm afraid that he may have to use a stick sometime in the future. Marshal Pilsudski died today, and he was good to the Jews. Now, whoever becomes Marshal, only God knows what will happen to us?"

"Don't worry, Mama. Tata will protect us," I told her, and she kissed me several times and went back to her laundry.

I have never forgotten the frightened look on mama's face, but she was right.

Smigly Ric became marshal and the Endeks, an organization who's main function was to intimidate, brutalize, or kill Jews, had little opposition from the new marshal.

Penc's son, Zigmund, was a young teenager, and rumors were that he had joined the Endeks, causing Pec's Jewish tenants to be wary of him.

Three months before I was to begin first grade, Penc had decided to evacuate his buildings. He wanted to restore and rent them for more money.

The Altman's were the first to move to Plac Stare Miasto (Old Town), only a short walking distance from Pec's place.

Pan Franciszek was a Droszkasz. He owned a fine droszka and two horses. He built his own home only a short walk from Penc' property. They had a garden and grew fruits and vegetables, even potatoes. The Franciszek family had two daughters and a son. Irka, their youngest daughter, was my only friend, and now, she too moved.

I stood, gazing at the aged, wood floor that had been scrubbed and painted red many times, and I remembered the Franciszek and the Sztraiman children sitting in a circle on that same floor, for there weren't enough chairs. Each of us had a spoon in our hands, eating from the same bowl of noodles with farmer's cheese soaked in butter, sugar, and cinnamon; or potatoes and sour cream soup; or whatever Mama could afford to cook. I made a mental note to visit the Franciszek family right after I opened the door where I saw my family for the last time. I was hoping to see the new tenants or, at least, the painter. I had many questions about Penc, Zigmund, and Ola, but the entire building seemed vacant.

I ambled out to the back yard and listened for sounds of the past. My eyes traveled to the roof, and I remembered the large cage and white doves, but the roof was covered with torn black tar paper. The entire back yard was deserted, as if a beautiful painting of a landscape had been splashed with gray paint covering every speck of green. I didn't hear dogs barking or chirping birds or children. The silence was deafening. I wondered if Zigmund was alive? If he were alive, whom did he hate now? There were no Jews left in Radom.

As I looked around, I waited for Hanna, the gray cat, to jump into my arms, and Madia, the rooster, to greet me with a loud crow. I remembered Snow after giving birth to three fluffy white puppies was very tired and slept all the time. Tata hand-fed Snow, but the loyal dog finally died in his arms. Our family was in mourning many weeks. We could never forget our beautiful Snow. Though it broke my tata's heart, he had to give away the puppies so that they could live. Tata took our puppies to a dog that had given birth to dead puppies. The dog's teats were swollen, but the owner refused to let her nurse our puppies, unless Tata would let him keep them. Tata loved Snow too much to let her babies starve. Every day we stood by the short, white picket fence and talked to our three little puppies. Each time we were chased away by the homeowners, but that didn't stop Bela, Edzia and, me from returning with Citra's tail wagging all the way. We were certain that Citra knew she was going to visit her sisters and brothers. She never wanted to leave the fence. She stood on her hind feet and barked softly, until the puppies came running to the fence wagging their tales.

Our family was the last to move from Penc' building. Each day the building had become more eerie, especially at night.

On the morning of our moving day, Tata discovered the empty birdcage, and there was no sign of the cat and rooster. Though it was too early in the morning for Sonny to have let the white doves out of the cage, it didn't occur to Tata that theft was a possibility, until he opened the stable to mount the horse onto the wagon. He was shocked to find our stable empty as well. Rumors were that it was Zigmund who stole all of our outdoor animals. My parents were devastated to find that our goat, the horse and wagon, the cat, the rooster, and the doves were all gone. Zigmund had dozens of killer Endeks behind him, and there was nothing my family could do. We all carried our belonging to Plac Stare Miasto six and prayed that some day we would leave that country leaden with hate for us. Like everything else that had happened to Jews, the whole thing was hushed up as if it had never happened.

"I have to visit one more place before I open the door I have been unable to open in 1945," I told Carla.

"Aren't we standing in the apartment where you were born?" Carla asked.

"Yes, we are standing in the apartment where I was born, but the door I need to open is where I saw my family for the last time."

Carla silently followed me without question. We walked three blocks before I recognized the little house. I knocked on Pani Franciszkowa's door hoping to see Irka. A woman in her sixties, a bright smile on her face, opened the door. I knew that this woman with the round dimpled face and round body couldn't be Irka. Irka was a gaunt girl with a long somber face.

"Does Pani Franciszkowa still live here? I asked.

The smile had vanished from the woman's face. Why do you ask?" She queried suspiciously.

"I'm very sorry to bother you. My name is Jadzia Boren. A very long time ago, we were neighbors at Penc's building. Pani Franciszkowa and my mama were friends," I said apologetically. "I mean no harm," I added.

The smile on the woman's face returned. "Yes, she does live here. Please, come in," the woman said politely.

As I stepped through the door, I saw a man in his thirties sitting on a gray couch in the small living room with a plate of food in front of him. He looked very familiar, as if I had seen him before, but I knew that I hadn't. I turned my head to the right and saw a very old, wrinkled woman propped up in a recliner. Her head was covered with a scarf, babushka style. Though there was no resemblance to the energetic, Pani Franciszkowa, I remembered her being a tall woman who never had a smile on her thin oval face, but we all knew that she was not a bad person. I was unable to stop my tears from flowing as I placed a gentle arm around her shoulders and kissed her leathery face. As if she felt that I was someone from her past, the old woman muttered, "My God, my God…." During our short visit, I was informed that Pani Franciszkowa had lost her husband, her oldest son, Janek, and oldest daughter, Franka, but not to the Germans. They had died some years ago. Her daughter-in-law, Janek's widow, was taking care of Pani Franciszkowa, and she told me that her mother-in-law had dementia. I knew that the old woman didn't recognize me. How could she? Having dementia was bad enough, and the last time she saw me was when I returned from the camps in 1945. By the way she looked at me when I said that I was Mindala's daughter, in that split second, I was sure that she remembered me, or at least the name Mindala brought back a recollection.

The young man, sitting on the gray couch in front of a simple brown wooden coffee table eating cabbage rolls, stood up and offered his hand.

"My name is Stasiek. I'm Irka's son."

"Why didn't I see it immediately. The resemblance to Irka is evident in your face and slim body? Where is Irka? Does she live close by?" I asked, anxious to see her again.

"No, she lives in Warsaw, but you wouldn't recognize her. She is very fat," he chuckled.

"I would like to see her, but our time is limited. If I knew that she lived in Warsaw I would have looked her up, we just came from there," I said.

Carla whispered that she needed to relieve herself. I asked Helena if my friend could use the bathroom?

"Certainly," Helena said smiling and asked Carla to follow her.
A few minutes later, Carla returned and said in sotto voce; "The woman put a bucket in the middle of the floor and draped a curtain around me. I stood looking at the bucket and didn't know what to do, but I couldn't hold it much longer, so I used the bucket to relieve myself."

After I assured her that she did it correctly, she let out her breath.

Helena returned a few minutes later with a steaming plate of cabbage-pierogi, and Carla ate hungrily. The thought of the bucket and not having running water took my appetite away, but I also remembered growing up with the same facilities. Ironic, I thought, how easily I adapted to the good life. I remembered the times when Mama would buy a life fish for the Friday evening meal, usually a carp. She would club the head with a blunt object, then slice the fish, and place it in a basin with cold water. She changed the water two or three times and boiled the fish with onions, carrots, salt, pepper, and sugar. In the evening after mama lit the Sabbath candles, we all ate and enjoyed the fish, never giving it a second thought that the fish wasn't cleaned under running water. Now, the mere thought of it makes me queasy. How my life has changed, I mused as I was leaving Pani Franciszkowa's house.

Walking towards Plac Stare Miasto six, I recognized the old age home. The short white picket fence was still there. I didn't see the old people sitting in the garden or the lilac tree. I remembered when every spring the large, old lilac tree suffused the entire neighborhood with the sweetest scent. On hot summer days, if I had five grosze I earned for running errands for Fraida or

Sonny, I bought an ice cream cone at the corner store, only a few feet from the old age home. How I savored every tiny lick from the small cone. The store was still standing, and I wanted to recapture the taste, but the sign had said, "Closed." I looked through the glass door that sold the best vanilla ice cream, the only flavor available, and I was saddened to see it dark and aged. The paint was chipping from the walls and ceiling, the high counter I could barely reach to pay the five grosze and had to stretch my arm to receive my ice cream cone was cracked, and the once shiny wood floor was dingy and splintered. It was hard to believe that behind that counter, once stood a proud man and woman selling groceries and ice cream cones.

I looked over my shoulder and was too excited to tell Carla why I had suddenly begun to run. Though from the moment we entered Radom, she had learned not to ask why I did what I did, and she just followed me with her camera dangling on her wrist.

I jumped up on a three-foot high, cement ledge and grabbed a hold of the wrought iron fence.

"This is the apple tree the neighborhood kids reached for. Sometimes the branches were close enough to the fence, and we were able to pick a green apple or two and run like hell," I bantered excitedly while Carla aimed the camera at me.

As I stood on the ledge holding on to the fence and telling Carla how our hearts were pounding as a bunch of us kids tried to steal an apple, my eyes caught a familiar building across the street. I jumped off the ledge and ran towards the building with Carla panting behind me. I stopped in front of a tall wire fence and saw a woman digging in her garden. "What is your name?" I asked.

The woman put the shovel down and reluctantly sauntered towards the fence. "What do you want?" she asked.

I could see that she was frightened. "I went to Maria Konopnicka School. I remember that a girl in my class lived here. Her name was Janina."

"What is your name?" she asked suspiciously.

I had to remind myself that Poland was under the Communists rule, and apparently, the woman may have had good reason to be frightened.

"My name is Jadzia Boren." I hadn't forgotten that I wasn't allowed to have a Polish name when I started school, but if I had said that my name was Jenta, she would remember me as being Jewish. I pointed to Carla. "This is my friend Carla Stevenson. She was born in America. I immigrated to America in 1949 and am an American citizen," I said proudly and automatically touched my purse with my passport inside.

She looked at me with scrutinizing eyes and suddenly exclaimed, "Yes, I remember you!"

I was glad that she didn't remember my Jewish name, and I said, "A girl named Alina lived here too. Does she still live here?"

"She still lives here. She's married to my brother. Please, come in," she said getting ready to open the gate.

"I would like that very much, but I would like to see my neighborhood before it turns dark. May we come back later?" I asked.

"Oh yes. Please, come back. I'll have Alina here when you return."

Chapter Ten: Opening the Door to My Home Where I Saw My Family for the Last Time

My heart pounded as my tennis shoes imprinted the cul-de-sac. There were tall trees, now, where there was only sand in the summer and deep snow in winter. Suddenly, about ten children surrounded us. All of them were beautiful boys and girl. Most of them had blue eyes and blond hair, and fair complexions were visible through smudged faces. They ranged from five to twelve years of age. All of them wore shabby outgrown clothes, and they followed our every step.

Carla was wearing a digital watch, and the boys were fascinated by the fact that it showed not only the time, but also the date.

While Carla was busy with the neighborhood boys, I stood in the middle of the cul-de-sac and remembered every nook and cranny. I looked for the tiny grocery store at the cul-de-sac's entrance. The dim wooden hut consisted of a counter, a scale, and a few essential groceries. The storekeeper was a short thin Jewish man. I'm not sure if Putki had been the man's real name or if it was his nickname. In winter Putki was selling Halvah, a delicious candy made from crushed sesame seeds and sugar. With five-grosze I could buy a thin slice of halvah and savored it for as long as I could hold out. Now, Putki's little store had vanished the same as Putki had vanished. The ground had been flattened as if Putki and the store had never existed. I looked to the right in the middle of the block for the larger more elaborate grocery store that was owned by a Jewish woman named Marmel. Because Marmel had dark hair on her upper lip, she was nicknamed Marmel-Mustache. She was a tall, heavyset woman, and because she was overweight, everyone in the neighborhood was certain that she was rich. Marmel-Mustach had a fat daughter about my age, with thick blond braids. Nobody knew the girl's name, for everyone called her fat doll. Marmel Mustache's apartment was situated directly above the store, and she was the only one in the neighborhood that owned a radio and played it loud enough for the entire neighborhood to enjoy.

I inched over to Marmel Mustache's store, and I didn't see anything resembling a store. The door was closed and a white curtain hung on the window. Everything looked the same, yet nothing was the same. All of the buildings were still standing, though more rundown, in bad need of repair, but the people in the cul-de-sac didn't seem to mind.

I watched Carla holding her wrist up for the boys to get a better look. Though she didn't speak Polish, somehow they seemed to understand each other.

I asked the children to follow me to a building near the cul-de-sac's entrance. "I would like to tell you something," I said and pointed a finger to the ground. "During World War II, right here on this very spot, a man was shot by the Germans for no reason what so ever. His blood stayed on the concrete until I was taken to the Concentration Camp, and the blood was still there when I returned in 1945. The boys were looking for the bloodstains, but I saw that the area had been cemented over, and I told them so.

The children nodded their heads and were polite, but they were more interested in Carla's watch. I wanted so badly for these beautiful children to learn tolerance for people with different cultures and religions. Poland is a Catholic country, and these children had never seen anyone different from themselves. After I experienced the bigotry in Warsaw only two days ago, I was hoping that the schools would teach truth and tolerance to these young boys and girls.

So many memories came to mind as my eyes took inventory of each rundown building. I wondered what had happen to our landlord, Pan Jakubowski. Mama had always addressed him as Panie Dziedzicu (Squire). When Mama spoke to him and said "Panie Dziedzicu," it sounded as if she were addressing royalty, and maybe he was royalty, for he owned the entire cul-de-sac.

I asked the people in the street, "Who owns these buildings, now? Do you know Pan Jakubowski?"

They looked at me as if I were an Alien from out of space, and I never found out what had happened to the tall, distinguished-looking man, my Mama so highly respected.

The sun had gone down, and I knew that I couldn't stall any longer. I motioned to Carla, and she followed my footsteps into building number six.

On the first floor to the right, the window in Fraida's apartment was covered with a whitegauze curtain.

"This is where my oldest sister lived with her husband, Joel, her five year old son, Abraham, and her three year old daughter Eva," I told Carla as my throat tightened.

The wide entrance to the hallway had no door, and I stepped inside with

Carla nervously lagging behind. The walls had the same gray chipped paint, only more weathered. The cement floor was chipped and cracked. The marble stairs looked as if they had never been washed, and the cracks were filled with dirt. As we continued to climb the stairs, I felt as if I had never left, for everything looked the same. There were no lights on the stairs, only one very dirty window on the third floor, high above the stairs, close to the ceiling, which added enough daylight that kept us from tripping over each other. As we reached the top of the third floor, I had been unable to stop my heart from pounding, and the lump in my throat had begun to swell. I swallowed several times to ease the pain in my throat and took several deep breaths as I had learned in the yoga class. I was able to breathe better, but the pounding in my heart continued. I looked to the right at the large dark hallway. No windows were in that area, and no lights. I knew that there were other apartments on that side, but I had never known the occupants. It was always nighttime in that area, unless someone opened a door. Because there were no windows in that long corridor, during thunder storms, all the neighbors would gather in that area to avoid being hit by lightening. I turned into the very narrow, windowless corridor on the left and remembered the three apartments. My eyes were adjusting to the darkness, the same as when I was a child, and focused on the first apartment on the right where I had lived with my family. Immediately across, on the left side, Motek the shoemaker, his wife, two sons, and a daughter lived in two very narrow rooms. The droszkosz, with his wife, two daughters, and two sons, lived at the far right in two small rooms. The door on the left opened ajar, allowing some light into the ink-dark corridor. As I remembered, the same dusty, unlit light bulb hung from the ceiling on a long black wire. I wondered if this lonely unadorned light bulb had ever been changed or connected to electricity.

"Come on, Yaja. Knock on the door," Carla urged.

I was glad I had plenty of tissues in my handbag, for the tears were gushing down on my face beyond my control. I made several attempts to raise my hand to the door, but I couldn't control the tremor. I took so many deep breaths that I was beginning to hyperventilate. With Carla's urging, I lifted my right hand with the help of my left and put my knuckles to the door, but there was no answer. A middle-age woman on the left held her door wide open. I quickly wiped my tear-smudged face and turned to face her.

"The woman that lives here is outside visiting neighbors," she said politely.

"I'm sorry to disturb you, but I grew up in this apartment. While I'm visiting Poland, I would like to show my friend where I lived," I said, trying hard not to show my emotions.

The woman was anxious to be helpful and offered to go and find the occupant. After waiting ten minutes in the dark corridor, I was beginning to get very nervous and asked Carla to follow me downstairs. As we walked out of the building, I saw a short heavyset elderly woman with short gray hair, wearing a cotton print dress, rushing towards us. Her neighbor had informed her of the reason for my visit. Though she seemed a bit nervous, she was willing to cooperate. The three of us walked up the stairs, and I stepped aside, giving her room to unlock the door. When I saw the woman insert the five-inch-long, black metal key into the lock, the lump in my throat returned, and my teeth locked so tight my ears had begun to ache.

"It's the same key," I muttered in English. Only my lips were moving. The woman stepped inside her apartment first, and I followed behind. Though the door was already open, I gripped the door handle and pushed it down. So great was the need for me to open the door where I saw my family for the last time. Although there was no sign of the furniture I grew up with, as I walked through the threshold, I felt as if I had returned to a time when I was only a child. The only thing that had remained the same in the apartment was the tiled wood-burning stove, but the tiles had been painted over with thick beige paint.

"This is the same stove my mama used," I told the occupant.

The smile from the woman's face disappeared, and her demeanor reverted as I remembered May 1945, to a truculent scowl.

"Oh no, this is not the same stove," she argued.

I was suddenly under the impression that she was afraid I would be claiming the stove and immediately reassured her that I must have made a mistake. The scowl from the woman's face had disappeared, and the smile returned. I breathed easier and asked her if she would allow me to stand at the window for a few minutes.

"Take your time," she said.

I stood at the open window, looking at the lace curtains waiving in the gentle breeze, and remembered our moving day from Penc's house to Jakubowski's house. Bela carried Citra in her arms and introduced her to our new home, but Citra preferred Penc's house and jumped from her arms and ran outside until she saw the Altman's German shepherd, Wilk. Everyone was busy fixing up the apartment. I ran errands, Sonny fetched buckets of water, Bela washed the only window in the apartment, Mama cooked, and

Tata painted one of the walls with stencil, making the room look like the garden he didn't have anymore. It was a beautiful mural with red tulips on a white wall. Fraida polished the wood floor with shiny red polish, and the potted plants were scattered throughout the apartment. On the left side of the window were two side-by-side mahogany double beds with newly stuffed straw mattresses, clean sheets, and new, ivory color, damask bedspreads. The two beds were for all the women in the apartment. On the right side of the window was Tata's and Sonny's single, white, metal bed. The sleeping arrangements were the same as at Penc's house. In the morning my tata came home from work with a still warm bread under his arm and rolls in his pockets, and once in a while, he surprised us with a large cookie for everyone to share. After breakfast, Tata went to sleep in the white bed, Fraida and Sonny went to a dressmaker to learn how to sew, Bela went to school, and Edzia and I were the only ones left at home, but I, too, was soon to start school. I couldn't wait until September. Friday nights were different. Tata didn't work on Friday nights, and all the girls including Mama slept in one bed, and Tata slept in the other. Mama, Edzia, and I slept with our heads against the headboard. Fraida and Bela slept with their heads against the footboard. When one of us turned, the other automatically turned as well. Though Edzia and I complained that Bela kicked us during the night, it never occurred to us that, somewhere, other girls had a bed all to themselves. In the middle of the room stood a large, brown wooden rectangular table with chairs all around. My tata installed an avocado-green curtain to separate the stove from the rest of the room, giving the elusion that we had two rooms. The stove stood three feet away from the door against the right wall. The white tiles on the wood-burning stove were scrubbed until they shined. Mama was so proud of her stove, for it also had an oven were she could bake cookies and cakes.

After we had settled into our new home, Mama baked cookies and cakes and had sent each of us to invite her sisters for a celebration. Uncle Jacob had promised in his letters that he was planning a trip to Radom, and Mama wished it had been today when everything looked so new and beautiful, and Tata had a steady job. I couldn't remember a happier time. Aunt Hudesa took time out from her busy day and brought her two sons, Julek, the professor, and Shulim, still in school. Her husband Josef never left the hospital grounds. He was an invalid. Hudesa's two older sons were living in France. Shlomo was the oldest. He went to Paris and established a better life for himself, his wife, Sylvia, and adopted son, Dudek.

Lopek went to Paris to study medicine. He had changed his name to Lucian because he knew he would never want to come back to live in Poland. Aunt Hanna, too, came with her two daughters, Edzia and Hudesa, and her son, Lopek. Everyone was impressed with Jeremy's artwork on the wall, and Mindala listened with pride and said, "My Jeremy has golden hands. What his eyes can see, his hands can do. Give him a piece of land, and he could build a house."

She took her sisters hands and strolled over to the stove. "This is a very special stove," she said proudly. "It isn't just a stove with four burners. No, it also has an oven." She bent down and pulled opened the oven door. "Look at the size of this oven. I baked the cake and the cookies right here, I and didn't have to leave the house," she said her face flushed with happiness.

The sisters hugged Mindala and wished her always to be prosperous and use the oven often. Pearl and Mendel didn't come, for they were too busy in the bakery. Mindala knew that Mendle wouldn't come because Jeremy's house wasn't kosher enough for him. Aunt Hudesa brought a letter from their brother Jacob, promising to come for a visit, and the sisters hugged again when Hudesa read the letter. Jeremy's brothers also came with their wives and children and admired their brother's artwork.

There was no place to sit, but everyone enjoyed Mama's cheesecake and other pastries.

Chapter Eleven: Starting First Grade

All summer, wherever I went I carried my teczka with me, pretending to be a schoolgirl. September had arrived, but my teczka had lost its newness, even though I polished the leather and buckle to a glossy shine. Mama filled my teczka with a note pad, a pencil, a pencil holder, and an eraser.

Three weeks before I was to begin school, Mama had saved a navy blue dress from the last America package and took me to Rachel, the dressmaker. Rachel was a flashy spinster with bulging eyes. I had to see her for fittings several times, and when she looked at me, I was afraid that her eyes would pop out and bounce like little balls on my face. After the second visit, when she smiled and asked me to carefully put on the dress because it had temporary stitches and she began to shape the dress on me, while asking me to turn in different directions, I didn't notice her eyes at all. On the fourth fitting, she said, "Tell your mama that your dress will be ready tomorrow."

The day before school began, my new clothing had been neatly folded on a shelf.

Along with my new dress were new undergarments, new shoes and stockings with garters, and new three-inch-wide, navy blue ribbons for my pigtails.

After Tata went to work, I waited until it was dark and everyone went to sleep. I tiptoed out of the warm bed, and in the dark, I put on my new clothes and new shoes and stockings. I pulled up my garters, combed my hair, tied the ribbons on my pigtails and curled up on Mama's hope chest. Mama woke up during the night and was shocked to find me shivering on the hope chest. She physically tried to pull me off the chest, but I tenaciously wouldn't let her move me.

"I don't want to be late on my first school day," I defended.

As many times as she pleaded and promised to wake me on time, I refused to listen to reason, until she covered me with tata's heavy coat and went to sleep.

Since we didn't have a clock, I stayed awake all night until the sky turned from black to gray.

I stood up and pressed down my new dress with my hands and touched my ribbons, making sure they were still in place. I picked up my teczka and quietly left the house. I took two stairs at a time, for my new shoes made squeaky noises, and I was glad when I was outside of the building. I held the handle of my teczka securely in my hand and walked briskly trying not make too much noise, for it seemed as if the entire cul-de-sac were asleep.

The school grounds matched the gray sky and even the little candy store next to the school had a padlock on. I didn't know what time it was, but I was sure that I had left the house too early. Other times when I walked by the insane-asylum, only ten yards from the Maria Konopnicka School, loud noises were heard from the patients. Now, all I could hear was dead silence, and I wished the noise would begin. I wished Sara, who was always at the little window on the second floor asking the children to talk to her, would now be talking to me. My imagination took me from the man with the black hand to the man with the long sideburns. All the scare tactics my aunt Hanna used to keep me from leaving her apartment at night had come to life.

That morning, my first day of school, September 1935 had been as if the town had been swallowed up, and it took forever before the sky changed from gray to azure.

I turned the doorknob and tiptoed inside the school hallway.

As I began to walk up the squeaky stairs combined with my squeaky shoes, I panicked. I wanted to turn back, but it would have made the same noise, so I quickly ran up two stairs at a time. It seemed forever before I reached the upstairs classroom.

I had been on the school grounds many time, for the school was right outside the cu-de-sac, but I had never been inside, and the darkened unfamiliar room was very frightening, and for a while, I was sure I went to the wrong school. I sat quietly in the corner behind the last desk, until the middle age caretaker, a short, obese woman, walked in and saw that my teeth were chattering.

"What are you doing here so early?" she shouted, making my teeth bang louder against each other.

"Is this the Maria Konopnicka School?" I whimpered.

"It is, but you didn't answer my question?" she said, her hands on her hips waiting for an explanation.

"This is my first day, and I didn't want to be late," I muttered.

"Well, it will be two hours before you are assigned to a teacher. Go home and come back later," her authoritative, harsh voice frightened me, and I felt as if I was being scolded.

"Thank you, but I don't want to be late, so I'll stay here and wait. Is it all right?"

She must have seen how frightened I was for her expression softened. "The first graders will meet downstairs, you can go down and wait there," she said in a softer voice.

I stood up and curtsied. "Thank you very much," I said, still shivering, but I began to breathe easier after she left the room.

An hour later, another girl sauntered in and sat down next to me. "What's your name?" she asked.

"Jadzia Sztraiman," I said, "and yours?"

"Joasia Grosicka. My older sister's name is Jadwiga, the same as yours."

"Doesn't everyone call her Jadzia?"

"Yes, mostly."

"Where do you live?" she asked.

"Plac Stare Miasto, six," I said.

I live around the corner from you," she said.

Joasia told me that her mother had been sick for a long time and was waiting to go to heaven. Her father owned a slaughterhouse for pigs, and her oldest sister limped because she had been born with one leg shorter than the other was. Joasia had two older brothers, Mundek and Zbiszek. I told her about my family, and she soon found out that I was Jewish, and she made sure I knew that unless I converted and became a Catholic, I would surely go to hell when I die. In Penc's building, Catholic boys threw rocks at Jewish kids and old men with beards. "Jews to Palestine," they shouted, but it had been the first time someone looked sincerely into my eyes with concern about what would happen to me after I die, especially when dying had never entered my mind. No one in my house ever spoke of hell, but Joasia gave me to understand that I would be wise not to go there. I was becoming very nervous and was glad when the classroom filled up with girls. Maria Konopnicka was a school for girls only.

The teacher arrived and wrote her name on the blackboard, Pani Ulatowska. Pani Ulatowska was a tall, gaunt, middle age woman with deep-set blue eyes, wispy blond hair, and large teeth. She stepped up on the podium, the same brown color wood as the floor, and sat down at a large mahogany desk. She placed her briefcase on top of the desk and removed sheets of paper, books, and a colorful tin can. She opened the can and removed a pink hard candy and dropped it in her mouth. My eyes were fixed on her face as the candy outlined her right, hollow cheek. I wondered if the hard ball could break through her thin skin.

Pani Ulatowska looked around the full room and removed a thick ruler from her desk drawer. A moment later she banged the ruler on the desk and the room had become soundless. Each desk had two inkwells. Two girls were to be assigned to a desk, and Joasia and I remained at the same desk were we sat for at least an hour.

Using an authoritative voice, Pani Ulatowska said, "Sit up straight with your hands behind your backs. I will call everyone's name now. When you hear your name, stand up and raise your right hand." She began with the letter "A"

When I finally heard her call, "Sztraiman!" Nervously I stood up and raised my right hand.

"What is your first name?" she asked.

"Jadzia."

"On your enrollment application, it states that you are a Jew. What is your Jewish given name?" she asked and waited impatiently for my answer.

I was confused for a moment, then I remembered Mama calling me Jentala, and I hated it each time. I lowered my head and looked down at my hands.

"Jentala," I muttered feeling embarrassed.

"Your name is Jenta, sit down Jenta." I wanted to protest and tell her that I was Polish, only my religion was Jewish, but my mouth locked. I felt as if I had been buried in a grave made of ice. With trepidation, I accepted my name and from that moment on I was known as Jenta. Only after school, I made sure the girls on my street called me Jadzia, for I hated being called Jenta, and as of that day, I hated being Jewish. It was of no use asking anyone at home why we aren't Polish? The answer would be the same as always, "You are too young to understand."

At recess Joasia told me that she was very happy to be sharing a desk with me.

After school Joasia took my hand and together we walked home. Joasia's apartment was situated around the bend from the building I lived in. My new friend invited me to do homework together in her house. Her house looked more impressive than our apartment did. Joasia's apartment was attached to the main building, and it had the same address, but because the apartment had a separate entrance and only five wooden steps, it gave the impression of being a single house.

Before we entered the Grosicki home, Joasia showed me the basement that was located under the house. Chunks of pork, large sausages, and lard hung from the ceiling on hooks and were laden with salt.

"This is where my tata smokes kelbasa and all kinds sausages, but the live pigs are kept at a different location," she said with pride.

I knew that Mama wouldn't approve of me being around so much temptation. Up to now I had never seen or tasted pork before, but it was getting late, and though I was hungry, still Mama's cooking sounded better than what I saw in Joasia's basement.

I had promised to do homework together, and I was anxious to get started so I could go home. Joasia's one room apartment was larger than ours was. The kitchen area was dark, for a curtain was drawn to give privacy for Joasia's bedridden mother. I stopped at the clay stove where a large kettle filled with potatoes in the skins was boiling. Joasia saw me gazing at the huge pot and said, "That's for the pigs." When her older sister stopped in front of us, waiting for an introduction, Joasia said, "This is Jenta Sztraiman. She lives in the main building, and we are going to do our homework together."

Panna Jadzia limped over to us and looked me over. So your name is Jenta? That's a Jewish name, right?"

"Yes, but why am I not Polish? You are Catholic, and you are Polish. Why can't Jews be Polish? Everybody in my family was born here. I don't understand. Everybody always called me Jadzia. Today Pani Ulatowska said that my name is Jenta because I'm not Polish, I'm a Jew," I whimpered, trying hard to hold back the tears.

"You don't look Jewish," Panna Jadwiga said with half a smile, "but your religion is that of Moses, so you are a Jew. If you convert to Catholicism, then you could be Polish and go to heaven when you die."

I was confused and needed to ask more questions, especially about dying. I never heard so much talk about dying as I had today on my first school day.

Joasia took my hand and put her index finger to her mouth. "Let's see if my mama's awake?"

Soundlessly, we tiptoed towards her mother's bed, and I was startled at Pani Grosicka's ghostly complexion. Her thin fingers entwined with each other on top of the feather quilt, and her pretty oval face was chalk white. A long brown braid lay on her thin chest. A faint smile graced her delicate face when she saw us standing next to her bed. She stretched out a thin arm and invited us to come closer.

"Who is your pretty friend, Joasia?" She asked weakly.

"Her name is Jenta Sztraiman. We are sitting at same desk, and we were the first ones in school today. Jenta wanted to be called Jadzia, but Pani Ulatowska said that she's only permitted to have the name of Moses," Joasia said excitedly.

Pani Grosicka's chest raised as she took a breath. "Come closer, children," she said in a small voice. She lifted a tired hand and touched my face. "You sure don't look like other Jews, Jenta."

I didn't understand what she was talking about. Other Jews didn't look any different than I or Joasia did, or Panna Jadzia.

"I look like my sister Fraida. She will soon marry Joel Altman. My tata doesn't approve of her marrying a shoe repairman. He said that a pretty girl like Fraida deserves better, and my mama would like her to wait for my Uncle Jack to send us visas to go to America so Fraida could marry a rich American, but Fraida loves Joel," I said in one long breath.

Pani, Grosicka, picked up the rosaries that lay on her pillow next to her. "When you are older, you can convert, and you can have the same name as my daughter, Jadwiga, and you will be Polish," she gasped.

Her lips moved without sound while she gently touched each bead with her thumb and index finger, giving Joasia a signal for us to leave her bedside. We didn't have much homework on our first day, and I was glad to go home, yet I wasn't anxious to face Mama. I was afraid that if she would start to ask me too many questions, I might tell her about Joasia and her family.

Before I left, Joasia made me promise that we would walk to school together every day. For the first time in my young life, I had to keep a secret from my family, and I didn't like the feeling. Had I told mama about Joasia and her family's pressure to be converted, I would have been forbidden to be friends with her. I liked Joasia, and I liked Panna Jadzia and Pani Grosicka. They tried to protect me from burning in hell.

Mama was busy at the stove. She always made sure that Tata ate supper before he went to work, and I was glad when she didn't ask me too many questions about school. I didn't want to tell her that she could now call me Jentala all the time because that's what my name was going to be at school, and I didn't have to lie about my new friend.

I continued to see Joasia and began to learn all the Catholic prayers. I was glad when no one at home questioned my whereabouts. It allowed me the freedom on Sundays and often on weeknights to go to church with Joasia and Panna Jadzia. I was introduced to the nuns, who urged me to convert. I had been so impressed with the young nuns, and I had told them that when I grow up, I would convert and become a nun.

Sonny worked as an apprentice for a garment maker and earned tips for delivering the garments. I began to save every penny I had earned by running errands for Sonny. Each time he would send me on an errand, he gave me five-grosze. Mama, too, gave me a grosz or two for running an errand. Although I would have enjoyed spending my money on ice cream, or halvah, I didn't give in to temptation. Every Sunday when I went to church with Joasia and Panna Jadzia, I put all my pennies into Holy Mary's cup.

Our class had three aisles of desks. Three months into the school season, each girl was assigned a seat according to how well and fast she was learning and how she looked in general. The right hand aisle and the middle aisle were assigned to the best students. The left-hand aisle was for the worst students. Joasia and I were assigned to the right aisle.

Pani Ulatowska was always calling my name and asked me to read out loud, and I was always receiving yellow ribbons for best reader and best handwriting. She openly, in front of all the other girls, praised my reading and my handwriting. One day she singled me out from the entire class and ordered me to meet her every morning in front of her house.

"Every morning you will carry my teczka briefcase to school," she said with a soft, but authoritative smile, adding more lines to her already wrinkled face.

From that moment on, I had become the envy of all the girls in my class. On the first morning, I had arrived at her house forty minutes too early and waited outside until my fingers and toes were frozen, but I felt a great honor when Pani Ulatowska and I arrived to school together for everyone to see her teczka in my hand.

During school ours, especially during mathematics, she chose me to run her errands. She started by sending me to the store for her hard candy. As time went on, I had become her companion and lackey. She had sent me to the butcher-shop for the ground meat. I carried wooden boxes filled with sand for her cats, of which she had many. All those items I delivered to her home and handed them to her husband. Her husband was of German descent. He was a short, stocky man with a face that resembled a full moon. He was always at home wearing an apron around his large belly. He only opened the door ajar, being careful that his dozen or more cats wouldn't run out. Though many times I was cold and soaked during rainstorms, or I felt that I couldn't walk another step with the heavy box of sand, I never complained. It had been a great honor to be singled out by the teacher and given that much responsibility. Every girl in my class wished that the teacher would favor her as she did me. Many times she kept me after school and told me to walk home with her, but she never invited me inside her house. She would say, "wait out here, and I'll be right out." A few minutes later she took my hand as if she were my mother, and we often walked on the main business streets, mostly Ulica Riwajnska or Zeromskiego. Several times during our walk, she had me read the billboards above the stores or a street address. She would smile proudly and say, "Very good, Jenta." I wanted to ask her why I couldn't keep my Polish name, but that would be disrespectful. During such times, she told me how important it was for me to convert if I wanted to go to heaven. I promised that I would when I was older.

Chapter Twelve: The Wedding and Uncle Jacob

Many years my tata watched Fraida and Joel play house and make mud-pies. One afternoon, he woke up to get ready for work and saw the family rummaging through a carton with clothes from America. He was still in his little white bed when he saw Fraida try on a chiffon dress. He suddenly realized that his oldest daughter was not a child anymore, and it never occurred to him that one day she would tell him that she wanted to marry Joel Altman, the shoe repairman.

Joel grew up to be a tall handsome young man with large brown eyes, sharp facial features, and straight black hair, combed back. My tata also knew that Joel Altman will never be more then a shoe repairman, and he couldn't accept that. Now, Mama and Tata quarreled often.

Each blamed the other for allowing Fraida to get too far with Joel. Tata told Fraida, "Under no circumstance will I allow you to marry the shoe repairman. You could at least try to date other boys. You have never dated anyone other than Joel. How could you be so sure that you love him?" Tata argued.

"What about you and Mama? Did she listen to anyone? Tata, I love Joel, and I don't want to marry anyone else," she sobbed.

"You are too young. You have to wait another year. During that time, you will have to date other boys. After a year, if you still want to marry Joel, you have my permission."

Fraida began to cry uncontrollably. "Tata, I cannot live without Joel. If you forbid me to marry him, I will commit suicide," she whimpered.

Tata put his arms around his firstborn daughter and held her tight. "I won't interfere," he said simply, but I can't go to your wedding. I cannot watch my first-born child throw her life away.

June 1936, my first report card had only "fives." A five in Poland, was the same as an "A."

No one in my family expected me to be a bright student. I was timid, and in my sibling's eyes, I was stupid, and they didn't mind reminding me often enough, and I tried not to believe them. It never made sense for me to respond. I knew I wasn't stupid. I felt closest to Fraida, for I still had the memory of her dressing me, before I had learned to dress myself. Still, I knew that she, too, didn't think I was too smart. She was often surprised and would look at me in disbelief when I made an intelligent statement or suggestion. I knew that she loved me because she always fussed with my hair, making sure the navy blue ribbon was tied perfectly on my pigtails.

Bela would never allow Sonny or Fraida to call her names. The biggest insult to Bela was to call her "pig hair." Bela's hair was very blond, almost white, and very straight. Her hair was much longer than the hair of a pig, but because it was so very white, the nickname pig hair had been attached to her. Bela did fight back when teased by Sonny, and often Mama had to intervene when fists began to fly in the air. Because Bela fought back, she had gained the reputation as the smart one.

I had learned from the beginning that Sonny could do no wrong in the eyes of our parents. He was an only boy among four girls and had learned early on how to show his superiority, sometimes with his fists. When he sent me on an errand and gave me five-grosze, I thanked my big brother. He had always been good to me and never showed anger towards me. He would pat my hair and tell me that I was a good little girl, and I truly loved him. Though I also knew that while he told me that I was a good little girl because I was obedient and never asked for anything and never talked much, he would often chuckle and say "little dummy." I would walk a way wondering if he was right.

We had no plumbing in our home. Several times a day we needed to go to the dumpsite near the outhouse and empty a pail filled with waste. Other times we needed to fetch a pail of water from the nearby coin hydrant. Fraida and Sonny were the oldest children, but they both worked for garment makers. Bela was the only one old enough to help. When Mama asked her to fetch a pail of water, she almost always threw a tantrum. After a minute or so of watching Mama pushing the empty pail at Bela begging her to go, I grabbed the coin and empty pail and ran to the hydrant. I filled the pail to the brim. By the time I reached the third floor, I had spilled half of the water all over my feet, and my arm felt as if it had been pulled out of the sockets, but we now had some water, and I didn't have to hear the pleading and whining. My reward was when Mama kissed me and said, "You are too young to carry a pail of water." She would kiss me again and say, "You are my best child." It bothered me, though, that Mama didn't say that I was a smart little girl, the way she would often emphasize to her friends about the smart things Bela had said yesterday. I respected Bela and tried to emulate her, but she was after all three years older and read many library books. She would often correct my grammar or my demeanor. "It's not polite to laugh so loud; don't eat with your mouth open; and if someone pays you a compliment, you should say thank you, not giggle." Always before her friends would come over, she never failed to tell me ahead of time, "Don't follow me around when my friends are here; you have your own friends."

School was just the opposite for me. From the very first day, after I got over my name change from Jadzia to Jenta, my teacher often praised my good manners, my school work, and very often said to the other Jewish girls in my class to take an example from Jenta. "Look how clean she eats. Not like you, Szepsman! You have jam all over your face. Why can't you be like Jenta?" That part I didn't like. I felt bad for Szepsman or my cousin Ester. Pani Ulatowska ridiculed her reading or writing in front of the other girls and praised my Polish. "You see how smart Jenta is?" she would say, and I felt bad for my cousin and sat in my seat trying not to look her way. After school with Joasia and her family, I felt special, too. They were always happy to see me. All I had to do was learn the Catholic prayers and promise to convert when I was older.

Every morning before school I stopped at Joasia's house. We said our prayers together and went to school.

I had divided my young life in two parts. Though, Bela showed off my perfect score on my report cards to her friends, at home, I was loved. I knew that, but I also knew that I was the good, stupid child. I was also completely Jewish at home. I enjoyed Friday nights when Tata was home at night. I loved watching Mama light the Sabbath candles and say the Hebrew prayer welcoming the Sabbath. We all sat at the table for a festive meal without praying or any kind of traditional ritual. After dinner, our playful Tata would get on the floor on his hands and knees, and Edzia and I would ride him as if he were a horse.

My tata wasn't religious. He never prayed, but he would never stand by and watch a Jew being beaten without stepping in and often risk his own life. Mama kept kosher as every Jewish housewife in Poland did. She never mixed dairy dishes with the meat dishes, and if we accidentally used a butter knife on a meat dish, Mama buried the knife in the soil of a houseplant and kept it there over night. Afterwards, we were allowed to use it again.

I had never learned about traditions, such as a Seder on Passover or High Holidays. I never saw it at home, though I knew that such traditions existed in Jewish homes, but not in ours.

Though my tata never practiced his religion, Mama would go to Temple on the High Holidays and fasted on Yom Kippur. Both my parents were committed to the Jewish faith, and I could never tell them what I was doing when I wasn't at home.

As soon as I left our apartment, I had left my religion and had begun a secret life.

Walking down the street, I crossed myself and curtsied in front of a nun, I crossed myself and curtsied in front of a priest. Since I knew all the Catholic prayers, I was their equal. I felt Catholic in every way, and my Catholic friends never treated me differently.

Some of the Jewish girls in my class lived on Walowa Street, a Jewish neighborhood. It was the same street where my Aunt Hanna lived. During summer vacation, when most of my Polish friends, especially Joasia, were away on vacation, I enjoyed spending time at my Aunt Hanna's apartment. Whenever I stayed overnight, I played with the girls in the neighborhood. All wanted to play school. I was always chosen to be their teacher, and I wasn't just playing. I was teaching them to read and write and speak Polish correctly. Those were the times when I knew that I wasn't stupid. I sat in front of ten or more girls, some from my class and other girls from the neighborhood, and I was their teacher, and they listened to my every word. Their mothers begged me to do it more often, for their children did better in school after vacation. Sitting in front of the Jewish girls, I felt the same as when I walked through the door of our apartment and heard the Yiddish spoken words. I was Jewish again.

Now, as I was standing in the apartment of my childhood, I had a vision of Fraida sitting at the table, a page from a notepad and inkwell and pen in front of her. Mama began to dictate a Yiddish letter to her brother Jacob, telling him how wonderful it would be if he came to her daughter's wedding.

"My Fraidala tried to wait, but she and Joel would like to get married this summer. We set the date for August. It would be so wonderful if you would honor us with a visit." Uncontrolled tears were dropping onto Mama's lap. She kissed her daughter's chestnut hair. "You finish it Fraidala," she said and went to the basin and washed her face.

Mama never received a reply from her brother. Everyday she stopped the postman and asked if he had a letter from America for her. "Maybe it got lost among all of your other letters? Please check it again."

The postman pretended to look, then said, "No, Pani Sztraiman."

Finally, Mama gave up waiting for a letter and began to concentrate on her daughter's upcoming wedding.

One week before the wedding, Tata was out of work. Whether or not he quit his job on purpose so that his daughter would hold off on marrying Joel. No one said anything, but Tata stayed away from home.

Without money for a wedding, Mama didn't know what to do next. The wedding wasn't going to be costly since it was going to take place in our one room apartment. Mama would do all the cooking and baking, but she needed money to buy the food.

As always, whenever Mama was feeling sad or happy, she always went to visit her sister Hudesa.

Bela was busy with her friends, but Edzia and I tagged along.

On the way to Aunt Hudesa's, Mama asked me to go and bring Aunt Hanna to Aunt Hudesa.

"We need to talk about Fraida's wedding," she said.

Aunt Hanna's daughter, Edzia, had married a garment maker and now had a two year-old daughter named Cesia. Aunt Hanna's younger daughter, Hudesa, was in her twenties, and Aunt Hanna was anxious for her daughter to be married. Hudesa was not pretty, and Aunt Hanna didn't have a dowry for her. The chances for Hudesa to find a husband were very slim. I loved my aunt Hanna. She never made me feel as if it were a shameful thing to wet my bed, and I did many times when I stayed overnight in her house. She washed the sheet in a large basin and hung it on a rope in the storage room.

Aunt Hanna was just returning from the market place with the large empty baking shied and saw me climbing up towards her apartment. "Are you staying over tonight?" she asked, happy to see me.

"Mama is waiting for us at Aunt Hudesa's. She wants to talk about the wedding," I said, taking the baking shied from her hand and ran up to the fifth floor to her apartment to drop it off. Mama waited at the entrance for us before she rang the bell to enter the hospital grounds. She didn't want to disturb the caretaker twice. As always, Aunt Hudesa was happy to see her two sisters. All three sisters shared a special bond, poverty.

Aunt Hudesa never judged my tata, unlike their sister Pearl and Mendel. She never said, "I told you so," the way Mendel often did. We were greeted with hugs and kisses, and Aunt Hudesa spread out a blanket on the grass and wanted to know the latest news about the wedding. This time no one had a letter from uncle Jacob to share.

Aunt Hudesa's sons, Julek and his younger brother Shulim, sat under the chestnut tree, playing chess, and ate strawberries. I walked over to them, and Julek sat me down next to him. He put a strawberry in my mouth and patiently answered my endless questions on the names and functions of each chess piece until I became bored and went back to sit with the women.

Aunt Hanna and Aunt Hudesa reassured my mama that they would help with the cooking and food. They cried and hugged and talked about the least expensive way to make a wedding that would seem expensive.

Everyone stretched out on the blanket, arms folded under our heads and with closed eyes; the sisters continued to talk.

"Wouldn't it be wonderful if Jacob surprised us and came to the wedding," Mama said.

"What would you do if Jacob walked through the door right now?" Hudesa asked.

Before anyone had a chance to answer, Bela came running towards us gasping for breath. "Uncle Jacob and his wife Sala are in our house! He told Fraida that he wanted to see his youngest sister first!"

The sisters stood up, stretched out their arms, and hugged each other. Suddenly, they began jumping up and down until all of their hairpins fell from their long chestnut hair onto the grass. Still holding on to each other, the sisters began to run, leaving their shoes on the blanket.

Following Julek and Shulim's lead, Bela and I picked up everyone's well worn shoes, some with holes, and chased after our mothers.

As we ran up three flights of stairs to greet our American relatives, a barrage of every Jew in Radom flooded the cul-de-sac. Each straining his or her neck to get a first hand glimpse at the American.

Mama was the first one to run into her brother's welcoming arms. "You honored me by coming to my home first," she cried, her tears soaking her brother's shoulder.

"You are my little sister, even though you have such beautiful children yourself. I haven't forgotten when you were a little girl, at the time when our parents died, " he said, his large green eyes misting.

Aunt Hudesa and Aunt Hanna waited patiently for that long awaited hug from their brother.

Pearl, Mendel, and their children arrived within minutes. Pearl embraced her brother, who a long time ago had promised he would bring the family to America, but no one reminded him. Everyone was too happy to see him.

My eyes were fixed on Uncle Jacob's second wife, Sala, from Warsaw. I wasn't impressed with her looks. My mama and Fraida were much more beautiful, I thought.

Aunt Sala was about five feet four inches tall, of medium built. She wore a black hat on red, tight, curly hair and a pretty, two-piece, black, silk dress with white and gold buttons, beginning at the neck and ended at the waist.

Unlike Uncle Jacob who spoke only Yiddish to everyone, Aunt Sala spoke only Polish to me, and I was grateful, for I was more comfortable speaking Polish.

I was fascinated with the tiny gold wristwatch Aunt Sala was wearing. Before school was over for summer vacation, we had begun to learn how to tell time. Since we had no clock in our home, I had nothing to practice on. I followed my new aunt around and kept looking at her little watch. She was quite pleasant and didn't mind my tagging along. In fact, she seemed to enjoy my company and answered my many questions, mainly about how to tell time on such a tiny watch.

I remembered when on past occasions the sisters would get together to read a letter from Uncle Jack. They would talk about a time when Sala became insane, soon after she had married their brother, Jacob.

"That is because she had to have her insides removed and could never have children, poor thing," Aunt Hudesa said, her eyes misting.

Maybe, that was why Pani Ulatowska often wanted me to walk with her and hold my hand? I cerebrated. I knew that she had many cats, and I was certain that she didn't have children. As I stood close to Aunt Sala, I wondered what it would have been like to be her child and live in America? When I saw Uncle Jacob opening a suitcase and unpacking beautiful gowns for all his sisters, I pictured my Mama in the beautiful beige, lace gown he gave her, and I knew that I'd rather have hungry days with my family than live in luxury with Aunt Sala in America.

Uncle Jacob had a wedding dress for Fraida and one for Aunt Hanna's daughter, Hudesa. Hudesa looked as surprised as I was when Uncle Jacob said, "This is your wedding dress." Hudesa was a quiet girl. I seldom heard her speak, and I was certain that she didn't date anybody, much less get married on such short notice. She accepted the dress and walked away, her head hanging down as if she had dropped something on the floor and tried to retrieve it.

After the suitcase was empty, Uncle Jacob unpacked a large moving camera from another bag and told everyone to go outside while he stood at our window and pointed the camera down at us. He told us to line up and walk and make a circle and walk again. He joined us outside and continued to point the camera, and he asked us to form circle again and back up and move forward, line up and walk. Wherever Uncle Jacob went, all of the town's Jews followed, and the camera kept on rolling. He had lined up all of the town's beggars and handed out money and food, and the camera continued to roll.

I wasn't photographed too often. I enjoyed standing quietly in the background and observed how anxious the people were to be photographed. I liked looking at my uncle. Unlike my tata, who had a thick head of brown hair, Uncle Jacob was completely bald on top with light brown hair on the sides. I saw him as a very tall handsome man with large green eyes, the same color as my mama's eyes. He had a square face with high cheekbones and little spectacles pinched onto the bridge of his small nose. He held his head up high. His back was straight. His demeanor exuded self-confidence, unlike most Jews living in Poland. His round body matched a well-fed paradigmatic American.

Now the summer of 1985, I was standing at the same window pointing down my little camera, the way uncle Jacob did with his in the summer in 1936, and I remembered the cul-de-sac being crowded with Jews. I had no Jews to take pictures of and bring back to America to show to my children the way Uncle Jacob did. I turned off my little camera and thanked the woman for allowing me to visit what once was my home, and we returned to the hotel. I was suddenly very tired, and I stretched out on my bed and closed my eyes, letting the tears roll down on my pillow.

So many memories had begun to jumble my brain that I had to line them up and place them in correct sequences.

Through my silent tears continued to flood my pillow through closed eyes, I suddenly remembered Mama asking uncle Jacob to stay in our home.

Now that I was older and wiser, I wondered why Mama would think that her rich American brother, who doled out money to beggars as if it were confetti, would accept her invitation to sleep in the same room with seven people. My mama's heart was in the right place. She truly believed that since she had been so proud of her one room apartment with the beautiful tulips on the walls and shiny red floor that her brother would gladly accept her invitation. And why wouldn't she believe? She had never in her life stayed in a hotel, and it never entered her mind that her brother would stay in a hotel suite, having twice the space that we had for all of us.

Uncle Jacob kissed Mama on her cheek and said he was staying at the Europa Hotel. It was the same hotel where Carla and I stayed and probably the same beds my aunt and uncle slept in.

I recalled the hotel in 1936 being very elegant. The shiny, rich, mahogany stairs with Persian rugs covering the middle of every step, the lustrous mahogany curved banister, and the crystal chandelier lighting up the lobby did not resemble the Europa Hotel in 1985. The lobby was dark, and the stairs and banister were scratched and dirty. It was no more than a cheap motel, but the memories of 1936 were as vivid as if it had only happened yesterday.

Night after night, there were constant meetings with the town's matchmaker. Mama and Aunt Hanna were busy in Aunt Pearl's bakery, baking for two weddings, and my tata was nowhere around, and everyone had been too preoccupied to notice.

We had all been inured to Tata's disappearances, and now, at least, we knew it had to do with Fraida marrying Joel. Another reason was the letter Mendel had sent to the relatives in America, telling them that, "Jeremy was not a good husband and father. He didn't want to work and neglected his family." Since Jeremy knew about the letter, he also knew how low his brother-in-law thought of him.

Everyone in the family knew that Mendel was devious and mean, but I couldn't understand how a man who was always praying to God would do such a thing. My tata was fun to be with, especially when he worked and was coming home every morning with warm bread and rolls and often a large cookie for everyone to share. And when he woke up in the afternoon, he played with us on his hands and knees pretending to be a horse, and Bela, Edzia, and I climbed up on his back and we all laughed so hard until our bellies hurt. I was sure that Aunt Pearl and Mendel's children had never experienced such fun. That would have probably been a sacrilege in their parents' eyes.

Except for the table, which was needed for the food, all the furniture in our apartment, including the beds, had been removed. Our apartment had been filled to capacity with people. The door to our apartment was wide open. Even our next-door neighbor's apartment to our right had been utilized for the occasion. Everyone was standing. There had not been a chair in the entire apartment. I strained my neck standing on my tiptoes, trying to get a glimpse of Fraida.

Fraida had been the first bride I had ever seen, but I could not imagine a more beautiful bride. I often heard Mama and Aunt Hanna say that I resembled Fraida. I didn't think I would ever be as pretty as she was. I studied her face as she stood next to Joel in front of the Rabbi, smiling nervously.

As the afternoon sun danced through our window, Fraida's thick chestnut hair sparkled with rich copper. Her almond, green eyes and long thick eyelashes emphasized her ivory complexion.

No one asked how Uncle Jacob knew what size dress Fraida would wear, but the silk lace embraced my oldest sister's body as if it had been part of her. If America had such beautiful things, I wished Uncle Jacob would take us all with him, but he only stayed long enough to help find a young man for Aunt Hanna's daughter, Hudesa.

Uncle Jacob rented a hall for Hudesa's wedding. Aunt Hanna's home wasn't large enough for guests. I liked Hudesa; after all, how many times did I wet the bed and blame it on her? On the night of my cousin Hudesa's wedding, which took place only days after Fraida's wedding, I became sick with dysentery, and Mama told me to stay home.

The entire building went to the wedding. I didn't mind being alone while it was still light outside. I was too busy running to the outhouse every few minutes. When the sky turned gray and I knew that it would soon turn dark, I was terrified of being alone. I remembered Aunt Hanna telling a story about a man with a black hand. I imagined a giant with a big, bushy mustache. He had a very long arm and a giant hand as black as coal. When it turned dark, I suddenly remembered Mama telling her stories about how both her parents had died of dysentery. I was sure it was an omen because uncle Jacob was here, and he once touched my face and said, "You look just like my mama." Though it had been a hot August night, I got under the covers with my night potty next to me. I no longer used a potty, but since my stomach cramped every five minutes, I didn't want to soil the bed before I died. Once I was in bed, I would have been too cowardly to step on the floor and use the waste night bucket. I put the covers over my head, closed my eyes, and willed myself to fall asleep. I didn't want to be awake when death came for me.

When I woke up to the bright sun coming through the window, I knew that I must be alive. My stomach didn't hurt, and I was hungry. If I were dead, I would be burning in hell because I wasn't Catholic, I reasoned. Mama saw that I was awake and gave me a glass of tea with sugar and lemon and a piece of sponge cake from the wedding.

Uncle Jacob, his wife, and his moving camera went home to America, and we all remained in Poland, still hoping that some day he would send for us. The next letter had arrived from Aunt Sophy in America, and Mama knew that Tata was right. Uncle Jacob did bring Aunt Sala's sister and brother from Warsaw to America. Uncle Jacob was the only one who had the wealth to send visas for his sisters, and Mama never lost faith in her beloved brother.

Chapter Thirteen: Life Goes On

Fraida and Joel lived with us while waiting for an apartment to become available.

Shortly after the wedding, Fraida became pregnant, and Joel had been drafted to the army. Because he was tall and strong, he was given a horse and was trained to be a horseman.

On his first furlough, Joel rode into town on his huge brown horse, but he wasn't home when his son Abraham was born. Abraham was a beautiful boy with big blue eyes and straight blond hair, but he kept us all awake crying most of the night.

In the fall of 1937, I began second grade, and a new girl joined our class. On roll-call, we found out that her name was Halinka. She had dark blond hair and blue eyes. She was wearing a new navy blue dress and new shoes. We soon found out that Halinka was an Evangelist of German descent. 'Halinka' was a Polish name, and since she spoke perfect Polish, we soon forgot her nationality. No one asked where she was from, though it was obvious that she wasn't from Radom, and Germany seemed too far away. She was the only Evangelist in our school, and no one knew anything about her religion, and no one befriended her.

I had been chosen to perform in every school play and continued to receive yellow ribbons for excellence in reading and writing. Pani Ulatowska continued sending me on errands, and I continued carrying her teczka.

One month after school began, Halinka approached me and asked if she could be my friend. She would like to walk with me every morning and bring the teacher to school. I was glad to have a companion, for it was still dark on winter mornings. I admired her pretty, light blue coat with a gray fur collar, her new, high to her calves, laced up shoes, and her warm wool hat and wool gloves. In February, while I was freezing at the teacher's door in Mama's thin shabby gray jacket, many sizes too large, Halinka was eating a brown banana with a spoon. I wondered what her tata did for a living? Even when my tata had a steady job, I could never dream of ever wearing such beautiful clothes or eat bananas. I had never tasted one. Bananas were imported, therefore, very expensive.

Though I wasn't walking to school with Joasia, because I had to leave my house much earlier to pick up Pani Ulatowska, Joasia and I were still best friends, and I still said my Catholic prayers every morning, though I had to say them discreetly at home. After school, Joasia and I walked home together and did our homework in her house.

Before I left to pick up Pani Ulatowska, I knelt on a chair at the table, making sure no one was watching. I crossed myself and put my palms together and whispered the Morning Prayer. One such morning when Mama was making the beds, I knelt on a chair at the table facing Mama's back and began to whisper my prayer. Suddenly, Mama turned around in shock, "What are you doing Jentala? Are you praying the Goyisher prayers?"

My heart pounded, but I had learned early on how to cover my tracks and said, "No, Mama. I'm reciting a poem for school."

I had become so bold that during religious hour, when a nun or priest came to our class to pray with us, all the other Jewish girls and my new friend, Halinka, the Evangelist, left the classroom for that hour, but I stayed. At first, I didn't want to disappoint Joasia or my teacher. As time went on, my life outside of my home had been as Catholic as any good Catholic could be. In class during religious hour, I crossed myself the same as all the other Catholic children and said the prayers out loud as they did.

When I walked down the street and saw a priest or nun, I automatically curtsied and crossed myself.

Pani Ulatowska had been very pleased with me and that had been most important to me. The more she praised me, the harder I tried.

At lunch time, the poor children received a piece of bread and jam, and when my tata was out of work, I too stood in line for that piece of bread and jam and sat at my seat and savored every bite. The hardest thing I had to endure was when Pani Ulatowska scolded a Jewish girl when the jam touched her face and ordered the girl to look at my clean face. I felt as if a large rock had landed on my chest and wished I had been someplace else. At such times, I wished I didn't have to run her errands or carry her teczka, but nothing had changed, and she still praised me and ridiculed the other Jewish girls.

"When Abraham was three month old, he had stopped crying. His face filled out, and he became the little king everyone loved.

Day after day, Fraida sat at his blue musical cradle with hand painted flowers all around. Every Sztraiman child, including Fraida, had been rocked in the same cradle. It wasn't really a musical cradle. The body was made of metal, sitting on hinges. When pushed like a swing back and forth, the hinges made a squeaky sound, and we called it the musical cradle. Fraida was constantly talking to little Abraham. She called him every endearing name, "sweetness, fantastic baby, beautiful child, my heart," and much more. Little Abraham moved his lips as if he understood.

On a very warm day in August 1937, the sun coming through the window of our apartment was so bright I had to squint while standing on the other side of Abraham's cradle.

As always, Fraida was having a conversation with her three and a half month old son. "I'll make sure that you will not be a shoemaker. Even if I have to scrub floors for some rich people, you, my beautiful sunshine, will get the best education. If Poland won't let you go to college to become a doctor, you will go to France or America. Your tata and I will make sure of that, don't your worry."

Abraham looked into his mother's loving green eyes and cooed like a dove.

Fraida kissed her son, "I wish your tata could see you now? He would be so proud of you."

Abraham's hands and feet went into motion. He grabbed a handful of Fraida's shiny, chestnut hair and smiled, showing pink gums.

"Did you see that, Jadzia? Did you see that? He understands!" she exclaimed.

Fraida had been so enthralled in her baby she didn't hear the knock on the door. Our door was never locked during the day. The only key we had, which was about five inches long, was always in the lock from the inside, but the door was always unlocked. After dark, we turned the key. It was unusual to hear a knock on our door. Everyone simply opened the door and walked in. Since it was such a novelty to hear someone knocking on our door, I was curious and opened the door. I was surprised to see Joel standing in the dark corridor squinting against the strong sun. He looked handsome in the Polish uniform and high boots. His straight black hair and brown face looked even darker now, for he had spent much of his time outdoors. He put his index finger to his lips, letting me know not to spoil the surprise. Joel's black eyes sparkled as he looked at his wife and son from behind the curtain. With two wide steps, he enveloped Fraida's tiny waist, lifting her off the chair, and they stayed in each others arms for what seemed to be a long time.

I felt out of place when they began to kiss, and I quietly slipped out of the house.

Joasia was still at the farm with her family. I had a choice, to play with Hinda next door or teach Sara across the hall to read and write. Sara was a diabetic and couldn't go to school because she often fainted. The neighbors always saw me with my yellow or red ribbons pinned to my dress, and Mama boasted, explaining what they meant. "Every subject in my Jadziala's report card is always a five."

Sara's mama offered to pay me if I would teach her sick little girl to read and write, but my mama wouldn't allow me to take money from her. "Motek is a poor shoemaker, and he can barely feed his children. It would not be right to take money from his children's mouths."

Sara was a pretty eight year old with light blond hair and blue eyes. She only spoke Yiddish, for she was too sick to interact with other children in the cull-de-sac, and since she couldn't go to school, Yiddish was all she heard at home. Sara was a fast learner, and I liked teaching her. Since I had finished the second grade and would begin the third grade next moth, I considered myself knowledgeable. I used my first grade book and began to teach her the abc's. My Yiddish had not been of the best quality because I only heard Yiddish at home. When Mama asked me something in Yiddish, I answered her in Polish. It had been so automatic that we had not been aware of it. I understood whatever was asked of me in Yiddish, but Polish had been much easier for me to answer.

When I began to teach Sara, I only spoke Polish to her. By the time I had started the fourth grade in September, Sara was able to quote the alphabet and put together words.

My cousin, Ester, sat in the left aisle in the back of the classroom with the other underachievers. I felt sorry for my cousin Ester and divided my time between being with Joasia, teaching Sara, and now tutoring Ester.

Sara had made good progress. She could read words and sentences, but Ester wasn't participating, and her grades only improved slightly. I didn't give up, for her mother begged me to continue. The only good thing that came from tutoring Ester was that she didn't fail.

Joasia and I did our homework in her apartment, and I had never seen Pani Grosicka out of her bed. I had developed a great love for the sick lady, and she for me.

Once I had a toothache and my cheek was swollen. She immediately told Panna Jadzia to bring a special poultice to her bedside. Pani Grosicka dipped a frail hand into the mixture and gently massaged a brown thick liquid on my cheek. Within minutes, the pain had subsided, and so did the swelling. There were times when I wanted to put my arms around the pretty sick lady and hug her the way my mama often hugged me and all my sisters and brother, but I was afraid that if I touched her, she would die. So, I curtsied and thanked her.

Joasia never wanted to come to my house. She knew that my tata was a baker, and she was afraid he would catch her, kill her, and use her blood to make the Passover matzo. Many times I tried to convince her that Jews don't kill anybody and that the matzo had to be made of flour and water only, but she refused to listen to reason. It was more stressful at Easter time. Passover often fell around the same time as Easter. Hardly a day went by when Joasia didn't try to convince me that the Jews kill Polish children for the blood.

"Didn't the Jews kill Jesus?" she challenged.

"No," I told her. "The Roman's killed Jesus," I said. "Besides wasn't Holy Mary Jewish, and she was Jesus' mother, so why are we praying to a Jew and hate Jews?" I said, not able to understand.

"That's a lie," Joasia spat," Jesus and Holy Mary were not Jewish, and the Jews killed Jesus. And if you don't convert, you will surely go to hell."

I was so confused I didn't know what to believe. I asked Joasia to come with me to my tata so he could tell her the truth, but she took my hand and ran to her house.

Never again did the subject come up, and I never found the answer as to why the Jews were not considered to be Polish. I remembered Mama telling us that her parents and her grandparents were born in Poland, and being Jewish was a religion, just like being Catholic was a religion, but the Catholics were allowed to be Polish, but not the Jews. I never did get an answer. When I questioned Mama, she told me I was too young to understand, but I had a feeling that she herself didn't understand, and everybody accepted the situation.

Joasia's tata, Pan Grosicki, would often smoke kelbasa and other pork sausages in his basement. He handed me a piece of still warm sausage dripping with fat and a drop landed on my notepad. I was sure I would get a two on my homework. A two was the lowest grade, and I cried. Pan Grosicki bantered, "You don't want to eat pork! You have been faking all along! You never intended to convert, did you?"

I pointed to my notepad. "Pani Ulatowska will give me a two for the spot on my notepad," I hiccuped.

He softened his tone and suggested I tear out the page, and the teacher wouldn't know the difference. "Now, eat the sausage," he ordered.

I was very hungry. It had been at least two hours past my dinner hour, and my tata had been out of work. I stopped crying and pulled out the page, knowing that I would have to do my homework all over again, and eagerly ate the sausage.

I was glad that Pan Grosicki and his son Mundek weren't home very much. Rumors were, that Mundek was an Endek. The youngest Jewish child knew that an Endek was capable of murder. He would have no remorse about cutting the throats of as many defenseless Jews they could lay a knife to. Pan Grosicki and Mundek frightened me. They were tall men with stern expressions. Unlike my tata, who was affectionate and laughed easily, I never saw Pan Grosicki hug Joasia or Panna Jadzia.

One Sunday morning, two days before Christmas, Joasia and Panna Jadzia waited for me to go to church. When I walked into their apartment, the table had been decorated with foods I had never seen. Pan Grosicki stood at the table talking to a very distinguished looking man with long sideburns.

Joasia whispered to me that he was from Warsaw.

Pan Grosicki called me over and said, "This is Jenta, Joasia's Jewish friend. When she is older, she will convert," he said proudly.

I stared at the man's sideburns and felt as if my worst nightmare had come true.

The man looked me over as if I were about to be sold to the highest bidder and smiled approvingly. "I have a son waiting for her in Warsaw," he said to Pan Grosicki.

From the corner of my eye, I saw them sizing me up, winking at each other, then shook hands. I felt as if they were about to make a transaction. I couldn't wait to get out of the apartment.

I remembered that one time Fraida was reading the Yiddish newspaper out loud for everyone to hear, and there was an article about young girls being caught on streets and sent to Buenos Aires to be sold into slavery. As far as I was concerned, the man with the sideburns in Joasia's apartment fit the description.

Aunt Hanna's way of keeping me from leaving her house after dark was to tell me that the Man with the Black Hand and the Man with the Long Sideburns would catch me. I was terrified of these two men.

After the encounter with Pan Grosicki's guest, I became afraid of the dark. Waking up during the night and having to relieve myself had become as bad as having a nightmare about the Man with the Black Hand or the Man with the Long Sideburns. I was afraid to get out of bed, and I held it in as long as I could. When crossing my legs didn't help, and I was about to wet the bed, I woke Mama. She had to hold my hand and walk me to the night bucket and stand next to me until I was finished.

Christmas Eve at Joasia's house, we lit the candles on the Christmas tree that had been decorated with pieces of cake and cookies wrapped in pretty paper. Joasia, Panna Jazia, and I sat next to the tree singing carols and looking directly at the tree as if it were holy. Sometimes Joasia's brother, Zbiszek, joined in, but I was glad that Mundek and Pan Grosicki weren't home.

The next morning Panna Jazia placed a communion wafer on Joasia's tongue, my tongue, and her own, and the three of us went to church, and my family never knew what I was doing when I wasn't at home.

Chapter Fourteen: Going to the Grosicki Farm

June 1938, I had finished the third grade, and again, every subject on my report card was a five. Joasia and her family went to the farm. A week later, Panna Jadzia returned and saw me sitting on a rock teaching Sara. She asked me to help her with some chores, and I was eager to help. There were large sacks of cherries spread out on the floor. Our job was to sort the good cherries from the bad ones. Panna Jadzia stayed two days, and both days I helped assort cherries.

When we were finished, she said, "Come with me to the farm. Everyone misses you."

I didn't answer. I just followed her. During the long walk to the farm, Panna Jadzia asked if I had been saying my prayers while they were gone. I assured her that I had. She stopped on the road and told me to make the sign of the cross. She wanted to be sure I had been doing it right.

She smiled and said, "Very good."

Just before turning on to the dirt road towards the farm, a priest passed us, and we both curtsied and made the sign of the cross.

Panna Jazia ran her hand over my hair. "You're a good Catholic girl," she smiled.

That had been a very big complement, for Panna Jadzia did not smile very often. As we entered the farm, I was surprised that there were no fruit trees, only tall golden grass. By the time we had arrived, it was late afternoon, and the entire Grosicki family was happy to see me, especially Pani Grosicka.

There may have been other rooms in the small log cabin, but I only saw one large room. The only furniture in the room were two twin beds, a round table, and a rocking chair that Pani Grosicka sat in with a blanket on her lap. I went over to her and curtsied, and she touched my face with a soft hand. Even Pan Grosicki smiled when he saw me.

There were other people who I didn't know, and I asked Pani Grosicka to say that my name was Tola Wasilewska. Tola was a girl in my class I liked, and I also liked her name.

"I don't want these people to know that I'm Jewish," I told her, remembering my tata being an orphan because they lived on a farm, and his parents were killed by Catholics for being Jewish.

91

Pani Grosicka smiled. "I like Jenta much better than Tola. These people are our friends, and they know all about you. Now, go say your prayers and go to sleep."

Joasia and I knelt next to the statue of Holy Mary. We folded our hands in prayer and recited "Our Father" and "Hail Mary." We went to sleep on the wood floor, on top of blankets.

The morning sun was bright when I went to the outhouse. Zbyszek watched me from a distance as I knelt down alongside of the log cabin and said my prayers in silence. Joasia returned from the outhouse in time to hear her brother gloating.

"If you don't say it out loud, how do we know that you are not saying some Jewish prayers?"

I was too proud to answer him.

Joasia gave her brother a warning look to back off. She took my hand and said, "Let's go and say our prayers. I'm hungry."

I didn't tell her that I had already said my prayers. I didn't mind the repetition. It was like reciting the same poem over and over.

I felt as if I were on stage with an audience. Everyone, including the family's friends, paid close attention as I recited the prayers out loud. After I finished "Our Father," Pan Grosicka's friend patted my hair and said, "You recite the prayers better than the Polish children do, Jenta." Again, I was reminded that I wasn't Polish.

Pani Grosicka gave me a hard-boiled egg and a piece of bread. I refused the egg. I was afraid that she had given me the egg meant for her and I told her that the bread would be sufficient.

"You should eat the egg. It will give you strength," I told her.

She tried to convince me to eat the hard-boiled egg, but I wouldn't eat it. She looked so pale, and I was certain that the egg would make her stronger. I ate the bread, and Joasia and I went outside. It was a beautiful morning. The sky was cloudless. Joasia and I ran in the field where there wasn't another house for miles away. I had never seen a place where there was only one house in midst of high grass as far as the eye could see. Zbyszek was three years older than Joasia. He joined us and tried to teach me to ride his bicycle. Though he lowered the seat all the way, my feet still could barely reach the paddles. He held on to the back, and I tried hard to paddle, but I didn't feel secure enough, so I jumped off the bicycle and rolled in the grass with Joasia. I never felt so free in my entire life. All morning, the thought about being Jewish had never entered my mind.

When I left the farm in the afternoon and said good bye, little did I know that I would never see the beautiful Pani Grosicka again. Only one week later, the Grosicki family returned to town to hang out an announcement in their window, stating that Pani Grosicka had died, and the family would be moving to Lublin.

I cried for the pretty lady, not only because she tried to save me from going to hell, but also because she accepted my Jewish name.

Now that Joasia was gone, I was lonely, and yet I felt free from the constant pressure of going to hell. Having only Joasia for a friend wasn't easy to begin with new friendships, especially when school was still out for summer vacation.

Bela belonged to a Jewish organization named Hashomer, Hatzair. She would come home at night singing Hebrew songs. I never knew the purpose of the organization, only that she seemed happy with the group of kids. One day she said, "When I'm older, I'll go to Palestine and help build a Jewish homeland." Bela had many interesting friends from her organization, but I was the stupid kid sister she did not want in her circle. One evening, I silently followed her all the way to the organization. When she opened the door to let herself in, I was right behind her. She was very angry that I followed her. Before she closed the door, she whispered, "Go home this minute. When you are older, I'll take you with me. If you stay here now, you'll embarrass me. Now, go home."

I cried all the way home. Before I reached our building, I wiped my eyes with the back of my hand and mumbled, "I'm always too young and too stupid for my family." I wished I were more like Bela. She was smart and always said the right things. Everyone listened intently to whatever she said and laughed at her jokes. Wherever she went, she always had followers, and I always lagged behind her, and more often than not, she ended up being angry, and I ended up turning back with my shoulders hunched into my head. The only time my sister, three years my senior, allowed me to follow her was when she went to the river. She could out-swim anybody. Bela wasn't afraid to slide down the waterfall and coaxed me to follow her, but I couldn't swim and was afraid of drowning.

The neighborhood kids tried to emulate Bela when she tumbled on the grass near the river and walked on her hands. Her body looked as if it had been made of rubber when she did somersaults. All any of us were able to do was crawl under her when her body formed a bridge.

Fraida was happy now that Joel was back from the army, and they were talking about renting an apartment for themselves. It had never occurred to me that my oldest sister would ever have a need to live any place else. I felt very close to Fraida. It didn't seem so long ago when she helped me pull up my stockings and tie my shoes. Now, it was Abraham she was helping.

Chapter Fifteen: New Friends

September 1938, I began fourth grade. Since Joasia had moved to Lublin, I always came straight home unless Pani Ulatowska asked me to walk her home. Many girls from my school lived close by, but it wasn't the same as it had been with Joasia. I felt a kinship with Joasia, Panna Jadzia, and Pani Grosicka. With the other girls, it was only someone to play with.

I now played more with Tola Wasilewska. Tola was a very pretty girl with black hair, brown eyes, and a kind face. She lived around the corner from me, in a single house with a garden. The garden had two tomato bushes and a large apple tree. On warm days we sat in her garden on the wooden bench and did our homework. Tola's tata was a plainclothes police officer, but she never talked about her family, and I had never been inside her gray wooden house with one flight of steep wooden stairs. I couldn't wait for the fruit to ripen. One spring day, I picked a green tomato and ate it. When I saw Tola looking strangely at me eating the green tomato, I told her that I liked green tomatoes. The truth was, my tata was out of work for several days and I was hungry, but to say so would be admitting that I was poor and that would not be dignified. Tola never tried to encourage me to convert to Catholicism. It was possible she didn't know that I was Jewish because I never left the classroom during Catholic religious hour. Since all the other Jewish girls and Halina, the Evangelist, left the classroom for that hour, and Tola always saw me stay and participate in all of the prayers, it didn't occur to her that I was Jewish.

I had also made friends with two Jewish girls from my class, Lusia Royal and Henia Wertchaim. They too were good students. Henia's parents owned a little candy store next to our school. Henia, Lusia, and I were the same height, somewhat smaller than the other girls were in our class. Henia had brown eyes and curly blond hair. She was very friendly and anxious to be my friend. She liked to play a game called I arrest you. It was a very simple game. All we had to remember was, before one of us was allowed to sit down, we had to say, "I report!" If one of us forgot to say the word and sat down, the other had to say "I arrest you" and begin to count. Each count was worth one grosz.

Next to Henia's store was a long bench, and Henia almost always sat down and forgot to say, "I report." It was a good thing that I always won, because I wouldn't have been able to pay my debts. Henia always owed me money and paid me back with pumpkin seeds. Whenever her parents left her in charge of the little candy store, she paid her debt by digging into the pumpkin seed jar. This game often went on day after day, until one of us would call off the game. Henia always forgot to call off the game, and I didn't mind the pumpkin seeds, but I also didn't want her to get in trouble with her parents, and I would call off the game until she asked again to play the game, and I was hungry.

Lusia was the youngest of three sisters. Lusia had black hair and brown eyes. Her two older sisters also went to Maria Konopnicka School. Ida, the oldest sister was a pretty girl with blond hair, blue eyes, and a tiny turned up nose. A dimpled smile always graced her face. If there had been such a thing as looking Jewish, Ida would never be in that category. Renia was the middle sister and the tallest of the three. She had black hair and kind brown eyes.

When we started first grade, Ida had guided Lusia into our classroom after our seats had been assigned. I remember admiring her pretty blue coat and the shiny little shoulder strap purse.

Before Lusia's seat was assigned, Pani Ulatowska said, "What is your last name?"

"Royal," Lusia said.

"Your first name?"

"Lusia."

"What is your Jewish name?"

Lusia didn't answer, for she had never been told of any other name.

"Laia," Ida said.

Pani Ulatowska said, "Your name is Laia," but Lusia's name was only changed for one day. Everyone called her Lusia.

Lusia's parents owned a large grocery store. The girls were well dressed and friendly. Once in a while, after school, I came with Lusia to her house, which was located in back of the store.

Lusia's father was a tall, thin man, and her mother was a short round lady, with the same dimples on her friendly round face as Ida's.

At first glance, I could tell that my friend, Lusia, never knew the meaning of hunger.

I had my pride and never let on that there were days when my tata didn't work, and my stomach growled from hunger.

Once, Lusia took a large red apple from the store. She cut it in half and gave me the other half. We went outside to play, eating half an apple. Had it been bread or cooked food, I would have said, "Thank you, I'm not hungry." Since it was an apple, I accepted. You didn't have to be hungry to eat an apple, and therefore, it wasn't charity.

At Christmas, each girl in fifth, sixth, and seventh grade sewed a little, white, cotton sack to be filled for the lower grade children. The girl sewing the little sack embroidered initials for the girl of her choice. The sack could have been filled to capacity or scant, depending on the older girl's afford ability.

A week before Christmas, a girl from the seventh grade dressed up as Santa Claus and "Ho-Hoed" into our classroom, carrying a large sack filled with little sacks and called each name separately. Next to each name, she gave the girl a progress report on her schoolwork. She praised the good student and gave her the little sack with her initials. She ridiculed the bad student and gave her nothing.

Each year, several girls spilled silent tears as they went back to their seats. Since my name began with an 'S,' I was always close to the last on the list to be called. As Santa Claus handed me the little sack with candy, she said, "You are a very good student, but learn better." I curtsied, thanked her, and went back to my seat with my hurt feelings. I didn't know how much better I could learn than to have all fives on my report carts.

Though we were not supposed to know that it wasn't Santa Clause who gave us the gifts, I knew it was Renia who had sewed and filled my sack.

December 1938, after Santa Claus had finished giving gifts to all the good students, Renia stood up and called my name. When I stepped forward, she gave me a pretty blue sweater. I was embarrassed in front of all the other children to have been single out, and at the same time, I was overwhelmed by the generosity. I thanked Renia for the beautiful wool sweater, for I could never remember wearing anything brand new. When I returned to my seat and looked again at the sweater, as blue as the sky on a sunny, cloudless day, I suddenly felt very poor. It didn't feel like a present, it felt more like charity, and I never wore the sweater.

Though it was two years since Halina joined our school and the two of us had been proudly walking every morning to school with our teacher, Pani Ulatowska only intrusted me with her teczka.

Halina was a quiet girl. She never talked about herself. I was her only friend, yet I never knew where she lived. She never invited me to her home or cared to come to my home; though, she did know where I lived, and most mornings, she waited outside my home, and we walked together to pick up our teacher. On recess, Halina often stood at a distance and ate her lunch or a snack and watched us interact. I never saw her laugh or be willing to participate in conversation with other girls, not even me, though we were friends. At the end of a school day, she left immediately. I once asked her if she would like to do homework together? She shook her head without an explanation.

At least three times a week, I was ordered by Pani Ulatowska to walk home with her and carry her teczka. She continued with same routine, leaving her teczka at home, then took my hand, and we went strolling in the park or on the most popular streets. She smiled when she saw me curtsy and do the sign of the cross each time we passed a priest or a nun, and we always passed several, for the church was close by.

One warm afternoon on the way home from walking with Pani Ulatowska, three high school boys circled around me. "Let's get that little Jew girl," one said, and they all laughed, and their hands began reaching for me. Suddenly, I never felt more Catholic and more self-assured than I did that moment. With the palms of my hands I pushed them away from me as hard as I could.

"How dare you call me a Jew girl! If you don't take your hands off me and step aside this minute, you'll soon be limping all the way home!" I shouted aiming my foot for the first kick.

"She's not Jewish; leave her alone," one said, and each boy apologized separately. They were still apologizing as they crossed the street.

For the first time in my young life, I found out what it was like not to be Jewish. The rest of the way home, I was feeling as if nobody could ever hurt me. Just as I kept the secret from my family about my double life, that too had become my secret. I was afraid that if I would tell my tata about the boys, he would go out looking for them with a stick.

Chapter Sixteen: From Joy to Tears

I loved springtime, when the snow began to melt, and the warm sun relaxed my hunched shoulders. Soon, the large lilac tree in front of the nursing home would begin to suffuse the neighborhood with the wonderful scent. I liked that particular time, because my tata always worked, baking matzos for Passover. It meant, a new dress. Not really new, it was a makeover from a larger dress, but the sandals and socks were new, and sometimes I would get a new ribbon for my pigtails. I couldn't wait to wear my new clothes. It felt good to be outside without Mama'a ugly gray jacket.

Spring 1939 was a happy time for our family. My tata had begun to build his bakery, a dream he had since the day he sold his first bakery and took off on a journey to Palestine.

"By the end of this summer I will be my own boss," he said proudly.

Mama kissed him. It was nothing new for they always kissed.

"Your tata is building the bakery with his own two hands. He has golden hands," she said, as tears of joy glistened in her large round green eyes.

My mind was many years in the past when Carla reminded me that I promised my school friend, Janina, a return visit.

Janina and I went to school together six days a week until Jun 1939, when we finished four grades. During the entire four years, though we lived close to each other, I never saw the inside of her garden or her house. She would stand at the gate of the open door, and we would greet each other, but she never invited me in. Janina was the richest girl in our class. Behind the rod-iron gate, Janina's family owned an entire block with large houses and a lush garden with flowers vegetables and fruit trees. Now, an elderly woman, not a child any more, Janina unlocked the gate and excitedly invited Carla and me in to her home. As we passed through the gate, I remembered another girl.

"Didn't Aalina live here?" I asked.

"She still does. She's married to my brother," Janina said.

"As long as we are on the subject, do you know where Tola Wasilewska lives?" I asked, being sure she wouldn't know.

"Tola lives only a short walk from here. Would you like to see Aalina and Tola?"

"I would love to see them," I said.

"Then, I'll arrange it," Janina said happily.

Janina's house wasn't at all what I expected it to be. As a child I visualized a palace as in a fairy tale. To my disappointment, I stepped into a small, drab living room-dining room combination. An expensive Persian rug set under an old mahogany dining room table. Janina didn't offer to show us the rest of the house. She introduced an elderly woman sitting in the living room on a small, dark, non-descriptive, old sofa and said, "She's my boarder and sleeps on this sofa."

The dining table was filled to capacity with imported sardines, pate's, and other delicacies. It was a very generous table for a Soviet Union Occupied Country. Janina told me that she was making mink hats to supplement her income and offered to make us mink hats for twenty dollars each. We knew that it was a bargain even though twenty American dollars had been a lot of zlotys in Poland. I told her that we were going to Krakow for two days, and she promised that the hats would be ready when we returned.

"Please, eat," Janina said, making a hand gesture towards the table.

Carla immediately made herself comfortable and began to eat.

I was amazed at how quickly the ways of my childhood had returned. In America, when I'm invited to my friend's homes for dinner or lunch, I never hesitate. I feel perfectly comfortable sitting at the table and helping myself to servings of food. Now, after forty years being back in Poland, I was sitting next to Janina and suddenly felt as I had when I was a child. Accepting food meant that I was poor, and I told Janina, as I told others' decades ago, that I wasn't hungry.

Before we left, Janina gave me her telephone number and promised to have Aalina and Tola in her house when we returned from Krakow.

I lay in bed in our drab hotel room, trying to remember my school, but I was too tired to think. After a poor night's sleep, I woke up early and found a little store with the best cheesecake I had ever tasted. Carla and I ate as we walked towards my school. When I finished the last bite, I found myself standing in front of my school.

The very small, single house, only a few feet from the school, intrigued me. All the years I lived on Plac Stare Miasto and went to Maria Konopnicka, school, I didn't remember the little house being there. As I focused my camera on the little house with the sloped roof, I couldn't believe what I was looking at. Immediately above the front door, my lense focused in on a large, brown, wooden Star of David nestled in a wooden circle. The Star of David and the circle were the same color as the house. A short, overweight, elderly woman sauntered out of the little house and introduced herself. I wondered if she was Jewish, for that would be a good reason not remove the Star of David. I soon found out that she was indeed a good Catholic. She was very friendly and anxious to show me the beautiful church that was being built in the same place where the insane asylum once was.

When I pointed to the Star of David and asked her if she knew the significance of it? She shrugged her shoulders and said, "It's always been there."

She invited us to her home, and I felt a stabbing pain in my chest when I saw the amount of furniture in the tiny living room. She could barely open her front door as we squeezed through the large mahogany dining room table and hutch.

As I looked around her small house, filled to capacity with furniture, I remembered August 1942, the day after the liquidation of the ghetto, when the soldiers marched us inside the silent ghetto. Homes filled with furniture, but the people had been swallowed up. I tried hard to keep from asking which Jewish house her beautiful furniture had come from, and I wondered if I looked hard enough, would I recognize a piece of furniture from my own home?

The woman saw me in deep thought and pushed her ample bulk between her couch and table to reach a chest of drawers and returned with a box of prewar pictures. I recognized Ida Royal, Lusia's oldest sister, sitting in front of a group of children. Her dimpled smile was hard to miss. I told the woman that Ida Royal survived the war and lived in San Diego, California.

"I would appreciate if you could give me the picture. I'll make sure that she will make duplicates and returns the picture to you."

The woman didn't want to part with her picture. After I gave her my word that the picture would be returned to her, she reluctantly gave me the picture and again reminded me that she would like to have it back as soon as possible. The woman volunteered to be our guide, though I felt that I could find my way around. Before I had a chance to say, "Thank you, but I would like to see if I still remember my way around," she began walking with us to my school.

My school had been condemned, and nobody was allowed inside. The little candy store once owned by Henia Wertchaim's parents had been torn down. My eyes searched for the tiny cell my mama was kept in several days and interrogated every day to tell the police where Tata was hiding. That too had been torn down. The doors to the main entrance of my school were locked.

Just as I needed to open the door to the home of my past, I now needed to step inside the classroom where I began first grade and had not been allowed to continue after finishing only four grades. For some time, until the ghetto had been formed and my school became a police station, I heard the school bell and children's laughter on recess, but I was forbidden to join my schoolmates because I was Jewish.

Now, forty-six years later, the property's caretaker appeared and told me that it was too dangerous to enter the building. I told him that I wanted to show my friend my classroom. He saw the disappointment on my face and said, "be very careful," and unlocked the back door and carefully guided us in. Except for one wooden chair, the room was empty. My voice echoed as I was describing the layout of the classroom to Carla.

Yesterday, Janina told me that Pani Ulatowska had died of cancer during the war, and I felt very sad because I was sure that she would have remembered me.

I picked up the wooden chair and placed it on the right side near the window, the same spot where I sat four years. Carla told me to sit down while she snapped a picture of me. As I sat at that window, my mind was flooded with memories. I remembered spring 1939. A priest came to our classroom and asked the teacher, "Which one is your favorite Jewish girl?"

Without hesitation, Pani Ulatowska pointed to me. "Sztraiman, Jenta!" she said loud enough for every girl in my class to hear.

"Come here, Jenta," the priest said smiling.

Standing in front of the priest, I felt my heart thumping so loud. I was afraid everyone in class could hear it. I curtsied, but I didn't cross myself. I was afraid the other Jewish girls would tell my mama.

The priest reached in his shiny, leather, teczka and removed a naked doll as black as coal and gave it to me.

"That's for being a good Jewish girl," he said.

I curtsied again and said, "Thank you very much."

I felt my face burn as I went back to my seat holding the shiny black doll. The only time I had seen a black person was the chimney cleaner. We called him Murzyn. He was always covered from head to toe with soot, and nobody ever saw what he looked like. Except for his eyes, his face and hands and clothes were as black as the doll.

The girl sitting next to me in Joasia's seat touched the doll and said, "Murzynka," a girl chimney cleaner, and all I could think of was that I was in fourth grade, and what was I suppose to do with a doll? Especially a chimney cleaner, girl doll?

When the priest left, Pani Ulatowska announced that today was only half day. We were to go home and let our parents know that in one hour, our parents had to come to school for a progress report.

This time, I ran straight upstairs to inform Mama about the progress rapport. I knew that Tata couldn't go, for he had been working steady now and left the house early to build his bakery.

After Mama left with Edzia tagging along, holding onto Mama's dress, Tata sat at the table reading the Jewish newspaper.

I placed my teczka on the other end of the table and sat down to begin my homework. As I reached in for my notebook, my hand touched the doll I had forgotten about. I looked at the shiny chimney cleaner doll and put it back in my teczka. I hadn't thought of dolls for a long time, not since I had started first grade. The last time I played with a doll was before we had moved from the Penc house.

I remembered Mama taking a towel from the hook and rolled it up like a sausage then folded it in half. She secured it with a shoestring and said, "Here is your doll." I carried and cuddled my towel doll around all day. When someone needed a towel, I reluctantly gave up my doll, but I understood that my doll was also a towel.

Until the priest had given me the chimney cleaner doll, it had never occurred to me that there would be any other kind of doll except a towel doll.

My friend Irka from Penc house had a porcelain doll. When I touched the doll's face, it felt cold. I cradled my towel doll and thought it felt more like a baby doll.

As I put the notepad on the table, I was startled by the sound of my tata's voice.

"The stinking Germans didn't do enough damage in the last war and are now coming back for more. We're going to have a war again!" he bellowed to no one in particular, and he never noticed how frightened I was.

I threw my notepad back in my teczka and ran downstairs and found Fraida playing outside with Abraham.

"Are we going to have a war?" I asked her.

"No, who told you?"

"Tata is reading about the stinking Germans and said we will have a war."

"If we were going to have a war, would Joel be home? Don't worry. We won't have a war," Fraida said reassuringly.

Little Abraham's big blue eyes rested on my teczka and began squirming in his mother's lap, pushing at her round belly until his feet touched the ground. He ran towards me and began pulling on my teczka.

I removed the doll and offered it to him.

Abraham shook his head and began to back away from me.

"What have you got there?" Fraida asked. When I showed her the doll, she said, "It's a Murzynka. Where did you get it?"

I told her about the priest, and she kissed my face and said, "I'm proud of you Jadziala."

I liked it when she called me Jadzia. Jadziala was endearing.

When Abraham saw his mother holding the doll, he pulled it from her hand. She tried to retrieve it, but I stopped her. "I don't want it. I'm too old for dolls," I said and I went back upstairs to do my homework.

Tata was about to leave for work when I heard Edzia through the open window shouting, "Pociecho, Pociecho-------!"

Mama burst in the apartment and was followed by Fraida and curious neighbors. She enveloped me in her arms and began to kiss me, and Edzia pulled at my dress and repeatedly bantered, "Pociecho, Pociecho-----!"

"What's all the excitement about?" Tata asked.

Still holding on to me, Mama sat down and told everyone that Pani Ulatowska said in front of all the other parents, "Pani Sztraiman, Jenta jest moja pociecha. Jenta is my joy! You know what else she said?" Everyone looked at mama. "Pani Ulatowska said she wants to adopt my Jentala! She said that she and her husband had no children and could give Jentala a good home and a good education! Would you believe this? She thinks that children grow on trees, and I could just pick one and give it to her!" Mama bellowed and held me tighter.

"Relax Mama. Nobody is going to take Jadzia away from us."

I was glad to hear that Fraida hadn't forgotten my name, except that Jenta or Jadzia had stopped being my name. As of that day, the whole neighborhood called me Pociecha or Pociecho, Joy. I was glad that at school I was still Jenta. I had enough nicknames. After being called cat's eyes, just because my eyes happen to be green and slightly slanted, and red, just because my cheeks were pink, another name had been attached to me. At least, no one called me stupid today, I mused.

Easter came and went, and the teasing had stoped, but the name Pociecha belonged to me forever, and I answered to all three names, Jadzia, Jenta, and Pociecha. And sometimes, but not too often, my brother still called me stupid.

Pani Ulatowska continued choosing me to perform in every school play. I performed in a play celebrating our new President. Another show was at a real theater in town, and everyone had to pay admission. People were dressed up and were being ushered to their seats. I had a big part, and when I looked down from the stage, I saw my sister Fraida smiling up at me.

A letter arrived to our school from Joasia, and Pani Ulatowska read the letter to us for everyone to hear. In closing Joasia wrote, "I have many friends here, but I will never have a wonderful friend like Jenta." Pani Ulatowska read the address, "Joasia Grosicka Lublin, Sieroca 11."

How wonderful, I thought, it would be to write letters back and forth with Joasia and to tell each other about all the good things that the future would soon bring. I would write to her about the bakery my tata was building and the pretty short blue dress Wladzia Wachowicz loaned me to wear for the performance in the big theater.

Joasia would write back because her tata was his own boss, and she would have plenty money for postage. She would tell me all about her new school, and maybe some day when we were older, we would visit each other. I could have torn a page out from my notebook to write to her, but I didn't have the money for a postage stamp or an envelope, and I didn't have the heart to ask Mama for money. My parents needed every grosz for building the bakery, though my tata did all the work himself.

I was still reliving my childhood when the caretaker coughed to get my attention. "I have to close up," he said politely.

We had reservations to stay two days in Krakow, and I knew that it was time to leave Radom, but there were so many memories spinning in my head. Everywhere I looked, every street corner had memories. I told Carla that we would take the afternoon train because I needed to look for my tata's bakery, but I didn't remember the street, for he had begun to bake bread only one month before the bombings.

"Let's go to Krakow, you can visit other places when we return for our mink hats," Carla suggested, and I could see that she was anxious to leave Radom.

As I sat with my U rail ticket in first class, I was thinking that tomorrow we were to visit Auschwits, and all the horrors beginning in 1939-1945 had begun to revisit my mind. Though rumors of war and looting Jewish businesses in Germany were on everyone's mind, it hadn't stopped my tata from building his own bakery. He was determined to finish it. As much as he hated the Nazis, for he was reading in the Jewish newspaper about atrocities, he didn't believe that there would be a war. He too remembered the Great War and the Cossacks, but he also remembered that the Germans always paid for the bread, and having a bakery would be a good thing, he told mama.

I had never seen my tata work so hard. He worked six nights a week for a baker. He slept a few hours during the day and went to work building his bakery, brick by precious brick, until it was time to go to work at night again.

"Your tata needs to be his own boss," Mama told us with pride.

June 1939, Bela proudly carried my report card around and showed it to all of her friends, and she promised that when I was older, she will let me come with her to the Shomer Hatzair organization. I had several Polish friends from my class and also some Jewish girls, who always wanted to play school and chose me as their teacher. We also put on shows and sold tickets.

Debra Friedman's parents owned a bakery on Rinek Street. Debra was a Jewish girl from my school. Their living quarters were situated directly above the bakery's store. Part of the kitchen floor had been removed. A staircase leading from the store to the family kitchen was the only entrance to the small, dark apartment. The only daylight came from the bakery's glass door. A curtain was drawn to separate the living quarters from the bakery store. The curtain also created a stage. Friday afternoon, all the pastries and bread had been sold out, and the store was bare until Sunday morning. Debra's parents had given us permission to put on our show on Saturday afternoon. The girls sold tickets a day in advance. I was writing skits, and rehearsals had begun. I was the director, producer, and the star. Saturday afternoon, the storefront had been filled to capacity, not with children of our age, but with teenagers and adults. It was standing room only, simply because there were no chairs available and not enough space in the bakery store. Many people were standing outside at the open door. When the curtain opened, it felt like being on a real stage, and the audience looked up towards the family kitchen and applauded loudly after the finish of each skit.

When we took our bows after the finale, applauds lasted several minutes.

When I climbed down the stairs, a man, Joel's age, I had never seen before, put five zloty in my hand. "Because you are the prettiest and the best performer, this is only for you. Don't share with the other girls," he said and left. I never saw the man again.

I was overwhelmed by such a gracious complement, but I didn't think it would be proper to keep the money. The five zloty had been more than the take from everyone in the audience. I didn't want to hurt the other girl's feelings and never told them that the five zloty was mine to keep. We divided the take equally.

As the summer lingered on, everyone was worried, especially the Jews. From the moment my tata woke up until he went to work on his bakery, he was reading the newspaper. When I saw his lips and fists tighten, I left the house to give Sara a lesson.

One morning in August, Sara's mother was unable to wake her up. I had never known anyone who died before, and I felt a great loss. I cried each time I saw Mama trying to comfort the shoe repairman's wife.

Rumors of war had become stronger each day, but the people went about their business. The shoe repairman, the baker, the droszkasz (couch driver), the garment maker, and other men who couldn't afford to miss a day's work or his children would go hungry continued to work, and it had never occurred to them that the cancer that began in Germany would spread to Poland and to Radom.

Everyday the neighbors gathered in the cul-de-sac and listened to the radio blasting from Marmel the Mustache's open window. She was the only one in the entire cu-de-sac who owned a radio and graciously turned it up loud enough for the neighbors to hear.

The announcer's voice sounded threatening as he bellowed: "Halo-halo, Polish radio, Warsaw, Krakow, and the entire Polish Country!"

I understood the words, but when they began talking politics, I didn't understand the meaning. Before the threat of war, I loved to be with my tata, especially when he had time to linger while Mama prepared our afternoon supper, which had been served at three o'clock. He always played with Edzia and me. He would tickle us and kiss us and pretended that we were a sack of flour when he threw us over his shoulders, and we laughed and asked for more. Now every afternoon, he read the Yiddish newspaper. When I saw tata crumble the newspaper in tight fists and his lips turn into straight lines, I ran downstairs and listened to the screaming radio.

Mama was cooking supper to be served at two o'clock so that Tata could spend more time building the bakery. I was happy to know that our bakery was almost finished. When tata is his own boss, he wouldn't have to work so hard, and he would be in better moods. Most of the time, I wasn't sure if his bad moods were caused by being overworked or by reading the newspaper about the stinking Germans?

I was sitting on the little wooden chair watching Edzia play on the floor with the chimney cleaner doll. From our open window, I heard a loud voice, that sounded more like a dog barking, followed by thousands of loud cheering voices. I ran downstairs and sat down on a big rock and listened to the blasting radio.

My friend, Boba, saw me sitting alone and sat down next to me.

Suddenly, a very frightening voice began to shout with the same voice as Joel's dog, Wolf's, bark. In seconds all the neighbors in the cul-de-sac were outside listening to the frightening voice.

"Ich habe kein angst fur der ganze welt! England, America, Rusland!" ("I'm not afraid of the entire world! England! America! Russia!) Shouts were echoing from thousands of exited people, "Heil Hitler!" Though at the time I didn't understand the words, the voice itself and the roaring voices, over and over, shouting, "Heil Hitler!" was so frightening that I memorized every word, and I wanted to understand. After supper I followed my tata to our new bakery. As he dipped the paintbrush into the white paint, I asked, "Tata, what do the words, "ich habe kein angst fur de ganze welt, mean?"

Tata looked at me with large green eyes as if he had seen me for the first time. He turned his back to me and began brushing a wall.

"You are too young to understand," he said, speaking to the wall.

I had a feeling that he didn't want to frighten me.

"I'm not too young," I said tenaciously standing against the wall he was about to paint. When he realized that I wouldn't stop asking until he told me, he put the brush back in the bucket and said, "I'll tell you, but I don't want you to worry. It's just talk." When I learned the meaning of the words, I had never forgotten them. When I returned from the bakery, the radio was silenced, and everyone went back to his or her home.

Everyday, sitting on rocks and listening to the blasting radio had become the neighborhood's routine.
The next·day Boba and I sat on rocks next to each other, hoping to hear some good news. "Do you know whathappens during a war?" I asked her.

"Yesterday, I asked my mama, and she told me not to worry. She said that soldiers fight with each other," Boba said. Boba didn't have a father or brothers and wasn't concerned about a war.

Joel received a notice to immediately return to his platoon in Baranowicz. Fraida cried and held on to him, and Abraham wrapped his little arms around his legs and clung to him. When I saw my Mama and Fraida cry, I couldn't hold back the tears. Mama was happy that Sonny was too young to be drafted.

Bela was so involved with her organization that all she ever talked about was going to Palestine and building a homeland.

Everyday, the radio blasted with Hitler's rage, and the Jews in our cul-de-sac had gathered in groups and spoke in whispers about what the Nazis had done to the Jews in Germany. Everyday, airplanes were flying over our heads. A man in a Polish uniform had been stretched out on the rooftop, pointing a rifle at a low flying airplane. He then bellowed down to the people in the cul-de-sac, "It's ours! Maneuvers!"

With each passing day, more airplanes were flying over our heads, and the soldier continued bellowing that they were our own Polish airplanes, not to worry.

Each morning Hitler's barking voice and loud crowds in the background awakened us with ear piercing shouts of, "Heil----Hitler------!"

At two o'clock in the afternoon, the neighbors were in their homes preparing their supper. At four, everyone was back, sitting on rocks or standing and looking up at Marmel the mustache's window, to hear Hitler's threats about how he was not afraid of the entire world.

Just as my tata was waking up and Mama was cooking supper, a boy appeared in the cul-de-sac with an armful of newspapers, screaming from the top of his lungs, "Poland has Schlazen; we won't have a war------!" Within seconds, people sat on rocks and stood in doorways, and many sat on the edge of the abandoned water well in the center of the cul-de-sac. Two years ago, a child had fallen in the well and drowned. The well was now half full with debris and covered with rotted wood. All our neighbors, including my tata, were engrossed in the newspaper, and the newspaper boy left the cul-de-sac, change jingling in his pocket.

I was happy that we wouldn't have a war, and I looked forward to the third of September when I would begin the fifth grade. Nobody would talk about war at school, and I would try harder than ever to get good grades. This Christmas, I would be the one to sew and embroider and fill the little sack so that Santa Claus could give it to a younger student. After all, my tata now owned a bakery and would give me the money so I could fill the sack with real good things. I would even have money for postage to write letters to Joasia, for I had memorized her address. Maybe, one day I would be the one to give a pretty sweater to a poor child. I ran upstairs and polished my teczka and filled it with a new notebook Mama had bought for me. I sharpened my pencil, and I put a new ink pen on my pen, being careful not to chip the tip, and placed the pen, pencil, and eraser in the pencil holder.

An hour before Tata had to be at work in his own bakery, he took my hand and said, "Let's go and get your fifth grade books. I was proud that my tata remembered, for I had learned very early in life not ask for anything. I heard the answers when my older sisters were asking for things, and Mama's answer was, "When tata has a steady job." Most of the times Mama struggled to keep us from going to bed hungry.

Today my tata was the boss, and today he went with me to Szkolna, a street where students were selling their last year's books, and he bought me my fifth grade books. My tata held my hand as we walked home with my new books under my arm, and I had never loved him more than I did at that very moment. Though airplanes circled the streets as we walked home, I felt safe with my tata's hand in mine. I couldn't remember when I had been happier than that day.

When we came home, my tata went to the bakery. I put my books neatly next to the notebook and the pencil holder in my shiny teczka. With my new winter shoes and a navy blue Princess dress with a white blouse, all remodeled from a large American dress, I was ready to begin the fifth grade.

Chapter Seventeen: No One Was Prepared for the Evil

Only two days before the sound of the first explosion that rattled our windows, a soldier lay on his belly in the street cleaner's rooftop, aiming a rifle at a circling airplane and shouted down to the worried neighbors, "It's our plane! Maneuvers!"

I wasn't worried at all. The sound of the newspaper boy shouting, "Poland has Schlaizen; we won't have a war!" stayed in my mind and that was all I wanted to think about.

More planes circled our sky and a large piece of shrapnel landed in the middle of the cul-de-sac. The soldier that had been flattened on the rooftop began shooting up and was showered with a barrage of gunfire from an airplane at close range. He scurried down from the rooftop and disappeared.

Everyone was busy taping the windows with dark papers, and many windows shattered with each blast.

Friday, September 1, our airport, including several buildings, was bombed, and the town's men began digging trenches. All the neighbors in the cul-de-sac gathered in the dark, windowless hallway of the sturdiest building to wait out the bombing. People came with their blankets and pillows and slept on the floor in the hallway. Our entire family, including Fraida with her large belly, and Abraham holding on to his mother's dress, huddled next Mama. We all felt as if we were little chicks protected by Mama's touch, even if it meant holding on to her hand or her clothing.

Though the bombing continued, my tata went to his bakery to make sure that the people standing in line at dawn for a loaf of bread didn't leave empty handed. On the third bombing day, Tata came home early, his face was ashen as he told Mama that a bomb had fallen on the outhouse, and a baker was killed. Tata refused to sleep in the sturdy building's hallway and went home to sleep. I followed him home and lay down in his little white bed next to him. I knew my tata would protect me, and I fell sound asleep with my head on his chest. I didn't wake up until I smelled Mama's cooking.

"We didn't want to be without you, Jeremy," Mama said embracing her husband.

While the bombs were falling, Jews were leaving for the Russian border in horse drawn wagons, on foot, or on whatever transportation had been available, depending on how much money one had for such a journey. Sonny was eighteen years old and the apple of Mama's eye. He stood in front of Mama, begging her to pack up and leave.

"They'll kill us all, Mama. We'll all die."

Mama cupped Sonny's face with both of her hands and kissed the top of his head. "My son, my only son, your tata worked so hard for so many months building the bakery. As soon as the bombing stops, he will bake bread, and he'll never have to sweat for other bakers again. You know how he always hated to take orders from bosses. Now, he is the boss, and he is so proud."

"Mama, we'll never live long enough to sell the bread. The Germans are killers, Mama!"

Mama's tears had begun to roll down on her cheeks. "You've got the Germans mixed up with the Cossacks, Sonny. During the Great War, it was the Cossacks who were the rapists and killers. The German soldiers always paid for the bread, and they were polite. Why would they want to kill people like us? We mean them no harm. They couldn't possible kill us for no reason."

"Mama, do the Polish Endeks need a reason to make pogroms and kill Jews? The Germans have been killing Jews in Germany for a long time, and they will kill us all. Please, Mama, let's take Joel's droszka and horse, and Joel's father will take his own droszka, and we'll save our lives."

"Fraida has a small child, and another is due any day, and Joel is in the army. And what about your little sisters? Who knows what the Russians would do to little children?"

While Sonny was pleading with Mama to leave, Tata came home and told us that the Germans were marching in, and he began helping Joel's father to hitch up the horses to the two droszkas. Joel's three older brothers had left a day before for the Russian border. With Joel in the army, his parents, Garshnazik and his wife Laia, had two daughters and the youngest son at home. Their ages ranged from eighteen to fourteen.

"If Joel comes home alive, and we all survive, we'll find each other after the war," Laia said and began climbing into the droszka and was followed by her three children. Just as we were beginning to climb into the second droszka, a Polish soldier approached our building.

"Do you know where Fraida Altman lives?" He asked my tata. "She is my daughter," Tata said, turning white as the shirt he was wearing.

Fraida was upstairs getting Abraham ready for the journey when the soldier came through the open door.

"I'm coming," she said before looking up.

Tata walked past the soldier, placing himself next to Fraida, and we all followed. The soldier took off his hat and handed my sister a piece of paper.

"Pani Altman, Joel Altman died on the battlefield from a chest wound."

"No, there must be some mistake. My husband was at home only ten days ago. You have the wrong Altman."

"I'm very sorry Pani Altman, but I saw him fall at my feet," the soldier said and disappeared.

Fraida stood motionless. Then suddenly, her eyes rolled up, and all I saw was the white of her eyes, as if her green pupils had been stuck inside her head. Her body fell limp into Tata's arms. Tata and Sony struggled to get Fraida onto her bed and began gently slapping her face.

We all cried until Fraida's eyes flew open, and she began to cry out in pain.

Joel's family stood motionless, as if their feet were grounded and their faces had turned to stone. Fraida's scream brought them back to reality, but they were unable to stay in our apartment and ran downstairs. I watched from the window as Joel's mama hunched her gaunt shoulders and walked away from our building, leaving her husband to turn the droszka with the horses towards their own home.

Mama placed a wet cloth to Fraida's forehead, and Abraham jumped on her bed and cried. When his mother's piercing scream reached his ears, he jumped of the bed and ran into Mama's arms.

Dusk had left our window, and darkness fell upon us. Tata covered the window with a dark cloth and lit the naphtha lamp.

"I'll be right back with the Akuszerka"(midwife), he said as Fraida howled, holding on to the bedpost.

"You can't go, Jeremy. It's too dangerous; they'll mistake you for a soldier. You stay here, and I'll go," Mama cried.

"I'm going to bring the Akuszerka," I said before running out the door. I ran down the stairs before Mama had a chance to protest.

The Akuszerka lived approximately two miles from our home, and I ran to the sound of marching boots. I had no idea how I found myself unlatching the short, white picket fence. My heart pounding, I knocked softly on the door of the only midwife in town. When she didn't answer, I was afraid that she might have gone to help another woman deliver her baby. The marching boots were getting closer and louder, and I knocked harder, but still there was no answer.

"What am I going to do?" I cried, "Fraida needs the Akuszerka. What will

I tell Mama and Tata? " I began knocking with my fist. "Pani Akuszerka, please open the door, my sister needs you!" I cried loud, and I prayed that the marching boots wouldn't hear me. Through tears, I saw the door opening ajar, and the Akuszerka saw me crying and gasping for air.

No one new the midwives name, she was only known as the Akuszerka. She was a tall stout woman with kindly blue eyes. She had delivered all of us, and I was sure she wouldn't remember me, and I didn't care. I only wanted to persuade her to help Fraida.

"Who are you, and what are you doing here at this hour, with Germans at our door steps?"

"It's my sister, Fraida Sztraiman...I mean...Altman," I stammered.

"I can't leave the house now. Didn't you see the tanks and motorcycles?"

"I wasn't paying attention."

"The Germans are everywhere. We'll get shot being caught on the street."

"Please, Pani Akuszerka. Fraida just got news that Joel had been killed at the front. She fainted, and now she is screaming from the pain."

"Oh, Fraida, that pretty girl who married the shoe repairman?"

"Yes," I cried.

"I saw Joel in June when he was home on furlough. He gave me a ride in his droszka to deliver a baby on a farm and didn't charge me. It was a gift for delivering his son, he said. Nice young Jewish man and handsome too, big black eyes," she said, and I saw a faint smile on her round face. What's your name?" she asked.

"Jadzia...I mean Jenta."

"Jenta, help me get the horse from the stable," she said, and I ran following her footsteps and her instructions, and together we hitched up the horse onto the buggy, and she climbed up. Just as I turned to run home, she reached her hand out to me and pulled me up. She took the reins in her hands, and the horse began a fast gallop. Through sounds of hoofs and motorcycles, Pani Akuszerka shouted, "Joel told me that Fraida's uncle from America bought him the droszka as a wedding present. Is that true?"

"Yes, my uncle...that's my mama's brother, visited Radom in 1936 and gave my mama some money to make the wedding. My uncle asked Joel what he wanted for a dowry, and Joel said that he didn't want to be a shoe repairman, and he could support Fraida better by being a Droszkasz. So my uncle Jacob bought him a droszka," I said, hoping she would stop asking me questions and make the horse go faster. I was afraid that Fraida's belly would pop open from the pain.

The sound coming from heavy motors and motorcycles frightened the horse, and every few minutes, he bucked, and Pani Akuszerka crossed herself each time, and so did I, and I knew I confused her. She knew that my family was Jewish. She also knew that Jews wouldn't think of crossing themselves. I was glad she was too busy trying to steady the horse to be asking me questions about why I was crossing myself. I wouldn't want to explain about Joasia and my teacher and that crossing myself had now become a habit.

At one o'clock in the morning, September 8 1939, Fraida gave birth to Eva. She was named after Aunt Hudesa's daughter who had died of tuberculosis.

By daybreak, the Germans had taken over our town. The thought of leaving Poland was now out of the question.

Nazi rules began immediately and were meant for Jews to obey or die, and die even if we did obey their rules. The first rule was that Jews were not allowed to go to school and not allowed to step foot on sidewalks.

Tata did fire up the oven and baked bread. People stood in line since dawn, and the bread left the bakery as soon as it left the oven. Tata only managed to bring home one loaf. Three days later, the ration cards began. Since no one would have been able to survive on the rations, my tata began baking bread for the rations and for black market sales.

It didn't take long before the Germans settled themselves in our town, dishing out orders. Each order had tightened the noose around our necks a little tighter.

Hardly a day went by that I didn't witness an elderly Jew getting his beard cut off with a knife by the SS. Though as humiliating as it had been for the bearded man, it was a fun game for the young Nazis and still the mildest punishment for being a Jew.

Notices to young and old men with orders to report at certain places for forced labor began to arrive. People staggered home bruised and bloody, and many didn't return. I was standing outside our building with my friend Hinda when her oldest brother, a young man in his twenties, limped towards us, his face and clothes smeared with feces. He told us that the SS had him clean outhouses, and when he was finished, they ordered him at rifle-point to cover his face and clothes with feces. His tears left clear lines on his face and brown liquid dripped from his chin onto his clothes.

Hinda and I ran upstairs and picked up buckets and filled them at the hydrant with water. We told Jidel to sit down on a rock, for we were unable to reach up to him. When he sat down, we poured the water on top of his head.

Other neighbors did the same, and as he stumbled towards his father's stable to get clean behind closed doors, he left a trail of brown water. Buckets of water were brought into the stable, and his mother brought a basin, soap, and clean clothes. It took a long time before the door to the stable opened.

"I will never feel clean again," he mumbled, and the next day he disappeared. Rumors circulated that he had taken off for the Russian border, but no one knew for sure if he had made it.

My tata and Sonny were getting notices to appear for forced labor and returned as everyone else staggering home, their heads bashed in.

As long as Tata baked the bread at night, we were secured with a loaf or two for ourselves.

The rule for photo identification had not as yet been enforced, and younger men often replaced their fathers, uncles, or people who had money and were able to buy a substitute to take their place at forced labor. Sonny often took our tata's notice and went to work in his place. Since he knew how to sew, he often worked in a sewing room for the SS altering their uniforms or shined their boots.

For a short time while Tata was able to bake the bread, our family including Fraida with her two children were surviving.

There was hardly a night when I didn't hear Fraida crying. "You are not dead, you are not dead---,"she whispered to her wet pillow.

It was a cold evening in October. The naphtha lamp flickered low to preserve the little fluid at the bottom of the lamp. Fraida sat at the edge of her bed where Abraham slept. She had one hand on Abraham and the other on the musical cradle where Eva slept soundly and sang to her children in a soft whisper.

"Your tata's alive. He will soon come home and kiss away the tears from my face." As she sang, she leaned her head on the cradle, her tears dripping on Eva's face, and the infant began to squirm.

Fraida felt a hand pass over her hair, thinking it was our tata and lifted her head. Her red-rimmed eyes gazed up and looked into Joel's eyes. She closed her eyes and opened them again. This time, Joel folded his right arm around her shoulders and his left arm was in a sling. Fraida stood up abruptly and began to scream, "Mama-------!"

We all saw Joel enter the apartment, but Joel put his finger to his lips.

Mama turned up the naphtha lamp, and we happily watched Fraida and Joel standing in an embrace. Abraham woke up, and so did Eva. They picked up the children and held them close.

Joel kissed little Eva, whom he met for the first time. He later explained that indeed he was hit by a German bullet and fell unconscious. "I don't know how I got there, I only know that I woke up in a hospital in Baranowicz," he said, and Fraida didn't care about the details. She thanked God for sending her husband back to her.

The old woman on the ground floor directly beneath our window had died a week before Joel returned home. Joel and Fraida rented the apartment. It was a large airy room, and Fraida was happy to have privacy for the first time since she and Joel were married. As soon as Fraida and her family moved into their new apartment, Joel's German shepherd, Wolf, came to stay with them.

Joel's horse and droszka had been confiscated, and once again, he began repairing shoes in their apartment.

Notices for forced labor without pay kept coming, and Sonny went to work in everyone's name. Since Joel's chest wound still needed healing, and he also needed to repair shoes so his family could survive another day, Sonny took Joel's place at forced labor.

I never saw my Catholic friends. It was as if the Jews were suddenly a disease, and they were afraid of catching it.

It was an unusual sunny day in March 1940. I heard the school bell and was afraid to trespass. Still, I couldn't help myself from inching closer for a better look. The recess bell rang out, and from a distance I saw my friends playing outside. I was afraid to come closer, though I wondered what Pani Ulatowska would have done if she saw me? Would she invite me in and send me to the store to buy sand for her cats? I remembered her husband being of German descent. He was a short fat man, who only cared about his cats and was always angry with Pani Ulatowska. Once when I brought the cat's medicine too late, one of his cats had died. His watery blue eyes flashed with anger. "Tell your teacher to go to hell," he shouted.

I hiccupped all the way back to school. I only told my teacher that the cat had died.

As I stood watching my friends playing volleyball, I wondered if my teacher had forgotten all about the child she called Pociecha, Joy, and wanted to adopt. I was suddenly cold. My shoulders hunched, I walked back to the cul-de-sac and saw the dogcatcher chasing Wolf. I ran as fast as I could and caught up with the dog and pushed him with my body into Fraida's apartment. When I told Fraida that I saved the dog from the dogcatcher, she told me I shouldn't have tried to save him. "We can't feed ourselves now, and the dog would be better off dead rather than starve.

My eyes were blinded with tears, and I didn't see the dogcatcher waiting for me as I left Fraida's apartment.

"I should throw you inside the truck with the dogs and let them chew you up into little pieces!" he roared, a thick vein bulging in his neck. When I tried to turn and run up the stairs, he caught my arm and slapped my face so hard that I fell on the first two steps and hit my head. When I regained my composure, the dogcatcher was gone, and I felt as if a horse had kicked me in the stomach. As I ran up the rest of the stairs I felt something warm and wet inside my underpants. I was sure I had wet my underpants.

Mama was standing at the stove cooking potato soup and saw me holding my abdomen. I quickly told her about Wolf and what the dogcatcher did to me.

"My stomach hurts, I think I wet my pants," I groaned.

Mama put her arms around me. "I told you to stay close to home. Anything can happen these days. Take off you underpants, and I'll rinse them out."

When I lifted my dress to take off my underpants I screamed, "Mama! I'm bleeding! I'm going to die of dysentery like your parents did!"

Mama turned around and looked down at me and smiled.

"I just told you I'm going to die, and you think there is something to smile about?"

Mama kissed my face. "No you are not going to die, you've got you first period," she said and ran a hand over my hair. She put a basin of warm water on the floor and told me to clean myself. She gave me a piece of white cloth and explained what a period is all about. "From now on you should be expecting it once a month. If you remember approximately when it should come again, you won't soil you underpants," she said and gave me several pieces of the white cloth. "Every night you'll need to wash them and reuse them. When there will be no more blood, you'll wash the rags and save them for next month."

I was in too much pain to eat the potato soup and went to sleep with a hot water bottle to my belly.

All of my efforts in saving Wolf two days ago were in vain. One of the many anti Jewish decrees had been to give up all pets. That had been the worst day in Bela's life, for she had shared her own meager portions of food with Citra and promised that the Germans would soon leave, and everything would be all right again.

I remembered, in 1935, Bela was walking home from school and saw the dogcatcher grab her Citra. She ran home and cried until Tata bailed out her dog and brought Citra back to her. Now, nobody could bail out her beloved Citra. Wolf and Citra had been the first in our family to perish by the hands of the Nazis. Not a single day had passed without a new rule. All Jews over the age of ten had to wear a white armband with the blue Star of David insignia, and every Jew had to have a picture ID with the initial 'J' for Jew on it. Non-compliance was punishable by death.

A curfew was enforced between nine p.m. and five a.m., and everyday people were disappearing from their homes. It was called relocation, but the people were never seen again.

Hunger was beginning to show on Jewish faces, and the name 'Muzelman' was invented. I couldn't find the word in the dictionary. The emaciated cadaverous look, the Muzelman look was the biggest fear. Once the look of the Muzelman set in, there was no hope, it was only a matter of time before the skeleton would fall to the ground and die.

Jews were not allowed to own anything of value, beginning with furs, jewels, electrical appliances, paintings, and Oriental rugs. Everything had to be turned into the German Police Headquarters.

The only radio in our cul-de-sac had been silenced.

Though there were daily house-to-house searches, and the penalty for hiding valuables was death, many Jews hid their valuables so they could trade with our Polish neighbors for food, and soon Jewish lives had quickly become worthless.

Now that the armband and ID could recognize every Jew, it wasn't safe to leave the house. Pick up-trucks with SS were constantly circling the streets, rounding up everyone they saw. May it be a teenager, a child, or older person, depended upon which work place the SS would drop them off. Often some never returned, and others were beaten so badly, they wished death would come quickly.

Sonny continued to beg Mama to take a chance to make our way to the Russian border, but Mama had been at home most of the time, except when she went to pick up our meager rations. The store was in the cul-de-sac, only a few feet away from our building. She didn't see the two SS in the back of the building lighting a match to an old man's beard. She still couldn't believe that they would be heartless enough to kill innocent people. When Sonny or Tata came home bruised, she put cold compresses on their bodies and cried, "How can we take a chance trying to cross the border with small children? If we don't die from hunger, we'll die from the bullet." And so day after day we had learned to accept out fate.

Mama sent me to Rachel the dressmaker to learn how to sew and to earn a little money for delivering garments and also to keep me off the street. The dressmaker had a younger sister named Stella, whom she loved and protected as if she were her child. Stella was a tall, beautiful girl with big brown eyes and black curly hair. She was well dressed, for Rachel made sure of it, but Stella had tuberculoses. We all knew she would die, but she wasn't at all like Aunt Hudesa's Eva. Stella wasn't in bed. She was out with her friends and always looked pretty. Her cheeks were rosy, and her large brown eyes shined. One day when I came to work, everyone was crying and getting ready to go to Stella's funeral. Two weeks after the funeral, Rachel handed me a navy blue dress that belonged to Stella and told me to carefully rip apart the seems. While I was ripping up Stella's dress, Rachel took my measurements. I didn't know that the dress I had been ripping apart was to be a new dress for me. Mama sent me to a brassiere maker and had two brassieres made for me. Now that I had a monthly period, a brassiere, and a new dress, I felt all grownup, though every morning before I went work, I ran downstairs to Fraida, handed her my navy blue ribbons, and asked her to tie my pigtails.

It was May 1940, the snow was melting, and being outside in the warm sun helped me to forget for a moment or two that tomorrow may be darkness. There had been a time when I would shy away from the sun, of which I had taken for granted. I didn't like to be teased about my freckles. Now, my freckles never entered my mind. I ignored Mama's warning and sauntered outside wearing my new dress, and I craved to get a glimpse at my school hoping to see my friends. I knew that I was forbidden to walk on the sidewalk. With the armband pinned to my sleeve and the identification card with an extra large 'J' for Jew in my pocket, there would be no question of my religion.

I walked close to the sidewalk and, in defiance, limped on and off the sidewalk. Leaving the cul-de-sac, I slowly walked towards my school, trying to build up enough courage to look through the window and see who was sitting in my seat. I was startled by a shrieking noise. I turned, and my heart pounded when I saw a pickup truck in front of me and heard a harsh voice shout, "Halt!" An SS man jumped from the truck, pointing a rifle at me, and bellowed, "Get in the truck! Mach schnell!" (make it fast) The truck was cramped with teenagers wearing white armbands with the blue Star of David insignia.

We huddled together, looking like a bunch of frightened rabbits, afraid to move for fear the rifle in the SS man's hand will go off. During the long and frightening truck ride, I knew how Bela's dog Citra and Wolf felt when the dogcatcher caught them. I suddenly realized that all of the neighborhood animals had vanished and wondered if they were killed because they, too, were Jews. I was so angry my jaw was aching from clenching my teeth. Why did I have to be born a Jew? I hate being Jewish. I want to feel free like all my Catholic friends. I mused. At least before, I could go to school, and outside of my home, I felt Catholic. Now, with the armband and the picture ID with the large 'J' for Jew, if I crossed myself in front of a priest, he would probably turn his head for fear of being identified with me. I pondered until the truck came to a stop at the airfield. Rifles poking at our ribs the, two SS shoved us off the truck, whips whistling in the air and slicing into our backs. They sped away with the empty truck. To catch some more dogs, I thought.

Two soldiers stormed out from a small building, wearing boots and fur lined coats, whips in one hand and rifles in the other. They marched us out to a field, gave us shovels, and ordered us to clear huge mounts of snow. The shovel felt like a stick of ice. Shivering, we began pushing the shovels while the soldiers bellowed, "mach schnell!" With each shout, I felt a whip burning into my back. It didn't take me long to learn how to dodge the whip. I saw a soldier man coming towards me, and I began to push the shovel as if my life depended on it. He stopped in front of me, but he hadn't raised his whip, and I was sure he was going to shoot me any second.

"How old are you!" he shouted.

"Fourteen," I said. Learning right from the beginning that Jewish children were of no use to them and being fourteen meant I would be in seventh grade and was not a child.

"So klein"(so little), he muttered, but couldn't resist burning into my back with his whip anyway.

I remembered Mama often saying since the invasion, "The person is stronger than iron. There is no limit to how much we are able to endure."

As the day wore on, the shovel became as heavy as lead, which gave the soldier a reason for lashing the whips across our legs and backs.

At six o'clock, we were ordered, with the help of rifle jabs, into a pickup truck and dumped like sacks of potatoes on the Walowa Street.

I saw Mama and Tata running towards me. Tata picked me up as if I were an infant and carried me home. When I next opened my eyes, I saw Mama sitting next to me, applying cold compresses to my back and legs.

121

Chapter Eighteen: Loss, Hunger, and Spilled Blood

Not a day went by that Sonny didn't beg our parents to take our chances and leave for the Russian border, but our parents knew that it was too late. The Germans were everywhere, yet there were still some young people who got out, and I silently prayed that Mama would take Sonny's advice. After my last encounter with the sadistic SS and their whips, I was certain that next time I wouldn't survive.

Though the Germans continued robbing the bakery of the bread my tata baked, he somehow managed to buy more flour and to supply the ration cards and a little extra for the black market.

After twelve hours of sitting on a hard wooden chair altering clothes for the SS, Sonny returned home starved, his fingers had many needle punctures. Some fingers were still bleeding. Each time an SS man screamed at him to sew faster, the needle punctured a finger. Mama placed a plate of potato soup on the table in front of Sonny. Before picking up the spoon, Sonny took Mama's trembling hand in his.

"Today, a bunch of SS men laughed as they talked about cleansing every country of all the Jews. Mama, we have to run before we all die," he pleaded yet again.

Mama now knew that these Germans were not the same as the Germans from the Great War. She also knew that wayfaring towards the Russian border with her family, on foot, would be suicide.

"It's too dangerous, Sonny. How far do you think we could go without getting stopped? If we get caught without the armbands, we'll get shot."

Sonny's face was red with anger. "Mama, if we don't take a chance, we'll all die anyway. You should've heard the SS talk today? They didn't think I understood. Mama, they said that soon there wouldn't be a single Jew left in all of Poland."

Tears showered Mama's face. "Whatever our destiny is, there's nothing we can do now. We are caged in like animals. If I were sure that they would shoot me first, I would take the chance. I can't take a chance watching my children get shot in front of my eyes," Mama sobbed.

June 8, 1940, my tata came home from the bakery without the loaf of bread under his arm.

"Again, the Germans confiscated a sack of flour and took all the bread I shoveled out of the oven," he told Mama, and I watched my helpless parents accepting whatever was dished out.

"What happened to the people in line for the bread?" Mama asked.

Tata sat down at the table and rubbed his tired eyes.

"When the people formed a line for the bread, they walked away thinking I didn't want to give them the bread with the ration cards. I will have to find a place to hide the flour and the bread, as soon as it's baked, otherwise we will all starve." While Tata was drinking tea with saccharin, a messenger handed Sonny a note. Sonny's face turned as white as the curtain on our window. I saw him splashing water on his face before he approached Tata.

"Tata, I need money for a deal. I could double the money and give it back to you before you will need it for the flour," Sonny said, avoiding Tata's eyes.

Being that the SS took the flour and bread, Tata knew he wouldn't have enough money to buy flour on the black market. He took out a pack of money from his wallet and counted out one hundred and fifty zloty. That was all a Jew was allowed to have in his possession. Tata didn't see the desperation in his son's face, for all he could think about was money with which to buy flour.

"Here, take it, but I need it back this afternoon to buy flour on the black market," he said, placing a hand on Sonny's face and pulling him close for a hug.

"I only need fifty," Sonny said, and he cut a piece of bread Tata managed to save for us and ate the bread as he was leaving the apartment.

By mid afternoon when Sonny didn't return, Tata was becoming concerned. In two hours he would have to buy flour, and there was no sign of Sonny. Tata left the house and began searching the Jewish sections and asked everyone he knew. A man told him that he saw Sonny with Szama-Lipa hitching rides.

When Tata went to see Joel Malach, the shoe repairman, he found him and his wife, Chaja, pacing the floor and twisting their hands. Now, both fathers knew that their sons would never return.

Standing at the stove peeling potatoes, Mama was blinded with tears. She looked for something with which to wipe her eyes and noticed a white armband and a piece of paper on the little worktable, next to the stove. The only thing she could think of was who forgot to put on the armband?

She looked at Bela's arm, then mine and saw that we were wearing ours.

123

She worried that Tata may have forgotten to put his armband on and never gave any thought to the piece of paper, until Tata ambled in, his face ashen.

"He's gone, Mindala," he whispered.

"I know," Mama sighed and showed him the armband.

"What's this?" Tata asked, looking at the piece of paper next to the armband.

Mama wiped her eyes with Sonny's armband. "I don't know; it was there next to Sonny's armband," she whimpered.

Tata began to read out loud. "This is to inform you that, immediately upon receiving this notice, you are to appear at the headquarters to be shipped out to a forced labor-camp for no less than two years."

It had become clear to all of us why Sonny had to leave. Mama cried and prayed that he would reach the Russian border and find sanctuary. I silently wished that he had taken me with him.

One early morning in August, only two-months after Sonny's disappearance, a Polish police officer in civilian clothes stormed into our apartment. "Where is Jeremy Sztraiman?" he bellowed.

Immediately, when the authorities came looking for someone, we were conditioned to lie. For whatever reason the authorities came to your home looking for a family member, it was never good news.

Mama lied and said that she didn't know.

"He never comes home," she told the Police Officer. While Mama tried to convince the officer that her husband had deserted us, the Police Officer was eyeing our tall lustrous ficus plant Tata had nurtured many years. It was the only plant left from the time since we lived in Penc's building. Mama knew that bribery was alive and well and was desperate to get the officer out of our home. She feared that Tata might come home any moment and would be taken away in handcuffs; though, she didn't know why.

To get rid of the officer before Tata would come home with a loaf of bread tucked under his arm, Mama said, "Would you like this plant?"

Before the officer had a chance to answer she lifted the heavy plant and handed it to him. That ficus had been in our home as long as I could remember. I remembered Tata often told us how the plant grew from a tiny stick. Now, it was saving his life for just a little bit longer. As Mama handed Tata's pride and joy to the police officer, she said, "Please, could you tell me why you are looking for my husband? Not that it matters; he has deserted us."

"He's a Communist," the officer grunted.

"He's a bad husband; he deserted us, but he was never a Communist. He always minded his own business," Mama said, trying to sound as if she didn't care.

"He's on the Communist list. If he shows up, you would be wise to turn him in," the officer snarled and stormed out, carrying the heavy plant.

Minutes after the officer left our house, Tata came home. Mama saw him eyeing the bare lifeless stool and told him about the police officer.

Every night, I had rolled my pigtail ribbons and placed them under the ficus plant to keep the creases out. I couldn't think of another heavy object to place them under. Now, looking at the damp, weathered stool was as if a death had occurred. The plant had been sitting on that stool ever since we moved from Penc' building.

My parents always hugged each other, on good occasions and bad. After the hugging was over, Mama asked, "Why are you on the Communist list?"

"You remember the time when I was beaten half to death, because I passed through the same spot where Communists had murdered a Polish official? Now, I have to give up my bakery and go into hiding," he said acquiescently.

His sad eyes were fixed on the empty stool where his beautiful ficus plant once stood. I remembered how my tata loved gardening and how much pleasure he derived from planting tiny twigs and bringing them to life. When they grew a bit taller, he transplanted his houseplants into larger pots. On rainy days, he carried his plants out to soak in the rainwater. When his dogs, cats, rooster, and white doves followed him around as if he was their best friend, and he was; or when he had begun to build his own bakery and the triumph when he had baked his first bread; there was pleasure in those eyes, but no more. His eyes were open, but there was no life left in them. He had worked so hard building his bakery and as many times the Germans confiscated the bread and flour, he somehow always scraped together the money to buy yet another sack of flour.

"I have to go and find a place to hide before they come back for me," he said, leaving his home and family.

Since the Germans hadn't yet tied in Tata's name to the bakery, he took chances and continued to bake bread, but he didn't come home in the morning to sleep.

Every morning, Mama disappeared and returned with a loaf of bread and a little money to supplement the meager rations.

Friday nights without my tata was worse than going to bed hungry. I was used to going to bed hungry, but I felt protected when I knew that Tata was home and sleeping in the little white bed. I would have felt better if I knew where he was hiding and could go to see him.

Mama was the only one he allowed to know of his hiding place.

Chapter Nineteen: The Ghetto Was Enforced

March 29, 1941, a decree had been issued to establish a Ghetto. All Polish people within the designated areas had to move out. All of the surrounding villages were vacated and turned into military camps and maneuver areas for German soldiers.

The Jews from those areas were relocated to Radom, bringing the Jewish population in the Ghetto up to thirty-five thousand.

In order to execute orders, the Germans established a Jewish council. They later became spokesman for all the Jews in the Ghetto.

Our area had been enclosed as part of the Ghetto. In our one room apartment, we had to take in a family of six, two parents, two spinster daughters, and two grown sons. Suddenly, our two carved mahogany beds had disappeared. Mama explained that the people living with us now were older and needed their beds. Our one room apartment was divided in two. Our half was on the right side with the table in the middle, and since my Tata had to go into hiding, the only bed for our family was Tata's little white hospital bed, which Mama shared with Edzia.

Our four straight dining room chairs had become beds for Bela and me. We each slept on two straight chairs pushed together and lined with bedding.

My school, Maria Konopnicka, had been dismantled, and the Jewish police headquarters was established. Jewish young man were hand picked by the Germans and ordered to become policemen. They wore no uniforms, only blue-red caps with the Star of David insignia and armbands.

Suddenly, all my school friends had disappeared. Even the few Jewish friends stayed home.

I missed my tata. I missed tiptoeing around him while he slept. I missed Mama saying, "Be quiet. Tata has to work tonight." I missed seeing my parents hug and kiss. Now that Tata had his own bakery, we would never have to go to bed hungry. If only the Germans would get out and leave us alone, I often prayed when I said my Catholic prayers. When my prayers didn't work, I was thinking that God was punishing me for trying to be Catholic. I tried praying in Yiddish, but I didn't know how, so I just asked God to stop punishing the Jews and to throw the Germans out of Poland. No matter how I prayed things only got worse. If I knew where Tata was hiding, I would visit him and wouldn't feel like crying all the time. I missed my aunts. I hadn't seen them in a long time and decided to visit Aunt Hanna. I fantasized that Tata had been hiding in Aunt Hanna's attic.

I knew it was dangerous to walk outside. I could get stopped and pushed into a truck. When I thought of staying home or sitting at Rachel's and ripping apart old dresses day after day on a warm day, it made me want to cry again. I didn't want to think anymore. I wanted to lift my head high from my neck and allow the sun to warm my sad face.

As I walked towards Walowa Street, I was startled to see three people in Gestapo uniforms walking towards me. A tall man, equally tall woman, and a girl, my age, wearing a Hitler youth uniform, walked in step with each other towards Gestapo headquarters. My first instinct was to run. If I did, they could shoot me in the back. So, I lifted my head up high, and continued walking. As I came closer, I saw that the Hitler youth was my friend, Halina, the girl I shared the honor in bringing our teacher to school every morning. Everyday like two good friends, we waited together at Pani Ulatowska's door to walk her to school. Now, Halina was my mortal enemy. Her parents could kill me for looking their way and go to lunch to the Gestapo headquarters and have themselves a good laugh. I saw Halina turning her head. Our eyes met, and without a word being uttered, she looked straight ahead and continued walking in step with whom I assumed were her parents. I realized, then, why she never stayed after school. I also realized that the girl who had been my friend for two years had the power to kill me without blinking an eye, and I was suddenly very frightened. As I continued to walk towards Aunt Hanna's house, I wondered what Halina or her parents would do if I had said "hello" to Halina? My heart pounded at the thought. I stopped walking and stood frozen, unable to stop thinking about Halina. I watched the strangers in uniforms pass through the gates and raise their arms in a shout as if all three had only one voice, "Heil Hitler!" I knew that I was standing on enemy grounds, but I couldn't keep my eyes off the gates. What I had just seen was an evil metamorphosis. Halina was my friend. She was the Evangelist I befriended. For two years, during the Catholic religious hour, she left the classroom the same as the Jewish girls. She played with them on the schoolground for an hour, until it was time to return to class. I shared my beloved teacher with her, who only wanted me to carry her teczka. I let her take pride in arriving to school together. Though it was a warm day, I was shivering, and my teeth were chattering.

Suddenly, the distance to Aunt Hanna's seemed too far. I turned around and ran back home, praying that I wouldn't run into Halina and her parents.

When I stormed into my home, I was out of breath, but to my delight, Aunt Hanna was sitting on a chair next to the stove, eating a bowl of potato soup Mama had just finished cooking. Aunt Hanna told me that she was now living with her daughter, Hudesa, and helped Hudesa with her two baby boys. I hugged my aunt and remembered the many nights I had spent in her tiny apartment and how I loved the now gaunt woman. Though I was hungry and knew that my portion was going to be smaller, I was glad to see my beloved Aunt Hanna and would have shared my last bite of food with her.

Joel was forced to work in a shoe factory without pay. At night, he repaired shoes for the neighborhood. As time went on, people didn't have the money to pay for the repairs, and there was no leather to put on the soles of the torn shoes. It was easy to see the hunger on Abraham and Eva's faces. Little Eva's belly protruded, and we all had learned it was from lack of food. Fraida, at twenty-three, looked shriveled. We all did.

Every once in while, Mama would send me to the slaughterhouse where Uncle Gershon worked. The slaughterhouse was located outside of the Ghetto. I stood close to the Ghetto's gate, and while I waited for the guard to turn his head, I took off my armband and stuffed it in the gate's crevice. I was on the other side before he turned his head towards me again. The minute I was two feet away from the Ghetto, I lifted my head up high and thought the way I used to think, like a Catholic.

I was completely without fear. I curtsied and crossed myself on passing a priest or a nun. When passing a German, I smiled and said, "Good morning," in Polish.

He would smile and say, " Grus-Gott"! It translates, salutes or regards to God.

I pretended I didn't understand and continued on my way. The Germans knew that the Polish people didn't understand German. The Yiddish language is similar to the German language, and the Jews had no problem understanding or speaking German.

My only fear was to encounter a Polish boy, girl, or an adult who would recognize me and point me out to a Gestapo or SS. Now that I knew Halina's identity, I prayed that I wouldn't run into her. That was the reason why many of us wouldn't dare leave the Ghetto. I waited outside the slaughterhouse, and Uncle Gershon pointed to a more secluded area and gave me a package wrapped in newspapers. "Go quickly," he said, looking in every direction and disappeared back into the slaughterhouse. I put the little package in the wicker basket and walked home, swinging the basket until I came close to the Ghetto's gate. I didn't get too close until I saw that the guard was busy. Like a mouse, I was back inside the Ghetto and retrieved my armband.

It was the same each time. We all watched Mama unwrap the package and remove a few scraps of meat, or a kidney, or part of the cows' stomach, or a little piece of fat. It was a real feast. We all knew it wasn't kosher. Mama washed the scraps several times, salted them, and again rinsed three times, and now, it was kosher. If she had the money to buy a few potatoes and an onion, she stood next to the stove making sure that not the tiniest scrap was wasted.

Mama served some of the food to Bela, Edzia, and to me. She ate a few spoonfuls, and the rest she divided in two portions and left the apartment. She dropped off one portion at Fraida's apartment and disappeared with a little pot of food.

We all knew she went to see Tata in his hiding place, but no one asked any questions. When she returned, she would tell us how very thin Tata had become.

Though Tata was in hiding, he still took chances and worked a night here and there, and sometimes, when he scraped together some money, he would bake some bread and sell it on the black market. Otherwise the bakery was dark, and Tata hoped that the Russians would soon liberate us so he could go back to baking bread and be his own boss. One or two nights a week of work wasn't enough to feed the family, and we were always hungry.

Typhoid fever and dysentery were rampaging. Bela was taken to the hospital with typhoid fever. When she returned two weeks later, her golden hair had been shaved and her already thin body was now gaunt.

Until her hair grew back, Bela resembled a little boy and her friends nickname her Bela-Boy. The name stayed with her for as long as she lived.

It had always been more difficult for Bela than it had been for me to go without food. Now, since her illness, it was much harder for her. She was always hungry, and her stomach would hurt when there was no food. Since Bela's return from the hospital, Tata took bigger chances. He worked more nights and would often sneak home at dawn to surprise her with something he had baked for her, mostly a large cookie made with sugar and butter.

It didn't take too long before Bela regained her strength, and her hair grew back from straight to wavy, with the same golden luster.

July 1941, Mama was arrested for withholding information on her husband's whereabouts. She was kept in a holding cell at the Ghetto police headquarters.

The tiny wooden structure was no bigger than a doghouse. The only difference being that it was high enough for Mama to standup, and it had a little bench to sit on, but not long enough to stretch out. With the door locked, the only air Mama breathed had been through the cracks. When the Germans were not around, the Jewish police kept her door open, otherwise she would surely suffocate, for it had been a very hot and humid month. Mama was kept in that cell three days and nights. The SS questioned her every day for several hours. Each time she gave them the same answer, "My husband, Jeremy Straiman, has deserted us, and I haven't seen him in a long time."

Bela, Edzia, and I stood next to Mama's cell, until we were chased away, but we kept coming back. When Mama was released, her legs wouldn't move. We had to help her walk home.

To avoid being hauled into a truck and driven to a place of no return, many girls in the Ghetto volunteered for work places, where they were treated a little more humanely. The girl was given a pass stating that she worked for a German Company everyday.

Bela's friends, two sisters in our cul-de-sac, Fela and Junia Wisnia, went to work in a warehouse, called AFL, located outside of the Ghetto. Their job was to load and unload boxcars from the railroad train that stopped several times a week directly in front of the warehouse. On the days when the trains didn't come, the girls sorted and made hundreds of bundles consisting of confiscated shoes and clothing from every country in occupied Europe. Russian military winter uniforms and boots, wooden shoes from Holland, woolen socks, and knitted ladies sweaters. After the goods were assorted, the girls loaded the boxcars marked for Germany.

Three non-ranking soldiers with whips guarded the girls. If a girl didn't run fast enough up or down the three flights of stairs, often with potato sacks of wooden shoes on her back, she felt the whip on her legs.

The good part was that at noon, each girl received a bowl of soup.

The Wisnia sisters told Bela about AFL, and Bela was anxious to get a bowl of soup. Her friends brought passes for her enabling her to leave the Ghetto. When she arrived on the first morning, she found most of her friends were already working at AFL.

Since Mama's arrest, there was hardly a day when the police didn't search our apartment and every bakery looking for my Tata.

Now that Tata couldn't take a chance at being seen at home or in any bakery, we were starving and dying a little every day.

Since Mama had returned from jail, we guarded her as if she were a precious jewel. At night, Bela moved her bed of two chairs close against Mama's and Edzia's little white bed. I moved my bed of two chairs all the way to the foot of the little white bed. At night, the four of us lay listening to our own growling empty belies, too hungry to fall asleep. On the third night, Mama began pacing the floor.

"If I don't do something, we'll all die from hunger," she said, more to herself. She turned to me, "Yentala, you will have to help me."

"Rachel taught me how to sew on the sewing machine. I could ask her if she would pay me, now. I'm pretty helpful to her," I said feeling grown up.

"No, that's not what I have in mind, but I do need you to help me. Where did you put your clothes? You'll need to get dressed in the dark."

"On the chair next to my feet, Mama."

"Will you be able to get dressed in the dark?"

"Yes, Mama."

"Alright, I'll wake you in the morning. Now, go to sleep."

Since the beginning of the war, sleep had been the best part of my life. When I slept, I wasn't afraid to walk on the sidewalk, I wasn't hungry, and my tata was home and asleep. We tiptoed around him, for he worked all night in his new bakery. If I could have slept until the Germans marched back out of Poland, and Mama would wake me up to go to school, that would have been the happiest day of my life. But dreams are only good when you're asleep, that is, if they are good dreams.

Mama woke me at dawn. "We are going to bake cookies, and you will help me," she whispered.

I knew we had no money for potatoes to cook soup, much less for cookies, but I didn't ask any questions. I got dressed quickly, and we were out of the apartment within minutes. The streets were dark, and we walked like thieves against the buildings. Mama knocked softly on a dark, little storefront. The storekeeper urged us in and quickly locked the door behind us. He was a short, thin man. He could have been twenty-five or forty five years old. I'm not at all sure. When you are young, everybody over twenty is old. His beard was now only one-inch long, his shoulders hunched, and his lifeless eyes reminded me of my tata's eyes when he told mama that he had to go into hiding.

Mama and I were standing in front of the counter, weak with hunger.

"How many cookies a day can you sell?" she asked the storekeeper, her voice so weak the storekeeper asked her to repeat the question.

"You are a baker's daughter, so I would have no problem selling your cookies. The only problem is, the Goyim are buying our precious possessions and giving us less and less for them, but I'll do my best for you because I remember you well, Generous Mindala. I also remember your Mama. No one could duplicate her cheesecake. Tell me what you need?"

"I wish I had listened to my son and escaped with my family to the Russian border," Mama sighed, her tears running down her bony cheeks faster than she could wipe them away with the handkerchief her mama had embroidered for her. She handed him our wicker-basket and named several items.

"I also need two slices of bread and a tablespoon of honey."

The storekeeper looked at me then mama and sliced two half-inch slices of bread and poured a generous amount of honey on each slice. While the storekeeper filled our wicker basket, Mama and I stood at the counter making every bite count. After we finished our bread and honey, the storekeeper put the wicker basket on the counter. "I know you don't have the money to pay me, but don't worry. I trust you, Generous Mindala."

"No need to trust," Mama said proudly, as she removed the bandage from her finger that covered her thick wedding band she was concealing from German eyes.

I had never seen Mama without her wedding band. She placed the ring on the counter and for only a moment looked down on her bare finger and turned to leave.

The man followed us and put some money in mama's pocket. "This ring is worth much more than the few cookie ingredients," he sighed, as he unlocked the door for us.

It was still dark when we left the tiny drab store with the naphtha lamp giving barely enough light to see which way to turn. Again, we walked briskly like thieves against the walls until we arrived at my tata's bakery. Mama knocked softly on the door.

I recognized the baker who opened the door ajar. I had seen him in my tata's bakery before, but I didn't know his name. When he saw my Mama, he quickly let us in and closed the door behind us. He was a tall thin man. His face was clean-shaven, like my tata's. He looked at Mama with sad brown eyes and sighed. "Jeremy worked so hard for this place," he whispered as he guided us inside. Mama spoke softly to the man, and he nodded. After Mama emptied the basket upon the worktable, she rolled up her sleeves and washed her hands with a little piece of soap sitting on top of the sink, then slipped the soap in my hands and told me to do the same.

133

"No matter how hungry we are, if water is available, there is no reason not to be clean," she whispered and began cracking the eggs. First, she whipped the eggs and sugar with a wooden spoon. Then, she placed the spoon on the table and added the rest of the ingredients and began working the mixture with her hands. With quick strokes, she had turned the mixture into pliable dough. She put two pieces of dough on the table, covered them with the palms of her hands, and rolled them into little balls. She flattened the two perfectly uniform balls with the heels of her hands and ran the rolling pin over each cookie twice, and I put them on a large bakery size cookie-sheet. When one cookie-sheet was filled, she stepped into the pit of the oven, placed the cookie sheet on a large wooden shovel, shoveled it in the oven, and immediately began to fill the next cookie sheet.

The scent of the cookies baking made my mouth water, but I now knew that these cookies were not for us to eat. They were to be sold. Even only eating one cookie would mean eating the profit and less money for our supper.

After Mama removed the first batch, my job was to loosen the baked cookies from the cookie-sheet.

Mama was happy that not a single cookie was sticking to the sheet. Light as feathers, they were all the same size. With the slightest touch of my fingers, the way mama had demonstrated, the cookies came easily off the sheet.

When the next batch was done, I lifted the cookies and carefully placed them on top of the first batch. When the third batch of cookies was finished, mama told me to put one on top of the others. She quickly figured out how much she would have to give the grocer for tomorrow's baking and how much money she would have left to buy some potatoes, a few grams of barley, an onion, and maybe even a piece of fat to make a thick soup. After she had it all figured out, she told me how much to ask for the cookies and placed the large cookie-sheet filled to the brim in my outstretched arms. She kissed my face and said, "You go directly to Synagogue Street and sell them, but be careful. Watch out for the Germans," and kissed me again.

As I walked towards Synagogue Street, the cookie sheet was not only becoming heavier with each step, but I couldn't see the uneven cobblestones. Twice I tripped, but the thought of dropping the full cookie sheet, after all the work and mama's ring, was enough to keep me upright.

Synagogue Street was filled with black-market vendors such as myself, selling saccharine and used clothes. Teenagers were selling pastries their parents baked. The noisy slogans were ear piercing.

The first half-hour I didn't know what to do, and nobody was buying my cookies. My arms began to throb, and my knuckles became white. I saw other people selling their goods, and I felt like a failure. What would Mama think of me? I visualized the disappointment on her face, and that was unacceptable. I stood quietly for a few minutes and began listening to the slogans of the other vendors. Each screamed, praising his or her merchandise loudly, trying to convince the customers why his or her product was the best.

I remembered the ingredient mama bought with her ring, and I began screaming as loud as the other vendors did. At first I felt uncomfortable. Words didn't leave my lips loud enough. Each word was more like croak, but I wasn't about to come home with a full cookie sheet and continued practicing as if performing in a school-play except louder.

"My cookies…are made with pure butter, eggs, and sugar! Once you taste my cookies, you will never buy any other!" I shouted and saw customers turn their heads.

One man was standing two feet from me and every two minutes bought another cookie and ate it. He must have eaten about six cookies before he walked away.

In three hours, I had sold every cookie. When I walked in our apartment with the empty cookie sheet and emptied my pocket of change onto the table, I never felt more proud of myself.

Mama had sold the rest of the cookies to the stores and was already home cooking soup. When the soup was finished cooking, she filled a little pot and put it aside. After dishing out a bowl for each of us, she filled a little pot to take downstairs to Fraida, then scraped out a few spoonfuls for herself and ate quickly before leaving the apartment holding the two little pots close to her bony chest.

We all knew she went to bring the soup to Tata's hiding place, but we were not allowed to ask.

She had told us in the beginning that it would be too dangerous for us to know where our tata was hiding.

I had become proficient in selling the cookies; though, I never tasted one. I was always very hungry, and eating one cookie would lead to another. My mouth watered, and I tried not to look at the same man, day after day, as he was buying my cookies and ate them in front of me.

Six days a week, Mama and I woke up at dawn and knocked lightly on the little storekeeper's door. Mama often changed bakeries, in case the SS or Gestapo would be looking for my tata.

The SS or Gestapos were frequent visitors on Synagogue Street. Someone always warned us a few seconds ahead of time giving us a chance to hide inside a building before we heard running boots and shootings.

Everyday, more people were disappearing, and the ones still in the Ghetto looked thinner, and it took me longer to sell the cookies. It was easy to see that the people were running out of things to sell, and cookies were a luxury. The Gestapo had been frequent visitors, and the casualties were great. At least once a day, the SS or Gestapo raided Synagogue Street, but I managed to run fast enough and hide inside buildings the same as the other vendors. Some vendors were caught and shot on the spot or clubbed half to death, but that didn't stop us from coming back the next day. We were given a choice, dying from a bullet would be the easiest way to die, or getting our brains splattered on the cobblestones from a blow to the head with the butt of a rifle. Or, not do anything and become emaciated and die a slow death. I chose to help Mama and hoped we would be liberated before we all vanished.

I screamed my heart out on Synagogue Street, trying to sell the last cookie, while constantly dodging the SS or Gestapo.

With each passing day, it had become harder and harder to sell the cookies.

Everyday, another steady customer had vanished, and I stood in the middle of the street screaming to smaller groups of people. Each day I returned home a little later than the previous day. By the time I sold the last cookie, my right arm ached and my fingers were numb.

The Ghetto police were steady visitors on Synagogue Street, but they looked the other way. Their own families, in order to survive one more day, had to do the same as us. Only the few who were lucky enough to have been rich before the invasion didn't have to risk their lives on the black market, but they were the minority. The rest of us struggled any way we could to survive one more day, and the black market had been the only way to keep from starving to death.

I had been lucky until one Friday, when without warning, the SS stormed in on Synagogue Street, and people began to run. Shots from rifles went off every few seconds.

My hands were fastened to the cookie-sheet with half of the unsold cookies spread neatly for my customers to see.

As I began to follow the crowd and run for cover while steadying the large baker size cookie-sheet, I was knocked to the ground by vendors and customers. With my right hand still fastened to the cookie sheet, I lay face down in the mud from last night's rain.

Countless feet were running and tripping over me. I was certain that I was very close to death. A few minutes later, I stopped feeling feet on my back, and my head felt as if I was buried in hollow ground. I was certain that I was dead and waited for my soul to leave my body.

As if from a far away place, I heard two voices sounding like barking dogs. Did Fraida's Wolf and Bela's Citra come to welcome me to heaven? Each bark sounded as if they were asking me to follow them, but how do I get there? Oh no, "I can't get to heaven, I didn't convert. I'm doomed to burn in hell for all eternity," I mused, thinking the dogs heard me. When I felt rifles poking at my ribs and boots kicking both sides of my hips and I heard roaring shouts, "Get Up, Jew!" I had no doubt that I was in hell.

When I didn't move, they began to laugh, "Save your bullet; this one is dead," one shouted, sounding again like a bark in the German language.

Another voice howled, "One Jew less. Let's go!"

Loud laughter continued to echo until it was quiet again. No, I was thinking these were not our dogs. Our dogs wouldn't make my sides burn. I'm in hell, and these two voices were devils. Now, I was certain that I was dead and in hell. I lost consciousness. I don't know how long I laid in the mud when I heard familiar voices crying, "the poor child." I heard several voices talking about Generous Mindala's child. I felt hands slapping my face and lift me off the ground. After falling several times, I opened my eyes and saw that my cookies were crumbled and mixed with mud. The people helped me gather the broken cookies, and I was angry that I didn't die. Dazed, I cried all the way home. Not because I had almost died, but because Mama wouldn't have enough money to buy the ingredients for tomorrow's baking.

Mama's face contorted when she saw me coming through the door. I was sure she was angry with me. "I'm sorry, Mama. I should have been running faster. When the SS   started shooting and people were falling down, I was knocked to the ground, and the cookies fell in the mud. I emptied my pocket with the little change. What are we going to do? Will you have enough money for tomorrow?"

Mama kissed my soiled face. "Thank God you're alive, and don't worry about tomorrow," she said as she drew the curtain for privacy from our boarders. She added a piece of coal to the stove and emptied the tea kettle onto the basin and filled it with fresh water from the bucket and placed it on the stove. She took the largest pot we had and filled it with water and placed it on the other burner. Mama helped me out of my soiled clothes. As she lifted my white cotton slip over my head, pulled down my underpants, and unbuttoned my brassier, her face turned as white as my slip, and she covered her face with both hands.

"How much more agony are we suppose endure?" she cried as she dipped my muddy hair into the basin filled with warm water. She changed the water and finished washing my hair. She changed the water again and washed my back. With each touch of Mama's gentle hand, I cried out in pain. When I finished bathing, Mama used the same water to wash my muddy clothing and rinsed it in clean water and hung it on chairs.

"I'll make some tea, and tonight we'll eat the best cookies in Radom for supper. If we survive tonight, I'll have enough money to buy the cookie ingredient, but you will stay home, Jentala," Mama said, as she placed the bedding on the two chairs and told me to get under the covers.

It was the first time since Mama and I had begun baking cookies that I had tasted a few pieces of the broken cookies with the mud scraped off. Now, I knew why people were buying our cookies. They were truly the best tasting cookies in Radom.

I tossed all night on the two chairs, unable to find a painless spot. When I finally did doze off, I dreamed that I was begging Pani Grosicka to take me out of hell and allow me to join her in heaven. She placed a hand on my bruised face and smiled. "Yenta, you are still a Jew," she said. I woke up with a startle and fell between the two chairs with my heart hammering in my chest. I stood up to push the chairs together, and my body felt as if it were broken in a million places. It was still dark outside, but I couldn't fall back asleep. I lay with my eyes open and heard mama getting dressed. I reached for my clothes in back of the chair, but it was wet. My eyes were adjusted to the darkness and saw that Edzia too was getting dressed. I knew that Edzia couldn't possible carry the large baker's cookie sheet. She was much smaller than I was. I struggled to pull myself up and reach for my wet clothes, and again, I fell between the chairs and woke up everyone in the apartment.

Mama lifted me off the floor and, with difficulty, guided me to the little white bed.

"You stay in this bed until you are better. Edzia will come with me to the bakery," Mama said and helped Edzia dress quickly.

An hour later, Bela got dressed and went to AFL.

The next ten days, Edzia helped Mama in the bakery, but Mama was now selling her cookies to the vendors and the little stores. The problem was that the vendors didn't always pay up front, and Mama had to knock on their doors every evening to collect the money. There were those who always had an excuse for not paying, and our soup had become thinner with each passing day. It seemed forever before my body stopped hurting. After staying home for five days, I climbed downstairs to see Fraida. Every step was agony. I was shocked to see how yellow little Eva's skin had become. Her belly was larger than ever. Abraham's blue eyes were enormous, and he had the look of a little old man. Fraida herself was so gaunt the dress she wore looked as if it were hanging on a hanger instead of a person.

I never looked at myself in a mirror, so I could only see how my family had quickly become emaciated.

When Mama and Edzia returned home that evening, I said, "Tomorrow evening, I'm going to collect money from the customers so you can rest." Mama was grateful for the help. She knew that after dark was easier to hide inside a building in case I would encounter a German. There was also less chance of getting stopped and pushed into a truck, since the workday would be over.

Every evening I left the apartment and knocked on doors asking for money owed us. Most people were gracious and paid, but there were some that asked me to come back tomorrow, and when I did, it was another excuse. I understood when Mama said that she wasn't going to sell to him or her anymore.

One evening, Mama returned home with the little pot of soup untouched, her eyes were swollen from crying all the way home. Gasping, she told us that Tata had been taken outside of the Ghetto to the hospital with typhoid fever. While Tata was in the hospital, Mama was afraid that no one would feed him, and he would die. Saturday, she filled the wicker basket with one of our bread rations and a cookie and handed me the little basket. "You will have to take this to your Tata. Be careful, and walk close to the buildings so you won't get stopped."

I was glad that it was a warm day, and I didn't have to wear Mama's ugly jacket.

Fraida combed my hair and tied the navy blue ribbons to my pigtails. I was wearing the dress Rachel had remodeled for me, and I felt certain that I would blend in with the outside. I took off my armband and left it on the table. I took the little basket and walked towards the Ghetto gate, lingering a few moments until the policeman turned his head the other way, and I slipped out. As soon as I left the Ghetto gate, I felt the same as I did before the invasion. I didn't feel Jewish. I didn't walk behind the buildings the way mama instructed me. I walked on the sidewalk with my head up high as if I belonged. Several times I passed priests and nuns on the streets. I curtsied and crossed myself and continued strolling. I passed two Gestapo, and I didn't turn my head the other way. I smiled and said, "Good morning," in Polish.

They smiled and said "Grus Got."

"When I arrived in the hospital, I rang the bell at the gate. A nurse wearing a white armband with the blue Star of David insignia came to the gate and told me that I wasn't allowed inside. "But I brought food for my tata," I told her, tears stinging my eyes.

"What is your tata's name?"

"Jeremy Sztraiman."

"I'll take the food and give it to him."

"Could you please bring back my basket, and could you please tell me if my Tata is getting better?"

The nurse looked at me and saw the built up of tears about erupt.

"Alright, stay here, and I'll be right back," she said.

After what seemed as if she was never returning, although it couldn't have been more than a half an hour, the nurse returned with the empty basket and told me that my tata is still very sick. He didn't have the crisis yet. When she saw my chin quivering and a storm of tears gushing down on my face, she said, "Don't worry your tata is strong. He will get well."

While my tata was struggling for his life in the hospital, the police were our steady visitors, looking for him, and Mama continued telling them the same story, that he had deserted us.

Several times I left the Ghetto and took food for my tata, never knowing if he was receiving it. Different nurses came to the gate, and I always asked the same question, "Is Jeremy Sztraiman better? Has he gone through the crisis yet?"

The nurses were evasive, and I had the feeling that they had no idea who Jeremy Sztraiman was, but I always told Mama that he was getting better, and I prayed that it was the truth.

Two weeks later, I walked with less pain, and during the day, I was too hungry to stay home and watch our boarders eat. I began to venture out into the street. I was being very careful to watch out for trucks. I knew that my body wouldn't be able to withstand another beating. I walked close to buildings and looked over my shoulder. I stopped at the now vacant white picket fence of the old age home and wondered what had happen to the old people. I knew that the home was not for the Jewish elderly, and the old people may have been relocated. I figured that our boarders would have finished eating, and I turned to go back home. As I turned away from the fence, a truck stopped in front of me. Here I go again, I was thinking. No sooner does my body heal, and I go out and ask for more punishment. I hoped that this time I wouldn't return alive. I had caused Mama enough heartache. I pretended as if I didn't see the truck and began to walk towards the cul-de-sac. I didn't care if he pulled the trigger. The truck stopped an inch away from me and a middle-aged soldier jumped out and grabbed my arm. Though the uniform he wore had not been SS or Gestapo, he was a German, and that had been an immediate threat.

"Get in the truck, little one!" He didn't shove me in with his rifle the way the SS did, not too long ago. He gently helped me with just a little push.

The truck was filled with teenagers, most of them were two to three years older than I was. When the kids inside the truck saw how frightened I was, they assured me that this soldier was one of the good ones. Several boys and girls had worked for him before and were glad to go back every morning to be picked up. "We get a bowl of soup at midday," the girl standing next to me, whispered.

We were driven to an empty field piled high with bricks. The ones working there before knew what to do. I followed their lead and lined up. One boy, in front, began the assembly line. He handed bricks to the one next to him and each handed a brick to the next in line.

One boy was standing in the truck, placing one brick on top of the other until the truck was full and driven away by a soldier. Another truck arrived, and we continued to load one truck after another.

At noontime, we were given a bowl of yellow pea soup, and not once did the whip touch our bodies. Although it had been back breaking work, I didn't mind it at all. At the end of the day, the truck dropped us off at the Ghetto gate, and we all promised to return in the morning and wait for the truck. Before I went home, I stopped at Mama's customers to collect money. Mama was home cooking potato soup with barley. I put the money on the table and told mama about the builder and the bowl of soup I had received at noontime. Mama was worried that I took chances and wandered out, but she was glad that I didn't go hungry all day.

At the end of my fourth working day for the builder, I entered the Ghetto and saw an old, gaunt man stumbling through the gate and falling against the wall. I only recognized my tata by the clothes he was wearing and ran towards him and caught him just before he was about to fall. I was unable to hold on to him and was losing my grip.

Our neighbor, Joel Malach, saw me struggling and helped me walk my tata home.

Mama saw us from the window and ran down the three flights of stairs as if she had been chased. She took over my job and helped Mr. Malach get Tata upstairs. "God help us. He won't survive in the hiding place in his condition. He will have to stay home until he's stronger," Mama cried. She dished out a bowl of soup she had just finished cooking and spoon-fed my tata.

After he ate, we all helped him out of his clothes and guided him to the little white metal bed.

"Now, sleep," Mama said, as if speaking to a small child, and like a small child, my tata closed his eyes. It was hard for me to see my strong tata, the avenger of the Jews, in such debilitated condition. I ran outside and sat down on a rock and cried.

I was so angry with the Germans and the world for not coming to our rescue. I looked up at the black sky.

"Why does everyone hate us? What did we do to deserve such hatred? Doesn't anybody care?" I cried, sitting on the rock shivering with cold, until Fraida saw me from her window and urged me to go home.

At AFL, where Bela worked, every end of the day, the soldiers lined up the girls and physically checked each one for theft. Bela knew that she was the only one who could speed up our tata's recovery. He needed food, and she risked punishment or even death to nurture him back to health. She stuffed socks and other small articles inside her underpants where the soldiers didn't check. The first time Bela brought the items home, Mama twisted her hands fearing for her daughter's life, but she sold the stolen goods, and within three weeks, Tata began to regain his strength and returned to his hiding place. After dark, he came home to eat and sometimes remained over night.

Mirka, Bela's friend, lived next door to us. Her youngest sister Hinda, was my friend. Bela had brought Mirka to AFL and warned her not steal. She had told her all about the soldiers frisking everyone, but Mirka was sure that she had a foolproof hiding place. When she was caught on the first day with socks in her brassier, she was whipped and ordered never to return.

I continued working for the builder, and when there were no more bricks to be loaded, Herr. Builder drove us to a village named Wolanow. There, we were given a shovel and were told to dig the ground. Herr. Builder didn't scream at us or used the whip. We did what he asked, and he praised our work. He was especially impressed with me. I knew that the Germans had no use for Jewish children. The unproductive Jews were the first to vanish. Since I was the youngest and the smallest, I had to work the hardest. I always had to prove that I was as good as the older boys and girls.

One day in December, the ground was hard, and we had to work harder to dig. A young SS man came to check on our progress. The SS did that to check up on the low ranking Germans in our charge. Herr. Builder told him that we were hard workers, but the SS man had to see for himself.

The SS man pointed a finger at me and laughed. "Are you trying to tell me that she is going to dig your foundation?"

"She is one of my strongest workers," Herr. Builder said, but didn't laugh.

"She's a child! You're wasting precious time! Get rid of her, or I will!" he shouted

Herr. Builder picked up a shovel and handed it to the young SS man.

"This little one is not only strong, but she speaks perfect German. Now, let's see which one of you can dig faster," he said.

The SS man's laugh sounded like a barking dog, the same barks I heard when I lay face down on Synagogue Street with the cookie sheet next to me.

"Builder! Are you are trying to tell me that this child can dig faster than me?" he laughed so hard and loud. All the other kids began to work harder, and shovels of dirt were flying in the air.

"Why don't you try it and find out?" Herr. Builder quipped. "I'll count to three!" Herr. Builder shouted and began, "one…two…three!"

I knew I had to prove Herr. Builder right, for my life depended on it, and my shovel took on a life of it's own. By the time the SS man had dug up one shovel, I had been working on the other. He was blinded with perspiration and kept wiping his forehead with his uniform sleeve. The SS man laughed and threw the shovel into the ditch. He gave a Heil-Hitler salute and quickly disappeared. Herr. Builder was bursting with pride.

To this day, I don't know where my strength had come from. Certainly not from enough food, for even with Bela risking her life for us every day, I was still going to bed hungry every night, and I waited for morning when Mama would pick up our bread rations that tasted like sawdust.

After the foundation for the first structure was finished, Herr. Builder took me on as his personal assistant. He stood in the ditch laying bricks, and my job was to hand each brick to him.

Just as I was beginning to fear every living German, I realized that not all Germans were bad.

Soon, buildings were erected, but no one knew for whom these building were being built. We only did what was asked of us.

Herr. Builder was kind to us, and I didn't mind running twelve hours a day stocking up piles of bricks, then get on my hands and knees and hand him each brick as needed.

Herr. Builder himself worked very hard. He was standing on his feet all day in dampness, laying bricks.

One day, he asked me to follow him into an unfinished wooden structure and gave me a piece of stale bread, and another time, he gave me a little square of chocolate and told me I was a good little worker.

He asked us all to bring pictures of ourselves, and we all did. He told us that it was going to be for our identification cards, which we never received.

One afternoon, Builder climbed out of the ditch, and I saw him turn behind an unfinished building. While I waited for him to come back, I piled up enough bricks to last until the end of the day. When he didn't return, I went in the direction he had gone. I turned a corner and saw him stretched out on the unfinished floor, holding on to his stomach.

"Herr. Builder, what is wrong?" I asked frightened. It had never occurred to me that I would ever be concerned for a German's welfare, but I was for Herr. Builder. He wasn't the same German every Jew feared. He was more like the Germans my mama remembered from the Great War.

He looked at my frightened face and said, "Don't worry, little one. I get stomach pains sometimes. I'll be fine in a few minutes. Go back to work."

I knew he didn't want me to get caught talking to him, in case the SS or Gestapo showed up unexpected. I continued piling up the bricks, and a half an hour later, he returned and stepped inside the ditch and said, "Hand me a brick little one."

Day after day, the truck picked us up and drove us to Wolanow, and one building after another was being erected. The bowl of soup at midday made it a bit easier on Mama. I never asked for anything to eat when I came home. I knew I wasn't as gaunt as Fraida was.

Chapter Twenty: It Had Only Just Begun

Winter starts early in Poland. Cold rains in October, with hail the size of small rocks, and snow lags behind. Harsh December frost and cold winds raged on, and Mama's thin worn out jacket hadn't been enough to keep me warm at the construction site. Each time I picked up a brick, it was like picking up a block of ice with my bare hands.

By the time the middle of January came around, I wasn't sure if I could make it through another twelve hours. The wind was blowing through my body in Mama's thin gray jacket. Each hour was becoming more unbearable. Even the soup that arrived at midday was cold by the time they finished dishing it out.

My ankles were frostbitten and bleeding. My toes and fingers were constantly numb.

Every night I sat with my feet an inch from the brick heater my tata had built for us. We were grateful to our boarders for supplying the coal that kept our apartment warm. At night, I slept on the two chairs pushed together, wrapped in our feather quilt, but my feet never warmed up. Day after day, I walked around on two sticks of ice in worn out, one size too small shoes.

When a blinding blizzard made my teeth chatter and my throat constrict, I told Builder that I wouldn't be able to return to work anymore.

"I'm freezing to death," I confided.

He became flustered. "Don't leave Jadzia," he pleaded.

I was flattered that he remembered my name, for he always called me 'kleiner,' little one. Though Builder made me feel that being a Jew was not a bad thing as long as I was a good worker, I knew I couldn't survive in that freezing weather, not-with my thin dress, worn out shoes, mama's thin jacket, and no gloves.

Herr. Builder continued pleading with me not to leave. "It will get better once the buildings are finished. You will work indoors, but you must continue to come here…" His mouth opened and closed as if he was trying to tell me something, a forewarning, but my stiff fingers told me that it was impossible for me to continue with snow and wind beating down on me. Whatever he had been trying to tell me, I knew that if I stayed, I would die from the cold.

When I came home that night and told Mama about the cold, she ask Bela to take me with her to AFL. Bela promised she would ask the soldiers.

Now that my tata had regained his strength, thanks to Bela, he became braver and worked in a bakery some nights, and other nights, he stayed home, instead of going to his hiding place. Of course, we loved having our tata at home. We felt as if nothing would happen to us as long as we had our parents, but the Germans never slept. Everyday they thought of new ways to destroy us. There were bloody Wednesdays, bloody Thursdays, bloody Jewish holidays. And on those bloody days or mostly nights, the Ghetto was raided, and men drawn wagons pulled dead naked bodies piled one on top of the other on the slippery roads. Blood drained from the wagons, staining the snow all the way to the morgue in the Jewish hospital. The morgue wasn't large enough for hundreds of dead bodies. The martyrs were laid out like sardines, one on top of the other.

One such night, because he was a butcher, my youngest uncle, Gershon, had been rounded up along with other butchers and shipped out to Auschwitz, leaving his wife and two young sons to starve.

Wednesday, February 1942, my mama and tata slept together in the little white bed with Edzia at their feet. We had no watches or clocks in our home, and we went only by the color of the sky. The sky that night was black when loud banging at our door woke us up.

My tata quickly climbed out of his little white bed and slid under our boarder's beds.

Two young, tall Gestapo pushed in the door shouting, "Which one of you is Jeremy Sztraiman?"

Mama stood up and put her dress over her nightgown. "He is not here," she mumbled.

One Gestapo, young enough to be Mama's son, pushed his fist into her face. "Where is he? If you are lying, we'll kill everyone in this room!" both shouted in unison.

"He's not here. I don't know where he is," Mama's small voice pleaded.

"Turn on the lights!" one barked. Whenever I heard Germans shout, I always thought of dogs barking.

I wondered if that was the way Germans normally spoke? Then, I remembered Herr. Builder. He was a kind, soft-spoken man.

"We don't have lights," Mama said, trembling.

The two Gestapo began lighting matches and looked in every corner. One Gestapo pointed a lit match under the bed where my tata was hiding, and I prayed like I never prayed before.

146

"Please God…make them run out of matches…Please…God…please …God…please… make them run out of matches…."

At that moment, I was sure that God heard my prayer and created a miracle. The Gestapo bent on his hands and knees with a lit match. Under the bed, he ran out of matches. He stood up and shouted, "Do you have matches? Give me matches!"

"We have no matches," Mama cried.

Again, they looked in every corner and turned the covers away from all of us, then pointed the rifles at Mama.

"Where is Jeremy Sztraiman? If you don't tell us right now, we'll start shooting and kill everybody in this damned house!" two voices bellowed in unison.

Mama knew they wouldn't hesitate. Trying to get them out of the apartment, she mumbled, "He is…in the bakery…."

The two Gestapo left our apartment, and Tata crawled out from under our boarder's beds and quickly left the apartment.

We were sure that they wouldn't know in which bakery to look for Tata, and they would forget about us, at least for now, and everyone went back to sleep.

At dawn, Bela left for work.

Mama was in bed with a damp towel to her bruised face, but it was time to get dressed for her days work and cookie baking.

Just as she began to wake Edzia, the same two Gestapo stormed in, pushing my Uncle Laizer forward.

"Is he your husband?" they bellowed at Mama.

"No, he's my husband's brother," Mama said as she sat up in bed, holding the wet towel to her face.

One of the Gestapo hit my Uncle Laizer in the head with his rifle butt. Uncle Laizer fell against our stove, hitting his head against the large teakettle, and fell to the floor. While the two Gestapo were busy brutalizing my mama, Uncle Laizer crawled out of the apartment on his hands and knees.

The top of my head was pressed against the metal footboard as I lay on the two chairs. I could hear each blow with two rifles. One rifle pounded Mama's upper body and face, and the other pounded her lower body. Edzia lay trembling under the covers at Mama's feet, her head covered with the quilt.

The two young Gestapo, in their immaculate uniforms with their belt buckles, read, "Got mit uns" (God with us), and they did not resemble any human I had ever seen and certainly not anyone who believed in God. They stood next to the little white bed and without mercy brutalized my mama's gaunt body with the rifle butts.

"This is your last chance!" they barked in unison.

Each time my mama cried out in pain, I lifted my head and cried out as well.

The Gestapo standing at Mama's feet turned his attention to me. "If you don't shut up I will shoot you like a dog!" he barked.

I couldn't help myself. The two rifles were flying in the air and down at my mama's body, and she cried out in pain. I cried out again, and the Gestapo standing at Mama's feet hit me on my head with his rifle. I may have lost consciousness for a moment. When I lifted my head, I saw both Gestapo lowering the butts of their rifles on Mama's body, and her crying voice was that of a sick baby.

The Gestapo standing at Mama's upper body shouted, "I will count to three! If you don't tell us right now where he is, we will start shooting until everyone of you, "verfluchte Juden" (damn Jews), is dead!" He began to count, and both Gestapo aimed the rifles at our boarder's beds.

On the second count my mama suddenly stood up, her face and head soaked in blood. "Come, I will show you where he is. Come," she muttered and began stumbling towards the door with the two Gestapo following behind and shouting, "If you are lying to us, we'll kill you like a dog and go back and kill everybody in you house!" I heard them threaten Mama, all the way down the stairs.

For a moment, I lay on the two chairs, shaking, unable to move. As if the apartment had been haunted, I couldn't stay there another moment. I got up and pulled my clothes over my head. As I was running out of the apartment, Edzia followed behind. All the way down, the stairs were stained with my mama's blood. We ran to Fraida's apartment and found her standing at the window, her tears washing her face. The three of us were standing at Fraida's window and watched the two Gestapo poking at our mama's back with their rifles, and she stumbled until they disappeared from sight.

Edzia and I stood at the window, unable to stop shaking.

Fraida gave us a cup of hot tea with saccharin. After a few gulps, we calmed down, but the three of us didn't move from the window.

I don't know how long we stayed at the window, witnessing one wagon after another being pulled by gaunt men mounted to the wagons like horses. The starved men strained on the icy road pulling dead, naked bodies piled high one on top of the other.

After countless bodies, we saw our tata between the same two Gestapo, his hands tied in back.

Suddenly, I found myself running to the open hallway leading to the street. I had one foot on the threshold ready to make a run towards my tata. As I opened my mouth to cry out, "Tata!" I felt Fraida's hand covering my mouth and pulling me back inside. With aching hearts, the three of us stood at the window and saw our tata turning his head towards us, and the Gestapo dug the rifles into his back pushing him forward. At that moment, I was sure that these two young men were not humans. They didn't fit the description of anyone who possessed a heart or a soul. They were marching entities conditioned to brutalize and murder. It wasn't possible that such men would have parents or possibly wives and children.

We didn't speak or cry, we just continued standing at the window and watched our tata leave the cul-de-sac.

When the street was quiet again, we realized that Mama hadn't returned.

Fraida told Edzia to stay put and watch Eva and Abraham. We took off looking for Mama. Since we didn't know where Tata had been hiding, we didn't know where to start looking. We decided not to separate and walked in the direction where we saw Mama and the Gestapo turning the corner.

It was a cold and gloomy morning that matched our broken hearts. I don't know how long we walked in the freezing mountains of snow stained with blood.

Except for the open wagons filled with naked bodies, Fraida and I were the only living souls outside. It was so eerie, and I felt as if we were the only people alive. Our teeth were chattering. We were just about to turn back and go a different direction when I heard a whimpering sound. Fraida heard it at the same time. We ran in the direction of the sound and found Mama curled up behind a barn.

It took all of our strength to get our mama to her feet. Her face had been swollen beyond recognition. She was unable to straighten her body. We pulled her bruised arms around our necks and pulled her towards our home. When she saw the building, she began to cry and pull away from us. "No, no, I can't go in there. They'll come back for me, and then, they will kill everybody," she whimpered, and we saw that all of her front teeth were missing.

No matter how much we tried to reassure her that they wouldn't come back, she wouldn't listen. Take me to Hudesa until they'll go away," she muttered.

Fraida realized that she wouldn't be able to persuade our broken mother to come home, so we stumbled with her to Aunt Hudesa and pulled and tugged our mama until we reached the hospital.

Aunt Hudesa wrapped her arms around Mama and tried to guide her to her apartment, but Mama wanted first to go to the morgue. After looking at the mountain of naked bodies, we were satisfied that Tata wasn't among the dead. We left Mama with Aunt Hudesa and visited her every day. After three days, Aunt Hudesa convinced her sister that her children were starving, and she returned home.

The cookie money was gone, and all we had for food were the ration cards and the occasional woolens Bela had stolen from AFL.

One week after our tata had been taken from us, Bela came home and showed me a pass. "Tomorrow you are going with me to work. I know you like to sleep late, but you'll have to get up really early. It will still be dark when you wake up, alright?"

"Don't worry. Didn't I wake up early when I worked in Wolanow and when I went with Mama to the bakery until...?" My eyes filled with tears, thinking about that day when my life had as much value as a worm, and I couldn't finish the sentence.

"Yes, you did, but lately you have been sleeping late."

I was sleeping late, hoping for the day to pass faster, so I wouldn't think of how hungry I was.

I didn't tell her that, instead I said, "Don't worry. I won't disappoint you. At least now, we won't starve. I, too, can bring home woolens and help out."

Bela became enraged. "Don't even think about it! The way your face gets red, you will get caught in no time. Promise me you will get the thought out of your head. If they catch you, we will both get killed. Promise, or I won't take you!" she bellowed.

"I promise," I said, worried she would change her mind and not take me with her.

Bela, too, slept on two chairs next to me. As soon as I heard her stirring, I sat up so abruptly that my chairs parted, and I fell through, waking up the entire household.

My clothes were folded at the foot of my chair, and I was dressed in two minutes time. As I began dividing my hair and tying the ribbons to my pigtails, Bela stopped me.

"You can't wear pigtails if you want to look older," she said and took the comb from my hand and combed my hair in an upsweep and put bobby pins on each side.

The ribbon for my pigtails had been the most valuable possession. When I looked at myself in the piece of mirror large enough to fit in my hand, I felt as if I had been wearing a disguise. But if that was going keep me working with my sister, whom I loved and respected, I accepted her hairstyle for me, for I also knew that she wanted me to have a safe place to work.

All the way to work, Bela reminded me about my promise not to steal anything.

Several times on our walk to AFL, Ukraine Soldiers stopped us at rifle point. Our passes saved us from getting shot. We arrived ten minutes before roll call.

Three low-ranking soldiers stood in front of us, whips in hand. They knew all the girls by their first names and seemed friendly.

Herr. Doren was a short, middle-aged man with a round belly and red face. Only among themselves, never to his face, the girls referred to him as Red. His loud voice could be heard throughout the warehouse. Each word sounded more like a bark, but he didn't seem too threatening.

Herr. Aurisch was a reticent, no-nonsense, middle-aged, overweight man with dark blond hair and a thin mustache. The feeling I had on my first day was to be wary around him. He held his whip tight in his fist, and the way he continually passed it over his shiny boot gave me reason to believe that he would enjoy using it on us for the slightest reason.

Herr. Linden was younger than the other two soldiers. He had a pleasant face, large blue eyes, smiled easily, and the girls didn't seem to be afraid of him. His left leg was amputated, and the crutches occupied both of his hands, leaving him no room to carry a whip, though I had the feeling that this man wouldn't use it.

The whistle blew for roll call. Bela took my hand, and we lined up in military fashion, facing the soldiers. My heart pounded when Red began to count us and stopped in front of me. He looked angrily at Bela.

"She is too little, she can't stay," he barked.

"Please, Herr. Doren, give her a chance. She is very strong. She was digging ditches in Wolanow," Bela pleaded.

He touched me lightly with his whip on my shoulder. "Alright, she can stay today, but don't bring her back tomorrow."

As soon as we heard the train whistle, Bela quickly told me that if I want to avoid the whip, I had to run like the wind up and down the stairs, no matter how heavy the load.

I soon found that out when I saw everyone running down the stairs. A soldier stood on each flight of stairs ready, to use the whip if anyone slowed down. Even Herr. Linden stood on the first floor, his back against the wall, his underarms leaning on his crutches, and a whip dangling from his right had. Still, I didn't think he would use the whip.

I saw the relief on my sister's face when she saw me run up and down the three flights of stairs, carrying potato sacks on my shoulder, loaded with wooden shoes from Holland.

At the end of the day when we all lined up to be counted and searched, the red- faced soldier told Bela that I was a good worker.

"She is little, but strong, just like you. She can come back tomorrow."

I never thought that my sister liked me, but when I looked at her tired but happy face, I never loved her more. I would readily die for her if such a time should arrive.

"Thank you very much, Herr. Doren," Bela said humbly.

As time passed, I saw that Bela was very popular at AFL. Everyone liked her. Her thin body and short golden hair made her look boyish. "Bela boy," they called her. She could not only outrun anyone and never feel the whip on her back, she had a wonderful sense of humor. When the loadings and unloadings were finished, Bela made everyone laugh as we stood at the tables, sorting, folding, and packing. When our feet were cold standing on the cement floors without heat or windows for sunlight, Bela taught us a step to get the circulation going without having to leave the table and get in trouble. We jumped up on the balls of our feet, clicking our feet together in the air, and again touching the floor with the balls of out feet. Click, touch, click, touch. Our shoes made a drumming sound,…tra-ta-ta-tra-ta-ta- tra-tra-tra-ta-ta…. We all did this step throughout the day to keep our feet from becoming numb.

Red enjoyed sneaking up on the girls, grabbing them from behind, and tumbling them over on his back or wrestling them to the floor. He could never do it to Bela. Almost everyday, he would sneak up on her, and every time she made her thin body heavy, and he was unable to budge her.

I tried to emulate my sister's every move. I longed to be like her. The only way I succeeded was to make my body heavy the way Bela taught me, and Red couldn't tumble me over. "Genau wie die Bela" (just like Bela), he laughed.

As we walked home, Bela said, "I saw Red trying to tumble you. You did good." I could see the pride in Bela's eyes, and I wished she had put her arms around me and told me she was happy that we were together, but that had not been Bela's style. The only sign of affection from Bela was her index finger bumping the bridge of my nose. I tended to be demonstrative, but I learned quickly that Bela was different from Fraida. Fraida loved to hug. I also knew that Bela cared deeply, and today, when I saw the approval of me in her beautiful green eyes, was enough for me.

Mama was happy that at least two of her children had work passes.

At the end of March 1942, the snow was melting, promising warmer days to come. A messenger delivered a package, wrapped in brown paper, marked Auschwitz. We all stood around Mama and watched as she placed the package on the little worktable next to the door, near the stove. As soon as she untied the paper, we all recognized our tata's clothes. A short letter had been placed on top of his coat. The note stated that "Jeremy Sztraiman died in Auschwitz."

Mama's face contorted as she examined Tata's clothes.

My teeth were chattering, and I was freezing. Though I saw the Gestapo walk away with my Tata, I had never been able to visualize myself as a fatherless child. I had a friend who only had one parent. The thought of it happening to me was unthinkable. Seeing my tata's bloody underclothes, I refused to believe that he would never come home to us or to his new bakery he had worked so hard to build. Every brick he laid down in that oven were hours of sweat and deprivation of extra sleep and money to buy food and clothing for his children. No, my tata was not dead. They are lying, just as they had been lying about everything from the start. Maybe he was in Auschwitz, but my tata was strong, He was not dead, I told myself. I didn't cry. I refused to cry because that would be admitting to the fact that my tata had indeed died in Auschwitz.

Mama put Tata's underwear in a basin filled with cold water. Her tears spilled into the basin as she began to scrub, until there was no sign of blood. She finished washing Tata's white boxer shorts, t-shirt, and white long sleeve shirt with hot water from the teakettle and hung them next to the heater where they dried in no time.

When I saw Mama carefully iron and fold my Tata's clothes, I was sure she was going to put it away until he returned home, but she wrapped the clothes in the same paper it came in and put Tata's coat on top of the package and left the house without uttering a word.

Mama hadn't been very talkative lately, not since the Gestapo had knocked out her front teeth and took away her husband. She never forgave herself for taking the Gestapo to Tata's hiding place. As many times as the family and our boarders had told her that she had no choice, she held on to the guilt.

Mama returned an hour later and announced that she now had the money to begin baking the cookies again, and we all knew that she had sold Tata's clothes.

Mama left the apartment at dawn with Edzia holding onto her shawl.

Every day more people disappeared from the Ghetto, and it had been harder for Mama to sell her cookies. If it hadn't been for Bela bringing home a pair socks, a wool hat, or whatever article of clothing she could fit in her underwear, the family would surely starve to death. At least, Bela and I received a bowl of soup at midday, but what about Mama, Edzia, Fraida, and her family? The cookie baking brought in enough to cook a pot of potato soup, and Bela put another slice of bread on the table.

April 27, 1942 was known as the bloody Wednesday. On that day, several hundred Germans of the Security Service arrived to our town with lists and raided the Ghetto. Everyone on the list or who accidentally crossed their path were either shot on the spot or arrested. Again, we all stood at Fraida's window and watched a young garment maker, who had a wife and small child, being shoved down the stairs of his house. A Gestapo pointed a rifle at him and pulled the trigger. No matter how much rain had fallen on that spot, the bloodstain of the young father remained as a reminder of the worst was yet to come. Again, men mounted to wagons pulled countless, naked dead bodies, leaving trails of blood all the way to the morgue. Families crowded on the hospital grounds looking for their loved ones.

After the streets were quiet again, we found out that my Uncle Gershon, along with most of the butchers in the Ghetto, had been arrested.

Two weeks after the bloody Wednesday, Bela and I were getting dressed for work when Fraida came running breathlessly upstairs.

"Mama!" she gasped. "There are rounding up people on the Walowa and Buzniczna Street!"

Mama and Fraida began to help us with our clothes. They wouldn't give us a chance to comb our hair.

"Now, go quickly, and keep your labor card in your hands. Now go!" Mama shouted. When we hesitated, for we didn't want to leave our family, Mama and Fraida pushed us out of the door and ran down the stairs with us, making sure we wouldn't change our minds and return.

It was the longest day of our lives. Everybody was upset, and the soldiers were aiming their whips at us all day. At the end of the day, we all ran home. Bela and I were out of breath when we ran to make sure that Fraida and her children were in her apartment. We panicked when her apartment was empty.

We ran upstairs and burst into our apartment, being sure it too would be empty. When we saw Mama, Edzia, Fraida, and her two children, it felt as if we had received a gift from heaven. We all ran into each other's arms and accepted the wonderful gift.

Mama's eyes were red rimmed. When I wrapped my arms her neck, her face contorted and a storm of tears gushed from her eyes. She could barely speak.

"Except for Hudesa and us, the entire family is gone. All of Jeremy's brothers and their families are gone. Hanna and Pearl, together with their children, and everyone is gone, swallowed up as if they had never existed. We are all quickly disappearing, " she sobbed, and there was nothing Bela and I could say to her that would give our mother comfort.

As I lay on my two chairs that night, I couldn't stop crying for my Aunt Hanna. So many nights I wandered away from home and climbed to the fifth floor and was welcomed with hugs and kisses. Other than my own home, Aunt Hanna's home was the only place I felt comfortable to sleep over. Many times I would wet my bed. In the morning, I removed the wet sheet from the bed I shared with my cousin Hudesa, and my Aunt Hanna smiled as she soaked the wet sheet in a basin with warm water. She never made me feel guilty for wetting the bed. Other times, when I woke up crying during the night because I may have had a bad dream and wanted to go home, Aunt Hanna's son, Lopek, carried me all the way home. Now, my wonderful, loving aunt and my cousins and their children were all gone, too.

Everyday more people vanished, and we never knew if at the end of the day, we would find our family at home.

We had become so conditioned in trying to survive, our thoughts were only on holding on to our labor-cards. If we had a steady workplace for a German Company, there was hope to survive yet another day.

Our only prayers were for the Russians to liberate us before we all perished.

May was always a happy time, but not in 1942. After a freezing winter, the snow mixed with blood had melted and turned to mud, and the sun lit up the dreary streets.

Had my heart not been so laden with pain and sorrow, I would have breathed in the wonderful scent the lilac tree had so generously offered. It seemed a lifetime ago since I stopped wondering what happened to the elderly people in the nursing home, only a few feet away from the cul-de-sac.

We arrived at AFL and saw construction workers a few feet away from the warehouse, digging the same outline for houses as the ones I helped dig in Wolanow. Stocks of lumber were piled up on the grass, and men worked as if they were given a deadline.

We knew that these men were not Jewish, for they did not wear the armband with the Star of David Insignia.

As the days passed, the same men were hammering nails into wood. It was easy to see that two side-by side houses were being erected. Each little wooden house had an iron wood-burning oven. Wide pipes were fed through the roof. A small window had been installed in each little house. We still didn't know why or for whom these little houses had been built. We had become conditioned not to ask questions. It was easier to accept our blind destiny.

Saturday, three weeks after the construction had begun, the two little houses were finished. It had been an especially hard day. Twice, the trains arrived with confiscated heavy packs, filled with Russian uniforms and wooden shoes from Holland. We didn't just unload the boxcars, running up the stairs with sacks full with confiscated goods and running down the stairs, we loaded the train to capacity with assorted goods.

At the end of twelve hours, my back and shoulders ached from carrying heavy sacks up and down three flights of cement stairs.

At six o'clock, the whistle blew, and we lined up to be searched and counted. At that time, we were told to come back Sunday morning with our belongings.

We now knew that the two little houses were meant for us, and tonight would be the last night we would be sleeping at home.

As soon as Bela and I arrived home, Mama placed the wooden balia with the wooden cork securely in place and filled it with warm water. She drew the curtain separating the kitchen from the rest of the room, and Bela and I began to undress, but Edzia was quicker. She was the first one inside the balia and in the hot water.

As Mama began washing our backs, Bela and I flinched when her hand accidentally touched our shoulders. She was familiar with our sore shoulders, but it had been the first time she had seen my purple arms.

Herr. Doren's new hobby was to pinch my arms each time he passed the table where I stood sorting the merchandise. Sometimes I saw him coming and ducked in time, but he had a way of sneaking up on me. I only had a short sleeve blouse and didn't own another garment to hide the purple marks from mama. I immediately assured her that I wasn't beaten.

"I fell against a door," I said, and Bela's eyes met mine. Bela saw the red-faced man sneak up on me, pinch my arms, and laugh. His large belly shook with sadistic pleasure. We never talked about our predicament. There was nothing to be said. What choice did we have? It was still better than the threat of being shipped out or thrown in a truck and be whipped by the Gestapo or SS. Mama, too, accepted our painful shoulders and purple arms. She knew that it was still safer than being in the Ghetto.

Sunday morning, Mama left at dawn and returned with our bread rations and made tea with saccharine. I had never gotten used to the bitter saccharine aftertaste, but Mama said that it's good to have something warm in our stomachs.

The hugs and kisses we received gave me the feeling as if we were going on a long journey. Even Edzia wrapped her thin little arms around my neck. That was rare, for she favored Bela.

Our small family walked in step with us to the Ghetto's gate. At the gate, Mama kissed me and whispered in my ear, "Don't forget to use the bucket before you go to sleep."

I wanted to tell her that I had stopped wetting my bed a long time ago, but she hugged me until I was out of breath, and Bela urged me on. "We'll be late," she whimpered, trying to suppress the tears. Our pillows and blankets were under our arms, and we got one last kiss and a hug before we stepped through the Ghetto's gate. As we turned the bend, our family was still standing at the gate.

I couldn't stop the tears from flowing all the way to the camp. Bela, too, turned her head and wiped her eyes.

Before, when we returned home every night, we saw that our family was safe at home. Now, although the soldiers promised us a two hour pass every other week, it wasn't going to be the same as being home every night. A lot could happen in six days, and as of today, we would never know if we would find our families at home.

When we arrived at the camp Sunday morning, and the soldiers ordered us to line up on the grass in front of the two little houses for roll call. After we were counted, the soldiers pointed to the little house on the left.

"This barrack is for the girls," Herr. Auricsh shouted. He pointed the whip at the right barrack. "Here is for the men. Get water and rags from the kitchen and clean the rooms and wash the windows. Dismissed!" he shouted.

When our room was spotless, straw was spread out on the floor.

At twelve o'clock, we were given a bowl of soup, and as we had done so every night since the invasion, we went to sleep hungry.

I hadn't thought about wetting my bed until Mama reminded me not to forget to use the bucket before I went to sleep. As we lay on the floor on top of the straw, I prayed for a dry first night, for it would have been more embarrassing than I could have handled. It took me a long time to fall asleep, and I used the bucket again when I began to feel drowsy. I woke up during the night and used the bucket once more.

In the morning, when the loud whistle rang out, I was happy that I was dry and knew that as long as I used the bucket just before I would fall asleep, I wouldn't embarrass myself or my sister.

Most of the girls in our barrack were between fifteen and twenty years old, with the exception of a few girls that were younger and a few women that were over thirty.

I don't know how it started, but one older woman in her late thirties or early forties, we all called Grandmother, and she liked it. Grandmother stood up, her hair and cotton nightgown was covered with straw. She turned her head toward the window and stretched a thin arm towards the sky. "I sleep between the oven and two night buckets, and the sun is shining directly on my face." Grandmother made that statement in German accented with Yiddish, causing roaring laughter, and every girl had memorized the statement. That statement had become the joke of our barracks.

By week's end, three layers of bunk beds were assembled in our barracks. The bunk beds, the oven, and the night bucket took up every inch of space in the room.

Bela chose two top, side-by-side bunks for us and was happy that the ceiling had loose movable plywood boards, a perfect place to hide stolen merchandise, and the girls prayed that the soldiers wouldn't discover it. The ceiling also served as shelving for our shoes and clothes.

Some girls still had money and were able to smuggle in food and cook it on the stove.

It wasn't that way for Bela and me. We had to depend on the piece of bread in the morning and the soup in the afternoon.

Though the soldiers made unexpected searches of our barracks while we were at work, it didn't occur to them that the ceilings were loose.

When my first pass had been handed to me, Bela still refused to let me steal. She had become quite proficient and didn't need to worry about me getting caught.

As I walked through the Ghetto gate, I prayed to find my family as I left them a week ago.

Fraida saw me coming and ran out to embrace me, with Abraham and Eva trailing behind, and followed me up the stairs.

Mama's sad green eyes lit up when she saw me come through the door. Her arms felt like a warm blanket on a cold winter night. My entire family, even our boarders, were happy to see me.

Mama held the door open. "Where is Bela?" she asked worriedly.

"They don't allow us to leave together, but she will come next Sunday," I reassured her.

Mama held my face in both hands and kissed the top of my head.

"Mama we need a basin for washing ourselves and our laundry," I said timidly.

"You didn't bathe the whole week?" she asked surprised.

Embarrassed I shook my head. "The soldiers promised to take us to the showers next week," I said.

Mama placed the large, blue, aluminum teakettle on the stove. "Mama, there's no time for a bath. The water is still ice cold," I protested. The truth was, I didn't want her to see the new purple marks on my arms. Whenever Red was in a playful mood his fat fingers made imprints on my arms.

"Don't worry. You have plenty of time. I don't want you to get lice in your hair," she said and placed a plate of cabbage and potato soup in front of me. "Eat while the water is heating," she said and sat next to me, making sure I ate the soup.

"Mama, I get food at the camp. I want you to eat it," I said and moved the plate away from me. I worried that she gave me her portion.

Mama's eyes were larger than ever, and her checkered dress hung on her as if her body had become invisible. She wouldn't let me leave the table until I finished the soup. "I ate plenty," she said, running a hand through my hair.

White puffs of steam were beginning to leave the spout and like a locomotive, and thicker and thicker clouds coughed up until the cover on the teakettle danced with the boiling water. Mama placed the basin on a chair. While I undressed, she filled it with hot water and added cold. As always, since I began working at AFL, Mama counted the bones on my back, but it had been the first time I heard mama curse, "The cholera should take the sadistic murders! Pinching a child, making her black and blue, and getting pleasure from it!"

I flinched when she touched my bruised shoulders, and Mama's tears began dripping into the water. "All the bones are showing," she sobbed, and continued muttering about the murderous, sadistic Germans, pinching a child for pleasure.

The two hours seemed a minute, and once again, Mama, Edzia and Fraida walked me to the Ghetto's gate, and I prayed to see them again with my next pass, but I prayed harder to be liberated by the Russian's before we all perished.

Each time I came home for the two-hour visit and found my family at home had been a gift. Every waking moment, we prayed to be liberated by the Russians before we all vanished, but God, as well as the rest of the world, had forsaken us, and we were at the mercy of heartless murderers.

Next week, the soldiers marched us to the public showers located in the Ghetto. When we arrived, our families were standing outside hoping for a glimpse. I saw Mama, Fraida, Edzia, Abraham, and Eva. They wanted to come closer for a hug, but they were chased away by the soldiers. So, they stood and waved and smiled, and tears were rolling down from mothers and children faces. Our families were still there when we left the showers and were marched back to camp. I saw Mama straining her neck for a last glimpse of us.

August 16, 1942, the whistle blew at dawn, and all three soldiers entered our barracks. Startled, everyone woke up and quickly began to dress.

In his usual loud voice, Red announced, "Today, everyone of you will be given a one-hour pass to visit you families."

It was an unusual treat, and we were very grateful for the generosity.

My turn to go home was from two to three in the afternoon, and Bela's turn from three to four.

Ukrainians heavily guarded the streets leading to the Ghetto. There were always guards, but never so many. I was stopped three times at rifle-point.

Polish electricians were up on the electric poles installing spotlights throughout the Ghetto.

Fraida saw me entering the cul-de-sac and ran towards me with outstretched arms and hugged me much tighter than usual. When she loosened her grip on me, I asked, "Why are these men installing such big lights all over the Ghetto?"

"General Frank is coming during the night to inspect the Ghetto," she said.

It didn't make much sense to me. Why would a General be inspecting the Ghetto during the night? I wanted to believe with all my heart that it was a good thing. I ran upstairs to surprise Mama, but she wasn't surprised. Girls from the neighborhood had come home earlier and told her of the generous gift our soldiers had given us. Mama had the basin with warm water ready for me and began helping me with my bath.

"Mama, I saw Fraida downstairs. She said that General Frank is coming to inspect the Ghetto. Maybe, when he sees how bad things are here, he will do something to make it better," As I was saying the words, I tried as hard as I could to believe, but my mama continued helping me with my bath and changed the water to wash my hair.

As always, when I finished bathing, Mama placed a bowl of cabbage soup on the table in front me. "Now eat the soup. You are skin and bone," she said and sat down next to me, her eyes fixed on my face while running a hand over my hair.

As I stood up to leave, I tried to tell myself that I would see my family next week. But as hard as tried to tell myself that the lights in the Ghetto were to honor General Frank, I was unable to rid myself of the darkness I had felt in my heart.

As I was getting ready to leave, Mama wrapped her arms around me, being careful not to touch my shoulders or my bruised arms. "Jentala, I have a feeling that I will never see you again. Ask the soldiers to give you a pass for me to come to camp with you," she said as tears filled her eyes, and I felt her body trembling. I didn't want her to see me cry and blinked away the tears.

"I'll ask the soldiers, but things will get better after the Generals' visit, you'll see," I said and felt a lump in my throat. I could barely breath.

"Ask the soldiers, Jentala," she said again.

I wanted to tell her to come with me right now. Then, I remembered the Ukrainians on every corner, pointing the rifles at me, and without passes, I was sure that we would all be shot on the spot.

"I will mama, I'll ask," I said.

"What about me," Edzia whined.

"You'll be all right. You'll go to the hospital and stay with Aunt Hudesa," Mama said.

"No, I don't want to stay with Aunt Hudesa. I want to go with you," she protested.

Once again, my family walked with me to the end of the Ghetto and stayed at the gate until I turned the bend.

All the way to camp, I practiced how to approach Herr. Doren and beg him to let my mama come to work with us.

Several times I was stopped at rifle-point, and each time I was glad that I wasn't foolish enough to bring Mama along, for she would have been shot in front of my eyes.

As I entered the camp, the sun was still strong, and several families with small children sat on the grass on top of blankets.

How did they get here without being stopped by the Ukrainians? I wondered. I was hoping to find Bela before she left. Maybe, she saw all the other families and was able to get passes for our family. I looked everywhere, but there was no sign of my sister. How I wished she would come back with Mama, Edzia, Fraida, and her two children.

Suddenly, all three soldiers came running with whips in hand. "You must all leave the camp!" Red bellowed loudest at the families on the grass.

Within minutes, all the mothers and small children had left the camp crying, and I knew that Herr. Doren would never give me a pass for my family.

I waited by the gate for Bela to arrive. I was sure that it was more than an hour since she had left. Tears flooded my face as I stood close to the gate waiting for Bela's return.

The guard had become annoyed with me and pointed his rifle at me, shouting for me to move away from the gate. "If you come any closer I will shoot you!" he shouted.

I hunched my shoulders and slowly shuffled away, but I stopped five feet from the gate. I heard shots fired from a distance and flinched each time, wondering where my sister was. Each thought of why Bela wasn't back yet made me shudder. Did she lose her pass and get shot? Or had she decided to stay home? Did she take a chance and attempt to bring the family? Just as I decided to tell the guard that I wanted to leave the camp, I saw my sister show him her pass and walk through the gate.

I wiped my eyes and ran towards her, wrapping my arms around her neck and assaulted her with a million questions.

There was unrest in the barrack. Everyone was talking about the spotlights.

Since Bela had been the last one to return, the girls wanted to know what was happening in the Ghetto?

"All I can tell you is that everyone is worried. The Ukrainians have surrounded the Ghetto. I was stopped many times, and that's why I'm late."

When we climbed up on our bunks, I saw that Bela's eyes were red.

"What's wrong, Bela? Did Mama ask you to ask the soldiers for a pass for her?"

Bela stretched out and folded her hands behind her head and looked up at the ceiling. "No she didn't. I was at home when all the mothers and children returned. Why are you asking? Did she ask you to get her a pass?"

"Yes, she wants me to ask the soldiers for a pass to be together in AFL. She said that Edzia would go to the hospital and stay with Aunt Hudesa, but Edzia didn't want to. I promised her that I would ask Red for a pass."

"Did you ask?" Bela whispered.

"No, when I returned, the camp was full with mothers and children, but the soldiers chased them all out. I was looking for you, but you had already left. I was hoping that you got passes for our family."

"Tomorrow, I'll ask Red," Bela said, but we both knew that the answer would be a loud no.

"Was Mama worried about the spotlights?" I asked, risking the possibility of making my sister angry for asking too many questions.

Bela turned her head to the side, and I saw a single tear roll onto her pillow. "Yes, she was worried and asked me to take care of you because…" As if afraid she had said too much, Bela rolled over on her side with her back towards me.

"What exactly did Mama say that got you so upset? Did Mama tell you that I did something bad? Why can't you tell me?" I insisted.

"Mama told me…to…take care of you…because you are not smart enough…to take care of yourself." Bela said more onto her pillow than to me.

I was hurt but not surprised. I always avoided confrontation and stayed out of my sibling's ways and had earned the name 'stupid.'

I turned on my side, my back towards Bela. I looked at the girls in the lower bunks, several like Bela and me. The older sister comforted the younger one, and I wondered what instructions their mothers had given the older sisters.

I buried my face in my pillow and cried silently. I closed my eyes, willed myself to stop crying, and began making plans. Tomorrow morning I'll go to Red and beg him on my hands and knees to give me passes for my family. When I'll get the passes, I'll ask permission to go home and bring my family. Maybe then, Mama will know that I'm not her stupid kid.

The lights went out, and I dozed off. I dreamt that it was morning, and we were all still in bed. My tata came home from the bakery with a round-bread under his arm and pockets bulging with still warm rolls sprinkled with poppy seeds. He reached in his pockets, and we all held out our hands to catch a roll. Just as I was about to catch the flying roll, I woke up to lights filtering through the little window, followed by sounds of gunfire and locomotion.

Everyone in the room sat up. Within minutes, we heard more gunfire and loud cries coming from the Ghetto. We all jumped off our bunks and ran to the barbed wires.

The bright lights from the Ghetto lit up our camp. Ignoring the stabbing pain, we gripped the sharp points on the barbed wire. The only pain we felt were our families cries in the Ghetto and the blaring shouts in German.

We heard heavy doors slam and, minutes later, the sound of moving locomotives. Another train came to a screeching stop and cries from the Ghetto began again.

I clearly heard women's voices crying, "my foot, my hand, my baby!' For an instant, I was sure I heard Fraida's cry, "my arm, my arm!"

I was shaking the wire and cried, "Fraida!"

We all knelt on the grass by the wires, crying for our families. I willed my thoughts to my mama. "Hide, Mama, and please, take Fraida, her children, and Edzia and hide. I'll find you in the morning and bring passes for all of you, and we'll be together. Please Mama, take our family and hide until it's over. As soon as the trains leave, I'll come for you," I cried loud, willing the sound from my mouth to my mama's ears. I pulled at the wires oblivious to the blood gushing from my palms onto the grass. I felt no pain, only the ache in my heart.

Bela stood next to me, gripping the barbed wire, and cried silently.

One girl fell on the grass, her eyes rolled onto her head, arms and legs thrashing, her entire body was quivering like a motor. When she finally stopped thrashing, her mouth was bloody, her lips and tongue were cut and bleeding.

All night we listened to the screeching locomotives and slamming of metal doors. Helplessly we listened, but we were unwilling to believe that our families were being pushed into cattle trains and shipped out.

At dawn, all three soldiers, whips in their hands, appeared at the barbed wires and ordered us to line up to be counted. Oblivious to their threats, my ears were only tuned to the Ghetto and my helpless family, until three whips had begun flying in the air. As one whip burned into my back, I cried silently, "Hide Mama."

Like zombies, we stood in line to be counted then shooed into the warehouse.

We stood at the tables sorting Russian uniforms, leaving a mixture of tears and blood from our palms on the uniforms.

All day the soldiers threatened to march us into the Ghetto if we didn't stop crying, but we couldn't help it. How could we stop crying, knowing that we may never see our families again?

As if our vigilance would keep our families from being shipped out, no one lined up for the soup at midday. All we wanted to do was get back to the wires.

Monday evening when the whistle blew, we were lined up, counted, and dismissed. We all ran back to the wires and listened to the cries of our families in the Ghetto and the shouting in the German language, followed by gunfire.

When it turned dark, once again, the spotlights from the Ghetto lit up our camp.

The sounds were not as loud as the night before, and the locomotives were not as frequent, but gunfire was.

Tuesday morning, August 18, we were still at the barbed wire when the soldiers, this time didn't use the whips, but ordered us to line up outside our barrack to be counted.

Two young SS men rushed through the gate and spoke to our soldiers. Minutes later, the soldiers stepped aside, and the SS men stood in front of us, guns secure on the hips. The shiny, large belt buckles on their midriff read, "Got mit uns" (God with us). The two SS men walked back and forth from the beginning of the line to the end and back again. We were inspected with piercing eyes, the way a rancher examines cattle.

"Anyone born later than 1926, and anyone older than thirty-nine years of age leave the line and pack your belongings," one shouted.

Mrs. Luxenburg, somewhat older than thirty-nine, a lady we all loved, stepped out and walked towards the barrack.

I remembered, once Mama pointed me out to her lady friend, and said, "My Jentala is the scale. She was born on October six," but Mama never said which year I was born.

Seeing Lusia Rojal, my school-friend, her mother, and older sister leave the line and walk towards the barrack, I knew that I would have to do the same. Lusia and I finished the fourth grade in 1939, so if she was born later than 1926, so was I.

Bela was standing next to me and whispered in my ear, "Stay where you are, you were born 1926." I never questioned her, for I was glad to be among the living, even though it would only be temporary, and I remained in line.

Twice, one SS man stopped in front of me. I stood on my tiptoes and strained my neck to appear taller. The second time he touched my shoulder with his whip and asked, "How old are you?"

My heart pounded so loud I was afraid he would hear it and order me to join the group that was being send to the Ghetto.

"I was born October 6, 1926," I said in perfect German, making my voice strong.

I prayed he leave my sight before my toes cramped, and my heart popped out of my chest. The same SS man strolled to the end of the line and back to me.

"How old are you!" he shouted again.

"I was born October 6, 1926." I said gazing at his bobbing Adam's apple. It seemed forever before the SS stopped in front of another young girl.

After what seemed a lifetime, the two SS raised their arms to our soldiers and exchanged a loud "Heil Hitler!"

I allowed myself the luxury of a breath as our soldiers took over and ordered us to go to the warehouse.

As we passed our barrack, I heard Herr. Linden, our one legged soldier, tell the condemned, "Pack and unpack. Pack and unpack. Don't rush." He stepped outside and listened to the sound of boots and looked towards the gate. When he saw that the two SS had left our camp, he told the group to follow us to the warehouse.

In the last three years since the massacre of Jews had been legalized, I had been fortunate to know two kindhearted Germans, and I suddenly wondered what had happened to Herr. Builder? I was certain that I would never know and hoped he was well.

These two Germans helped me to hold on to the hope that not all Germans or all Polish people were bad.

As we ran up the stairs and reached the third floor, Mrs. Luxenburg fainted on the last two steps.

She was about to slide down a flight of stairs when the girls held onto her and positioned her on the cement floor in the hallway and sprinkled water on her white as a corpse's face. I had seen enough corpses since September 1939 to recognize the difference. When she regained consciousness, her color still hadn't returned to her gaunt face. She became hysterical and fainted again. The girls pulled her inside the warehouse and laid her down behind a large stock of shoes, on a pile of Russian uniforms.

When she regained consciousness, the girls didn't allow her to stand up and kept her calm until her color returned.

I was standing next to a large heap of women's sweaters, getting them ready for shipment. Herr. Doren and Herr. Aurisch strolled from table to table, whips swinging in the air as if it were an ordinary day. As I stood in front of the mountain of sweaters unable to control the tears, Herr. Doren stopped in front of me.

"How old are you?" he asked, his eyes narrowed to slits, and his face became red as smoldering coal.

My heart pounded as I remembered Bela's words, and I said, "I was born October 6, 1926." He pinched my arm and shuffled away, grinning like a Cheshire Cat.

The whistle sounded for our daily bowl of soup, but no one lined up. We all ran to the wires. We needed to hear that our families were still alive, but there were no human sounds coming from the Ghetto, only frequent gunfire and infrequent freight cars, slamming the doors shut. My empty stomach growled, but I wasn't hungry. We were ordered back to the warehouse, and we flooded the woolens with our tears.

At night we all ran to the wires, but we heard only dead silence. No more cries from our families. No more gunfire, and no sounds coming from locomotives, only ear-piercing silence. It was over. There was no point in kneeling and holding on to the wires. No need to beg Mama to hide, for she couldn't hear me.

No one uttered a word in the two barracks, only eerie silence.

Bela and I cried silently into our pillows. Exhausted, we fell asleep.

Wednesday morning, our soldiers had decided to march us to the public shower-house. A morbid stillness hung in the air. I looked for Mama, Fraida, Abraham, Eva, and Edzia. I wanted them to wave to Bela and me.

My eyes rested on the same spot where my family stood, and I wished that the last three days had been a nightmare, and I would see my mama holding on to Edzia, for she tried to pull away from her and run towards us. But my wishes hadn't come true in a very long time.

After three nights and days of kneeling on the grass and gravel and barbed wire spikes cutting into my palms, the cold water rushing down from the ceiling was soothing on this hot August day. We were allowed thirty minutes for bathing, but it wasn't enough time to wash away the pain in our hearts.

Herr. Doren lined us up to be counted. When satisfied that no one was missing, Herr. Aurisch, in his quiet manner said, "You have our permission to visit the Ghetto. We'll meet here in one hour."

The entire Ghetto was so still, as if every living thing had been swallowed up.

Everyone ran in different direction. Bela and I ran to the cul-de-sac and stood in total silence. I was sure that Aunt Hanna's Man with the Black Hand would materialize. He would stretch out his enormous long arm and huge black hand and make us disappear with the rest of the people in the Ghetto. I followed Bela into the hallway of our apartment building and walked through Fraida's open door.

The only things left in her apartment were the empty beds. Everything else had been stripped clean. There was nothing left of my beloved sister and her family. Our musical crib, little Eva had slept in, was gone, too. There was no sign of my sister's existence, nothing, not a picture or a little token to remember her and her beautiful children. Leaving Fraida's apartment, we ran upstairs and stopped in the dark narrow hallway. The dusty light bulb hung from the ceiling on a single black wire. It never occurred to me to wonder if that light bulb ever discharged light into the narrow, black little hallway or what color the three walls in the little hallway were. The door to our apartment was closed, and I prayed that everyone inside would be home and happy to see us. But such happiness was not meant for Bela and me. Like Fraida's apartment, ours too was stripped clean, not by our family, we were sure of that. Only our boarder's beds were left. Tata's little white bed was gone.

Bela and I sat down on our boarder's bare mattress and listened to the eerie silence. I felt as if I was a sand-castle and was being washed away bit by bit until no traces were left. We would cease to exist and nobody would be left to cry for us. We had no more illusions about being rescued by the Russians. It was only a matter of time before we all vanished. Dry eyed, Bela and I looked at each other, and without uttering a word, we knew what the other was thinking, *We only have each other, now.* We stood up, and with stooped shoulders, we walked back to the shower house with fifteen minutes to spare.

All the girls arrived before the hour was over. We waited outside for the soldiers to leave the shower house. They, too, had taken advantage of the cold showers.

Defenseless and hopeless, we lined up for our walk back to camp. With the knowledge that, once we outlived our usefulness, our barracks would be as empty and silent as our apartments. Yet, I had this strong need to hold on to just a glimmer of hope for a miracle. If it hadn't been for that tiny light called hope, I would have left the line and not look back. A bullet would enter the back of my head and end my misery.

At night I lay in darkness, but sleep wouldn't come. Where is my family? Are they still alive? Will I ever feel my mama's arms around me? Will I ever hear Fraida calling her children, "my sweetness?" Suddenly, a soothing violin sound broke through the men's barracks. Slowly, our girls joined in with the softest voices and saddest songs.

Edzia Horowicz was a beautiful, tall, blond girl with a voice of an angel. Her upper bunk was pushed against the wall of the men's barracks. When she began to sing "Mama," my tears soaked my pillow, and I fell asleep.

Every night thereafter, I fell asleep to the violin and our girl's voices crying for Mama.

Chapter Twenty-One: The Small Ghetto

A week after the liquidation of the entire Ghetto, a small Ghetto with three thousand men and women was formed in Radom, on Szwarlikowska Street.

Our soldiers announced that we would be given two-hour-passes to visit the small Ghetto every other Sunday.

I was among the first to receive a pass. My heart raced as I passed the Ukrainian guard on Szwarlikowska Street. The sun was strong, and groups of people sat on chairs next to their assigned apartments, having emotional conversations with tears streaming down each face like rain drops from leaves.

No one paid attention as I walked by and looked at each face, praying that at least one of the faces would belong to my family, or at least recognize me.

A familiar voice called my name. I turned my head and saw Joel standing next to a building. I ran to him as fast as I could. Fraida...Fraida's alive. I was sure of it. I strained my neck beyond Joel, being sure Fraida was somewhere inside the building.

Joel wrapped his long arms around me.

"Thank God you're alive. Is Bela with you?" he asked, looking over my shoulder at the same I was looking over his shoulder.

"Bela will come next Sunday. Where is Fraida?" I asked looking through every window, being sure she would jump up from behind the building and surprise me.

Joel's eyes hooded, his lips were moving, but I didn't hear a word he said.

"Where is your apartment?" I asked, being sure Fraida was in the apartment, hiding behind some furniture, waiting for the chance to jump out and wrap her arms around me, and Abraham and Eva would jump into my lap, and I would smother them with kisses.

Joel turned and I followed him to a small dark room. Each wall was covered with three layers of bunk beds, blocking the small window and the little light that would filter through. I strained my eyes looking for Fraida, but all I saw were men curled up on bunks in the fetal position.

Joel tried to tell me the reason why Fraida and the children weren't with him, but I wasn't ready to listen. As I left the dark room, my eyes squinted in the bright sunlight.

I looked at every face and visualized Edzia, who was always good at hiding from our mama and would suddenly tiptoe behind me and shout, "boo!"

As I continued walking back towards the Ghetto's exit, a red headed woman looked at me with curiosity. She was sitting on a chair next to a blond boy, Edzia's age. "Aren't you Mindala's daughter?"

"Yes," I said, wondering how she knew who I was, and I suddenly remembered seeing her somewhere. "Do you know my mama? Have you seen her? Is she around here? Could you tell me where I could find her?" I was asking so many questions in a single breath that the woman didn't have a chance to answer me, until my eyes filled with tears, and my throat formed a lump.

"No, child, I didn't see your mama, but I'm your Aunt Hudesa's daughter-in-law from France. My name is Sylvia, and this is my son, Dudek. Days before the bombings began, we came to Poland to visit Szlomek's mama, your Aunt Hudesa. During the bombing, my husband and his brothers, Julek and Szulim, took off for the Russian border. I should have gone with them, but it was too dangerous for Dudek."

"Did you see my mama and my sisters during the liquidation?"

"No, I was in the hospital with your Aunt Hudesa. During the liquidation of the large Ghetto, the Gestapo removed all the patients, fifty-nine of them. They were taken to Penc Park and shot to death. The staff and families were sent here. Your Aunt Hudesa is also here. She's working in the kitchen," Sylvia said and pointed towards the kitchen.

Before I ran across the street to see my aunt, I said, "You speak perfect Polish. You must be a quick learner."

"I'm originally from Poland. After Shlomo and I were married, we went to Paris to study. It must've been before you were born. As a matter of fact, in 1939 your cousin, Lopek, only had six more months before he would finish medical school. Hopefully, he finished and is practicing medicine in Paris."

I didn't remember my cousin, Lopek, but I often heard Aunt Hudesa speak of him with pride.

"I hope he finished. My aunt is very proud of him," I said and ran across the street.

I stood in the doorway and watched Aunt Hudesa scrubbing a large pot. Then, she wiped a wooden counter. She didn't recognize me until I identified myself and put my arms around her neck and kissed every inch of her face. She wiped her hands on her apron and tightened her grip on me. "I'm sorry, child. I didn't recognize you. My glasses broke during the liquidation," she said, holding me to her bosom.

My aunt's scent reminded me of my mama, and I never wanted to leave her embrace. "Bela and I are camped in AFL. We were promised two-hour passes every other Sunday. I'll come to see you in two weeks, and Bela will see you next Sunday, but I have to go now, Auntie. My time is running out," I said, as I reluctantly left my Aunt's arms.

"You must be hungry. You're skin and bone. Wait and let me give you some soup," she said, wiping her eyes with the back of her hand. She dished out a bowl of gray liquid and placed it on the wooden counter in front of me. The soup looked as if it had burned scrapings mixed with the dishwater from the counter. I was very hungry, for I hadn't eaten since the day before. I held the spoon with liquid to my mouth and swallowed quickly as if it were medicine.

"I have to go, or I won't get another pass," I said, knowing that the punishment would be worse than what I had told her.

"Come, child. I'll walk with you to the gate."

My aunt held on to my arm until we reached the Ghetto's gate. It reminded me of the time when Mama and my sisters walked with me to the Ghetto's gate and didn't leave until I disappeared from sight. When I kissed my beloved aunt's face, she hugged me tightly to her chest.

"The sun feels so good, but the cement floor in the kitchen feels like a block of ice under my feet. I wish I had some woolen socks. It would make my life so much easier," my aunt said, and all the anguish revealed itself in her contorted but still beautiful face, the same face, the same soft spoken words that for many years had brought sunshine to countless patience and to all of us. I hugged my aunt and promised that Bela will bring socks for her next Sunday.

Bela was waiting for me when I returned. She was anxious to hear if I found our family? I told her about Joel.

"What about Fraida?" she wanted to know.

I lowered my eyes. "She isn't with Joel. Aunt Hudesa is in the small Ghetto. The Germans liquidated the hospital and killed all the patients. I told her that you'd see her next week. Bela, she's working in the kitchen. She looks really bad, and her feet are freezing on the cement floor. I told her that you'd see her next Sunday and bring her warm socks."

"I'll take care of Aunt Hudesa's feet next Sunday, but don't you even think of taking socks from the table. I'll take care of it," Bela said, looking into my eyes and letting me know that she meant what she said.

"I promise I won't."

She poked my nose with her index finger, Bela's sign of affection.

Monday and Tuesday I stood at the table sorting, matching, and sizing woolen socks. Each time I came across a pair of soft heavy socks, I pictured myself kneeling in front of Aunt Hudesa and putting them on her feet. I could hear her sighing and telling me how good her feet felt.

Friday morning, a new shipment arrived with Russian uniforms, beautiful women's wool embroidered sweaters, and more wool socks.

My old navy blue sweater had been patched many times. The temptation to bend down between two girls, take off my old sweater, and put on a brand new powder blue one was great. It would have been easy to mix my old sweater with the new. But what if one of the soldiers remembered my old sweater? I felt my face burn and my hands shake. I quickly folded the pretty sweater and began tying the bundles. Early afternoon I had finished with the sweaters and began with the socks. The temptation to take a pair of socks for my aunt had been much stronger than the sweater. My sweater was patched, but I could still wear it, but my poor aunt was suffering, I reasoned. I came across a soft gray pair of socks. I put one on my hand and brought it to my face. Again, I visualized my aunt's face relax and tell me how nice it felt. I saw Bela scowling at me from the next table. I quickly removed the sock from my hand and paired it with the match.

All day Saturday, the soldiers were watching us very carefully, I was afraid that Bela wouldn't be able take socks for our aunt. The frisk at the end of the day had been more thorough than any other day, and I prayed that Bela didn't take any socks.

While still in line waiting to be dismissed, the soldiers were handing out passes to visit the Ghetto. I was surprised when Red handed me a morning pass. I didn't look the gift-horse in the mouth and said thank you. Bela's pass was for the afternoon. As we climbed up on our bunk beds, I wished I had taken the socks for Aunt Hudesa, for I was sure that Bela didn't. To my surprise, Bela reached her hand in her underpants and pulled out a pair of soft gray socks. She put a sock on her hand and rubbed it in my face.

"Will you listen to me from now on?" she said playfully. We hugged and I told her that I would never doubt her.

"Oh, I forgot to tell you," I said excitedly. "Red gave me a morning pass. He must have had an extra one, or he made a mistake. Since I'm going before you, I'll take the socks for Aunt Hudesa."

"No you will not! If you are searched at the gate, you'll panic."

"I won't panic. I know where to find our aunt. What if you don't find her. She will have frozen feet for another week. Please, Bela, trust me and let me go."

"We'll see," she said.

When the lights were out, Bela silently moved the panel on the ceiling and hid the precious socks.

Sunday morning, Bela and I were the first to wake up. Bela whispered in my ear, "Go pee in the bucket and come back up."

When I returned, she told me to get dressed. "Lift your dress up and take the socks and put them in your panties. Make them flat the way you do the rag when you have your period," she whispered.

It suddenly occurred to me that I only had two or three periods in my whole life.

"Bela, when was the last time you had a period?"

"I don't know. I don't think I had one since I started working here. None of the girls are having a period. We think that they are putting something in our soups to stop the periods. I don't care. I don't have to worry about rags."

"I'm glad too," I told her.

Bela lifted her dress and untied a rope from her underpants. "Lift you dress and pull up your panties."

She tied the rope around my panties and pulled them up tight for the socks to cling to my body. "Now, climb down and walk."

When I did, it felt as if I had a pillow between my legs.

"Come back up. I'll have to take the socks myself," she said.

"No," I protested. "You are always taking the risks. I can do it."

"Jadzia, listen to me. If the guard sees you walking through the gate this way, your life will have no value."

I unbuttoned my skirt and pulled my stretched out panties up and tucked them under my brazier. I tightened the rope until I could hardly breeze. Bela watched me walk outside and said, "good."

As I showed my pass to the guard at the, gate my heart was pounding, and I prayed that my face wouldn't turn red. I held my breath until the he motioned for me to go.

I took a deep breath as and began walking in the direction of the Ghetto. Halfway there, I felt my panties slipping. By the time I reached the Ghetto, the socks were dangling between my thighs. It was very early and Szwarlikowska Street was deserted.

I shuffled into a darkened hallway inside of a building and reached my hand to my inner thighs and pulled out the socks that were just about to fall out. I unbuttoned my skirt, separated the socks and hung them on the rope, like laundry on my abdomen. It showed a bulge, but my stomach was empty and flat, and with my sweater over, it wasn't noticeable. I pictured my aunt wearing the warm socks, and I rushed over to the kitchen.

The door was wide open and the stove and counter were clean. My first thought was that it was still too early. It was Sunday. I sat down on the step and waited.

Twenty minutes later, people were beginning to put their chairs out in front of their apartments. I observed much fewer people than a week ago.

The sun was strong now, and as I stood up, I became lightheaded and had to hold on to the wall. I should have been used to walking around with an empty stomach, but telling myself that didn't help. I crossed the street to the apartment where I had met Sylvia and Dudek. I was hoping that my aunt would be getting ready to go to the kitchen and knocked on the door.

A gaunt man stepped out and sat down on the old wooden chair.

"Excuse me, please. Did you see Hudesa, the nurse?" I asked. Everyone in Radom knew Hudesa the nurse. She had lived and worked in the hospital since she was a very young girl. She married the orderly and raised and educated four sons and a beautiful daughter, who died of tuberculosis.

"Hudesa, Sylvia, and Dudek, together with the entire hospital staff and others, were shipped out this week," the man said nonchalantly, as if it were a normal routine, of which it was. Only I was still unable to accept it. I ran to see if Joel was still among the handful left in the small Ghetto.

The door to his dark room was open, and Joel was sitting on his bunk talking to his roommates.

"I'm sorry about your aunt," he said when he saw me walk through the door. "They practically emptied the Ghetto," he said.

I turned towards the wall and removed the socks I had carried around my waistline. Quietly, so the others wouldn't see or hear, I handed the socks to Joel. "Here, I brought them for my aunt's cold feet, but she won't need them now. Sell them for some food for yourself," I said, unable to control the tears for the loss of the only relative I had left.

With hooded eyes, Joel humbly took the socks. There was no need for thanks or for any more words.

My time was up. I turned towards the door and left quickly before Joel saw the tears that began to flood my face.

175

I found Bela sitting on the grass facing the barbed wire, a pile of small rocks next to her. "Why are you back so soon?" she asked, although she already knew the reason when she saw my red eyes. I sat down next to her and told her about Aunt Hudesa, and I also told her that I gave the socks to Joel.

Bela picked up a little rock and threw it at the wire. The rock fell cleanly through the wire and continued to roll. "Freedom!" She blared as she continued throwing more rocks at the wire. No tears today, only anger.

I promised myself that if by some miracle I would survive, I would kill every tall German in uniform.

I didn't go to the Ghetto again. There was no reason. Seeing Joel reminded me too much of the family I once had and had no more. Bela and I had only each other now.

Bela had become more important to me than my own life. I would have gladly taken a bullet meant for her. I wouldn't want to live without my sister. She had become my mother, my mentor, and my pride.

Lusia Royal was my only friend in AFL. We went to school together, and she happened to be in the same camp, but Lusia had her mother and two older sisters with her. She was like a little chick kept warm by her family. I only had Bela, and Bela had many friends her own age. I often felt like an intruder. Bela was three years older, and her friends were her own age, not mine. I tried to partake in conversation or say something amusing, but I overheard a girl say that I was trying to emulate Bela.

Everyone loved Bela Boy. She made her friends laugh, and at night she sang along to the violin and carried a perfect tune.

No one knew me for myself, I was only known as Bela's sister, and I was very proud to be the sister of the strongest and funniest girl in AFL.

My sister was often rolling on her bunk with stomach pain, especially when she was hungry.

I heated water on top of the one burner for a compress and had to fight with Tusia Rosenberg, who had found out that she had tuberculosis and always had a pot on the stove cooking something. She had come from Warsaw with some possessions and was able to buy food through the barbed wires from the Polish people. Hearing the other girl scream at me for removing her pot, Bela was in more agony. When Tusia wouldn't listen to reason, I ignored her abusive language until the water was hot.

As I replaced Tusia's soup on the burner, I remembered my mama quoting Aunt Hudesa, "Patients with terminal diseases were envious of the healthy."

176

I felt sorry for Tusia. She was a very pretty girl. It was easy to see by the clothes she wore that she grew up in a wealthy home. She was always brushing her lustrous black curls. Her large brown eyes were like black cherries and set deep in her chiseled features. I was angry with Tusia. She didn't have to be so mean. She had always enjoyed being around Bela and could have waited a few minutes to eat.

When I applied the compress to Bela's abdomen and saw her relax, nothing else mattered.

My sister fell in love with a blond boy from the adjacent barrack, and he broke her heart when he fell in love with another girl. I felt her pain and cried with her all night.

In December 1942, the soldiers chose ten of the strongest and hardest workers to be sent to the outskirts of Radom to bundle and load freight-cars to be shipped to Germany.

Bela was one of the chosen ones, and I was told that the group was supposed to return at the end of the day.

All day I sorted and bundled shoes, socks, sweaters, and uniforms.

Herr. Aurisch and Herr. Doren were supervising the warehouse.

Herr. Linden had gone with the group.

It had been the longest day of my entire life. Every passing hour in my sister's absence seemed as if it were a year. At six o'clock, we were counted frisked and dismissed. I ran to our barrack, and my heart sank when I saw Bela's empty bunk. Though it was cold, threatening to snow, I ran back outside, straining my neck beyond the gate, hoping to see the truck coming back. I paced a few feet from the gate in total darkness. My teeth were chattering, and the cold wind took my breath away. I stumbled back inside and sat on my bunk like an abandoned child.

Just before lights out Herr. Aurisch and Herr. Doren stumbled through the door with bottles of vodka in each hand.

"This is a celebration. Everybody has to celebrate," Red shouted, his words slurring. The soldiers shuffled around each bunk passing the bottle, making sure that each girl swallowed a large gulp of vodka.

The girls didn't want to make the drunken soldiers angry and began to swallow small sips of vodka. The two soldiers, though quite drunk, could see that the girls were faking and tilted the bottles for the liquid to burn down each girl's throat.

I curled up on my bunk, pulling the cover over my head and pretended to be asleep, hoping to be overlooked.

"Wake up, little one," Herr. Aurish's voice slurred, poking at my ribs with the bottle, and Red laughed. When I didn't move, Herr. Aurisch stepped on the lower bunk and pushed the bottle to my mouth.

"You have to celebrate with us, little one!" he shouted.

I sat up and took the bottle from his hand, but when the bottle touched my lips, the smell of vodka contorted my face. I handed the bottle back to him and said, "Thank you."

Both soldiers laughed as Herr. Aurish anchored himself onto my bunk. "You have to take a drink," he said, an angry tone to his voice.

"Thank you, but I don't like it," I pleaded.

Herr. Doren's large belly shook with drunken laughter as Herr. Aurish grabbed my arm and forced the bottle against my teeth. I began to taste blood and opened my mouth. My throat was immediately on fire, but he didn't stop pushing the bottle against my teeth until he lost his balance. If not for the girls easing him off my bunk, he would have fallen backwards.

I suddenly got on my hands and knees and began to laugh. I found myself unable to stop laughing, and I began to hiccup.

The girls sat quietly on their bunks. I felt as if I was a very small child left alone among strangers that wanted to hurt me. "I want my mama! Please, Mama, come home!" I began to cry. Two girls climbed up on my bunk, trying to calm me, but I couldn't stop crying. "I want my Bela. I want my mama," I whimpered.

The soldiers were suddenly quiet. The entire barrack was very quiet, and I heard one girl say, "Bela will be back in the morning. Stop crying, or you'll make the soldiers mad." I wanted to stop, but the sound flew from my throat, and I cried louder and pulled away from the girls.

The soldiers slithered out from our barrack, so I climbed down from the bunk and ran to the door looking for Bela.

Hiccuping and crying, I opened the door and stepped barefoot into snow.

"It's after curfew. The guard will shoot you," the girls were shouting.

"I don't care. I have to find Bela. She's lost," I cried and stumbled off the step and fell in the snow and threw up. Trying to get back up, I saw Herr. Aurisch's back turned towards me. He was making large circles in the snow as he urinated.

He suddenly turned towards me and was transformed to my Aunt Hanna's Man with the Black Hand, in a German uniform.

I wanted to run back inside, but not without Bela. "Please, Bela, stop hiding from me. The black hand is going to get you, please, come back…," I whimpered and fell on my knees. I felt hands pulling me back inside.

"Bela's on her bunk," I heard a girl say as I was being pushed up. When I saw Bela's bunk empty, I began to cry until I couldn't catch my breath and passed out.

I woke up Sunday morning to a thousand drums banging inside my head. To add to my agony, my sister's bunk was still empty. I put my aching head back on the pillow.

All day, I lay on my bunk making plans on what to do if Bela didn't return. Two solutions came to my mind, and I settled for one. The first solution was to run through the gate and let the guard shoot me. That would be too painful, and I was also concerned that the girls would be punished for my deed. The German rule was "one for all and all for one." I had settled for the second solution. I would not line up for the midday soup, and I wouldn't eat the bread ration. After a few days, I would become emaciated and die. Now that my mind was made up, I went back to sleep. It had been a good time to start.

The girls were busy doing their laundry and getting in line for the soup, and as long as I didn't make any noise, I was ignored.

While the girls were lined up in front of the kitchen for the soup, I went to the outhouse. My legs felt like rubber, for I hadn't eaten anything all day yesterday, and I was glad, for I knew that death would come sooner than I figured. I climbed back up on my bunk and closed my eyes and waited to stop being hungry. I knew that it was the first sign that death was near. When I opened my eyes again, it was dusk. I heard a commotion. Before I could turn around to see what was going on, my sister was on her bunk, her arms tight around me. I was suddenly starving and was glad to see my two days bread rations at the foot of my bunk. I gave one to Bela, and though I wanted to devour my piece of bread, I reminded myself to slow dawn and make every bite count. While we ate, I filled her in on last nights horror and apologized for making a fool of myself.

Bela's eyes darkened. "The cholera should take the fat sadists," she muttered.

After dark, Bela stretched out on her bunk, her hands folded behind her head, and joined the girls in the sad songs. Once again, through the men's thin wall, the soul-soothing violin accompanied the singers. Once again, I felt safe knowing that my sister was on her bunk next to mine.

Life goes on. The cement floor in the warehouse was like standing on ice. Everyone was grateful to Bela for introducing us to a dance to keep our feet from becoming numb. While standing and sorting at the tables, we jumped up on our toes our feet clicked together, touched the floor, and jumped up again. The sound, tra-ta-ta-ta-tra-ta-ta-ta-tra-tra-tra-ta-ta…was heard throughout the building, and I was grateful to my sister for bringing me to AFL.

Many of the girls, including myself, didn't use the passes to go to the Ghetto. There were very few family members left, and the small Ghetto had been turned into a labor camp. Even if Joel had still been there, it would have been too painful to see Joel without seeing Fraida.

One Sunday morning in February 1943, we had lined up for our bread rations, and the snow on the ground glistened in the sunlight, but the air was cold as our murderers' hearts. The soldiers were in their warm quarters, and some of the girls braved standing at the wires and sold their possessions for food. I knew that Bela and I had nothing left to sell. We didn't have jewels or good clothes and depended only on the rations. After eating our bread, Bela went outside and told me not to leave the barrack. She returned a few minutes later with a package under her jacket. She filled our pot with water and placed it on the burner. She cracked two eggs and began to beat them with a spoon. She added water and a package of flour and mixed it together. She spooned dumplings into the boiling water and cooked it for a few minutes. She drained the water outside into the snow and carefully unfolded a piece of paper and added the contents of real sugar, not saccharine, but real sugar. I had almost forgotten what real sugar looked like. She unfolded a small package of butter, about one heaping tablespoon. My mouth watered as the butter melted on the sugar and dumplings. The last package was a thick slice of liverwurst. Keeping the pot on the burner, the liverwurst melted into the dumplings.

Under normal circumstances, it would have made me ill to look at the concoction, much less eat it. But when I tasted the first spoonful, I felt as if I had died and gone to heaven. I never asked my brave sister what she had exchanged for the feast. I feared she might tell me that she sold stolen woolens. We sat on our bunk, with spoons in our hands, and feasted on the dumpling concoction until the pot was empty.

That night had been the first and last time since the invasion that we went to sleep on a full stomach.

Chapter Twenty-Two: The End of AFL and the Beginning of Blizyn

Spring and the beauty of green grass began to show through melting snow. The trees and flowers on the other side of the wires had begun to blossom. People strolled freely on every street and on the sidewalks, and I couldn't stop wondering why the word Jew was cursed. I knew that the lilac would soon begin to suffuse our camp. Strong rains melted away the lingering snow, and grass came to life together with the glorious sun. The patch of grass in front of our barracks waved with the mild breeze, drying the ground, as if it were an invitation to roll on the grass and savor the delicious warmth. And that's what we all did. After standing on the cold cement six days, twelve hours each day, without a window, on Sunday everybody tumbled on the grass, especially Bela. The name Bela boy suited her well. She turned cartwheels, walked on her hands upside down, wearing quilted Russian army pants, then stretched out on the warm grass, her hands folded behind her head. She closed her beautiful green eyes and allowed the warm sun to turn her face golden. Other girls tried to emulate her, but none came close. My Bela, how proud I was to be her sister.

As we lay on the grass soaking in the sun, no one asked where the birds went. Maybe they didn't visit because we had no trees, or maybe it was too sad for them to be around us. We didn't miss them. All we cared about was to keep from starving and freezing and survive another day.

We all knew about Auschwitz and crematoriums from pieces of German newspapers found by the girls who were cleaning our soldier's rooms. I knew about Auschwitz when my tata's clothes came wrapped in brown paper that read, "Jeremy Sztraiman died in Auschwitz."

The food our girls had smuggled in through the wires was wrapped in Polish newspapers, giving us hope that the Russians were close to our borders ready to liberate us. We prayed to be liberated before we were shipped out to Auschwitz and turned to dust, but God and the entire world had turned a deaf ear.

I would have been grateful for the constant hunger and cold cement floors and being chased up three flights of stairs by the German civilian, who was old enough to be my father. He was in charge of the shoe department on the ground floor. Each time I was ordered to carry a sack of shoes to his department, he chased me up three flights of stairs. My heart pounded each time I reached the third floor and managed to hide under a heap of merchandise. I dreaded to think what would have happened had he caught me. I would also accept being pinched by Red and having continues purple marks on my arms and see his belly shake with laughter. I would endure any hardship to be in AFL another day with the glimmer of hope to soon be liberated, but our time in AFL had run out.

On Saturday at six o'clock in the evening, May 1943, as always ,we lined up to be frisked and counted. Before we were dismissed, Herr. Doren announced that tomorrow morning we should be packed and ready to be transferred to another camp.

Bela and I didn't have much packing, only the clothes on our backs, an extra skirt, and a few meager essentials.

Saturday evening, many of us sat on the grass under the brightest stars. It felt as if the entire universe looked down on us yet were unable or unwilling to save us.

After curfew, we lay on our bunks and listened for the last time to the violin and songs that would break a heart of steel. Most of us were awake the entire night.

Two pickup trucks arrived at dawn, and our soldiers pushed our door open. Whips flying in the air, they shouted, "Rous rous, ale rous!" (Out, out everyone out!) We were rushed into the trucks, and in the shuffle, I had lost sight of Bela. I panicked and ran through the crowd looking for my sister, asking every person if he or she had seen Bela Boy, but nobody had seen her. I ran back to the barrack calling her name. I ran to the outhouse and to the kitchen. I called her name in every nook and cranny. I ran around each truck that was filled to capacity with weeping people. The motors were running, and the soldiers were screaming at me to get in the truck! I didn't care if they whipped me or shot me. I wouldn't leave without my sister. She had vanished, and I had nothing to live for. Suddenly, I remembered the young, short, round bodied SS man. He had blond hair and light eyes. He often came to AFL for merchandise and always asked Bela to help him with his chores. The last time I saw him talking to Bela was only a week ago. That night, Bela told me that he had asked her to run away with him.

"He said that he would have false papers for me, marry me, and take me with him to Germany," Bela said with hooded eyes.

"What did you tell him?" I asked, knowing well that any of us would die first before we would consent to marry a German, especially an SS man, even if he appeared to be sincere.

"I told him that I couldn't leave my sister alone," Bela said, and she stretched out on her bunk, laced her fingers behind her head, and looked up at the ceiling.

Now, I wondered if the SS man showed up and took her away. "My God, did he take her by force? What would he do to her? I cried, covering my face with my hands. We had heard so many horror stories about Nazis using young girls and killing them in brutal ways. Frightened for my sister's safety, I ran like a mouse being chased by a cat. I cried hysterically up to the truckloads of people, calling Bela's name, but my sound was muffled by the roaring motors and shouting soldiers. Only seconds before the first truck began to move, Red appeared behind me, grabbed my bruised arms and pushed me up on the second truck. Although we stood like sardines unable to turn, being little gave me the advantage, as if I was a thread pushing myself through the eye of a needle, and maneuvered in very direction of the truck. Whatever our fate, I wanted to stand next to my sister. I pushed myself to the front of the truck and called Bela's name in the wind. When I didn't see Bela, I pushed through the crowd and held on to the side of the truck. The upper part of my body hung over the side. As we turned the bend, I saw the first truckload of people in front of us. I screamed, "Bela! Bela! Bela!" so loud that I felt my throat tearing to shreds. Just as I was unable to utter another word, I heard Bela's voice, "Jadzia! I'm here!" She screamed and waved her thin arms in the air from the side of the first truck.

The rest of the way to our unknown destination, Bela and I didn't take our eyes off each other until the trucks came to a sudden stop in front of a large gate. On top of the gate, a sign in large letters read, "Blizyn Lager."

We all breathed a sigh of relief that we were not in Auschwitz.

Maybe it won't be so bad, I told myself, until a chill went through my bones when the gate opened, and the truck in front of us, carrying Bela, kicked up dust and came to a full stop in the middle of an enormous unpaved camp.

Our truck followed, and we all turned our heads to the high, curled barbed wires on top.

Everywhere I looked, I saw armed Ukrainian guards standing watch around the barbed wires. Yes, AFL was paradise, I thought.

As in the Ghetto, young Jewish men wearing hats, identifying them as police, unlatched the flaps on the trucks.

I pushed through the crowd and ran into my sister's arms where she was waiting for me. From that moment on, I never lost sight of her.

Our three soldiers stood at a distance, looking towards us. I could see that they were not enjoying what they saw. They spoke to a tall thin SS man holding a German shepherd dog on a leash in one hand and a whip in another.

Our soldiers were the first to click their shiny heals together and stretched out a right arm in a "Heil Hitler!" shout, and the tall SS man returned the salute.

I watched as our soldiers were leaving the camp, and all three looked back and held the gaze for several minutes.

The Camp's Police had ordered us to line up in military fashion, facing the SS man with Ukrainians protectively on each side of him. After we were counted, we were given numbers written on a piece of one inch by two inches cloth, and we were ordered to sew the numbers onto our garments below the clavicle. It was to be visible at all times or suffer severe punishments.

Barbed wire separated the man from the women. There were two female barracks, and Bela and I clung together so as not get separated again. Our barracks were made entirely of wooden boards. A brick oven stood in the middle of the room, close to the door. If there were windows, I don't remember seeing any, but the wall-to-wall door was wide open. Three layers of bunks, not bunk beds, were held together by posts and layered with boards. Wooden ladders were nailed on to the posts.

I followed Bela to the farthest end of the barrack, and we climbed up to the top shelf. We put our pillows and covers down on the board and sewed the cloth with the number onto our blouses.

As I stretched out on the board next to my sister, I suddenly felt as if I was a thing being shelved.

All of Bela's friends were assigned to the other barracks. I knew that she would miss them.

At the end of the day, we were given a piece of bread. Starved, I bit into the bread, and a tiny splinter had lodged itself between my teeth. We heard rumors that sawdust was being added to the flour of our bread. In AFL the bread tasted dry, but I was always so hungry and never gave it much thought. Here, in Blizyn, was the first time I had proof, but I ate the bread filled with sawdust hungrily. I closed my eyes with the knowledge that Blizyn might bring us closer to our demise, and the hope of being liberated was only a dream.

The lights were turned off. As I began to doze off, I felt as if a cat or dog was walking on top of me. I opened my eyes and looked into the eyes of a rat the size of a full-grown cat. Frightened, I pulled the cover over my head and began bouncing convulsively until the rat jumped off.

Bela, too, woke up. We moved close to each other and slept with our heads under the covers, feeling and listening to rats chewing on our covers. At dawn, shouting policemen awakened us from a restless sleep. We didn't need time to get dressed, for we slept with our clothes on. Within minutes, we were assembled at the dusty arena.

The men were now wearing prison striped suits and hats. Men and women stood at attention on the same turf, but not in the same rows. We stood lined up in military fashion.

The SS man holding the German shepherd dog on a leash stood tall on a cement stage in front of us. A cement wall shielded his back. Armed Ukrainians and lower ranking SS man guarded him from each side.

Jewish police made sure that the rows were uniform and that everyone stood at attention, and the hat exercise for men had begun. "Hats off! Hats on!...Hats off!...Hats on!" This exercise, we soon found out, was routine.

The tall thin SS man with the German shepherd dog in one hand and the whip in the other stood facing us. I shuddered each time my eyes caught a glimpse of his thin, pinched face. There was no sign of compassion in the small piercing eyes. The thought that our lives were in his hands didn't leave us much hope for survival.

"I am, SS Unterscharfurer, Paul Nell," the SS man shouted in a strong authoritative voice. "You are in Blyzin Konzentrations Lager (Concentration Camp), and this is the Appellplatz (Roll-Call-Place)! You are Haftliger (detainees)! Every morning and every evening, you will be counted. If one Hatflig is missing, you will all be punished! One for all, and all for one! You are verboten (forbidden) to stand close to the barbed wires!" To the men he shouted, "Failure to remove your hat in the presence of a German will be severely punished. If you are found in the women's barracks, you will be severely punished!"

Three gaunt men were brought forth and pushed against the cement wall. "This is an example!" he shouted.

A Ukrainian placed himself in front of the three men, aimed his rifle, and fired three times. Each man, one by one fell to the ground like a marionette.

Nell continued shouting orders with the same nonchalance, as if murdering three men was like swatting a fly. "Now stand at attention while you are assigned to a work place!" he shouted and gave orders to the Jewish Police that were lined up in the front line. He gave the dog's leash a tug and strolled away.

The Jewish Police gave orders to several men. The men ran and returned with an open wooden wagon. They picked up the bodies and laid them out on the wagon. Two armed Ukrainians followed the men pulling the wagons. The bodies were wheeled out of the camp to be buried in the woods.

We were marched inside a large factory lined with sewing machines.

"If you know how to use a sewing machine, pick a machine and sit down," a man in charge shouted.

Bela and I were glad to have learned how to use a sewing machine. A mountain of precut men's shirts was placed in front of us. We were shown, only once, how to sew the seams on both sides, and I found that it wasn't difficult.

"The shirts have to be finished by six o'clock," the policeman announced.

The next day, we were assigned shifts. Bela was assigned to the night shift, and I the day shift. A week later, I was assigned the night shift, and Bela the day shift. Bela and I only saw each other on the appellplatz mornings and evenings. Sunday was the only day we didn't work. We were counted on the appellplatz in the morning and evening and to be dismissed to be outside on the campgrounds or the barracks. It was the only day my sister and I spent together.

When there were no more shirts to sew, we were sewing buttons or made buttonholes on German uniforms. Each of us was given the same amount of garments to finish. If, during a twelve-hour shift, one person failed to finish his or her allotment, we were all rounded up and chased by two German shepherd dogs into a large barbed wire cage. Once inside, Nell removed the dog's leashes and gave a command for the dogs to chase us around the cage. Anyone falling behind or tripped suffered the fate of the dog's teeth, and we were all conditioned to the consequences for being disabled.

"One for all, and all for one!" Nell shouted from the outside of the cage.

Our food rations were not enough to sustain life. Each day, the ladle of watery soup at midday and the piece of bread mixed with sawdust in the evening brought us closer to becoming skeletons, Muzleman. I'm not sure if there is a correct spelling for the word. The people in the Ghetto had made up the word for those who had become emaciated from starvation and that had been our biggest fear. Once you became a Muzleman, death followed.

On my third morning in Blizyn, a young man fell at my feet on the appellplatz. His bony, rubbery legs buckled. The hat flew off the shaved

186

head and, like a paper airplane, glided onto the dusty ground and was finally at peace. It was hard to tell if there was a person inside the striped uniform. Only the skeletal face with the open mouth and bulging eyes were visible.

I knew that sooner or later, unless a miracle would happen, my sister and I would succumb the same way or by a Ukrainian's bullet.

Every day, Polish people approached the wires offering food for money, jewelry, clothes, and anything of value. The food consisted of loafs of bread, butter, and a chunk of ham. It depended on the valuables the inmates had to offer. Everyone knew the consequences for being caught buying food at the wires. If caught, the punishment was being thrown in a deep hole in the ground for several days and covered with a wooden cover. When the time in the hole was over, the smuggler received seventy-five lashes. The next punishment was death, depending on Nell's mood. Nothing deterred some of the men from buying food at the barbed wires. Mostly, the electricians and policemen were given the freedom to roam throughout the entire camp. At dawn, the electricians paid off the Ukrainians to look the other way, then threw the money or what ever they had to offer over the wire.

Once the Polish people had the valuables in their hands, they threw the food over the wire.

Bela was constantly massaging her hungry stomach, and I never felt more helpless. Sunday, I approached an electrician and sold him my only new remodeled skirt for a quarter loaf of bread. I cut the bread and quickly took a bite from my piece, and Bela didn't know that she was getting the larger piece. We sat on our bunk and made every bite count, being careful not to let the tiniest crumb go to waste.

Bela and I had nothing left to sell, and we knew that it was only a matter of time before we would turn into Muzlewomen.

With each passing day, the rats were bigger and more abundant. On Sunday morning, we stood what seemed endless on the appellplatz. We were counted and witnessed two men being shot. We returned to our barracks and were greeted by hundreds of rats on our sleeping shelf. Since there was no food on our board, they chewed up our quilt. It wasn't until Bela took a stick she had found and began banging on the board that the rats slowly strolled away. When Bela's arm was tired, the rats returned to claim their territory. The rats were winning, for they were getting stronger from feasting on the many dead bodies. Although, by the time the bodies were buried, all they could chew on were bones and the skin covering the skeleton. As we lay quietly stretched out on our bunk trying to combat hunger, a rat sat next to Bela's feet and began nibbling on her left toe. She banged the stick on the wood, and the rat strolled away.

Every night someone screamed from fear. A rat was tangled in her quilt or her hair, but one night everyone was awakened when a rat hooked his teeth onto a girl's lip. Her scream brought a Ukrainian into our barrack. The girl was still screaming as he pulled the rat from her lip.

On Sundays, the SS weren't roaming the camp as often as on weekdays, and the Ukrainians were paid off by men with money for the privilege of visiting the female grounds and barracks. One Sunday early afternoon in July 1943, the sun was so bright and the sky so clear, I could have sworn that I looked directly into heaven.

Bela and I sat on the patch of grass between the two female barracks and ate our watery soup. I rinsed out our bowls and went inside our barracks to put away the two bowls and spoons on our bunk. As I walked through the open door, a man in his late twenties or early thirties was standing next to a bunk closest to the door, conversing with the girls on the bunk. His cheeks were full and pink, no sign of hunger. He blocked my path. A ham sandwich in one hand, he gripped my bony shoulder with his other hand and smiled into my eyes.

"Cat's eyes, but beautiful. Would you like a ham sandwich?" he asked, pressing his well-fed body against me.

I felt my face burning with anger. With all the strength I had left, I pushed him away from me.

"I have survived without ham sandwiches up to now, I will try to survive a little longer," I said, and I turned away quickly so as not to give him the satisfaction of seeing the tears stinging my eyes.

I climbed up on my bunk where a fat rat was chewing on my cover. I picked up the stick and banged on the cover with so much anger that I almost hit the rat that ran to the next bunk. I shook the cover, making sure one didn't get caught in the quilt. I stretched out on the board, letting the tears fall freely where they may. Feeling very lonely and forsaken, I closed my eyes. Will I ever see my mama? Will I ever feel her reassuring arms around me? Why, why did the world turn against us? Why did good people in my family disappear and let a man like the sandwich eater live?

My mama and my tata would always share the last bite of food with the hungry and never ask for anything in return. "Mama where are you?" I cried and didn't bother wiping the tears. I must have dozed off, for I woke up, startled by screaming policeman chasing us out again to be counted and to receive our daily portion of bread.

Most of us saved the bread for the next morning, in order to function at work, but Bela almost always took a bite from her piece of bread. She was often doubled over with stomach pain from hunger, and I felt helpless.

Every night we put our meager portion of bread in our pot and covered the pot with both bowls and put a rock on top, so the rats wouldn't get to our bread.

I was always able to withstand hunger better than Bela. In the morning, I took our bread from the pot and ate the one Bela had taken a bite from. She was so hungry, she never remembered that I gave her my whole piece.

On one lucky occasion after a twelve-hour night shift and two hours standing on the appellplatz, I was about to step through the door of our barrack. A man approached me and promised me a bowl of soup if I come to the kitchen and peel potatoes.

After two hours of peeling potatoes, the cook poured a full ladle of thick soup into my bowl. I was afraid to look at the bowl of soup for fear that I might be tempted to eat some of it or get carried away and eat the whole thing. I walked briskly, being careful not to spill a drop of the precious soup before I reached the factory where Bela worked.

I found my sister sitting in a closet on top of German uniforms, holding on to her stomach and silently moaning in pain. She was surprised to see me and gazed at the bowl of thick soup with the potatoes being clearly visible.

I could see the confusion in her eyes, and I quickly told her about the cook and placed the soup in front of her. "Now eat," I said.

She fished out the spoon from her pocket and made room for me to sit next to her. "Where's your spoon?" she asked.

"I ate my portion," I lied and watched her eat one spoon after another until she finished the bowl of soup.

"Is your stomach better?" I asked.

Her gaunt face was now brushed with a bit of pink. "Yes, much better," she said.

As I was leaving the factory to get a few hours of sleep before the appell and my night shift, I felt as if nothing could stop us from surviving the war. I climbed up on my bunk and chased the rats off my cover and stretched out. It seemed I had just closed my eyes, and the whistle was already blowing to be counted. All night, while sewing buttons onto uniforms and rushing to finish my allotment I was making plans, for tomorrow. I would go back to the kitchen and ask the cook, no, beg the cook to allow me to peel potatoes or what ever he would want me to do to keep Bela's stomach from hurting. I ignored the hunger pain in my own stomach and concentrated only on my sister.

As soon as the shift and the appell were over, I ran to the kitchen. My heart pounded as I braved through the kitchen's open door. My eyes didn't take in any part of the large dim kitchen, only the large pots that lined the stove. The cook was a tall well-fed man with an air of indifference. I stood at the door like a hungry puppy dog.

"Would you allow me to peel potatoes or do any other chore? I'm strong, and I could do a lot of work," I said in a pleading tone.

"No, no potatoes to peel. Now go before someone catches you here," he said, shooing me out the door. I hunched my shoulders and trudged towards my barracks. Yesterday's euphoria became today's melancholy.

As the days passed, I listened to my beloved sister moaning from pain, and I watched her become thinner and more listless. Slowly, I had given up all hope of surviving. I would do anything to take Bela's pain away. I would have gladly changed places with her and suffer her pain.

Bela's two friends in the next barracks weren't hungry. Their boyfriends made sure of that. Rusty's, (not her real name) boyfriend was a policeman with a wife, but he made sure that Rusty's stomach was full. Dimple's (not her real name) stomach was also full. Her boyfriend worked in the kitchen.

Sunday morning, Bela took one of our portions of bread and told me to go to the next barrack to give our bread to Rusty in exchange for a bowl of soup.

"I talked to her, and she's expecting you," Bela said.

I took our portion of bread and briskly walked the few feet to the next barrack. I was appalled when I stepped inside a cubicle with two bunk beds, only for the privileged. At the entrance stood a little wooden table bedecked with several bowls of soup and about ten portions of bread.

Rusty took the portion of bread from my hand and handed me a bowl of soup. I was angry with my sister for thinking that these two girls were her friends. They could never have eaten all that bread and soup. When I told Bela about the mountain of bread and soup on that table, she said, "Let's eat the soup."

I could not forgive Rusty for taking the piece of bread from me. I made a pledge that, if by some miracle we would survive that hell, I would let her know how she treated her friend. Each time I saw her on the campground, I looked away. I couldn't look into her greedy eyes. Yet, Bela still considered the two girls her friends. My sister always saw the good in others.

Chapter Twenty-Three: Blind Trust

Several men from Blizin were ordered to go to the Radom Ghetto to do special work and to bring back supplies.

Sunday morning after the appell, a tall boy with special skills and privileges to roam in the women's camp, approached me in front of the door to my barracks. I had seen him look at me several times in the past when he visited the group of bunks next to the door, but we never spoke before. Ever since we arrived in Blizyn, my mind was only on my sister's hunger pain. Boys never entered my mind. When he blocked my passage, I was thinking that he was another one trying to offer me a ham sandwich, and I tried to get past him.

"Wait a minute, I only want to tell you something," he said sounding sincere.

I stopped only to hear what he wanted to tell me, and if he would hand me some food, I would grab it, push him out of the way as I did the last man, and give my sister the food. But he didn't touch me, and he didn't smile, and he didn't offer me food.

"I'm being sent to Radom tomorrow, and I'll be in the Ghetto one or two nights.

"Do you have a relative in the Ghetto who could send you a package?"

"My brother-in-law is in the Ghetto. I'm sure if he could, he would help," I said.

"You could give me a letter to take to him, What's his name?"

"Joel Altman," I said hopeful.

"Go write a letter, and I'll wait for you here."

I found Bela and told her the good news.

Bela was as exited as I was. She sat down on the bunk and wrote, "Dear Joel, please help us."

I took the piece of paper and gave it to the boy. After he read it he said, "I have a perfect hiding place. You can write whatever you want, and nobody will find it."

When I hesitated, he continued to reassure me.

"Look, if I didn't have a perfect hiding place, would I risk my life to take letters at all? I'm telling you that you have nothing to worry about. You can

191

write whatever you like, and your brother-in-law will get the letter." I thought for a moment.

"Are you sure that your hiding place is secure? I wouldn't want you to get caught. If I rewrite this and tell the truth about what is happening to us here and they find the letter, I don't have to tell you what the punishment will be."

The boy was becoming annoyed with me. "I told you that you could write whatever you like. Nobody will find your letter. Other friends gave me letters to take to Radom. Do you think that I would want to risk your life or mine? Now, go write your letter and don't worry. You can write whatever you like. I'll wait for you here."

I tore up Bela's letter, and with my fourth grade education, I wrote a full page.

Dear Joel,

This letter is written with blood, not ink. Everyday, people are falling down and dying from starvation or by the bullet. Bela and I are starving to death. You are our only hope. If you won't help us, we'll surely become Musleman and die.

I signed the letter, Jadzia, Bela.

As I was folding the letter into the size of half a cigarette, I was thinking that when Joel reads it, he'll do anything he could to help save our lives, but as soon as I placed the letter in the boy's hand, my heart began to pound. I wanted to ask for the letter back, but I was afraid he would think that I didn't trust him.

All night, sewing buttonholes on German uniforms, I was so nervous I felt like a pincushion. I hardly had a finger left that wasn't stabbed by the long thick needle.

In the morning after the appell, I looked for the boy, hoping he wasn't chosen to go or that the transport had been canceled. If only I could find him, I would ask him to destroy the letter, but he was nowhere to be found.

Suddenly, I heard the motor and saw the boy in the truck, leaving the camp, and I knew that I had put my sister's life in jeopardy.

I couldn't tell Bela what I did. I knew she would be very angry and tell me that I was stupid to put all those words in writing.

I remembered how I felt when I found out that Mama had asked Bela to look after me because I wasn't smart enough to take care of myself. Now, I know Mama was right. I am stupid. I castigated myself.

Though the boy said he had a foolproof hiding place, my gut told me not to listen, and I knew that I shouldn't have torn up Bela's letter, and now it was too late. Bela was always the smart one. She knew what she was doing, and by signing her name to my stupid letter, I may have cost her, her life. I should have known that you couldn't hide anything from the Germans, and now it was too late.

I was glad that I had the night shift, for I would have been unable to sleep. When at midnight there was a blackout, and I heard the sound of airplanes followed by explosions. I wished a bomb would fall where I was standing and kill only me. I didn't want anyone else to get killed because of my stupidity. The next two days until the trucks returned, I didn't sleep at all. Every night, during the air raids, when the lights were turned off, I prayed for my quick death from explosions. Though we did hear explosions every night, our camp remained intact, and I lived until the trucks returned.

Rumors that the letters had been discovered had begun circulating throughout the camp. I still didn't tell Bela what I had done. I only prayed that the boy was right, and he did have a foolproof hiding place.

Unterschafrurer Paul Nell called for an emergency appell. Nell and his lackeys, fully armed with rifles and whips, stood at ready in front of us.

Nell stood tall, his weathered face expressionless, his shiny boots sparkled in the sunlight. He began to read names from a list. His ear-piercing voice could be heard on the other side of the fence.

Each time he called a girl's name, she stepped out of line. A circle of the accused was formed. After calling all the names on the list, about fifteen girls, he called, "Jadzia, Bela!"

I pushed Bela back in line and cried out, "My name is Jadzia, Bela!" Bela refused to stay back and placed herself beside me.

"Who is Jadzia Bela?" he bellowed.

"I am Jadzia Bela!" I cried and continued pushing my sister back, but like a magnet, she stayed glued to me.

"Who wrote the letter?"

"I wrote the letter, only I. My name is Jadzia Bela!" I cried louder.

"If you don't stop crying, I'll have you shot right where you're standing!" he bellowed, and two Ukrainians standing on each side of him pointed rifles at me and waited for Nell to give the order.

"Do you see blood here?" Nell shouted.

Instead of answering his question, I pushed Bela behind me and continued to cry, "I'm Jadzia, Bela!" To say that I didn't see blood would have been a lie, and the words got stuck in my throat, and all I could answer was that I was Jadzia Bela.

"Did you see blood here?" he shouted so loud that his face puffed out as if air had been pumped into his wrinkled cheeks.

I cried louder, ignoring his question and continued pushing Bela behind me, hoping the Ukrainians would spare my sister and finally pull the trigger and kill me. I was unable to stop crying.

"It's all my fault," I pleaded. "I'm Jadzia Bela. I am the guilty one. I wrote the letter, only I!"

I was relieved to see that all the soldiers were pointing rifles only at me. I didn't give Bela a chance to stand next to me. With the strength of a lioness protecting her young, I kept pushing her back, almost knocking her down, and waited to catch the bullet.

The other girls stood silently and were not questioned. All of the attention had been directed towards me.

"Please God!" I cried in the only language I new best, Polish. "Don't let the others die because of me."

"Shut up?" Nell shouted. When I continued to cry, he bellowed, "If you don't stop crying and shut up, you will be shot to death!"

I couldn't stop crying, and through my hysteria Bela and I heard Unterscharfurer, Paul Nell, shout, "You will be shot! Dismissed!"

Condemned to die, we climbed up on our bunk waiting for the Ukrainians to come and take us to the woods. I prayed, as I had never prayed before, that they would only come for me. I visualized myself being walked out from camp into the woods. A bullet to my head, I would fall into the grave I would have dug for myself. I tried only to concentrate on the Ukrainians coming only for me.

Bela stretched out on the board, her hands folded behind her head, gazing up at the ceiling and listening to the rats between the roof and ceiling, as they scurried and chewed above our heads.

I turned towards Bela, my throat burning, "Please Bela, forgive me. We are slowly dying from hunger, and the boy promised that his hiding place was one hundred percent safe. I know it was a very stupid thing I did, and I shouldn't have torn up your note and written such a strong letter. I'm old enough to know better that there are no hiding places from the German's."

"It doesn't matter now how we die, by the bullet or starvation," she said resigned. I felt as if I were already dead, but I could not allow my sister to die for my stupidity.

"No, you won't die! Nell heard me say many times that I was Jadzia Bela and that I was the one who wrote the letter."

Bela turned on her side, away from me. I felt alone and worthless. If I could fall asleep and never wake up, I wouldn't have to dig my own grave, and I wouldn't have to face the bullet. Without me, my sister would have a better chance of surviving. I stretched out on the wood, closed my eyes and began to pray. "Please God, I don't deserve to live, but my sister is smart and good. She shouldn't have to die because of my stupidity. If my tata is with you, let me be with him, dear God. Please, I beg you. Let my sister live and allow me to sleep forever."

As if God heard my prayer, I felt drowsy and began to drift and roll on lush green grass, the same as on the Penc property, only greener and warmer. Tata sat quietly under an apple tree laden with juicy red apples. He waited for me to roll towards him. I felt no hunger, only warmth and peace, and I longed to be in my tata's arms. I was suddenly a very small child and rolled into tata's stretched out arms. He sat me down on his shoulders and held my hands. He ran with me around the large apple tree in the gentle breeze, then eased me down on the grass and looked into my eyes, a mirror image of his own. He smiled, showing beautiful white teeth. "From now on you will be smart," he whispered and disappeared.

I tried to chase after him, beg him to take me with him, but I couldn't run fast enough. My legs refused to move. I stretched out my arms, "Please, Tata, come back. I want to go with you. Don't leave me. I'm afraid."

I heard the whistle and shouts for appell, but my eyes stayed closed. If I sleep long enough, Tata will come back and take me with him. I heard Bela's voice and felt her slapping me lightly on my face. "Jadzia, wake up! It's time."

Whips were banging against wood and policemen shouted, "Rous, rous. Alle rous!" (Everyone out).

Unwillingly, I opened my eyes and followed Bela down the ladder. I didn't want to cause her anymore pain.

Like lambs to the slaughter, we stood facing Nell, his dog, and soldiers. During the counting, three men were pulled out of line and marched up front and shoved against the cement wall.

I stood next to Bela waiting for the name, Jadzia Bela to be called. I whispered, not in her ear, for we were not allowed to turn our heads, "Listen carefully," so as not to be overheard, but clear enough for her to understand. "My soul won't rest unless you do as I ask. When Nell calls for Jadzia Bela, don't move. You stay exactly were you are. He will only remember me. I told him enough times that my name is Jadzia Bela, and he knows that the name is for only one." I squeezed her hand tight. "Remember, do not move from this place no matter what. I'm tired of this life anyway, but without my stupidity, you might have a better chance to survive," I said and let go of her hand.

Bela stood silently, looking straight ahead, and I was unable to guess what she was thinking.

After the counting was over, the head of police gave a piece of paper with our count to Nell, letting him know that everyone was accounted for.

Without turning his head, Nell shouted, "Fire!" The three gaunt men fell like marionettes to the ground, and I waited for my name to be called next. I'll close my eyes and soon be with my tata, I mused. I now knew how it felt to be very old and tired of living. All the turmoil was over, and I hadn't felt such peace in a very long time. My euphoria turned to misery when I saw Nell walk away, and the head of the police shouted, "Dismissed!"

The dead men were wheeled away, and everyone lined up for the evening bread ration.

Bela went to sleep, and I went angry to the factory. Now, I had to wait another day before my execution.

The waiting had become unbearable. After three days, six appells, and five more men shot, it was Sunday, and I was still waiting to stand in front of everyone to catch the bullet. In the three days, Bela and I had barely exchanged a word. As I walked through the barrack's open door with my midday ladle of watery soup, I saw the boy, who only five days ago was friendly and reassuring. Now, as I passed him, he turned his head the other way. I didn't try to speak to him. I figured that he, too, was angry with me for putting him in jeopardy. My guilt was so strong, it never occurred to me to place the blame on him for offering to take my letter and telling me to write anything I wanted. I took all the blame on myself. I was glad that he wasn't punished. I figured that he must have hidden the letters inside the truck, and the Germans thought that the girls hid the letters there, themselves.

I climbed up the ladder and sat next to Bela and ate the soup in less than a minute. I was about to go back outside when three girls across from my bunk called my name. Two of the three girls were sisters. They shared a bunk with the girlfriend of a policeman, nicknamed Donut. Dizzy with hunger, I stopped and looked up. One of the sisters tossed a basin down the ladder, a piece of soap, and an armful of clothes. All three girls snickered and threatened to turn me over to Donut if I didn't wash their clothes.

The policeman was a short man, only known by his nickname. I didn't want to cause my sister stomach pain, so I stood and washed their dirty laundry. I couldn't see myself, the way I looked. We had no mirror, but seeing my sister holding on to her stomach and getting thinner and thinner, I knew it wouldn't take much longer before our bodies would become skeletons, and I prayed to go first.

Having Donut to supply them with food, the three girls had become arrogant. They looked at us the way the rich looked at the poor. I remembered Mama's words, "Only the poor understand the poor. The one with the full stomach couldn't understand the one with the empty stomach."

Starving to death, waiting to be murdered for writing a letter, and being tortured by the three girls on the bunk across from ours made my life a living hell.

Each time Donut saw me in the barrack on Sunday while visiting his girlfriend or on the campgrounds, he taunted me.

"Your brother in law is sending packages for you, but you'll never see them, because I eat them. Would you like to know what's inside? I'll tell you," he said and began to name items. "Salami, butter, ham, and a large loaf of bread," he snickered and laughed. Other times, he threatened to turn me over to Nell.

I made myself a promise that if I survived, which I knew for certain that I wouldn't, I would expose the three girls and Donut for what they were.

I left the barracks as soon as I finished washing the laundry. I couldn't stand watching my sister's tortured face while Donut and his friends made fun of me. As I walked out into the warm air, I saw that the soup line was still long, and the servers were hitting hungry men on their heads with the ladles for getting in line a second time. I was tempted to get in line for the second time and get a ladle of soup for Bela, but I was afraid to be remembered and punished. That would cause my sister more pain. My shoulders hunched, I walked to nowhere in particular, praying for the execution to be over and my sister spared. As for myself, I longed to be with my tata on the warm grass under the apple tree. I couldn't wait another day to die. It wasn't worth the effort. I was startled and flinched when I felt someone tap my shoulder.

"I'm sorry if I startled you," the soft voice said.

I lifted my head and looked up at a tall boy, about eighteen years old. He had the kindest, bluest eyes. His yellow hair matched his perfect features and fair complexion.

He lifted my chin with his index finger. "Why are you crying?" He asked with sincere concern.

I hadn't uttered a word to anyone in days, and he seemed easy to unload my heavy heart. "I don't want my sister to die because of my stupidity."

"Is your sister sick?"

"She does get stomach pain from hunger, but no she isn't sick, It's because of the letter I wrote to my brother-in-law, and I signed it Jadzia Bela."

"My sister is Nell's secretary. She translated your letter," the boy said.

I became very frightened. I didn't want him to tell his sister that my name wasn't Jadzia Bela. What if she would tell Nell that I was Jadzia, and my sister was Bela?

"Please don't tell your sister that my name isn't Jadzia Bela. I wrote the letter and signed both names. I don't want my sister to die. Please…tell your sister that I have two names, Jadzia Bela. Tell her that I alone wrote the letter, please. I need another favor. Could you please find out when Nell is planning to execute me? I'm praying that the other girls whose letters were found won't be shot. They only wrote short letters. I was the only one questioned. The waiting is worse than death…." I talked so fast he didn't have a chance to reply.

"Calm down," he interrupted before I was going to beg again for my sister's life."What makes you think you are going to be executed?" he asked. "Because of the letter," he clearly said, "you are going to be shot."

The boy smiled and ran a gentle hand over my hair, the way Sonny often did when I ran an errand for him. I was overwhelmed by the boy's kindness. It had been a very long time since anyone had shown me such tenderness.

"Could you please ask your sister when I'm going to die? But, please tell her that my name is Jadzia Bela and that I was the only one who wrote the letter. Please tell her."

The boy placed both hands on my shoulders and looked into my eyes, filled with tears like a dam ready to burst.

"Look at me," he said shaking my shoulders.

I lifted my head, but I didn't look at him. I didn't want him to see my tears.

"I don't want you to say another word. Just look at me and listen to what I'm telling you."

I did as he asked.

"Better," he smiled. "When Nell called your name, you cried so loud that all everyone heard was shut."

I lowered my eyes. "I don't mind dying. In fact, at this point, I'd welcome it, but my sister must not die because of me," I muttered looking down at my hands.

"You are not listening. I'm not finished," he said, scooping up my face with both hands. "What Nell said was, "You deserve to be shot, but since you are the first group of women to be shot, he will tolerate you this first and last time." Reluctantly, the boy dropped his hands to his side.

I was tempted to throw my arms around him in gratitude, but I was afraid he would misunderstand and think that I was throwing myself at him. Instead, I thanked him for giving us back our lives.

Though I was happy that Bela was being spared, I prayed she would survive. My dream of being with Tata on the warm grass and being a small child again bouncing on his shoulders was too much to give up, especially when I knew that there was no possibility of surviving the starvation in Blizin.

I lowered my head and began walking away.

The boy gripped my arm. "I just told you that you are going to live, and you look disappointed."

"I'm sorry. I'm very grateful to you. My thoughts are on a dream. I have to tell my sister the good news," I said and turned away in time to catch the tears with the back of my hand. I never ran into the boy again, and I never knew his name.

I found Bela on the patch of grass next to our barracks. She was stretched out on her stomach, and I could see she was in pain.

I sat down next to her and told her about the boy. "Thank God nobody will die because of my stupidity," I said.

Bela sat up and lovingly poked her finger on the bridge of my nose. "Don't ever do anything without asking me first, understood?" she said with the authority of a mother, though she was only three years older than I was.

"I promise I will never be stupid again," I said thinking of my tata's message. "From now on, you'll be smart."

Bela told the good news to all the other girls who wrote letters, but I still felt resentment and ridicule from Donut and his three friends.

As time passed, dates or time didn't matter. We had no calendars or watches. There was no need for such things. We were conditioned like animals in the zoo, only worse, much worse. At dawn, when the sky was still black as in a tomb, we were awakened with whips banging at our bunk boards. We were chased out of our barracks to stand on the appellplatz to be counted in total silence. After the count, gaunt men were dragged to stand against the cement wall in front of us and fell to the ground from a bullet to the head or chest. After the example, Nell dished out new orders and punishments while

Muzleman fell dead at our feet. The day shift went to work. The night shift went to sleep, unless chased by German shepherd dogs because one or two people didn't finish the assigned workload.

Thank God for Sunday. It was the only day that after the morning appell we were allowed inside and out of the barracks. Though the midsummer days were hot, I didn't feel the heat. In fact, I was always chilly. My shoulders were continually lifted towards my ears and my arms tight around my chest.

Bella loved the sun, and whenever she had a chance, she laid on the small patch of grass, her face turned to the sky, unless her stomach hurt. Then, she turned on her stomach.

I didn't want to face Donut or his friends and preferred to rest on the bunk.

Since the incident with the letter, Bela found a rag and made it into a curtain and hung it on a string for privacy. I stayed on my bunk behind the curtain, ignoring the rats. I closed my eyes, hoping my tata would come back for me. Though Tata didn't come back, I was glad to fall asleep. It was the only time I felt free in every way. No guilt for almost getting my sister and other girls murdered for writing a letter. No hunger, no cold, no taunting, and no more threads of dying. It would all be over as it was over for the muzelmen that were falling at my feet and for the men that were shot almost daily in front of us. I don't know how long I had been asleep when I opened my eyes and saw Bela leaning over me and pushing a piece of bread in my mouth. Disoriented I pushed her hand away.

"No," I muttered, "it's yours. You eat it. I'm not hungry. If you want to take two bites from yours, it's all right," I said, and I put my head down on the pillow. I was thinking that I'd just give her my piece of bread in the morning. I really wasn't hungry anymore, and I was glad knowing that death would come sooner.

Bela's large green eyes took on a frightening look. She lifted my head up. "Now, sit up," she demanded. "Do you know the meaning of not being hungry anymore?"

I nodded.

"Tell me," she said, shaking my gaunt shoulders.

"If I'm not hungry anymore, it means that I've given up, and I'll soon die," I said simply.

She slapped me lightly on my face. "No, I won't let you."

"Bela, please, it's all right, I feel free, now It's really not a bad feeling. Why don't you eat my portion of bread? At least, you'll live another few days," I muttered, not remembering that we hadn't been chased out for the evening appell or our bread rations yet. In my mind, I was sure that Bela wanted me to eat the bread ration we usually saved for morning.

"Now listen to me! Do you remember the organization Shomer-Hatzair I belonged to, and you always chased after me?"

I nodded, remembering how she always made me go back.

"A new group from Radom arrived a few days ago. My friend, David from the organization is here. I just saw him outside. He gave me this bread and promised that he will do what he can to help us. He was chosen with other stronger boys to works in construction every day outside the camp and made contact with some Polish people."

She cut the piece of bread in half and made sure I ate every bite.

After I finished the piece of bread, I was hungrier than before, and I wished I hadn't eaten the bread. I was already at peace, and now it was beginning all over again.

David kept his word to Bela, and almost every day on the evening appellplatz, he passed a canteen with boiled potatoes to her, and she gave him a clean empty one back.

I only glanced at David while standing at the appellplatz. He was a short muscular built boy, eighteen years old, reddish blond hair, and a moon-shaped face. He never entered the women's barracks, but thanks to David, we soon regained our strength, and Bela had stopped massaging her stomach, and I became more hopeful.

Chapter Twenty-Four: Typhus Epidemic in Blizyn

Two weeks after David gave us back our lives, Typhus fever struck our camp, and David was one of the first to fall victim to the epidemic. Within a few days of the onset of the Typhus epidemic, the hospital was filled to capacity. People were dying like flies. With so many people dead, the bunks in the center row was emptied and used for the stricken. Day and night, after work, Bela was at David's side, though she was well aware of the punishment if she were caught in the men's barracks.

Without the potatoes, we were starving again, and Bela looked exhausted.

I begged her to allow me to take turns in taking care of David, but she said, "Under no circumstances. I already had Typhus, so I can't get it again."

On the tenth day, Bela stood next to me for the evening appell, her face was flushed. "The crisis is over. David's fever has broken. All he needs now is enough food so he wouldn't get tuberculosis," she said, concerned.

Standing in line for our daily bread ration, Bela began to laugh. I couldn't remember the last time my sister laughed. I didn't want to interrupt her with questions. I was happy to see her in good spirits.

After collecting our meager bread ration, with the sawdust clearly visible, we climbed up on our bunk. Bela used her stick to chase away the rats and took a bite from her bread ration. Reluctantly, she handed me the rest of her bread, and I put both pieces in the pot and covered them tight. I couldn't wait any longer. I had to know what it was that made her laugh while standing in the bread line.

We stretched out, our hands behind our heads, and I waited for her to tell me why she was laughing before. Instead, she turned on her stomach and casually said, "Jadzia, I'm in love."

"With David?"

"No, his name is Moniek. I met him while I was taking care of David. He is tall blond and has the sweetest face and the kindest blue eyes."

"Do you think he is in love with you, too," I asked timidly, remembering the boy in AFL and how he broke her heart, and she cried for days.

"He's an electrician. He came to see me today in the factory and told me that he couldn't stop thinking of me. Jadzia, he told me that he's in love with me, and he wants to help us and won't ask for anything in return until we are free. He is so honorable."

"Is this why you were laughing when we where standing in the bread line?"

"No," Bela said and began to giggle again. Last night during David's crisis, his fever went very high, and he became delirious. As I was applying the cold compress to his forehead, he grabbed my hand and asked me to marry him. He asked me to lay down next to him on the sofa," Bela laughed again. "He hadn't seen a sofa in years. I wonder where he thought he was?" she said, as her face took on the usual somber, tired, and hungry look.

It was so nice to see her laugh. I wanted her to continue talking about David's marriage proposal, but she was suddenly very quiet. "Not bad," I said. "Two men are in love with you, and we are starving to death. I'm happy for you, Bela. I wish that the Russians would hurry up and liberate us so you could marry Moniek."

Sunday night we lay on our bunk, our stomachs growling, while airplanes were fly over our heads and explosions were more frequent. "Maybe tonight we'll be liberated, and tomorrow we'll have all the bread we could eat and maybe even butter. So let's eat our bread now and celebrate," I said and dipped into the pot for our bread ration and quickly removed the piece where Bela had taken a bite from and handed her my whole piece. As we lay on our bunk, taking small bites to make the piece of bread last, I wished that a bomb would fall on the cement wall of the appellplaz and stop the killings. Now that Bela was in love, wouldn't it be wonderful if the Russians would sneak in our camp, kill all of the guards, including Nell, and liberate us? I mused just before I fell asleep.

At dawn, just before the wake-up call, I opened my eyes and saw Bela holding two pieces of bread.

"The Russians are here!" I exclaimed as the wake up whips began banging on our bunks.

"No, Moniek was here a minute ago. He climbed up on the ladder and gave me the bread," she said and broke one piece in half. "You eat this. I'm going to give David the other whole piece, for now his appetite is very strong," she said, eating her half, then disappeared and showed up at the appellplatz.

"He is very weak, but thanks to Moniek, he will get his strength back," she whispered happily.

Moniek supplied us with two extra portions of bread everyday, and he also helped David to regain his strength.

Like the other electricians or men with privileges whose trades were important, Moniek dealt in the black market. He was buying bread from the Polish people and sold it to the inmates, and the profit was enough bread for himself, David, and us. Sometimes, he would leave a small peace of butter on our bunk, but Bela kept it for him when he visited on Sunday. When I looked at the butter, my mouth watered, and I reached out for a little piece, but Bela said, "That's for Moniek," and I put it back.

Typhus epidemic raged on. Many people died, and everyday more people became infected. The workload tripled. It had become impossible to meet the quotas.

At the end of August, during my night shift, I could hardly keep my head up. The pain in my head was unbearable. There weren't enough chairs for everybody to sit on. Only the supervisors sat on chairs. Many, including myself, sat on the large table leaning against the wall and sewing buttons on German uniforms and listened to the airplanes and explosions.

The more my head hurt, the more I prayed for a bomb to fall and take me away from this cruel world.

I was freezing and wrapped a uniform-jacket around my shoulders. Minutes later, I threw off the jacket and began burning up. I knew that if I didn't finish my quota, other people would suffer, so I continued to sew the buttons as fast as I could, until I finished, but others did not, and at dawn the chase began. As I was running inside the large barbed wire cubicle with the dogs chasing us, I became dizzy. Just as I was about to fall, I looked into the dog's mouth. His sharp teeth were about to bite into my leg, and I began to run for my life. In as much as I wanted to die, the thought of more pain was unacceptable, and I began to run as if in a race. When the chase came to a halt, and we were dismissed, I climbed up on my bunk board and fell asleep. I soon woke up and climbed down the ladder. I stumbled outside for some fresh air and found myself in the clinic, standing in line with other people, hoping to get some relief from the pain in my head and body.

Doctor Wainapel had been a very respected doctor from Radom, whose only reason for being trapped in this rat hole was that he was Jewish. He looked me over and said, "You have typhus. Go to your barracks and lie down. I wish I had some medicine to give you, but I don't have to tell you why I don't."

Holding on to my head, I climbed up on my bunk and blacked out.

Bela woke me up and guided me to the edge of our bunk where Moniek held out his arms to carry me to the middle bunk. He held me in his arms until two men finished removing a dead girl from the bottom bunk board, and I took her place.

Bela tried to feed me some soup, but I couldn't eat. My mouth was dry, and my body felt as if I had died and went to hell. I saw a bottle of liquid that looked like soda-water next to me, and I reached for it, but Bela took it away from me. "Please...let me have the soda water. I'm so thirsty."

Bela held my head up and gave me sips of water, but it didn't help. "I would like to give you that soda water, but I don't know how or where the dead girl got it from. She drank from it, and now she is dead. Please, Jadzia, drink the water," she said helplessly.

Days and nights, my body was burning up with fever. I was dreaming of an apple. I knew that if I ate an apple, I would magically feel better, otherwise I was certain that I would die. I opened my eyes and saw Bela applying a wet compress to my head.

I couldn't stop thinking of the apple. I gripped Bela's wrist: "I've got to have an apple or I'll surely die," I whimpered.

Bela's eyes darkened. "Jadzia, don't say that. You know that there is no possibility of getting an apple."

"Please, Bela, ask Moniek. He'll find a away."

"How can I ask Moniek for an apple? He's risking his life for a piece of bread. Asking him for an apple is like asking for freedom."

While I was pleading with Bela, Moniek walked in. "Ask me what?" he said softly and ran a gentle hand over Bela's hair.

"Nothing," Bela said, "It's the fever."

"Please...Moniek...I have to have an apple, a very small apple. If I don't get an apple, I'll die," I said and fell asleep.

I wasn't sure if it was the same day or the next. When I opened my eyes again, I saw Moniek sitting next to me, holding a small green apple in front of me. My eyes filled with tears when he placed the apple in my hand. I brought the little green apple to my mouth, but I didn't have the strength to penetrate the skin. As if in a dream, everything is so close, but you can't touch it.

Moniek saw me struggling and took the apple from me, reassuring me that he'll give it right back. He used the wire-cutting knife and peeled the apple and cut it in small pieces, the same as my tata did when I was little. Moniek made sure the peal was extra thin. He put a piece of apple in my mouth and patiently waited until I finished chewing and swallowed each piece before he put another piece in my mouth until I had finished the little apple. I didn't remember ever tasting anything better than that small green apple.

Moniek left soon after I had finished the apple, and Bela had worked the day shift.

I was alone with no one to take care of me, and I felt the apple coming back to my throat and to my mouth. I turned on to my stomach, and it took all of my strength to pushed myself up towards the edge of the bunk. My head dangled towards the floor and seconds later the slightly chewed apple flew from my mouth onto the floor, as a ruptured dam. I passed out with my head still dangling, until Bela returned and pulled me onto my side, giving me small sips of water.

It must have been night because it was dark inside the barrack, and I heard airplanes and explosions above my head. I was feeling very hot, and I knew that I was in hell. I felt the wood beneath me burning, and I was unable to move. I felt my body adhering to the wood and catch fire. Inch by inch, my entire body was burning, until I was only a tiny speck waiting for the wind to blow me away. As if turning a switch, I was suddenly at home with my family. I was very hot and tired, but nobody objected when my little sister Edzia picked up a large, straw broom, five times her owns size, and began chasing me. I was too hot and too weak to run, and she began hitting me mercilessly with the broom. I was angry that Edzia, being so much smaller than I was, would be that much stronger. "I'm bigger than her. Why is she hitting me with that broom?" I asked my mama, but Mama didn't hear me. Everyone in the house turned away from me, as if I were only visible to Edzia, and Edzia continued to bang the broom at my back, the way Mama banged at our feather bedding. Every spring, we all helped Mama carry the comforters outside and put them on two chairs to air out. Before we carried them back up, we all took turns banging at the comforters with the bamboo beater to get the dust out. That was the way I felt when Edzia was beating me with the broom, until I woke up exhausted but cool. I looked up and saw Bela standing next to me. "My fever's gone. Edzia knocked the fever out of me," I whimpered. As I fell asleep again in a pool of sweat, I knew in my heart that I was never going to see my family, but I refused to accept it. I needed to hold on to that flicker of hope that my family was alive in a different camp. As long as I believed it, I had reason to fight. When I next woke up, Bela's eyes were red rimmed. "Don't cry. I'm all right now. The fever's gone," I said.

"I know your fever's gone. I'm crying because Moniek is in the hole in the ground for last three days, and now he's getting twenty-five lashes every day. I hope he survives it," she sniffled.

My heart was breaking for Moniek and my sister. I suddenly remembered the apple and felt guilty. "I'm so sorry, it's all my fault. He took a chance getting me the apple, and now he might pay with his life," I whimpered.

"It's not the apple. He got caught at the wires buying bread. I pray he doesn't pay with his life. I don't think I could go on with out him. We'll know tomorrow after his last twenty five lashes."

I tried to comfort my sister, but found myself drifting off, and my head fell with a thud on the board.

When I next woke up, I was starving, but I was too tired to open my eyes.

I could hear the rain beating down on the thin roof and remembered Moniek in the bunker. It was just a hole in the ground covered over with boards. With the rain coming down strong, I was afraid he would drown. It must have been Sunday because each time I opened my eyes, Bela was near me. I was so tired I couldn't keep my eyes open for more than a few seconds.

I heard whispering voices, Miniek and Bela's voices. I opened my eyes for only a moment and saw that I was on my own bunk. The curtain was drawn and Moniek and Bela were in each other's arms making promises to each other. I closed my eyes again and heard Moniek's voice saying, "I love you too much to take advantage of you. I can wait. The Russians couldn't be too far. If we are lucky, our families will be at our wedding," he whispered.

I thought that I was dreaming and willed my eyes to remained open. I didn't want to lose the lovely sight of Moniek and Bela.

Bela saw me gazing at her and moved close to me. "How do you feel?" she asked, placing a hand on my forehead.

I didn't answer until I touched her hand on my face and saw Moniek's arm around her shoulders. I wanted to make sure that it wasn't a dream. "How did I get up here?" I muttered.

"Moniek carried you up the ladder," Bela said proudly.

"Moniek, thank God you're all right. How could you carry me up the ladder?" I said straining my voice.

Moniek smiled, "You don't weigh much."

Bela uncovered the pot and removed a stale piece of bread and a half a canteen of watery soup and placed it in front of me. "Eat. You need to get your strength back."

I tried to sit up, but I kept falling back. I felt like the doll Mama had made for me from a towel. I could never get it to sit, so I cradled it in my arms.

Bela sat in back of me, holding me up, and dunked a piece of bread in the cold soup and placed it in my shaky hand. "Now, eat slowly, and take small bites."

"What about you? Where is your food?" I asked worriedly.

"We ate our portion. This is yours," Moniek said, running a gentle hand over my mattered hair.

I had so many questions. I felt as if I had dug myself out from a burning grave and didn't know how long I was smoldering.

"Why is everybody on their bunks? How is David? Are your bruises very bad?" I asked Moniek.

Patiently, Moniek answered all my questions. "Today is Sunday, and my bruises will heal in time. Don't worry. I'm strong. I can take it, and David is back to work."

"Thanks to Moniek," Bela added.

I was glad Bela worked the day shift and was with me at night. I was afraid of the rats.

At dawn, when the policeman began banging on our bunks, I tried to stand up, but my legs felt like rubber, and Bela pleaded with him to let me stay in one more day.

He saw that I kept falling back and said, "You better be ready tomorrow. Cover yourself up until the appell is over."

Bela thanked him and quickly told me to eat the piece of bread from the pot, but I only ate half. I wasn't sure if Bela ate her portion.

The appell was over, the day shift had gone to work, the night shift slept, and the sick moaned.

The sick going through the crisis were delirious. Bony arms and legs waving in the air, and the dead were carried out.

All day I took baby steps, I climbed down from the ladder, holding onto the bunks. I walked towards the door through the stench from vomit and urine.

I stumbled through the open door, holding onto the frame, and took several deep breaths.

I lifted my face to the warm sun and wondered why God doesn't keep the sky cloudy and rainy to match our sorrow. Why does the sky have to be so clear and blue when we are being tortured and murdered every second? What kind of God, with the power to turn night into day, would not cause every whip and rifle to burn, in the murderous hands?

Edzia's little face with the big green eyes came into focus and tears began flooding my face. "Please, don't be dead," I cried. It was noon, and the people were lining up for the soup.

I knew that I needed that bowl of soup to survive, and I shuffled back to my bunk for my bowl. My legs felt as if they had no bones, and I was unable to climb the ladder. Several times I lifted one leg to climb the first step, and I was unable to lift the other. I became angry. "I have to get that bowl. If my little sister could knock the fever out of me, the least I can do is try to get stronger," I muttered to nobody in particular, as I kept on trying to climb the ladder a step at a time. I tightened my mouth and crunched my teeth together until my upper teeth were stuck on the lower and my jaw was aching. On the fourth attempt, I climbed up three steps, enough to reach for the bowl.

When I stepped off the last step, it felt as if I had climbed the highest mountain, but it felt good, though I had to rub my face to release the pain in my jaw.

Standing in the soup line, I didn't have to worry about falling. The people in line stood so close together it would have been impossible to fall.

The next morning, while the police banged on our bunks, Moniek appeared with two portions of bread and quickly disappeared. With the piece of bread in my stomach, I felt stronger than yesterday. As I stumbled towards the appellplaz, golden spots flying in front of my eyes blinded me.

Standing next to Bela on the appellplatz, I saw that I had been one of the lucky ones. Half of the people were either dead or sick. The people around me were swaying as I was, and some were unable to stand and leaned on the person next to them, the way I leaned on Bela.

I was assigned the night shift, which gave me an extra few hours of rest. As I climbed down ladder to get in line for the ladle of the noon soup, Moniek was waiting for me outside the barrack. He made sure nobody was watching and put a slice of bread with a thin slice of ham in my hand. "Eat it so you won't get tuberculosis," he said, running a hand over my hair. He saw me breaking the tiny sandwich in half and said, "You eat this. I have one for Bela, too."

Nell had been somewhat more lenient about being chased by the dogs.

Between nightly blackouts that lasted at least one hour each night and so many people dead and more getting sick, he and his soldiers didn't roam the camp as much.

Within ten days, thanks to Moniek, I was feeling stronger, and the spots in front of my eyes were disappearing, but there was no relief from the typhus epidemic. People continued to get sick, and more died every day.

Every free moment she had, Bela was on someone's bunk applying cold compresses to the forehead and giving sips of water. When I complained that she looked very tired, she reminded me that she already had typhus and wouldn't get it again.

Sunday morning, Bela stood at the appellplatz massaging her stomach.

"Is your stomach hurting from hunger?" I asked, knowing well the agonizing pain she had suffered before we got help from David and Moniek.

"I'm not hungry," she whispered.

The appell seemed endless, and Bela's pain was getting worse. When the counting was finally over, I put Bela's arm around my neck, and we stumbled to the clinic.

It was a very warm day, but her teeth were chattering. "I'm freezing," she cried.

There was a long line with sick people in front of the clinic. A friend or relative was holding up some, and some fell on the dusty ground, barely alive or dead. It was hard to tell if he or she was breathing.

By the time it was Bela's turn, her teeth had stopped chattering, and she felt as hot as the bread my tata had shoveled out from the oven. She was getting very heavy in my arms, and I was glad that it was her turn, for I was losing my grip on her.

After Doctor Wainapel finished examining her, he turned to me and said, "typhus. Next!" The next patient stood in front him ready to collapse.

"But she already had typhus in Radom. They even cut all her hair off," I insisted tenaciously.

"This is stomach typhus. She has to go to the hospital," he said and continued to examine the woman standing in front of him.

I was too afraid that if she went to the hospital, she might never return.

"The hospital has no medicine to give her. She'll just lie there, and nobody will pay attention to her. I'll take care of my sister, the way she took care of me," I said. I wanted to protest more, but when I looked at Doctor Wainapel's fatigued face, I didn't think he would remember one more patient needing to be hospitalized. I put Bela's arm around my neck, and we shuffled to our barracks. The lower bunk-board in the middle of the barracks where I had stayed during my sickness was vacant, and I helped Bela onto it. I used the basin Bela and I used for our bath and filled it with cold water. As I was dunking and ringing out our only towel for compresses, the same towel Bela had used on me when I was sick, my hands were shaking, and she held on to her stomach and moaned.

I ripped the towel in half and rang out both halves and applied one to her forehead and the other to her abdomen, but she threshed around and the compresses kept falling off. "Mama, help me. I hurt. Take away the pain!" she cried.

As I climbed inside the bunk and knelt beside her to keep the compresses in place, two men with a stretcher and Moniek, chasing behind them, stormed in. I was sure they had come to remove a dead body, but they came for my sister and began to pull her from the bunk.

"No, you can't take her!" I cried.

"Doctor Wainapell ordered her to be in the hospital," Moniek said softly, his blue eyes overflowing with tears.

"Please don't let them take her. What if she won't come back?" I cried, as the two men ran from the barracks with my sister on the stretcher.

Moniek walked briskly holding Bela's hand, and I chased after them.

As I tried to follow the men carrying my sister through the hospital door, the guard blocked the entrance. "Nobody's allowed inside," he said firmly, but he didn't stop Moniek from entering. Moniek followed alongside the stretcher as if he belonged.

Seeing my sister disappear from my sight was as if an entire half of me went with her. Though the guard warned that if a Ukrainian sees me near the hospital I would be severely punished, I refused to move. I only walked a few feet away and stood like a stone, never taking my eyes off the hospital door.

I stood on the mark, ready for the guard to leave the doorway, giving me a chance to sneak in, but he never moved.

Every time I heard a moan coming from inside the hospital, it sounded to me as if it was Bela crying, and I felt her pain and wanted to keep it. "Please God," I prayed. "Give my sister's pain to me and let her stop hurting and get well."

An hour later, Moniek came through the door and was angry with me for taking a chance of getting caught and urged me to go to my barrack. "You need rest. You haven't completely recovered, and you're working the night shift again, and in two hours will be the evening appell," he said and stood, waiting for me to leave the spot.

When I didn't move, he said, "Don't worry. I'll make sure that Bela gets the best care, and I'll keep you informed, but if you get caught by the Ukrainian, I won't be able to help you."

Like a bird with broken wings, I shuffled to the barrack and climbed up on the lonely bunk. Not until I picked up Bela's stick and banged hard on the board did six rats leave our chewed up blanket and saunter away.

I closed my eyes and prayed, "Dear God, please, don't take my sister away from me. We only have each other."

As the whistle blew for the appell, I opened my eyes and saw a rat sitting at my feet about to take a nibble from my big right toe. I didn't bother banging with the stick. As soon as I began climbing down the ladder, an entire family of rats surrounded our already shredded quilt.

All night, while sewing buttons, I prayed for my sister. In the morning after the appell was over, I ran to the hospital and stood outside the door, hoping someone would tell me something. Seeing a nurse leave the hospital, I ran to her and begged her for information, but all she would tell me was that Bela was alive.

It was the same as when my tata with typhus had been taken to the hospital outside the Ghetto. I took off my white armband with the blue Star of David insignia and stood at the hospital gate, hoping for some news. Each time, the nurse told me that he hadn't gone through the crisis yet. At that time, I didn't know what that meant. Then, I went through it myself. Now, the nightmare had repeated itself. The difference was that when my tata had typhus, I still had a family. Now, I only had Bela, and if I lost her, there would be no reason for me to survive.

Moniek had been the only source of information. I wasn't sure if I should believe him when he told me that she was getting better.

Day after day I stood in front of the hospital hoping for good news, until my shift had been changed to the day shift. By the time the twelve-hour shift was over and yet another hour on the appell, it was dark and too dangerous to be outside. I would have been an easy target for the Ukrainians. Moniek was my only lifeline to my sister.

Every night after collecting my nightly bread ration, I collapsed from exhaustion.

But first, I made sure that a rat didn't get tangled in our quilt full of holes, which took a lot of poking with the stick to free it. I had become so acclimated to the rats that I accepted them as fellow prisoners who shared my bunk.

Ten days since Bela had been taken to the hospital, I dreamed that I was playing with Bela and the neighborhood kids in the river. Bela was sliding down the waterfall in only her panties, the way we did when we were little. Bela was laughing, showing an array of white teeth and wet white hair. I was just about to jump in and slide down the waterfall when the Sunday morning whistle blew, and the whips were banging at our bunks.

I felt something tugging at my toe. With my eyes closed I reached for the stick and tried to stay with my dream one more minute, but Moniek climbed up on my bunk and shook me awake. "Bela passed the crises, and she's going to be fine," he said happily.

I wanted to hug the whole world. "Thank you, Moniek, for bringing me this wonderful news. Though you and my sister aren't married yet, and I pray to God that we'll soon be free, I already consider you my brother in law. You are the best brother-in-law in the whole world!" I said, hugging my torn quilt.

"If this is how you feel," he said, bringing his face to my lips. "Then, kiss your brother-in- law and make it legal," he said.

As I gave him a peck on his cheek, Tusia looked across to us, "shame, shame,"she sneered, trying to make me feel guilty. I refused to let her spoil my one moment of happiness in that God forsaken rat hole and ignored her accusation. I knew she had tuberculosis, but I hadn't forgotten her lashing tongue in AFL when I removed her pot from the oven to heat some water for a compress for Bela's abdominal pain. Still, I felt sorry for Tusia. She was sick and alone.

Two days later, Bela returned to our bunk, and I became a whole person again.

With Moniek's help, she soon regained her strength.

The epidemic subsided, and there were fewer people in our camp, but a new shipment from Maidanek arrived. Among the newcomers was Tusia's aunt.

I was happy for Tusia because she was sick, and the aunt had money and was able to buy butter or a piece of ham for Tusia.

Since the women from Maidanek had arrived, rumors were circulating that all of the people liquidated from the Ghetto were dead.

Sunday morning after the appell, we all went back to our barracks and gathered around the women from Maidanek and listened to the stories about Triblinka and Maidanek.

"Don't expect your families from the liquidated Ghettos to be alive. Every person was taken directly to Triblinka and put to death in gas chambers," Tusia's aunt said.

"You are lying," we all screamed in unison.

Tusia's aunt ignored our anger and continued. "The people were lined up in front of the gas chambers and given bars of soap. They were told to undress and step into the shower room. When everyone was inside, the door was locked and gas came through the shower heads," she gasped.

No matter how hard she tried to convince us that we would never see our families again, nobody believed her.

"Why are you trying to frighten us? Aren't we suffering enough?" one of the older girls shouted, and we all cried.

"Our group was ordered to pick up the clothes and check for valuables. While standing at the table, sorting and ripping out the linings from coats and jacket where people had hidden gold and diamonds, the smoke from the crematorium was puffing twenty-four hours a day," she said, wiping the tears from her tired eyes.

Everybody was angry with the Maidanek people for telling us such outrageous lies. I blocked what I had just heard from my mind and went outside, because I didn't want to have to look at Tusia's aunt and stayed outside until the evening appell. I collected my piece of bread and went to work the night shift.

The typhus survivors were so worn out that, even with the arrival of the new groups from Maidanek, Radom and Wolanow, it had been impossible to finish the allotted workload in twelve hours, especially at the night shift. Every night, the blackouts followed by explosions had become more frequent, and the dogs got their exercise chasing us inside the cage.

Chapter Twenty-Five: Basket Weaving

SS Unterscharfurer Paul Nell opened a basket-weaving workshop.

At the Sunday morning appell, Nell made an announcement. "Anyone willing to learn basket weaving may do so. Next Sunday, I will be giving tests. If you pass the test, you will go to Radom and work at weaving baskets. If you don't pass the test, you will receive twenty-five lashes. Dismissed!"

Rumors were circulating that the Russians were nearing, and camps were being liquidated and shipped out to Auschwitz. Many people, including Bela, were anxious to go back to Radom, hoping to be liberated before being shipped out to Auschwitz.

After the regular shifts, many people worked feverishly at the workshop, trying to learn basket weaving.

Bela wanted desperately to get away from Blizyn, and Moniek had told her that if she passed, he would take the test and was pretty sure he would pass. With that knowledge, Bela decided to take a chance. After the night shift and running from the dogs, she went to sleep without checking the quilt for rats. She only went three times to the workshop and wasn't sure if she would be ready for the test, but she decided to risk the lashes and take the test.

I had felt the whip on my back so many times that I didn't think I could survive another and decided to stay with my fate and didn't try to learn basket weaving. I knew that even if I learned the skill, knowing that Nell would be watching me perform, I'd surely fail the test. I also worried that I may pass the test, and Bela wouldn't. Either way, I would be left alone. If Bela did pass, and she and Moniek would be sent to Radom and were liberated, it would make me very happy.

Sunday morning, the day of the test, the sky was cerulean. The sun had dried the mud from yesterday's rain, and it felt good to walkout of the musty barrack.

I stood in the middle of the camp, a few feet from two tables. On top of one table was the weaving material, and the other was for climbing up for the punishment.

After watching several people failing the test and getting twenty-five lashes, I was frightened for my sister. She was so thin, and I was afraid that the whip would slice right through her bones.

The lines moved quickly with many punishments.

Each time a girl failed the test, she cried as the whip burned into her back. Some men screamed from pain, and others made no sound, and the whip was aimed higher.

Moniek inched over to Bela and reminded her, "If you take the test and pass, I'll do it too. I won't go without you."

Bela walked away from me. "I have to try," she said and got in line.

Though I couldn't see myself being left in Blizin alone and without Moniek's help, for I would surely starve to death, I tried not to think of tomorrow. If my sister survived, then at least, one of us would be a witness and warn the world to prevent the atrocities from happening again. Wasn't it what Mama said to me the last time she washed my back with more tears than water?

"Maybe, you will survive to tell the world," she sobbed.

I prayed for Bela to pass the test. I couldn't bear to see her punished. My heart pounded as I watched her getting closer and closer to the testing table.

Bela was handed the material, but her hands were trembling, and Nell ordered her to climb up on the table, face down. She made no sound while twenty-five lashes burned into her gaunt buttocks.

"Why didn't you scream? He wouldn't have aimed the whip so high," I cried, as I applied wet compresses to her back and buttocks.

"I wouldn't give the murderer the satisfaction," she moaned.

Poland's bitter cold winter came early. As the nightly blackouts and sounds of distant explosions had become more frequent, talk of being shipped out to Auscwitz had been on everyone's mind. I sat in the dark factory looking out from the only window and watched two airplanes shooting at each other, and one exploded in mid air, lighting up the sky, then fell to the ground.

I prayed that it was a German plane that exploded, and the Russian soldiers would rush in and tear the camp apart. At that moment, I thought back to the summer of 1939 when I sat on a rock listening to the only radio in our cul-de-sac, and Hitler's loud voice said, "I'm not afraid for the entire world! England! America! Russia!" I was now sure that the Germans had killed everyone in the entire world, and only Russia was still fighting.

With air raids being more frequent and lasting longer each night, it seemed as if the Russians were next door. All they had to do was break down the gates to our camp, march in, kill the guards and the SS, and shout, "You are free!"

It would have been a wonderful sound, but liberation was out of our reach, and our misery had only just begun.

At the beginning of 1944, SS Unterscharfurer Paul Nell left Blyzin, and a new group of SS arrived, headed by SS Obercharfurer Heller.

Nothing had changed. Only the rats were getting bolder and fatter.

The only things that gave us a will to live and a glimmer of hope were the nightly air raids. Throughout the winter months and spring, we hoped to be liberated before being shipped out to Auschwitz or some other death camp, but God and the world, if there was a God or a world, had been too far away to hear our cries for help.

Chapter Twenty-Six: 1985 - A Tour of Krakow and Auschwitz

As we were nearing Krakow, my American friend, Carla Stevenson, must've seen the distress in my face, and she took my hand in her own. "It's all right, Yaja," she cajoled.

I had changed the spelling of my name from Jadzia to Yaja. As it is, people have a hard time pronouncing my name, but it's a little easier with the new spelling.

"Look around you," Carla smiled, holding on to my hand. "We're sitting in a comfortable first class train, and you can come and go as you please."

"I looked into Carla's blue eyes and realized that my mind had been so deep in hell I had forgotten that my dear friend was sitting right next to me, and I apologized for being such a boring companion.

"I didn't come with you to be entertained. I knew before we left that this wasn't going to be a pleasure trip for you. Don't get me wrong. I'm not a martyr. This may not be a lot of fun for single women." Carla laughed.

"What's so funny?" I asked puzzled.

"Actually, we did have an adventure. I'm surprised that you have forgotten our romantic encounter in the park in Radom yesterday?" she said smiling. Her eyes twinkled as she waited for me to recall.

I suddenly remembered the toothless young man who sat down next to me on the park bench and invited me to his apartment.

"I'm sorry," I said, "my friend and I aren't interested in going to your apartment."

"I'm not interested in your friend; I'm interested in you. I don't want you to bring your friend," he said possessively.

When I asked why he wanted me to go to his apartment, he bluntly said, "because I want to make love to you."

He became angry when I said "no" and asked him leave me alone. When he refused to leave us and put his arm around my shoulder, I stood up and told Carla that we needed to leave the park.

Though she followed me to our hotel, she didn't understand why we had to leave. "It's such a beautiful afternoon, and the man seemed so polite," she said.

Once behind the closed door of our hotel room, I had told her what the man asked of me, and she couldn't stop laughing.

I too laughed as I visualized the man sitting next to me cajoling me to go to his apartment to make love to him.

Krakow was a modern city. The hotel too was new, unlike the hotel Europa in Radom. Our room was spacious and clean, not much different from a moderately priced hotel in the US.

Though it was late afternoon when we arrived, Carla wanted to explore the city.

We passed a park and heard people laughing. We were curious to see what the laughter was all about? As we entered the park, we saw a gaunt old man surrounded and taunted by a group of young people. He was running in circles holding a threatening stick in his hand. As we neared the crowed, the old man broke through the circle and ran towards Carla waving the stick at her.

I saw Carla standing pendulous, in disbelief, as the stick was about to fall heavy on her head. When I realized that she wasn't going to get out of his way, I placed myself between them. I pushed Carla, who is almost a foot taller than I am, out of his reach, but the stick crashed into my shoulder, and I cried out in pain.

Carla followed me as I ran from the park holding onto my throbbing shoulder. When we were safe in our hotel room, Carla sat down on her bed and began to laugh. "Why did you get between us? I could have handled the crazy old coot," she said.

"Carla, you were just standing there, and he was about to clabber you with that stick."

"My hero," she giggled looking down at me. When she stopped laughing, she admitted to me that she had been too stunned to move.

Before we went out to dinner, we stopped at the desk and made reservations for the tour to Auschwitz.

Though the restaurant, Wiezinek, was very elegant and the food very good, I was unable to eat. My shoulder was throbbing, and the thought of going back to Auschwitz after forty years was enough to make me lose my appetite and keep me awake all night. While I tossed and turned, I remembered June 1944.

Almost five years we endured loss of family, hunger, beatings, slave labor, and daily murder. Just when we believed that nothing could be worse than Blizyn, a notorious death camp, we were lined up and marched to a local railroad station where a freight train waited with open doors. On the side of each car was clearly written in large letters, "Auschwitz."

We were rushed inside like cattle and locked in. The only air we breathed was from the cracks in the wood of the boxed cars.

I'm not sure how many hours we stood in the cattle train, packed in like sardines, before it came to a full stop.

When the doors opened, I saw that it was dusk, and a group of men in striped prison uniforms and women wearing dresses stood at the open doors of the boxcars and shouted," Rous, rous!"(out) "Schnell, schnell!"(quick).

Bela and I jumped off the train, but Tusia was afraid to jump, and Bela turned back and took her hand, letting her jump into her arms. From that moment on, Tusia never left our side.

I remembered Eva before she died of tuberculosis. Aunt Hudsa wouldn't allow me near her daughter. "Tuberculosis is highly contagious," she would say. If you stand close to the sick person, you can catch it," she cautioned. I may have only been five years old at the time, but I had never forgotten the serious look on my aunt's face.

Remembering Aunt Hudesas' words, I was very frightened of catching tuberculosis from Tusia, and I was also worried for Bela, for she was standing too close to her.

I soon stopped worrying about catching Tusia's disease when I found myself standing in front of a large building facing an SS officer who looked me over as if I were the cattle that had jumped off the cattle train only minutes before. He pointed his finger and waved me over to the side with the young and healthy. Bela stood behind me, pinching Tusia's face to bring a bit of color to the surface. I let out my breath when I saw my sister coming towards me with Tusia following behind. I stood close to my sister as we were marched into a small room.

While being processed, we soon discovered that the men and women in our charge were shipped to Auschwitz a year or two before us and had suffered a great deal. Now, they were the privileged, and my observation told me to be wary of them.

Three girls were holding scissors, and two girls lifted our hair to check for lice.

While standing in line, Bela and I checked each other's hair and found no lice. We reassured each other that our hair would remain in tact.

Bela stood assured in front of the girl who had the power to say which one of us should keep or lose our hair. She looked at my sister's proud face and pushed her over to the girl with the scissors. "All!" she shouted.

My stomach turned into a knot as I watched Bela's golden blond hair fall to the floor. When all the hair was gone, the girl picked up a long razor and shaved my sister's head until her scalp, for the second time since the invasion, was smooth as a man's shaven face.

When my turn came, the girl looked at my contorted face, not knowing that my heart was crying for my sister, and told the other girl to only shorten my hair. What the girl didn't know was that I would have gladly changed places with my sister. I didn't care if my hair had been shaved off.

I wanted to comfort my sister, but there was nothing I could say that would make her feel better.

The line moved smoothly to the next large room. We were ordered to strip naked, leave our clothes in a pile, but hold onto our shoes.

Three SS men stood in front of buckets filled with water and ordered us to line up, one at a time, and take off our shoes and hand them to him.

After dumping each pair of shoes separately in the bucket, he filled them with water and rinsed them several times, making sure no valuables were hidden inside. After he was convinced that nothing was hidden inside, he threw the shoes back at us.

The next step was to stand under showerheads, with cold water running down from the ceiling. After we showered, water dripping from our hair and bodies, we were marched into the next room. A group of young men and women, I estimated them to be between nineteen and twenty-five, stood in the background and gazed at us.

I was next in line for the shaving. I stood in front of a young man, my arms tightly around my breasts.

"Lift your arms high above your head," he said. He didn't shout. His voice was rather gentle.

After my underarms had been shaved, I wrapped my arms around my breasts again while he used the same long razor to shave my pubic hair. I had an eerie feeling that someone was observing me, and I felt as if I were an animal in a zoo. At a glance, I saw a tall man in his early twenties standing from a distance looking directly at me. I tried to look away, hoping he would stop looking at me. When he disappeared from my sight, I breathed easier.

Suddenly, out of nowhere, he was standing in back of me, his arms wrapped around my naked body, while the other man was still shaving my pubic hair.

I stiffened and looked towards Bela and saw that she was ready to get out of line and come to my rescue. I shook my head, begging her with my eyes to

221

stay in line.

The man with the razor went to the next girl in line and the tall man was now facing me. He towered over me, wrapping his arms around me, but I kept my arms tightly wrapped around my breasts.

I tried to pull away, but his grip was much stronger. He had covered my face with his chest, and I couldn't breathe or see Bela's face.

"Please let go of me," I muttered into his chest.

"Don't be afraid. I won't hurt you," he said softly, and suddenly, he loosened his grip on me and disappeared.

I was shaking so hard that the girls in line with me had to hold onto me until Bela was finished shaving and stood in back of me. She touched my burning face.

"He's gone. It's alright; you're safe," she soothed, and she held on to me until I stopped shaking.

We each received an old, worn-out dress and no undergarments. Shivering from the cold night air, we were marched in darkness to a dark barracks in Birkenau.

We had no food for at least twelve or fifteen hours, and the thin dresses didn't keep us warm.

Bela and I curled up against each other on the lowest shelf to keep warm.

It was still dark the next day when we were chased outside to stand on the appellplatz to be counted.

After the appell was over, we formed a line to be tattooed and given a cloth number to be sewn onto our dress.

As the girl began to stipple in the number on the inside of my forearm, she realized that she had made a mistake. My number was to be, A-15791, instead of 7 she stippled in 8. When she realized that she had made a mistake she stippled a cross on the 8 several times and added 7 next to it. We considered ourselves lucky for being tattooed. It meant that we were still of some value to the Germans. The ones that were not tattooed were sent directly to the crematorium, and seeing the nonstop smoke from the chimneys and the smell of burned flesh, the tattoo looked pretty good.

After we were processed, we were given a piece of bread, which we immediately devoured. Again, we lined up and marched to different, more permanent barracks in Birkenau.

Two well-fed women in their late twenties, or early thirties, met us at the door of our new barracks. "My name is Magda," one of the women shouted, as if speaking to the hard of hearing. Magda had straight black hair, black eyes, and a dark brown complexion. Her shouts were ear piercing. I had never encountered a woman with so much lethal anger before. Looking at Magda's small wrathful eyes and listening to her rasping voice full of threats, I felt as if I was in hell facing the Devil. Magda pointed to the plump blond woman standing next to her. "This is Junuszka," she shouted, as if introducing the Queen. Junuszka was a pretty blond girl. She had blue eyes and fair complexion. Januszka seemed kinder in her demeanor; though, I wouldn't take a chance getting in her way. Both women were plump, well dressed, and spoke German, but to each other, they spoke Czech.

We were given a needle and thread and told to return it soon as we finished sewing the numbers to our dresses.

We were allowed inside our new barracks lined with three layers of wooden shelves as in Blizyn. Only here, we did not have our pillows or covers, only the boards. As always, Bela and I chose a top bunk. As we sat down and took off our dresses to sew on the numbers, I saw that my dress had a satin colorful lining with red roses and green leaves on a black background. I carefully tore out the lining and gave it to Bela to cover her bare head.

Bela covered her head with the cloth and made a knot on the crown of her head. "How does it look?" she asked me.

"You look beautiful," I said excitedly.

"Tomorrow morning, I'll go to see Moniek, I hear that the men are on the other side of the electric wires," Bela said with a glow I hadn't seen in a long time.

A half an hour later, Magda and Januszka ,our house elders and capos, chased us out of the barracks. "You will not be allowed inside the barracks until after the evening appell," Magda shouted.

There was no sign of any kind of work in Birkenau, and we were not stopped from roaming the campground. It was a warm day, and we didn't mind being outside.

Since her head was covered, Bela decided not to wait until the next day to see Moniek. She began walking briskly towards the men's camp, and when she was only five feet from the wire, Magda caught up with her and pulled off her head covering.

I saw Bela running back, tears stinging her eyes, yet not a drop fell on her cheeks. She didn't have to tell me what had happened. It was quite obvious when I saw Magda strolling towards our barracks, swinging Bela's head covering.

Early afternoon, we received a bowl of watery soup. It didn't kill the

223

hunger, but it was warm.

All day, we stood leaning against the barrack's wall and watched as the smoke bellowed from the crematorium. Except for a small patch of grass between the barracks, there was no place to rest. Finally, we stood at the evening appell, and I felt Magda's finger jabbing into my chest as she counted and recounted endless times. Each time she finished counting one of us, she wrote a large vertical line on a note pad. The lines took up several pages, and we all realized that Magda was elitterate. After standing at attention until nightfall, we were shooed inside the barracks.

On the left near the entrance was Januszka's and Magda's separate room. As I passed the room, the door was open ajar, and I couldn't help indulging myself in a quick glance. In that little room there was no sign of a war or Auschwitz. Our two capos, house elders, or whatever they called themselves, were wearing colorful silk robes and sat on comfortable wooden chairs at a small wooden table covered with an embroidered tablecloth. A loaf of bread and other delicacies were laid out on the table. I watched them spread thick butter on thin slices of fresh bread and bite into mouth-watering chunks of salami. I quickly disappeared from sight before I was caught spying on them. I put my head down on the bare board next to Bela and tried very hard to erase from my mind what I had just seen. I told myself that it wasn't real; it was only in my imagination, and I fell asleep exhausted and hungry.

The next thing I heard was Magda's ear piercing screams. "Appell! Rous, rous, alle rous! (Everyone out).

It was still dark outside when Magda lined us up military fashion to be counted for the morning appell. It was hot by the time she finished counting us.

Januszka followed Magda as if she was the Lady of the Manor, and Magda catered to her every whim. It didn't take long for us to find out that Junuszka's lover was an SS officer.

After we received our bread ration, Bela took one of our rations and told me to see Moniek and throw it over the electric wires for him. "All the man from Blizyn are standing outside," she said, her eyes hooded.

"Why don't you go yourself? Moniek loves you. He doesn't care if you don't have hair?"

"No, I can't let him see me this way; now go."

Moniek's face lit up when he saw me approach the wire. He looked beyond me, then asked, "Where is Bela?"

"Bela is fine, only her hair is shaved, and she doesn't want you to see her this way."

A warm smile formed on his face. "Doesn't she know that I love her no matter what she looks like?"

"I'll tell her, but get ready to catch the bread," I said and threw the bread over the fence, but it fell in the mud from last night's rain.

Tears filled my eyes, and I felt as if I had just killed my sister's future husband. I covered my face with my hands and began walking away.

"Jadzia, come back. It's alright; it's fine."

When I turned back, he showed me the bread he had picked up from the puddle.

He wiped it off with his sleeve and took a bite. "It just got a little wet, but it will fill my stomach just fine." As I turned to leave, he said, "Please tell Bela to come and see me."

The next day, Bela went to see Moniek with one of our bread rations. I didn't mind living on half a bread ration. I could never repay him for what he had done for us in Blizyn. I had never forgotten him risking his life for the little green apple.

On the fourth night, Bela was holding onto her stomach and moaned from pain. I too was beginning to feel lightheaded. On the fifth morning, Bela returned from seeing Moniek to give him one of our bread rations and returned with two dresses in her arms.

We moved to the very end of the barracks, shielded from the capos eyes. We stood against the wall and turned towards each other. Bela removed two portions of bread and handed me one. "Eat," she said.

"Where did you get all this?" I asked before taking the first bite of my bread.

"From Moniek. He ran into a friend from his hometown who'd been here a year before us. He promised to help as much as he can."

Within seconds, we had finished our bread, and she handed me a brown and red flannel-checkered dress. "Put it on quickly before Magda catches us," she urged me, as she was putting on a solid color navy blue wool dress.

As I was putting on my new dress over my old one, I remembered Mama having a dress just like that one, and I wondered if that dress was my mama's, but then I knew it couldn't be Mama's dress. Mama was much taller than I was, and Mama's dress would reach to my ankles. I remembered how much my mama loved her dress. She only wore it on Saturdays. I saw Bela looking at me, and I knew that she too was reminded of our mama when she saw me wearing the checkered dress. Bela went back the next morning to see Moniek and was told that he had been shipped out. "I hope he's in a better place," I mumbled.

We stood endlessly leaning against the barrack wall, but Bela found a patch of grass and stretched out in direct sun. Her face looked brown and healthy.

I was unable to tolerate the sun. I never tanned the way Bela did. My face would become red, and then my skin would peel.

Several times a week, one or two SS men lined us up and looked us over. If he found any sign of weakness or imperfection, or if he saw that my skin was peeling, he would send me to the hospital and that I quickly learned was as good a being sent directly to the crematorium.

Tusia was always standing next to us. Each day she looked weaker and paler.

Each time the SS man arrived, Bela pinched her cheeks, and lately she had to rub hard to bring some color back to her face.

As I stood in line for the inspection, I remembered a time when I was a child. I was angry when kids called me red, because of my pink cheeks. Now, I was grateful to have maintained some of the color in my cheeks.

We didn't have our basins anymore and only depended on the occasional march to the shower room. Each time on entering the shower room, our hearts pounded until we felt water coming down on us, instead of gas. Our first march to the showers was in August. The dresses Moniek gave us were taken away from us in exchange for another old dress.

Everyday, I wandered away from the safety of the barracks wall hoping to find my tata or my uncle Gershon. We knew that the Germans had lied to us from the very beginning. I hoped that the letter we had received from Auschwitz was also a lie, and I would find my tata alive on the men's side of the wires. I imagined my tata baking bread for the SS and their lackeys. My tata and Uncle Gershon were taken away early on and would be among the privileged. But they would be good to everybody, I was sure of that. Didn't my tata protect Jews from being hurt or killed by the Polish Endeks? My tata would never raise a hand to helpless people, nor would my uncle Gershon.

Sunday morning after the appell, I saw a short man my tata's age, walking towards the female capo's gathering house. He had the same proud stride and the same full head of straight brown hair. The resemblance to my tata was so strong that I couldn't help myself from following him all the way to the top of the steps. I heard him speak Polish to the female capos, and I dared to stand close and listen. The capos inside were the most notorious, yet I was unable to pull myself away from the man, even if it meant great bodily harm to me.

The man sensed that I was standing behind him and turned around. "Is there something you want?" he asked.

"Could you please tell me your name?" I gasped, feeling a lump as big as an egg constricting my throat.

"Why do you need to know my name?"

"Because you look just like my tata. He was taken to Auschwitz in 1942," I said, feeling my chin quiver and my eyes fill with tears.

The man told me his name, which I do not now remember. I only remember that it wasn't a Jewish name. I was trying to tell him my tata's name in case he knew him, but he wasn't interested. He was giving toothbrushes to the capo girls.and gave me one too, then shooed me away, turning his attention back to the strong, well-fed capo girls in the barracks. I lingered on the steps for another moment, but I could see that he would have liked for me to disappear. As I walked away, I was unable to stop the tears from gushing down on my face. I felt as if my eyes were broken water pipes.

September's heavy rains were constant. We now huddled in our thin dresses, against the barracks wall and each other, for warmth.

The SS picked rainy days to line us up for inspection. Everyday our group became smaller, and the smoke from the crematorium had been ceaseless. I still hadn't given up looking for my tata and Uncle Gershon. Giving up looking for them would have meant that they weren't alive anymore, and I refused accept that.

Everyday on my walks towards the men's camp, I witnessed a different tragedy.

One day as I passed what must have been the kitchen, I watched in horror as an SS Man ordered a young man to dance barefoot on red coals. I don't know what the outcome was, for I was unable to listen to the young man's cries and watch him being tortured. I also didn't want to be spotted and suffer the same fate. Another time, in the same area, I witnessed an SS man forcing a young man to eat an entire bucket of soup, until the man collapsed. I couldn't see if his stomach had split open, and his entire body was covered with his guts, or was it vomit? But, I had seen too many dead people in over five years since the invasion to know that the man was dead by the way he fell limp with his eyes bulging.

It was a cold and windy day in October when I approached the wire to the men's camp. A group of men huddled against the walls to keep warm, and I hoped that someone would tell me that he had seen my tata and Uncle Gershon. Or, by some miracle, they would be among them. I inched closer to the electric wire to get a better look. I was just about to call out to the men and ask the same question I have been asking since I arrived in that new hell, "Did any of you see Jeremy Sztraiman…Jeremy the Baker from Radom?" When I only saw heads shaking I asked, "What about Gershon Sztraiman?" He was taken with the butchers?"

A middle-aged man stepped away from the group and stood three feet from the wires. He was a short man, the same height as my tata, but I could see that he wasn't my tata. "Little girl, what is your name?" he asked.

"Jadzia Sztraiman,"

"What is your Yiddish name?"

I thought for a moment and said "Jenta."

"What did you say was your tata's name?"

"Jeremy Sztraiman. Do you know my tata? I'm from Radom, my tata was known as Jeremy the Baker. He was taken to Auschwitz on a bloody Wednesday early 1942, and my uncle Gershon was also taken to Auschwitz with the butchers. Did you see my tata or my uncle?" I asked. My teeth were chattering from cold, and my heart pounded while I was hoping for a "yes," answer.

"My name is Hakman. I am your uncle on your tata's side."

"Did you see my tata or Uncle Gershon," I asked, ignoring the details on how we were related.

"No, I didn't see your tata, but Gershon was here and died."

"How did he die? He was a strong and healthy man."

"Oh child, right now, this here is paradise. Not too many from two years ago or a year ago are still alive," he sighed.

I turned to leave knowing that my favorite uncle was dead, and I now wondered if my tata ever made it alive to Auschwitz? We may have overlooked him among the dead naked bodies in the hospital morgue.

"Wait a minute, child. I'll be right back," my newfound uncle urged. He returned in less than a minute with a plate of thick soup. "Now, be very careful. Don't touch the wire, or you'll get electrocuted," he warned and very carefully pushed the plate under the wire. "Now, carefully pull it out," he instructed.

After I had the plate of soup in my cold hands he said, "eat."

"Thank you very much, but I'm here with my sister, Bela. I'll be back tomorrow and bring back the plate," I said and ran, being careful not to spill a single drop of the soup.

Bela was huddling against the barracks. When she saw me running towards her with something in my hands, she left the barracks' wall to meet me half way.

We squatted behind the barracks, removed our spoons from our pockets and devoured the plate of thick potato soup. After we finished eating I told Bela about Uncle Hackman. "Did you ever meet him?" I asked.

"No, I didn't know too many of Tata's relatives. Maybe he was Tata's uncle?"

"Tomorrow, he'll be waiting with another plate of soup for us," I said feeling rich.

After the evening appell, when we were allowed to enter our barracks, we stretched out on the board, and I told Bela what Uncle Hackman had said about our Uncle Gershon. We didn't cry. It was, now more than ever, inevitable that it was only a matter of time before we too would succumb and turn to dust. The sad part was that there wouldn't be a single person left to cry for us.

The next afternoon, my uncle wanted to know why my sister didn't come? I told him that her hair was shaved off, and she was embarrassed. "It's unimportant, most people's hair was shaved off, but I understand. What did you say is her name?"

"Bela," I said, anxious to get the soup.

"Your sister's name is Baila. That was your grandmother's name. Your sister is named after your tata's mama."

I now wondered which dead relative I was named after? I always hated the name "Jenta." I didn't dwell on the name now; it didn't matter. I had more important things to think about, survival. Since we were not sent to work places, it meant that we were not productive. We all knew that we were only kept alive until such time when we would be walked to the showers and given gas instead of water. It was only a question of time. Each time we were walked to the showers, we all wondered if that was it.

After retrieving the soup from under the electric wire, Uncle Hackman told me to wait a moment and returned with two men's suit-jackets. "Put the plates down and catch the jackets," he said.

My heart pounded as he aimed and tossed the two men's suit-jackets, one at a time, over the high electric wires. If a jacket had gotten stuck on the wire, it would catch on fire or knock out the electricity or both, and we would all pay with our lives.

"The jacket will protect you and Bela from the wind," he said after the jackets were safely in my arms. I put one on immediately. Although it was only a thin summer jacket, I hadn't felt this warm since the end of last August. I thanked him for his kindness and his answer was, "No need. Come back tomorrow."

I transferred the soup from the plate to my bowl, filling it three-quarter full and pushed the plate carefully back under the wire. I had a feeling that my uncle was helping other girls and would need the plates. Our regular soup bowls wouldn't fit under the wires.

On the way back to our barracks wall, I tried to think if my tata ever mentioned a relative named Hackman? If we weren't related, how would he know my relatives better than I did? I was happy to have such wonderful uncle. For the next four days, Bela and I shared a plate of thick soup.

Nothing in Auschwitz stayed the same. People stood huddled against the wall one day and gone the next. On the fifth afternoon, I was told that my uncle Hackman had been shipped out. To make matters worse, today, the capo announced that it was Yom Kippur. "Anybody volunteering to fast will receive the entire ration in the evening!"

Several girls, including myself, raised our hands. Maybe if I fast, God would hear my prayers and perform a miracle.

Since half of us volunteered, Magda told us that everybody would be fasting.

After starving all day, we were lined up to stand on the appell to be counted. After the counting was over, we waited for our ladle of soup and the piece of bread. At nightfall, Magda chased us inside our barracks without food, and God hadn't heard our prayers. We wobbled up on our shelves knowing what we knew for a very long time that our days on this earth were numbered. The cold wind would soon carry our flesh with the smoke from the crematorium, and I only hoped to be dead before the fire engulfed my body. As I lay on the board, shivering from cold and hunger, I wondered why I wanted to go on under such horrid conditions? Then, I remembered Mama's words, "A worm under the ground fights to stay alive." I never stepped on a worm because of Mama's words.

I'm not sure of the date because we had nothing to go by. It had been some days after Yom Kippur and the evening appell. A capo from another section of Auschwitz asked for volunteers to follow her to a work camp. We all knew that the only way to stay alive one more hour was to be productive.

Bela and I stepped out of line, and all the girls from Radom, including

Tusia, followed our lead.

The night was black as ink. It was a long, tiring walk, late into the night. I had no idea what we were stepping into. The ground felt cold and muddy beneath my torn shoes. When I didn't think I could walk another step, I saw a dimly lit gate. On top of the iron-gate read, "FKL" (Female Concentration camp). After we passed through the gate, we still walked, what seemed like forever, to a dimly lit barracks, much smaller than the one in Birkenau. The only light was coming from a wood-burning hearth at the far end of the barracks. Wooden boards supported by thick wooden beams sat on top of one-foot thick cement. The cement beneath the boards was hollow in the middle, resembling a dome. A wooden ladder had been attached to each roll of shelves.

We were ordered to climb up on top of the shelves. The shelves were lined with plates of pea soup, the same plates my uncle Hackman pushed under the wire for us. Paradise, I mused. Hungrily, I began to eat the cold, half-cooked pea soup. After I finished the plate of soup, my stomach felt as if I had been poisoned. I was cold, and my stomach felt if a thousand fists pounded at me from the inside. To keep warm, I curled up against Bela's back as we had done so since the camps had begun. Tusia curled up against my back with her face against my neck. I was desperately afraid of catching her disease, but I was in too much pain to object.

It seemed that my head had only minutes ago touched the board when the wake up whistle blew, followed by capo shouts, "Rous, rous ale rous, appell!"

Climbing down the ladder, I felt as if my stomach was on fire. We were chased outside into the same darkness as when we arrived. I suddenly became very nauseous. I was glad to be standing at the end of the line and had enough time to turn my head away from the girl next to me. I squatted, and the round hard peas gushed from my mouth. My head was spinning, and my legs were rubbery. As the peas ejected from my mouth, I felt myself drifting. The girls standing next to me pulled upright. The sky was beginning to turn gray, and it took two girls to keep me from falling.

Bela urged me to straighten before I was pulled out of line and taken to the hospital. As far as I was concerned, the end couldn't be coming soon enough.

The counting was over, and my stomach was empty. For the first time since the Germans marched into Radom, I had welcomed an empty stomach. I lifted my head in time to see a middle-aged SS man shout, "march!" We turned and followed as if we were sheep going to the slaughter.

By the time we reached our destination, I was feeling better and ate the piece of bread the capo placed in our hands after the counting.

The SS man halted at a large field in front of a shallow square about two feet deep. The square was large enough to build a small barracks. He ordered us to pick up shovels that lay inside the square and dig. No matter how hard we tried, it was impossible to penetrate the frozen yellow clay. Each time I managed to pierce through a few inches, the shovel adhered to the clay, and I had to struggle to pull it back out.

Every morning, except on Sundays, we marched in darkness to the same field and the same square, and our cries echoed, but God didn't hear us. Each day the ground was harder and covered with snow. The SS man was wearing a fur coat, gloves, boots, and a fur hat. All day he sat on a chair several feet away from us, near a large metal barrel filled with coal and blasting fire. He barely paid attention to us. He knew very well that what we were doing wasn't work, only torture and a waiting period. There weren't enough crematoriums to accommodate us all. He didn't scream at us, as long as we stood in the square ditch holding the frozen shovel in our bare hand. The holes on the bottoms of my shoes were larger with each day, and my feet were always wet. Even at night when the hearth kept the barracks fairly warm, my feet never thawed out. We all slept with our dress on. We had no covers, only the bare boards. During the night when the hearth went dark, the only warmth Bela and I derived was from each other.

Tusia too needed a body to cling to for warmth, and I didn't have the heart to push her away. No matter which way I turned, I felt her breath on my face. I was certain that sooner or later I too would fall victim to tuberculosis. At that point of my miserable existence, it didn't matter, for I didn't think I would survive Auschwitz.

As much as I craved to fill my stomach, I craved to take off my dress wash my body.

One Sunday in mid November, the snow was high, and the winds and hail blew fears. I wandered out from the barracks, hoping to find a building with running water. If I could only wash my hands and face, I pondered as I continued walking in mountains of snow. When I turned the bend, I saw a brick building that didn't resemble a barracks. All of the barracks were made of wood. My life had so little meaning that I didn't care what would happen to me if I were caught. I opened a metal door and sauntered inside. I felt as if I were a tiny mouse looking for cheese. I looked around and saw a very large kitchen with enormous aluminum pots, but I didn't smell anything cooking.

Next to the door stood a sink and a faucet. Only my chin reached the sink. I reached up and turned the faucet. To my delight cold water was gushing from the spout. I was so excited to see the running water that I didn't see a man and woman in their twenties echoing from the far end of the stove. "What are you doing here?" The woman asked authoritatively, but not threatening. The man wore the striped prison outfit, and the woman wore a warm dress with a sweater over the dress. I recognized that these two people were the privileged, for there was no sign of hunger on the man or woman. From the accent, I knew that the woman was Jewish. I sized her up and didn't see anger, only compassion.

"Would it be alright to wash myself in the sink?"

The woman looked at the man for approval, and he lifted his shoulders and nodded.

I stood next to the sink and saw that I wouldn't be able to reach the faucet. I would be splashing water on the floor. I peeled off Uncle Hackman's jacket and pulled the dress over my head, paying no attention to the man that stood gawking at me. It didn't enter my to be embarrassed. I didn't feel like a sixteen year old girl. I didn't feel as if I were a human being. Only instinct told me that I needed to be clean. I stepped out of my torn shoes and, like an animal, climbed up on the counter and eased myself onto the shallow rectangular sink. I squatted directly under the faucet letting the icy water run on top of me. When I saw the woman striding towards me, I felt as if I were a small dog and was prepared to jump off the sink before she would pull me off and throw me out naked into the snow. To my delight she handed me a little piece of soap. "Here, you can use this to bathe with," she said softly. I was so overwhelmed that I couldn't stop the silent tears from flooding my face. I bent my head under the faucet and lathered my hair, then soaped my entire body especially my feet, for my shoes had large holes in them, and the bottoms of my feet were black. I turned the faucet on full blast until my body felt numb. I jumped off the sink, dripping water onto the floor, and it never entered my mind that it would have felt good to wipe myself with a towel. I looked at my dress and knew that it hadn't been washed before it was given to me. I threw the dress in the sink and scrubbed it with the tiny piece of soap. I wrung out and put the dress back on. I stepped into my shoes and put the jacket on top of the wet dress. I thanked the two people for the kindness and ran in the blizzard towards the barracks, feeling that if I had died tonight I wouldn't care, for I hadn't felt this clean in a very long time. Even in Birgenau, when they walked us to the showers, they never gave us soap. By the time I had reached the barracks, icicles hung from my hair. My dress hung stiff on my gaunt body, and my jacket was wet from my dress. I climbed up on my board and took off my clothes. I hung the dress on the edge of the board and put on the jacket and sat on the board with my bare bottom. When the dress began to thaw out water, was dripping onto the floor. When it was time to go to sleep, I placed my dress under my body, hoping it would dry before the wakeup call.

The minute I closed my eyes I felt an urgency to urinate. Wearing only my jacket, I ran to the bucket standing next to the open door. No sooner did I climb up on the board, I had to run again. I was feeling cold and hot and cold again, and I couldn't stop running to the bucket until the house elder caught me at a full bucket and ordered me to carry it out and dump it. I stumbled in the dark in knee high snow, urine and feces dribbling on my feet, and I had no idea where I was going, or where the dumpsite was? When my eyes adjusted to the darkness, I saw other girls walking with buckets and crying in the darkness. One girl dumped the bucket into the snow, and we all followed her lead. After returning the bucket, I went back outside and walked away from the barracks until I found a heap of clean snow. I took off my shoes and picked handfuls of snow and cleaned my feet and legs. I walked towards another clean heap of snow and cleaned my shoes and hands. Climbing up on my board, my body felt numb, and I didn't give it a second thought. I only knew that I was never going back towards the bucket. As soon as I climbed up on the board, I needed to urinate again. I climbed down again and slid under the boards and urinated inside the cement dome. This exercise continued until the whistle blew. My teeth were chattering as I put on my wet dress and the damp jacket on top. We were chased out into a blizzard and hail the size of mothballs. I could feel my dress stiffen against my body.

Chapter Twenty-Seven: The End of Auschwitz

The capo was a tall heavyset woman. As she began counting and recounting us, she reminded me of a large pit bull. It had been too dark to see the color of her eyes, but it was easy to see the evil in her demeanor. On the third count, she grabbed the collar of my damp jacket with so much force I felt as if I were a marionette. I stood dazed in front of her in the center of the arena, feeling as if I were a mouse in the jaws of a lion ready to be swallowed. "Where is your number?" she bellowed, slamming her fist into my bony face. She pulled off my jacket threw it onto the snow. "Why did you hide your number under your jacket?" she roared, as her fist collided with my head and nose. By the third or fourth blow to my head, I had lost count and had no idea what was happing to me. She pushed me back in line, and I collided with the girls, and Bela held me up as blood was gushing from my nose, mouth, and head. When my mind was functioning again, I had realized that, although I was always careful to have the number on my dress visible, this had been the first time when it was hidden by the jacket. I stood in line shivering in the blizzard, my legs buckling, and I felt as if I were a small damaged branch dangling from a tree, and I knew that any moment the wind would blow me away.

Every morning after the counting was over, a girl sat at a table with a pencil and notepad, and the capo announced, "If anyone is sick and wants to go to the hospital, get in this line and sign up!"

We all knew that signing up for the hospital was the same as volunteering to be sent to the crematorium.

I wiped the blood from my nose with my sleeve and stepped out. I turned to Bela and said, "I've had enough. I'm getting in line to sign up."

Bela only nodded, and I turned to stand in the death line, praying that I was dead before I was thrown in the oven. After I signed my name and wrote down the number tattooed on my arm, I suddenly felt free. All of my struggles for survival were over. No more hunger, no more beatings, and no more cold. I had never felt more at peace as felt at that moment.

After the signing was over, the sick were marched forward. I turned my head for one last look at my sister and saw that the capo was cutting off a large group from the end of the line with all the girls from Radom and marched them towards us. Daylight was braking through the heavy clouds. I strained my head trying to spot my sister and only saw Tusia. She always huddled next to Bela, but I saw no sign of Bela. Just before we were marched inside a large nearby building, I spotted Bela huddling around the bend behind the building. When the capo wasn't looking I stepped out of line and ran to my sister. "There's no place to hide. If the capo finds you, she will beat you without mercy. It will be worse than death," I pleaded.

"Every night there are bigger and louder explosions. I can't die now. We are too close to freedom," she argued and stood tenaciously as if trying to be one with the wall.

"Bela, please, look around. If I saw you, the capo will surely find you and beat you."

"No, I won't let them take me. The Russians are around the corner. I won't let them kill me now," she cried and shrunk her body against the cement wall.

I hunched my shoulders and walked as fast as I could, trying not to draw attention to Bela's hiding place. I followed the herd to the slaughter while praying that my sister lived to tell the world, if there was a world left.

Inside the building were three layers of bunk beds. I was certain that it was the hospital, the waiting place, next in line to the crematorium. We were ordered to undress and leave our dresses on a table next to the open door. As I placed the wet dress I had washed yesterday on the table, I saw Bela being pushed through the door by a capo, and I was grateful that she wasn't hurt.

Bela inched over to me and whispered, "There's no place to hide."

We were lined up and given a small piece of soap and lead into a large shower room. Holding the piece of soap in my hand, my eyes rested on the rows of showerheads fastened to the low ceiling. Each day, Jews from all over Europe arrived in Auschwitz and all said, "There are no more Jews left in the Ghettos." I was thinking that the Russians must be very close, for the Germans are making sure that there are no witnesses left to tell the world of our demise, if there was world left. We never heard any news about any other parts of the world. I remembered the frightening voice blasting through Marmel the mustaches' window; "I'm not afraid of the entire world! England! America! Russia!" The Germans may have killed all the Russians, but I was certain that we were the last of the Jews to be murdered.

In our own thoughts, we stood at the shower door with Jewish woman from all over Europe with the knowledge that the end of our suffering was finally coming to an end. When we were ordered to get under the showerheads,

Bela and I stood huddled together under one showerhead. We closed our eyes waiting for gas to overtake us. I began breathing deeply, for wanted to be sure I was dead before I'm thrown in the oven.

Just as it seemed an eternity, and I was beginning to hyperventilate, cold water began gushing down from the ceiling.

"It's water!" Bela exclaimed.

"It's water!" the girls screamed from under the showerheads.

Though I was prepared to die, I was happy for my sister whose will to live was still strong. I began to scrub with the little piece of soap as if it were my last time to be clean. I rinsed my shoes under the shower and put them back on. After the shower, we were given another worn out dress and marched to the room with the bunk beds.

The blood from my teeth and nose was beginning to dry up. The left side of my face was burning. My nose was throbbing. I felt as if my head was growing. I'm not sure if I fell asleep or passed out. I'm not sure if it was night or the next morning when the whistle blew. We were rushed through another door and lined up in front of a girl sitting in the middle of a pile of shoes. She looked at my shoes and asked me to take them off and throw them on the right on top of other torn shoes. She threw a pair of wooden shoes from Holland towards me. I carried potato sacks of these shoes on my shoulder in AFL, and I ran up and down three flights of stairs. I knew that wearing these shoes with the sharp edges on my frozen, lacerated, inflamed feet would be agony, and it showed on my face. I picked up my torn, old shoes and attempted to put them back on.

"My feet are too cut up, I won' be able to keep up," I muttered.

The pain of more than five years of misery and the last beating must have shown on my ravished face. The girl told me to leave the old shoes and threw a pair of old, but not torn leather shoes towards me. The shoes were two sizes too large. I was so use to feeling the ground with my bare feet that wearing these wonderful shoes was as if I were liberated. We were shoved out into a blizzard to a train station and loaded into a boxcar.

Chapter Twenty-Eight: Willischtahl by Sakson

I can't be certain how long we were sitting or standing on the floor in the boxcar, listening to the sound of the train's engine and the glorious sounds of gunfire, for I had been in and out of consciousness. I heard everything that was happening around me. I knew that my sister was near me, but I felt as if my head was too large for my body, and I didn't have the strength to carry it on my neck.

It was raining and hailing when the train came to a full stop, and the door opened. I stood dazed, looking at four women in SS uniform holding umbrellas over their heads, and listened to the shrill shouts, "Rous! Rous! Alle rous!" Bela jumped off the train and held out her hands for me, then Tusia. As I jumped off the train, though I had landed on my feet, it felt as if I had landed on my head, so severe was the pain.

We lined up and rushed through clean, wide, paved streets and stopped in front of very steep stairs. We were ordered to walk down about twenty cement stairs and lined up in front a barracks in military fashion.

A tall gaunt SS woman placed herself in front of us and shouted, "Haftlinger! (detainees) You are in Willyschtall by Sakson! In Germany! I am your Oberster (highest) Supervisor!"

After what I had lived through up until now, nothing should have frightened me, but the child in me still remembered Aunt Hanna's frightening stories when she didn't want me to leave her house at night and get hurt by Polish boys. Even the emaciated bodies in Blizyn and Auschwitz, dying at my feet on the appellplatz, hadn't frightened me as that woman had. Although I was alive and her voice was as powerful as her whip, her face resembled a Halloween mask of an angry skeleton head with big teeth. When she began to bellow, her teeth looked as sharp as the dog's teeth that chased us in the Blizyn cage. My chest tightened, and I barely breathed. I believe I took my first real breath when she shielded herself from the gusty winds and rain under the barracks awnings, and the lower ranking SS women took over. After the counting was over, an SS woman bellowed, "You will be answering loud, to the tattoo number on your arm only!" She pointed to the first girl in line. I couldn't remember when it was that we had anything to eat. The rain was so strong that it had filled the girl's mouth with water as she gathered her strength to shout out each number, and the SS woman shouted, "louder!"

The frightened girl raised her voice and called out her numbers, for we had memorized our tattoos.

By the time it was my turn to shout my number, the cold rain coming down on my head numbed the pain, and I gathered all of my strength and sounded off "A-15791."

It was dark by the time we were lined up facing the barracks and given a piece of bread at the door and allowed inside.

"Inside the barracks were two warm rooms. The main room was large with tri-level bunk beds as in AFL. An iron oven, red with heat, stood against the wall in the center. The room on the far end was small. In between the two rooms was a washroom with floor drainage. Small washbasins were lined up on wooden benches. A faucet with running, cold water protruded from the wall. On top of a roaring fire stood a large round clay tub capable holding six buckets of water. The tub was filled to capacity. The night bucket was also in the washroom, and everyone lined up to use it.

Bela chose the upper two bunks in the large room, and I followed her up. We peeled off our wet dresses and hung them on the edge of our bunks.

We sat naked on the bare boards, but the room was warm, and my head didn't hurt as much until I bit into my piece of bread. One hand flew up and held tight the left side of my face. I put my bread down and placed my other palm tightly on my mouth. Hunger soon won over pain. I tore off very small pieces of bread and tried to find a less painful side to chew on. Though my teeth were bleeding, I paid no attention until I finished the piece of bread and curled up on the board.

It seemed as if I had just closed my eyes when the morning whistle blew.

My dress was still damp when I put it on, but not wet; though, it didn't matter, for I could hear the rain falling on the flimsy roof. My head was still throbbing, but not as bad yesterday. Each of us receive a soup bowl and a spoon, and the house elder, a very pleasant, middle-aged lady poured a ladle of hot, black ersaz coffee in our bowl. I had never had ersaz or regular coffee before, and I didn't know what to expect and took a big gulp of the brew. My mouth contorted from the bitter taste, and I ran to the washroom and spilled the rest down the drain. I rinsed out the bowl, for we were told that the bowl and spoon were ours for our afternoon soup.

Before we were chased outside to be counted, we were ordered to leave our shoes at the door, and we were handed a pair of wooden shoes. These shoes had wooden soles and canvas tops with shoelaces. The shoes were comfortable, and my feet didn't cramp from the cold. We were counted by a light bulb hanging on a black wire from our barracks awning.

The SS women stood at attention in front of us. Every hair was in place, the boots sparkled, and the little hats were tilted to one side, shielded by the umbrellas. We were counted by one of the SS women. When she finished, she handed a piece of paper with the count to Skeleton Head, for that name was befitting for her.

Another SS woman shouted our Auschwitz number tattooed on our arm, and each of us identified ourselves. For many years our only identity was our number.

By the time the counting was over, it had stopped raining, and the sky had turned from black to gray.

It was a short march to a large factory. As we entered the factory, Skeleton Head handed to each of us a hairnet. "You must always wear the hairnet, or you'll be severely punished, she shouted.

Bela was assigned to work with a very large machine. She appeared dwarfed in front of the massive machine.

I was chosen with a group of four girls to stand in front of a table in a small room and test a piece of metal with another piece of metal. We were named, "the five little ones from the control."

Civilian German men and women worked at another table, only five feet from us. They glanced at us from time to time, but not a word was uttered.

We were given rectangular metal plates the size of a large palm. The plate had a rectangular opening in the middle. We were also given a metal rod. Our job was to push the rod through the opening on the plate and make sure that it fit. If the opening was too tight we had to file it until it fit. Although I had no idea what I was doing, it didn't take long before I found out that it was an ammunition factory. As I looked around the many different departments, I saw that our group was the only group kept as prisoners. There were other nationalities, and none had our frightened hungry look. We were not allowed to speak to each other or anyone. Even looking over our shoulders was dangerous. Our eyes had to be focused on the work. It was the same throughout our internment. We were not allowed to ask questions or say anything to our captors. We were not allowed to speak to each other at any time, except in our barracks after we were locked up.

Our group, the five little ones from the control, always worked the day shift. Bela was assigned alternate shifts. In comparison to Bela's work, mine was child's play.

SS woman Anna had been assigned to police our group. Anna was the prettiest of the four. She was in her late twenties or early thirties. She had very bright, blond, ear-length, pin-curl tight curls. She tried hard to be mean, but she was always too sleepy. She would raise her voice and shout, "Schnell! Schnell!" A moment later, she would stand against the wall, her eyes closed. Then, she slowly lowered herself to the floor, her chin pressing against her chest.

Monday through Saturday, day after day, we waited for our piece of bread after the evening appell and the ladle of soup at midday. Sunday was a real feast. In our soup bowl, instead of soup, we were given three boiled potatoes in the skins and a scoop of cottage cheese. On warm days, we sat outside on the ground, our backs against the barrack's wall and feasted on our Sunday bounty. On one such occasion, Bela announced, "If by some miracle, we survive this hell, we should choose once year, a Sunday to celebrate, by eating only potatoes in the skins and cottage cheese," and everyone agreed.

Our second pleasures were the nightly sounds of the air aids followed by sounds of explosions. Since we weren't in Poland anymore, we didn't know which country was throwing the bombs. But as long as the bombs were falling, we held on to a glimmer of hope. On such nights, Skeleton Head would come in our barracks and called us children. "Children," she would say, "the German Reich is winning the war. When the war is over, I'll make sure that you will get better housing and plenty of food to eat. We Germans will take very good care of you!" As soon as the air raid was over and the bombing stopped, she called us every ugly name and locked us in.

Although Skeleton Head often paid her nightly visits to our barracks, the house elder looked the other way as we took chances to fill our basins with warm water for our bath. Most of the time, she stood with her back turned towards the lower bunk, teary eyes listening as her daughter was being sexually molested by one of the SS woman.

The SS woman must have known the whereabouts of her superior, for she never got caught in our barracks. She wasn't on top of the girl on the night I was in the washroom with four other girls. Just as I began washing my hair, Skeleton Head stormed in and dipped a bony finger in each basin. She became enraged when she felt the warm water. One by one she grabbed each basin spilling the warm water down the drain and filled it with ice-cold water from the faucet. With the rage of a rabid dog, she threw the icy water at each girl and screamed, "Get out."

The girls ran dripping from the washroom as if chased by volcanic lava, leaving me for last. While I stood defenselessly, waiting for her to empty my basin and hit me with the ice water, Skeleton Head stood looking at me for what it seemed an eternity. By now, I was certain she would slice her whip on my bare back to set an example. When she spilled my warm water down the drain and filled the basin with icy water, I stiffened in preparation for the shock of the ice water. My eyes must have been enormous when I saw Skeleton Head place the basin with cold water on the bench in front of me. She placed her hands on my back "Cold water is good for you, child," she said soothingly.

I was so frightened of her touch and closeness that when she finally ambled away from me and left our barracks, I took my first breath. By the time I climbed up on my bunk, I was hyperventilating and passed out. I dreamed that I was in Blizyn Concentration Camp, running from a German shepherd. Suddenly, the dog's face was Skeleton Head's face. As the enormous teeth were about to devour me, the wake-up whistle sounded. I opened my eyes and jumped off my bunk as if running for my life.

I was glad that it was Sunday, and Bela's shift was changing to the day shift. I felt whole knowing that my sister would be close, and we would be together at night until the next Sunday.

After the morning appell, Bela was told that Skeleton Head ordered all the girls working with the large machines to sleep in the back room.

From the first day, all of Bela's friends had been sleeping in the back room. I was happy for my sister. She needed to be with her friends. Had I had friends, I too would have liked being in the same room. The friends I had before the war weren't Jewish, and the friends I had during the war were too young to work, and they were shipped out with their parents when the Ghetto was liquidated. The last four years I clung to my sister as if she were my only life support. When she told me that she was moving to the room where all of her friends, especially Rusty, were, I wondered, for only a moment, if it was really an order from Skeleton Head. I quickly pushed the doubt from my mind, for I knew that, although Bela would like to interact with her friends, she wouldn't lie to me. Bela put her arms around me, "Don't worry; it's not as if we were in different barracks or different concentration camps. You can visit me any time."

"Don't worry about me. I'm not a child anymore," I said, feeling a lump in my throat and hoping she would leave quickly before she saw how I really felt. As soon as Bela left her bunk next to mine, I had never felt more alone. I pressed my face onto my bunk board and cried silently. I didn't want the Rojal family to hear me sob and feel sorry for me. Mrs. Rojal and her three daughters were lucky enough to have stayed together, and I was lucky that their bunks were directly beneath my bunk.

Ida was the oldest sister, Renia, the middle, and Lusia the youngest. All of the three Rojal sisters went to Maria Konopnicka School, and Lusia was in the same class with me. Lusia and I played together after school, and we had finished the fourth grade on June 1939. From the beginning, we were together in every camp. Only now, the three sisters clung to their mother, and there was no room for anyone else.

Mrs. Rojal worked in the kitchen, and at night, I watched her throw potatoes on the fire in the iron oven. Like little birds, the three girls sat on their mother's bunk, and Mrs. Rojal divided the stash evenly among her children.

Once, on a Saturday night, Mrs. Rojal gave me a hot potato. I cut the precious gift with my spoon and ran to Bela's room. I climbed up on her bunk and gave her half of the small potato, leaving my piece on my bunk. I didn't want her to see that my piece of potato was smaller than the one I gave her. I wanted to stay a little longer, but I didn't want to get caught by Skeleton Head and went back to my lonely bunk and ate my piece of potato.

Some nights after Skeleton Head made her surprise inspections and left, I visited Bela on her bunk, but I never stayed long. Bela was often in conversation with her friends, especially Rusty. I couldn't forgive Rusty for taking our piece of bread in Blyzin in exchange for a bowl of soup, especially when she had plenty, and Bela suffered from hunger pain. I couldn't understand why Bela didn't see what I saw. Days went by, and I had nobody to utter a word to, only whispers at the worktable when nobody was looking.

A week after the encounter in the washroom with Skeleton Head, I was standing at the worktable with the other four girls running the rod though the slot.

Suddenly, I flinched when I felt a hand on my shoulder. I turned my head, and Skeleton Head was standing in back of me.

"Come," she said, gripping my shoulder and guided me towards the door. I was sure she was going to punish me, and I tried to think of what I had done to cause the trouble I was in. I could feel her hand tighten on my bony shoulder as she opened and closed the door to the small room. She pointed to a small table in a corner of the main, very large room. "Sit," she said, pulling out a round wooden stool next to the little table. A small lamp with a bare light bulb set on top of the table, though the room had plenty of lights. There were the same rectangular pieces of metal cut out in the center for me to run the metal rod through and make sure that it fit. The way her hand lingered on my shoulder made my hair rise up from my scalp. I couldn't ask her why she singled me out to be alone in the corner of the main room? We were not allowed to speak, but she looked pleased, as if she had done something special for me. I was beginning to think that I was destined to be alone and lonely.

Everyday, Tusia was a little weaker until she was unable to stand at the work place and was taken to a small room next to our barracks that had been converted to a four-bed hospital. One of our inmates was taking care of the sick. I wasn't sure if she was a nurse or only a caretaker. It didn't matter since there was no doctor or medicine at all. There were no crematoriums in Wilischtall, and the sick had a chance to live a little longer, though the threat of being murdered was on everyone's mind. Sunday, Bela and I saw Tusia, and it broke our hearts to see a pretty young girl turn into a shriveled up child. As Bela cajoled her to eat a few spoonfuls of soup, Tusia looked at my sister with enormous brown eyes, "When I could eat, I had no food. Now, I don't want the little food I'm given," she muttered.

"Do you hear the explosions every night? Soon the war will be over. With medical help, you'll get well," Bela soothed, running her hand over Tusia's damp face.

"If only I could live to see freedom, then I wouldn't mind dying," Tusia said, as a single tear spilled from her eye.

As I was leaving the hospital room, the nurse stopped me. "How would you like to work here and be my helper?" she asked.

From the very beginning of the occupation, I had learned that it was not safe to be sick, especially being in a hospital. What if the Gestapo or SS would come to murder the sick? I too could be a target, just by being inside.

"I can't," I said and stepped out.

Bela and I climbed up on my bunk, and we couldn't stop our tears from rolling down our faces. Although, I hadn't forgotten Tusia's name-calling for removing her pot of soup from the stove to heat some water for Bela's stomach pain at the AFL and for trying to put me to shame in Blizyn when she saw me kiss Moniek on the cheek for bringing me wonderful news of my sister's recovery from typhus, I felt great pain to see her so gravely ill. I wished with all my heart that we would be liberated, and our saviors would bring with them magical medicine to make her well.

Amidst the hunger and fear, we managed to entertain ourselves. The group in our barracks housed Jewish females from several countries, but in 1945 everyone spoke German. At night after we were locked up but before lights out, we tried to bring a little cheer to our morbid existence. Some girls danced, some sang, and I wrote and recited poetry. In rhyme, I described Skeleton Head's face, her evil demeanor, and the way she pushed herself on a civilian German gentleman. He was a tall thin middle-aged man who worked in the small room. At lunchtime, he always sat at a table close to the entrance and ate his lunch, usually a sandwich. Skeleton Head often pranced in, spread the man's legs apart, and pressed her pelvis against him while pulling his buttocks tightly towards herself. The man tried hard to pull away from her, but she wouldn't let him go until his lunch hour was over. After I wrote a poem, I quickly memorized it and burned it in the heating oven. I hated to think what my punishment would have been had she found it, and she would know that her secretary, one of our girls, supplied us with scraps of paper and broken pencils.

Our barracks had no windows, but we listened for Skeleton Head's unexpected nightly inspections. She would come in our barracks during an air raid and call us children. "Children, the German Reich is winning the war. The entire world will soon belong to the Reich! I will make sure that you will all get better housing and more food!" she shouted happily. After the all-clear sound, she would leave and lock us up. On other nights when there were no air raids, she would sneak up on us, and if she caught a group of girls standing and talking, the whip would be flying in the air and land on the back of the slowest runner. Just before she locked us up again, she called us every profane name in the German language, and there are many. She threatened us with shaving our heads, twenty-five lashes, and smaller food rations. As much as we listened for her footsteps, she often managed to sneak up on us and make our lives a living hell.

I knew that Bela had the day shift that week, but I didn't see her on the evening appellplatz. As we lined up for our bread ration, I figured that she was first in line and was resting in the small room. As I climbed up on my bunk, I was surprised to see her on the bunk next to mine. Seeing her red swollen eyes, I thought Tusia had died, for Bela had become very fond of her.

"Is Tusia all right? I asked.

She raised her shoulders. "I didn't see her since last Sunday," she said in barely audible voice.

After pleading with her to tell me why she was crying, she tried unsuccessfully to blink the tears away and whimpered, "If they shave off my hair, I'll commit suicide."

My empty stomach turned into a knot and my throat felt tight, as if someone was choking me from inside. "Bela, please don't talk about suicide. Tell me what's wrong?"

"My machine broke down, and I'm accused of sabotage," she gasped.

In case the answer would be "yes," I was afraid to ask if she sabotaged the machine, but something didn't sound right to me. I knew that I wasn't smart because all my life, though my report cards were always a hundred percent, my siblings called me stupid. I also knew that one didn't have to be smart to know that the Germans wouldn't just tell her that her hair would be shaved off for sabotaging an ammunition machine. She would be put to death for much less. I looked at my sister's beautiful blond waves that had grown back since Auschwitz and realized that the SS women were envious, especially Skeleton Head. Her bleached hair was dry and wispy. On Sundays, when we sat in the sun on the ground against the barracks wall enjoying our potato and cottage cheese feast, Skeleton Head and her lackeys would stand around watching us eat and lick the spoon clean. We didn't have to wear our hairnets in our barracks, and from the corner of my eye, I saw the SS women glare at Bela's hair as the sun brought out the golden luster in her waves. The same as at midday in the factory, all of the SS women stood around staring at us as we stood and devoured our ladle of soup, for there was no place for us to sit. One particular time, I found myself being watched as I licked the bowl clean and overheard one SS woman say to another, "She licks that bowl like a dog."

I remembered Mama's words, "The full belly is unable to understand the empty."

I was certain that Bela's hair wasn't going to be shaved off because of the machine. It was because of an excuse. They were always scrutinizing us, as if wondering from what planet we had come from. I could feel the resentment as Skeleton Head often looked at Bela's golden hair. I wished that I could take my sister's punishment. I wouldn't care if my brown hair would be shaved off. It broke my heart to see Bela cry. She always pretended to be tough. Even while her hair was being shaved off in Auschwitz, she had a smirk on her face. In Blyzin when she was getting twenty-five lashes for failing the test in basket weaving, she didn't cry. We stayed together on my bunk all night, holding onto each other, and cried ourselves to sleep. We stayed close to each other at the appellplatz, and afterwards, I didn't see my sister all day. I sat in my corner, running the metal rod through the opening on the rectangular piece of metal, and prayed that Skeleton Head would not stop in front of me. I was perspiring, my hands were shaking, and my stomach was burning. It was the longest day of my life. When we lined up for the evening appell I looked for Bela, but I didn't see her. My heart pounded so hard that I was afraid the SS women would hear it. After what seemed the longest appell, I ran into the barracks looking for Bela, but she was not on her bunk. I began to panic, asking every girl in the small room if she saw Bela today or at the appell. Finally, one girl broke her silence and told me that Bela was in the SS office. The SS office was located inside of our barrack next to the door.

I was about to knock on the door and beg Skeleton Head to let my sister go and take me instead. A girl pulled me back as I was beginning to turn the doorknob.

"You can't go in there," she whispered.

"I have to. Bela said she would kill herself if her hair gets shaved off again." I tried to loosen the girl's hold on me, but she was stronger. "Please let me go. I'll beg Skeleton Head to do whatever she wants with me. I'll offer myself instead. I don't care if my hair gets shaved off. I don't care if she gives me twenty-five lashes or as many as she wants, but not my sister. Please, let me go.

"You'll only cause more trouble for your sister and yourself. If Skeleton Head finds out that Bela has a sister, her punishment will be more severe. We are only known by our numbers, not our last names," the girl sighed.

Defeated, I sat down on the floor close to the door and vowed that if Bela committed suicide, so would I. I don't know how long I sat whimpering on the floor and having a silent argument with God. "Oh God," I whispered in anger. "Why does it always have to be my sister? I wouldn't care if my hair got shaved off, or if I got twenty five or fifty lashes on my back, or if I died this minute, but please, dear God, spare my sister. We only have each other; let me die, instead." Through my tears and an unfinished argument with God, I saw the door to the SS office opening, and Bela was shoved through it as if she had been discarded garbage.

For the third time in almost six years, my sister resembled a poor, skinny little boy. Although she was wearing a dress, her large, green almond-shaped eyes looked enormous and lifeless. She had always carried her head high, but not this time. Her spirit was broken, and I was desperately afraid that she would go through with her plan.

I tried to console her, but all she muttered was, "Please, Jadzia, I'm very tired. Let me go to my room."

I followed her, but she didn't look back. She climbed up on her bunk and stretched out, her arms folded behind her head, and she was looking up at the ceiling with vacant eyes. The bunk next to her was not occupied. I stretched out beside her and didn't care if Skeleton Head would catch me. Bela gave no indication as to whether or not she knew that I was close by until I whispered, "The war will soon be over, and your hair will grow back prettier than ever." When I saw tear drops flowing from her eyes onto the bunk board, I knew that she was listening, and I continued to talk, hoping to get her mind off suicide. I turned on my side to face her. "Please, Bela, listen to me. If we give up and let them see that we have stopped fighting for our lives, then they will be the winners, even if they lose the war. But if you don't give up, when the war is over, we'll catch the SS women, shave their ugly hair off, and dump their heads in the nearest outhouse, especially Skeleton Head. Can you picture her head covered with shit?"

"It would be an improvement," Bela grinned.

That was all I needed to hear. I reached out for her embrace, and we cried in each other's arms until we fell asleep.

In the middle of March 1945, air raids were nightly. Night after night we sat in the dark on our bunks and prayed for liberation, but we were afraid that as soon as our liberators would close in, we would be shipped out to a place with a crematorium.

Sunday morning, during the worst storm of the year, we were standing on the appellplatz to be counted. The wind whipped through our thin dresses, as if God finally woke up and was furious, but the guilty were not punished. All of the SS women were wearing boots and warm clothing, and they stood under the barrack's awnings to protect them from the cold rain and wind, while we, the innocent, stood shivering with only a thin dress and wooden shoes. We were counted and recounted. Our numbers were called out, and we all answered to them, except for one woman who did not answer to her number.

Skeleton Head repeated the number over and over, but the missing woman didn't raise her hand. We all turned our heads to see who was missing, for we knew everyone in our barracks. Suddenly, the girls began to whisper that Grandmother was missing. Grandmother couldn't have been more than forty years old when she came to work at AFL. She was old enough to be a grandmother and certainly old enough to be a mother to most of the girls at AFL, with the exception of Mrs. Rojal and Mrs. Luksenburg. The name, Grandmother, was befitting for her. Nobody knew her by any other name, and the woman, who looked much older than her years, liked being called 'Grandmother.' We were surprised that she would escape. Even if we had found a way to escape, there was no place to hide with our shabby dresses, wooden shoes, and tattoo numbers on our arms. We would stick out like branded cattle. All day, we stood at attention in the storm without food. I especially missed the Sunday potatoes in the skins and the cottage cheese.

At dusk, Grandmother was standing on top of the stairs between two SS women. The SS women gripped her thin arms and dragged her down the stairs as if she were a rag doll that a toddler would sweep the floor with. The SS women handed Grandmother over to Skeleton Head, and the appell was dismissed. We were allowed to get out of the rain, but not inside the barracks. We were marched inside a barn and forced to stand and look at Grandmother as she was ordered to take off her dress and climb into a long narrow basin attached to the wall. Skeleton Head snarled at Grandmother's emaciated body. The cold water added a green tint to her skin, and Skeleton Head howled at the shivering Grandmother, "You are filthy!" As I looked at Skeleton Head's face, I saw a demon. Her mouth was opened wide, and her lips spread to only a thin line. Her large teeth and gums looked larger than I had ever seen them. Her laugh sounded more like a wolf howling. She pulled several taller girls from line and handed the first one a bucket and ordered her to fill it with ice-cold water and throw the water at Grandmother. She handed a scrub brush to the next girl. It was the kind of brush one would use to scrub a floor, or heavy rugs. "Take that brush and scrub!" She shouted. Seeing that the girl wasn't scrubbing hard enough, she bellowed, "I said scrub hard until she is clean!" she barked as she took the brush away from the girl and pulled another girl from line. As she handed the brush to the second girl she shouted, "Scrub hard!" She picked more girls from line and ordered them to throw buckets of the freezing water on the shivering Grandmother and shouted for the girl to scrub harder.

Seeing Grandmother's blood roll down her back, Bela and I were unable to control our tears. I was glad when the familiar siren sounded, followed immediately by explosions.

Skeleton Head ordered the girls to pull Grandmother from the basin, and the SS women shooed us into our barracks and locked us up. We could hear running boots as if being chased.

As the days lingered on, hunger was becoming more and more unbearable. Some girls would sneak in the kitchen and steal potatoes they found on the floor or a rutabaga.

One Sunday in the beginning of April, I got up enough courage to sneak into the kitchen. The kitchen was located about twenty-thirty feet across from our barracks. I saw a rutabaga on the floor the size of an overgrown turnip. I picked it up and placed it under my dress, between my thighs. I had no underpants to hold it in place, so I had to balance myself as if walking a tightrope. With every step, I had to bend down and push up the slipping rutabaga. I finally made it to the barrack's door and found Skeleton Head in the doorway. My face felt as if on fire, and my heart pounded so hard that I was sure she knew what I had between my legs and would ask me to hand it over. I couldn't even think of what my punishment would be. Skeleton Head looked suspiciously at me but didn't move from the door. I felt the rutabaga sliding. A moment longer, and the rutabaga would pop to the floor. She touched my shoulder and stepped off the threshold. As she walked away, I could have sworn that I saw a smile on her face. I lifted the stolen treasure, which had slid down to my knees and went to the small room to get Bela.

Rusty saw me carrying the rutabaga and followed us to my bunk and sat down next to Bela, waiting for me to share. I had not forgotten that time in Blyzin when I humbly stood in her barrack looking hungrily at a mountain of bread portions and wondered what she was going to do with so much bread and bowls of soup. Had Rusty truly been Bela's friend, she would have given me the bowl of soup and not have taken our bread portion. Now, she had the nerve to ask for a piece of rutabaga, and Bela cut a large piece with her spoon and gave it to her. I never went against Bela's wishes, but I was very angry. I believe that I was angry with Bela for thinking that Rusty was her friend, but I didn't tell my sister how I felt.

Chapter Twenty-Nine: Goodbye Villischtal; Hello Theresienschtadt

After the morning appell, the end of April 1945, we were each given a loaf of bread and were told to line up to be shipped out to another camp.

With the now constant air raids and sounds of explosions, we knew that this would be our last stop. But where were they shipping us where there would be a crematorium?

I tried not to think of dying. Only a few months ago, when my head felt as if it weighed more than my body, from a capo's fist in Auschwitz, I wanted to die. Now that the end of the war was so near, it would have been a sin to die. I truly wanted to see if we were going to be put on display in a museum as Bela often jokingly said.

By the time, a truck picked us up to take us to a temporary camp, our loaf of bread was long gone. The truck dropped us off at a barracks, a short distance from Villischtal. The entire structure was constructed entirely of wooden boards inside and out. We were shooed up steep stairs to an attic. Two wooden pillars supported the low ceiling. The room consisted of a rectangular wooden table and benches on each side.

Groups from other camps had joined our group in the attic. Some of the girls in our group were united with childhood friends, giving us a glimmer of hope that our families might still be alive. Two hours later Skeleton Head opened the door and threw a loaf of bread in the air and disappeared. The hugging and camaraderie had taken second place, and the room had become a circus. Everyone was trying to get a hold of the bread, but no one held it in her hand very long. I too grabbed the loaf of bread from a girl's hand. There wasn't much left of the loaf. Each time a girl grabbed the bread from someone's hand it became a tug of war, and the bread crumbled. I was chased around the pillars with dozens of outstretched hands reaching for the bread, and I didn't get a chance to hold on to it very long. Within minutes the wood floor was covered with crumbs, and nobody ate a single bite.

Late afternoon, we were lined up and marched to the train station where a boxcar awaited us. We were lined up in orderly fashion, and each of us was given a little cloth sack, filled with about two or three tablespoons of sugar, and ordered to climb inside.

We all sat on the floor holding the little sack of sugar as if our lives depended on it. The boxcar slammed shut, and again, we were on our way to a place unknown, listening to the sound of "tapacatapaca tapaca...."

Tusia sat motionless against the wall, clutching the little sack with sugar. Her eyes were the size of large black cherries, deeply imbedded in her gaunt colorless face.

Bela sat next to her. "Don't give up," she cajoled. "Do you hear the gunfire?"

Tusia nodded.

"You can't give up now, Tusia. You said you wanted to see freedom. You will, if you don't give up." Bela untied Tusia's sack and held it up to her mouth. "Take a lick; it will give you strength to hold on."

Tusia shook her head, "I can't," she murmured, her breath shallow. Every few minutes, Bela tried to get her to open her mouth, but she refused.

I don't know how long we were in transit. The train had stopped several times because of air raids and bombing. With each air raid, we were locked up inside the boxcar, and through the cracks, I saw our SS women and other people on the train run to shelters.

Our sugar was long gone when the train came to a final stop. The door opened and gaunt men in striped prison uniforms helped us out of the train.

Dazed, I looked up at a large sign that read, "Theresienschtadt."

As two men transferred Tusia to a stretcher, Tusia held out her little sack with sugar and gave it to Bela, and the men began to run with her. I saw Bela holding Tusia's sack of sugar and told her that it wasn't right for her to keep it. Bela hesitated a moment, then ran alongside the stretcher and put the sugar in Tusia's hand.

As we were marched through the double gate, I saw the four SS women standing outside of the gates looking at us from a distance. Then, they turned away and disappeared. I had forgotten about revenge, as we were marched to a large structure with several equally large rooms. Our room looked as if it had once been a hospital ward. It was lined with narrow iron beds, thin mattresses, pillows, and covers. We hadn't seen such luxury in many years. There was also a wood burning stove and windows on each side of a mantelpiece. A large old clock stood on top of the mantelpiece.

Bela and I chose our beds and stretched out. My stomach was growling, but when I saw my sister massaging her stomach, I couldn't watch one more minute. It was breaking my heart. Why didn't I let her keep Tusia's sugar? She wouldn't eat it, anyway. She's probably already dead. I was so angry with myself that I was unable to rest. I got up and walked out of the room and saw men and women, resembling shadows, standing in line and walking away with a bowl of watery soup. I ran back to our room and told the girls what I saw, and within two seconds, the room was empty. I stood in line behind my sister and saw that her neck had broken out in large boils. Her hair had only grown in about two inches, and it was easy to see the lesions that had wrapped around her neck like a choker. After we drank our soup, I went with Bela to the infirmary where a nurse put some ointment and bandages around her neck.

Hungry, we lay in darkness, listening to gunfire. The welcome sound had become a lullaby. I awakened the next morning to a quiet room. It was the first time in many years that we were not ordered to stand on the appellplatz to be counted. No whistles were blowing, and no whips were cracking at our bunks to wake us up. It had been a very long time since I woke up and was greeted by the morning sunlight and listened to the sounds of chirping birds. Out of habit, as I did from the very first day since Bela and I had been torn from our home, I turned my head to make sure that my sister was in the next bed. This morning my eyes squinted in the sunlight as I looked towards Bela's bed and saw that it was empty. She was an early riser, and I was hoping that she was standing in line for some food. I put on my wooden shoes and left the room. I didn't see Bela or a food line. I was standing on the wooden porch searching the grounds. I saw a group of gaunt men in a heated conversation, as if trying to solve all of our problems. I was hungry for the slightest bit of news. I walked down the stairs and inched myself over towards the men.

"The crematorium is almost finished," I heard one man whisper worriedly.

"The Russians are at our doorsteps. We can't let them kill us now," another man whispered.

I was reminded of the time when the German's took over our town. I often watched my tata and his friends whisper about the Russians being at our doorsteps. In the meantime, my tata and his friends and my entire family disappeared, and men were still talking about the Russians being at our doorsteps. My stomach was caving in from hunger, and I wandered away. I had no idea where I was going. As I kept walking, I didn't see a single German, though I knew that they had to have been around; otherwise, why would the men be talking about crematoriums? Why wouldn't they open the gates and walk out? Lightheaded with hunger, I continued to walk. Suddenly, I was strolling in the midst of a lush garden taking highly scented breaths of flowers.

I hadn't seen such beauty since my tata had nurtured our garden when we lived in Penc house. The garden in Therasianschtadt was artfully nurtured with rows of roses of every color. Tulips, daffodils, and countless shrubs and flowers. I didn't know the names. I took off my wooden shoes and rolled on top of high green grass that had been warmed by the sun. I had forgotten about food. My mind went back to the time when I was a child, and the time when we rolled on the warm grass near the river, and Bela was tumbling, turning cartwheels and walking on her hands. Feeling the sun on my face, I closed my eyes, and I was sure that I had died and went to heaven, even though I hadn't converted. I opened my eyes and saw Bela riding towards me on a child's bike. It had been the first time in six years that I saw Bela laugh, as she paddled the little bicycle. Seeing my sister so carefree, I was more convinced that I was in heaven. She put the little bike on the side of the strolling path and stretched out next to me. We rolled on the grass as if we were toddles. Just as I was thinking about how much I liked heaven, Bela pressed a hand to her bandaged neck and cried out in pain. I stood up and saw people shuffling towards the food line. I urged Bela to get up and get in line. We stood in the long line, and it was dusk by the time it was our turn. It took us less than a minute to drink the ladle of watery soup. I went with Bela to the infirmary to have her bandages changed, and we went to sleep listening to our growling stomachs.

Though Theresienschtadt had beautiful gardens, one thing was a certainty; each day that we remained in here brought us closer to death. Our only hopes were the nightly explosions.

Chapter Thirty: May 10, 1945

I woke up at dawn and listened for explosions. Instead, I heard the sound of birds calling to each other. I grew up listening to harsh angry German shouts, sounds of whistles blowing, whips banging against bunks, and daily gunfire. It was dangerous to listen to the wonders of nature. I was Jewish, and I didn't deserve such pleasant sound.

Suddenly, I heard footsteps and voices coming from outside the door, getting closer and louder. I turned my head and saw that Bela's bed was empty. I panicked as I remembered yesterday and the group of whispering man about a crematorium.

"The Russians are here! The Russians are here...!" a man shouted.

I quickly put on my wooden shoes and ran outside to stand on the porch and look for Bela. I didn't see her. Groups of emaciated men stood on the grass, at the gate, and on the porch. Large eyes were deeply sunken in bony cheekbones, as though the flash had been neatly scraped from beneath the skin. The exposed ears on each side of the shaven heads looked enormous. The striped prison uniforms hung on bony bodies, as if hanging on wooden hangers. They shouted, "The Russians are here...!" I turned my head to the left and saw an image in the glass door. I hadn't seen my reflection in a very long time. I brought my hand up to my bony face and saw that the image I was looking at with horror was my own.

And so, we all stood around, still entangled in the German web. Such were the remains of human beings, stripped of all possessions, family, and dignity.

I spotted Bela at the gate and ran down to warn her. "Bela, this could be a trick. Yesterday, I overheard a group of men talking about a crematorium that is almost finished."

Bela put her arm around me and pulled me over to the gate. "See for yourself. The Russians are here!" she shouted over the noisy crowed.

The red flags on each motorcar quivered in the breeze, and the Russian soldiers, wearing the same uniforms we had assorted in AFL, shouted with pride. Arms waved from tanks, trucks, and motorcycles.

Bela was now anxious to see if Tusia lived to see freedom? We ran to the hospital and stumbled over people lying on the floor side by side. Some were moaning; others didn't move. A nurse was sitting at a small table writing on a note pad by a dim light bulb. "You shouldn't be here. We have typhus," she said in the Russian language, but we were able to understand most of what she said.

"We would like to know if Tusia Rosenbaum is here? She had tuberculosis," Bela added in the Polish language, and the nurse understood us.

"I'm sorry, but she died this morning," the nurse said sadly and looked surprised when she saw us looking happy.

"You see," Bela said. "She lived through the entire war with the disease, and all she asked for was to see freedom."

"Well, she did see freedom because I was here when she died," the nurse said.

Though the Germans were gone, we lined up for the same watery soup, and nobody came around with bread. Russian soldiers drove by the camp, waved, and drove away.

Bela went to visit her friends, two doors from our room. I stretched out on my bed and felt something warm between my legs. I pulled away the covers and saw other girls doing the same thing. We all got our periods at the same time. We never knew why we stopped having periods on the day we were camped in, and now, we didn't know why every girl began bleeding on the first day we were liberated. I tore off the corner from my sheet to stop the flow and went looking to find a shower room. Now that the Germans were out, I wasn't afraid to roam and found myself in a windowless room, lit only by a dim light bulb. A well fed girl sat behind a counter talking to a man standing in an oven pit, feeding wood to a roaring fire in a hearth. The cavity resembled a baker's oven, the same as in my tata's bakery. I had been conditioned not to ask questions, nor speak to anyone in authority, and I never asked why he was standing in the pit feeding the bakery oven since I didn't see anyone kneading dough. It would have been wonderful, I thought, if he was feeding the cavity with loafs of bread. The flow was beginning to break through the piece of cloth, and I chanced to ask the girl where I could find a shower room, and she pointed to the next room. I found a piece of soap inside the shower room and stepped under warm water. I stood lathering for a long time, as if I was trying to wash away years of pain and suffering. I returned to the girl at the counter with my dress in my hand, ignoring the man in the oven pit who was gazing at my naked body and winked at the girl.

I whispered to the girl about my period, and she gave me a pair of old but clean underpants and several rags. I went back to the shower room and put on the underpants and inserted the rag the way Mama had showed me four years ago, and I wished I had a clean dress, but the girl didn't offer. She took away my wooden shoes and gave me a pair of old leather shoes with shoelaces.

Bela was in our room when I returned with wet hair, and I showed her my leather shoes and told her where I got them. "You, too, can get shoes, I'll take you there," I said excitedly.

"I want to try on yours," she said.

I took off my shoes and handed them to her. After she tried them on, she said, "I like them. They fit me very nicely. I'll give you my wooden shoes for yours," she said.

"You can get your own, but we can share these," I said. "When you are outside, you can wear them. When I'm outside, I'll wear them."

Bela took on a hurt look on her face and left the room.

It had been the first time since we were separated from our family that I didn't do as she asked, and I was feeling very guilty for not letting her keep the shoes. I certainly didn't mind wearing the wooden shoes. When I offered them to her later that day, she refused to take them, and I couldn't forgive myself for being so selfish. That night, on the first day of our liberation, I wasn't hungry when I went to sleep, and I didn't care if I never woke up. But I did wake up at dawn to the sound of loud footsteps. Three Russian soldiers stormed into our room, shouting for watches. "Give us all your watches." Two lower ranking soldiers followed a tall soldier with medals on his uniform, and all three soldiers bellowed in unison. "Give us watches!"

I pulled the cover over my head and lay perfectly still as shouts for watches continued. It was apparent to me that the Russian soldiers didn't know that we had been prisoners in German Concentration Camps. Had they been informed, they would know that we were all starved and had no belongings, much less watches.

A soldier pulled the cover from my face and must have thought that I was dead.

He quickly threw the cover back on my face and continued shouting for watches.

I quietly removed the cover from my eyes and saw a soldier remove the old clock from the mantle piece. He placed the clock on his right wrist and held it securely with his left hand. He bent his head and placed his ear on top of the clock and listened to the ticking. "I have a watch!" he howled joyfully. The other two soldiers followed him out the door, taking turns listening to the ticking.

Afraid that other soldiers would come, we all quickly vacated the room.

I was standing at the gate and saw girls getting on motorcycles with Russian Soldiers and returning unharmed with bread and pork. I saw a girl from our room getting off a motorcycle. She was holding a package under her arm. I asked her if it was safe to get on a motorcycle with the soldiers, and her answer was, "yes."

"Did he give you bread?" I asked again, and the answer was again, "Yes."

I stood outside the open gate, hoping that a passing motorcycle would stop and give me bread.

Jeeps and motorcycles only slowed down, but none had stopped. Just as I decided to go back to my room and lay down, a middle-age soldier on a motorcycle stopped in front of me.

"Do you have bread?" I asked in my Polish language.

"Yes, get in, and I'll give you bread," he answered, partly Polish and partly Russian. The soldier looked older than my tata, and I didn't think he would harm me.

He'll give me some bread and bring me back. With that thought in mind, I jumped up on the motorcycle behind him.

"Hold on tight, or you'll fall off," he said as he sped away.

A jeep carrying two soldiers and two pretty blond Czechoslovakian girls appeared parallel with the motorcycle. A conversation was going on between my soldier and the two soldiers in the jeep. Although the Polish language is similar to the Russian language, I could only understand words, and I was unable to figure out what was said in the conversation. They did laugh a lot, and so did the two girls. I looked back and saw that the camp had disappeared from sight. I panicked, for I was afraid that I wouldn't be able to find my way back. Just as I was getting ready to jump off the speeding motorcycle, my soldier made a left turn into a park and was followed in by the jeep. He turned off the engine and told me to get off.

I suddenly became very nervous. "Can you give me some bread now, and I'll go back?" I asked pleadingly.

"Not now," he said, as he began spreading out a blanket on the grass.

Growing up in Concentration Camps, I was very naive, but my instinct told me to be wary. I looked over my shoulder to where the two soldiers were stretched out on a blanket, each next to a blond girl, passing a bottle and laughing. I suddenly realized that he was not about to give me bread and send me on my way. My soldier looked towards his friends and told me to sit on the blanket. My heart was pounding, and I begged him again to give me a piece of bread and let me go.

"Sit!" he said. His sharp voice told me to obey, and with great reluctance, I sat down. He placed a small package of ham on the blanket next to a loaf of bread, which I could have eaten all by myself. He broke off a piece of bread and a sliver of ham and gave it to me. I held the morsel of food close to my mouth, but I didn't eat it. When he wasn't looking, I stuffed the food in the sleeve of my dress and was grateful that the sleeve had elastic. He removed a full quart bottle of vodka from his motorcycle and held it to my mouth. "Drink!" he ordered.

"I'm not thirsty; I'm hungry. Please give me some bread, and I'll go back," I pleaded.

He gave me another piece of bread, and again, I pretended to eat and quickly shoved it in my sleeve.

"No, you can't go now. First, you drink; then, you can go!" he shouted as he tilted the bottle against my teeth. The force from the bottle against my gums was too painful, and I felt the vodka burn my throat all the way down to my empty stomach. I looked across to the two soldiers with the blond girls and remembered seeing myself in the glass door and wondered why he chose me. Next to the two girls on the blankets, I looked like a starved ten-year old. I knew that I had to get away now, or I'll end up under the soldier the same way as the two blondes did and seemed to enjoy themselves.

"Please let me go. You can have the beautiful, healthy girls," I begged.

"If you don't like the blanket we can go in the jeep," he said.

"I want to go back. My sister is sick, and she will worry," I pleaded.

"No! I gave you food. Now, you have to stay with me!" he shouted, holding on to my waist and gulping down vodka.

While he was drinking the vodka, I loosened from his grip and stood up feeling as if the park was moving, but a little voice inside my head told me not to let him pull me down again. Just as I was beginning to take small steps towards the park's entrance, he griped my arm and stood up holding onto me.

"Please," I pleaded, "I'm only sixteen. I have to go back to my older sister. You said that you'd give me bread and let me go. Please let me go now."

"How old did you say you are?"

I was hoping that he didn't hear me the first time and said, "I'm twelve."

He circled his arm around my waist and guided me towards the jeep.

Suddenly, I saw my entire life wasted for a piece of bread and wiggled out of his grip.

"Please let me go. I'm only a child. If you have a daughter, you wouldn't want anyone hurting her," I cried.

He pointed his rifle at me, and I was sure he was going to shoot, and Bela would never know what happen to me, and I didn't care. I would prefer to die by his bullet than be disgraced. My only regret was that I didn't give her my shoes when she asked for them. I continued to walk towards the gate. Five feet from the gate, I turned my head and saw his rifle pointing at my back. The soldier shouted, "Stop, or I'll shoot!"

I continued to walk, but I quickened my step. After I passed through the park's gate, I allowed myself a first breath. The gulp of vodka that the soldier had forced down my throat made my head feel heavier than my entire body. Now, I had the chore of finding my way back to camp and give Bela the bread and the sliver of ham. I remembered that he was driving straight and made a left turn to the park. I made a right turn from the park and turned around for only a moment and took a second breath when I saw that the soldier had turned away from the gate and was joining his friends on the blanket.

While staggering back to camp, I passed large trucks filled with soldiers, singing Russian patriotic songs and throwing hard candy to passers by. I picked up a few pieces of the candy and stuffed it in my sleeve.

When I finally reached the camp and the safety of my room, I found Bela sitting on her bed, her green eyes filled with anger. "I saw you get on that motorcycle. That was a stupid thing to do," she whispered, so the other girls in the room wouldn't hear.

I emptied my sleeves on her bed and said, "Eat, it will make you stronger."

"Why didn't you ask me before you decided to get on a motorcycle with a Russian soldier?"

"I saw other girls go on motorcycles with the soldiers, and they came back with bread. I asked them if the soldiers gave them food, and they all said yes. They didn't seem afraid at all, so I went too, but the Russian soldiers don't just want to give you bread for nothing. I was so scared," I told her.

"Did that old soldier touch you...? What did he do to you? Are you all right...? He didn't... I mean... Do you know what I mean...?" The questions rushed from her mouth in one single breath not giving me a chance to answer.

"I know what you mean. I'm not hurt, and I was very lucky. He forced vodka down my throat, but I got away."

"Good," she said and placed a bowl of very sweet cooked barley in front of me.

"Now, eat," she said softly.

"Where did you get the food? I didn't see any food this morning," I asked surprised.

"A little while ago, we lined up, and they gave us the barley."

Hungrily, I began to eat one spoonful after another. Halfway through, I became nauseated. Before I reached the door, all the barley mixed with the vodka flew from my mouth like water from a fire hose. My legs were buckling under me, and Bela helped me to my bed. I didn't wake up until the next morning. Just before I awoke, I dreamed that Mama was at home baking cheesecake. When I woke up, I prayed for my dream to come true. Now that we were free, I ached to go home, but I felt like a bird in an abandoned nest. Nobody came to our rescue with food and clothing, or direction.

Men and women from our camp were running into town searching abandoned houses for food and clothing the Germans had left behind while on the run from the Russians.

Bela and I followed the girls from our room into town. Everyone ran in different directions. Bela and I walked through an open door and saw a home that resembled our home after the liquidation of the Ghetto. The house had been stripped of everything except the furniture and bare mattresses. Either somebody had been there before us, or the owners took everything with them? We looked in the closet, hoping to find clothes, but all we found were shoes three sizes too big. We needed to be able to survive in a world without the protection of our parents. We opened a hope chest and found two pieces of material, enough to make two dresses. We took the material knowing that we didn't have a needle and thread or scissors. Even if we did have all the tools for making a dress, we didn't know how to cut out a dress-pattern. I looked in every part of the house, hoping to find something to help us make the dresses. Except for the two pieces of very thin very flimsy material, the house was bare. We were very hungry. The cooked sweet barley was only a one-time thing, and we didn't know when the next meal would come. We ran to the abandoned house next door, and it was the same as the first. While I looked in every drawer, Bela went to the back of the house. A few minutes later, I heard a noise. From the open door, I saw Bela running with a bucket of uncooked yellow split peas, about ten pounds, and was being chased by a man with a rifle. I caught up with her and grabbed hold of one end of the bucket, and we began to run with the man chasing behind, his rifle pointing at us and threatening to shoot if we ever came back. We ran to our room, huffing and puffing and feeling as if we suddenly became millionaires. We put the bucket down in the middle of the room for everyone to see, and Bela announced that we had enough peas in the bucket for everyone. Only, we realized that we had no pot or wood to cook the peas with.

I sat on my bed next to Bela, looking at the bucket full of peas we almost gave our lives for, and felt very sad.

"Why don't we try to go home?" I asked Bela.

"How can we go home looking like beggars? If we had scissors and a needle and thread, I would try to make us a couple of dresses. We'll go one more time to another area and see if we can get what we need," Bela said.

A woman in her late thirties or forties, in the bed next to our beds told us that she had been a seamstress in Poland before the war and offered to cut out our dresses with the material we took from the abandoned house

"On my trip to town, I found needles and thread and scissors. Don't worry. I'll help you make your dresses, " she said, running a hand over Bela's very short hair.

Excitedly, Bela thanked the woman and went to the showers, then to the infirmary to get her bandages changed. She returned with used but comfortable leather shoes and underwear. I still felt guilty for not giving her my shoes when she asked for them, but I was happy that she was able to get rid of the wooden shoes.

We worked feverishly to finish the dresses, and in only two days, both of our dresses, though simple and sleeveless, for there wasn't enough material, were finished.

On the afternoon before our departure, we went to the shower. Bela took off the bandages, and I saw that the boils on her neck were almost healed.

We woke up at dawn and put on our new dresses and left the room. We looked to see if there was a food line, and there was none. Happy to be free, we approached the gate, ready to leave Theressianschtadt.

A Russian soldier pointed a rifle at us and stopped us from leaving. "You are forbidden to leave the camp," he said.

"Why won't you let us leave?" Bela argued, "Didn't you liberate us? We are free, and we are starving here. We have to go home to Poland and find our family."

"You can't leave…quarantine…typhus."

"We had typhus in the camps. Let us go home!" Bela shouted.

The soldier became angry and shouted back at Bela. "Get away from the gate, or I'll shoot!" he bellowed, still pointing the rifle at us.

I took Bela's hand and pulled her away from the gate. Defeated, we stumbled back up the stairs where a food line was formed, and we received a bowl of soup and a piece of bread. After we ate, Bela went to visit her friends, and I followed her inside the small room. When I saw Rusty in an embrace with a very good-looking young man, I had a flashback of Bela's hunger pain in Blyzin. I remembered Rusty reaching out her hand for our piece of bread in exchange for a bowl of a little thicker soup. The picture of her taking our piece of bread and adding it to the mountain of bread on the little table stayed with me, and I was unable to forgive her. I left the room, but I was determined to get back at her, to let her know that I hadn't forgotten and would never forgive her for my sister's stomach pain that she could have prevented with and extra bowl of soup. I remembered the gossip about her affair in Blyzin, and I made up my mind to tell her boyfriend and never gave a second thought to the consequences. With that plan in my mind, I left the room. I returned to my room and took of my new dress and put on my old one. The Rojal family, as always throughout the war, sat on each other's beds not needing my intrusion. Two sisters, two good friends, and a mother, and a lucky daughter, all had each other. I missed my family. I missed Mama and Tata. I missed my brother and my sisters. I missed my school friends. I left the room to stand on the long porch. I looked beyond the gate to freedom. It was a cloudless day in Theresienstadt, and I decided to stroll in the park and take in the beauty of the flowers and inhale the fragrance. The sun felt like kisses from heaven. I stretched out on the warm grass and closed my eyes. As the sun filtered through the trees, warming my face, I had the feeling of being caressed by angels. I suddenly felt a chill as if the sun had disappeared. I opened my eyes and looked into the eyes of the man who an hour ago had been in an embrace with Rusty, and now, he was kneeling beside me.

"Aren't you Bela's sister?" he asked.

"Yes, I am," I said, and without giving it another thought, I added, "Did Rusty tell you about her Policeman in Blyzin? I think you should ask her," I said, and I stood up and walked away. I was sure that I would feel relieved. Instead, I felt as if I had just been hit on the head with a heavy rock, and I knew that I was going to be the one to be ashamed for what I had just done, but it was too late, and I couldn't take back. I had the same feeling of doom as when I tore up Bela's letter in Blyzin and gave my letter to the boy going to Radom.

An hour later, Rusty saw me walking up the stairs and showered me with a lashing of her tongue. She was so busy cursing me that I didn't have a chance to tell her why I did it.

Rusty was older than I was and much taller. She suddenly raised her hand and slapped my face. I ran to my room, climbed in my bed, and cried myself to sleep. I wished I could have slept forever so that I would never again see the hurt and disappointment in Bela's eyes. But as many times I wished not to wake up, once again I did wake up and see Bela's disappointment in me. I never told my sister why I did what I did, for it would have made no difference. Her low opinion of me would have been the same, for I certainly did not have a high opinion of myself. In only a few days of freedom, I had quickly learned that two wrongs do not make it right, and I had no excuse for what I had done. I have since learned that hate and anger is like standing near a smoldering fire in the middle of a forest. If you stay in it long enough, it will consume you with the slightest breeze. The next few days, I barely saw my sister. She spent most of her time with her friends, and I didn't blame her. I told myself that as soon as we would get back to Radom and I prayed, we would find our family at home. I would release her of all responsibilities. Even if we wouldn't find our family, I would never be a burden to her again.

The next few days, the only time I saw my sister was at night when we went to sleep and in line for our food. Even then, I felt invisible. On the fourth morning, Bela told me that we were going to escape. I only asked how I could help.

She said, "We'll dig our way out. Be ready after the sun goes down."

We met at the back end of the fence with three men and two other girls. We began to work like ants. We were all digging feverishly with our hands, and we carried handfuls of dirt and spread it all around the grass. We worked until curfew and went to sleep. We needed to wake up before dawn, finish the job, and slide under the fence to freedom.

Before Bela and I went to sleep, we made our way to the shower room to get ready for the next day. I was awake most of the night for fear I would oversleep. I looked over to Bela's bed and saw that she too was tossing and turning. Our room was still dark when Bela whispered, "It's time." I was dressed within minutes. We were the first to arrive at the barb wire fence. Moments later, the three boys and two girls followed.

It didn't take us long to scrape out the last few handfuls of dirt. We spied the area, making sure that there was no guard. Without sound, we lifted the fence, and one at a time climbed inside the hole, under the fence, and out. Once outside, we each went our separate ways. Until we were about a mile from the camp, Bela and I walked slowly so as not to attract attention.

We saw groups of survivors heading towards the train station, and we followed them. By the time we reached the train station, the sun was high, and the sky was cloudless.

Chapter Thirty-One: Going Home

I was glad that all the trains were free, for we hadn't seen money in a long time. We took the train that was marked 'Poland' and changed trains several times. In Kelce, we took the train marked 'Radom.' It was dusk when the train stopped in "Radom," My heart leaped from my chest as I stepped on the Radom platform. "Please, Mama, be home," I prayed. Many people were standing at the station, hoping to find family survivors, but no familiar face waited for us. We stood at the station and had no idea in which direction to start. I knew that if any family member had survived, he or she would be at the station waiting for us. We were about to walk towards our neighborhood when I heard a woman's voice call out, "Children!" I turned my head, aware that the voice didn't belong to my family, but the voice sounded again.

"Children come here!"

It was now dark, and I couldn't see the face until the voice sounded only about two feet from us.

"Aren't you Mrs. Hailigman?" Bela asked.

"Yes, I am. Did you see Mrs. Rojal, my sister, and her children?"

"Yes," I said, happy to bring good news. "We were together the entire time. They should be coming home soon," I said and followed Bela in the direction of our neighborhood.

"Come with me, children, and tell me about my sister. Is she well?"

"Yes, she is very well. In Willischtall, our last concentration camp before Theresienschtadt, Mrs. Rojal worked in the kitchen," I said, letting her know that her sister and her family didn't starve.

"Lusia and I are good friends. We went to school together. We both finished four grades when the war broke out," I added, but I was sure that after I had told her that her sister and nieces were fine, she didn't hear another word I said.

We followed Mrs. Hailigman up to the second floor and stepped inside a large living room, devoid of furniture. Only a large piano sat in the middle of the room, and a handsome young man sat on a short bench and played beautiful music. A pretty young woman stood lovingly next to him, her hand on his shoulder. Mrs. Hailigman didn't introduce us, but I assumed that it was her daughter and son-in-law, for I knew that she had a daughter. I knew that they too were Jewish and wondered how they survived so nicely. I later found out that during the war, they had moved to another city where nobody knew them and lived the entire time on Gentile papers. After the war, the family moved back to Radom and waited for family survivors. The couple at the piano seemed as if the war had never touched them. Bela and I felt invisible to the young couple. They only saw each other. I was too hungry to enjoy the beautiful music the man played. Growing up in concentration camps, I didn't know the difference between Mozart and Tchaikovsky.

Mrs. Hailigman showed us to a narrow room, large enough for one single bed, and Bela and I were grateful for the hospitality. In comparison to our previous accommodations, the room was paradise. She soon returned with a large pot of leftover potatoes and sour cream soup, about two ladles full on the bottom of the pot, and two spoons. "Eat, children. You can stay here as long as you like," she said and walked out, closing the door behind her.

As always, Bela and I shared every spoonful and scraped the bottom. We were still hungry, but not starved. We weren't sure if we should take the pot to the kitchen and wash it, or maybe, Mrs. Hailigman had a housekeeper. We were too humble to leave our room, but I got up enough courage to take the pot to wherever her kitchen was. I figured she would need it for the next day.

Mrs. Hailigman saw me looking for the kitchen and took the empty pot from me. I offered to wash it, but she declined my offer. I thanked her for the food and went back to our room.

Bela and I were awake most of the night, waiting for daylight. Mrs. Hailigman must have known how anxious we were and came to our room at sunrise with two pieces of bread.

"Good morning, children. I want you to know that you can stay here as long as you like," she said.

We thanked her for the food and hospitality, and she quickly walked out closing the door behind her. I suddenly felt very poor and humble. We ate hungrily, made our bed, and left the house.

Once outside Bela said, "We can't abuse Mrs. Hailigman's hospitality. We need to find a place to live until we find out what to do next."

"Do you want me to go with you?" I asked, trying not to sound needy.

"No, I'll go and see what I can find out. I'll see you later at Mrs. Hailigman's," she said and began to walk away.

"Don't you want to go home and see if anybody returned?" I asked timidly.

"Nobody returned, but if you want to go, then go," she said simply and turned away, but not before I saw the tears shining in her eyes.

Chapter Thirty-Two: A Bus Tour With My Friend, Carla

After we checked into a modern hotel in Krakow, we arranged for a bus tour to Auschwitz.

The only things that had remained in the death camp were the buildings. I showed my friend the barracks in Birkenau, where everyone from our barrack stood huddled together against the wooden wall trying to keep the November wind from blowing the cold air under our thin dresses. As I was showing her the bunk board I had slept on, my heart was breaking in a million pieces. I remembered the endless smoke belching from the crematorium and the stench from burning flash, and I was thinking of my tata and his brother with endless bodies in the same flame. I could see that Carla too was becoming stressed out. The only satisfaction I derived from the visit was that I was able to leave. Carla and I were the first ones inside the bus to leave Auschwitz.

Back in Radom, my friend Janina had finished our mink hats, but the price had gone up, and we didn't mind. Janina had two more friends from school at her house.

Tola Wasilewska and Alina, whose last name I didn't remember were there. It was a euphoric experience to see these women after so many years. Except for Janina, the last time I had seen the three women was June 1939, when we had finished the fourth grade. In May 1945, I saw Janina standing in front of her house. She was polite, but she didn't ask me where I had been the last six years. She didn't ask if I needed a place to stay. Although it was easy to see how gaunt I was, she didn't ask if I was hungry. Now, after forty years, when I didn't need her help, Janina decorated her dinning room table with a white embroidered tablecloth. Her best china was filled with imported sardines, cheeses, and other delicacies. As we sat around the elaborate table, my three friends took great interest in my life in America and very subtly quizzed me about my religion, mainly if I was Jewish. I wasn't afraid to remind my three school friends that I was Jewish. They were descent people and wouldn't cause me harm. I was concerned that if word got around and a Jew hater got wind of a Jew being in town, Carla would get hurt because of me.

Janina went as far as asking me my last name. When I said that my last name was Boren, Alina queried, "What is your maiden name?" I knew what she was fishing for and I said, "Sztraiman."

"Isn't that a Jewish name?" Janina quizzed.

As long as they didn't outright ask me if I was Jewish, I played it safe. "It could also be a German name. Maybe my tata was of German descent," I told them. When they realized that I wasn't volunteering, the interrogation stopped, and we took pictures with our new mink hats and promised to keep in touch.

It was Sunday morning, the day we were leaving Radom. I went back to the cul-de-sac for a last look. Everyone was in church, and the cul-de-sac took on an eerie silence. I stood at the entrance and looked up to the window where I once lived. The window was open, and the white lace curtain waived with the breeze. I had a warm feeling that my family was standing beside me. I stood in that silence, trying to hear the echoes of my family, relatives, and friends. I was waiting for the sound of Jewish children playing hopscotch in the cull-de-sac. I remembered the other reason why I returned to Radom after forty years. I needed to remember May 1945 when I climbed the familiar three flights of stairs, when I was standing in the dark narrow corridor, where the dusty light bulb omitting no light at all hung from the ceiling on a braided wire. Unless someone opened a door in one of the three apartments, the corridor was as black as a tomb.

My pride didn't allow me to knock on my door, and why should I have? It was where I had lived with my family. We didn't move willingly. The last time I had stepped through the threshold to the apartment was August 1942, three years ago. Nobody was at home then, but maybe, they had returned just like Bela and I did. My family had a right to be inside. The rent was always paid on time. Alright, maybe once in a while when Tata wasn't working, Mama asked Pan Jakubowski to be patient, and he was. So, why should I have to knock on my own door? While I held the door handle in my hand and argued my case in my head, my heart was pounding so hard it felt as if it would push through my chest and break down the door, but my hand froze on the door handle, and I was unable to push the handle down.

When the door across the hall opened lighting up the corridor, I could see that it wasn't Motek the shoemaker, who had lived in that apartment with his family and the daughter I had taught to read and write until she died of diabetes. It was Boba, my friend who had told me that only soldiers fight during a war. She had lived in another building before the war, and it was apparent that she was now living in Motek's apartment.

"Jadzia, come in. I'm having company," Boba said casually, as if I was her next door neighbor and had never been away.

"Who is living here now?" I asked as I followed her to Motek's apartment. It would always be Motek's apartment to me.

"Some people I don't know too well," she said, and just as Janina, she never asked me where I was for the last six years, or where I lived, or what had happened to my family?

Boba's mama was standing at the kitchen table, cutting up vegetables, bread, butter, sausages, tomatoes, and cheese. These were foods I hadn't seen in six years. Two tall teenage boys wearing suits and ties were standing at a larger table clicking glasses filled with vodka.

Boba filled a glass and handed it to me. She clicked her glass against mine, drained her glass, and waited for me to do the same.

The slice of bread Mrs. Hailigman gave me at dawn had long been digested. I knew that if I drank any amount of the vodka, I would get sick.

Boba's mother whom I remembered being an anti-Semite looked at me with a truculent scowl.

"You're still alive?" she grunted, making me feel as if I owed her an apology for surviving the war. The question and tone in her voice took me by surprise, and I was unable to respond. For only a moment, I stood looking at Boba and wondered why she was privileged to grow tall, and I stayed the same height as when I was ten years old. Boba was wearing a crisp navy blue dress, trimmed with a white collar, and navy blue shoes to match her dress. Her blond hair was professionally styled, and she wore a gold ring on her right finger. Though Boba was very friendly, her mama looked at me as if I were a leper. I felt out of place and gently placed the glass on the mahogany dinning room table that took up the entire room. I wondered which Jewish dining room that table had occupied before August 1942 and the liquidation of the Ghetto?

"Thank you very much for your hospitality, but I must go," I said and closed the door to Motek's apartment. Again, I turned to my door and held the door handle in my right hand. My heart was pounding so hard I could actually hear the thumping. My hand was shaking, and again, I was unable to push down the handle. I ran down the stairs and passed Fraida's apartment. I didn't try her door. I stopped at her window and recognized the same white curtains with the ruffles, though they were not as white anymore. I remembered how proud my oldest sister was when she hung the very same curtains. I tried to look through the window, hoping for a familiar face, but the curtains were tightly drawn, and I was afraid of getting caught.

Though Bela and I stayed in Radom until autumn, I never returned to the cul-de-sac. I never opened the door to my home, but the need to open the door and step inside my family home had never left my mind.

As I was leaving the cul-de-sac, I saw Bela coming from the direction of the Penc House.

"I went to visit Ola and Kaitek. Nothing has changed, only Kaitek is bigger. He didn't recognize me," she said, her eyes glistening with tears, but none were shed.

I knew that she would never return to the woman and the little boy she once loved.

The next few days we stayed at Mrs. Hailigman's house, but we didn't feel right about taking advantage of her hospitality. We had to find a place to live until we could figure out how to get out of Poland. We started out in the morning and walked all day, looking for a place live. By mid afternoon, we passed the abandoned courtyard that had once been Gestapo headquarters. It was the same place where I saw my Evangelist friend with her parents in Gestapo uniforms proudly march through the gate of the courtyard. As the gate opened, all three had lifted their arms to the guard in a Hail Hitler salute.

A chill went through my spine as Bela and I walked through the open gate. Beyond the gate were several small buildings. We opened the door to a small stucco structure leading to a dark, very small, entrance hall. There were no lighting fixtures. With the door closed, it was complete darkness. We held the door open and stumbled upon very steep steps. We climbed up a flight of wooden stairs leading to one large empty room with a splintered wooden floor. Three wooden steps above the large room was a much smaller room with a window looking down on the entire courtyard including the gate, allowing us a lookout for Russian Soldiers. The small room had a single bed, a small wooden table, and three chairs. We decided to make this our home, but we had no idea where our next meal would be coming from.

Other survivors had returned as we did, and each survived in their own way, for the town didn't offer a helping hand. In the morning, Bela and I went to visit Pani Franciszkowa, our neighbor from the Penc House. Her children were always eating in our house. Mama would have us all sit on the floor with a dish in the middle, often with pierogy filled with sweet cheese or blueberries in the summer or what ever she was cooking, and she made sure it would be enough for the neighbors children too.

We knocked on her door and asked if she had some mending to do. She gave us a bowl of potatoes and sour cream soup. It was a typical Polish

271

breakfast. When we finished, she placed a pile of clothes on the table with needles and thread, and we gratefully sat at her kitchen table and mended her clothes. It was late afternoon by the time we finished mending all her clothes, and we were hungry again, but we didn't ask her for anything more, and she didn't offer. I felt like a beggar. We were now free, yet we were trapped in Poland. We were not wanted, yet we were forbidden to leave, and we had no money with which to escape. Like homeless animals, we roamed the streets by day, hoping to earn our food, and night after night, we went to sleep hungry. We kept our bed and pillow close to the window, listening for footsteps of Russian Soldiers, afraid of being raped, or the Polish Endeks, a group of anti-Semites who took pleasure in killing Jews that returned from the death camps. Nothing had changed; it was the same as before the war. The police looked the other way. We were not expected to return alive, and our neighbors were very angry when a handful of us did survive and returned.

Three weeks after our return to Radom, two young survivors lost their lives on their wedding night. Endeks waited for them on the stairs and slit their throats as the couple happily climbed the stairs to their apartment. All of us survivors panicked and were anxious to leave Poland, but it took money to bribe the border patrol.

Many Germans had lived in Wroclawa. During the German occupation, it was called Breslau. The German women still living in Wroclawa were now desperate for money and were selling their clothes to survivors.

Train rides were still free, and many survivors, mostly men, began to travel to Wroclawa. They scraped together some money and bought the clothes or whatever the German women were selling. They returned to their towns with sacks full of purchases and sold the goods in the market place. After they saved up enough money to pay a smuggler, they were able to get to West Germany to be on the American side.

Mrs. Marmelsztain arrived with three daughters and moved into the courtyard and occupied a room filled with bunk beds.

It was a good thing that nobody asked for rent money, or we would all be sleeping on the sidewalks.

The courtyard had an echoing sound, and we could hear the softest footsteps. Each time we heard movements, we went to the window, hoping for new arrivals. We were also on constant alert for Rossian soldiers or Polish anti-Semites.

Mrs. Marmelsztain saw us standing at our window and asked us to come down. Once we were downstairs, she said, "Look, children. There are plenty of bunk beds in our room. Why don't you move in with us? It will be safer if we are all together," she said.

Of course, we accepted without giving it a second thought, and we were glad to be together with a mother, even though she was not our mother. We had no belongings, only what we were wearing. We followed Mrs. Marmelsztain to her room, hoping she wouldn't change her mind.

As always, Bela chose a top bunk bed and climbed up. Whenever she was hungry and there was no food, she would stretch out on her stomach and close her eyes. Today, she had checked out a book from the library to keep her mind off food.

I don't know where Mrs. Marmelsztain got the money from, but there was a large pot of potato soup cooking on the wood burner. I had nothing to eat all day and felt that if I stayed one more moment sniffing the aroma of the golden brown onions smothered in butter Mrs. Marmelsztain was adding to the soup, I'd lose my mind. I turned towards the door and was about to step out when Mrs. Marmelsztain said, "Don't leave now. The soup is almost ready."

"I'm sure it's wonderful. It smells delicious, but this is for you and your family," I said and turned to leave.

Mrs. Marmelsztain placed herself in front of me. "You are now part of my family. Stay and eat with us. It's a big pot," she said.

I couldn't remember when I had eaten anything cooked with butter, and I couldn't remember anything tasting better, not even Mama's cooking.

While we were savoring the thick, hot, potato soup, Mrs. Marmelsztain brought up the question of escaping from Poland.

"The only way to get out of Poland is with a smuggler, and we all know that takes money," she said.

Bela and I sighed.

"I know that you don't have money, but I have, though not enough to pay for a smuggler, not even enough for my daughters and me."

When we didn't answer, she said, "I have a solution." I looked at her, anxiously waiting to hear her solution.

"Many kids are getting on trains to Wroclawa. The German women are selling their clothes so they could get away from the Russian occupation." Young men go back and forth to Wroclawa and bring back sacks full of stuff. They sell quickly and go on the trains again."

I told Mrs. Marmelsztain that I knew of several men that go to Wroclawa on shopping trips. For a moment my thoughts went to Abramek. He was a handsome, tall boy with black hair and brown eyes. Each time he returned from one of his shopping trips, he treated me to the movies, and he loved going with me to the photographer and pose for pictures together. I never let him know how trapped I felt with no means of getting out of Poland. Abramek was only about a year or two older than I was, and he lived with his aunt. He once told me that he wished he was older. I didn't respond to his statement. I knew that he had to do what ever his aunt asked of him, and I pretended that we were casual friends.

"You could do it, too," Mrs. Marmelstain said, interrupting my thoughts. "You could buy clothes from the German women, bring it back here, and I'll sell it on the market place. After we save up enough money, we'll all get out of Poland together." She turned her attention to Bela and waited for an answer.

Bela turned to me. "It would be wonderful to have enough money to get out of Poland, but I can't go. I wouldn't be good at it. If you want to go, I won't stop you."

"I'll go," I said with determination.

"You can't go alone. It's not safe," Mrs. Marmelsztain said.

Mrs. Marmelsztain's daughter, Mania, put her spoon down and stood up, "I'll go with Jadzia," she said, looking to her mother for approval, as did I.

"It's settled then. The two of you will leave in the morning," Mrs. Marmelsztain said and added, I'll wake you early in the morning. Now, go to sleep girls.

I was excited about my contribution to get us out of Poland, yet I was frightened of the unknown and was awake most of the night.

Chapter Thirty-Three: Going on the Train to Wroclawa

The train station was mobbed with people pushing to get inside the already full train, with no place to sit or stand. People were climbing up on the train's roof, and Mania and I followed.

The roof was slanted, and there was no place to hold on to. Any wrong move, and we would slide off. Mania and I held on to each other until we needed to change trains, but each time we changed, the trains were full, and we ended up on the roof until the last train came to a stop in Wroclawa.

Stepping off the train, we had no idea where to begin or where we would spend the night. We were hungry and tired from keeping from falling off the roof.

An old woman was sitting on a chair at the train station selling hot soup. Mania bought a bowl of soup for herself and offered to buy one for me, but I thanked her and said, "I don't have money, and I haven't earned anything yet to pay back." I turned away while she was eating.

We began walking towards the town until dusk, and we still didn't have a clue where to begin.

I recognized a middle-aged man sitting in front of a building with a double glass doors. I rushed over to him with Mania trailing behind.

"Aren't you from Radom?" I asked.

"Yes," the man said.

"My name is Jadzia Sztraiman. In 1939 during the bombings, we were all huddled in the same building. You were selling little apples," I said, happy to have found a familiar face.

"You're right, but who are you?"

"My father was Jeremy the baker, and my mother was the pretty Mindala."

He sighed, "I knew your parents well. Your mother wasn't only the pretty Mindala, she had a heart of gold. What are you doing here, two young girls alone?"

I explained our predicament, and he offered us a place to stay the night. He gave us each a piece of bread and butter and burlap sacks.

"Tonight, get a good night's sleep, and tomorrow take the sacks, knock on doors, and ask if they have something to sell. Whatever you buy, put in the sacks. When the sacks are full, you can go home. "

YAJA BOREN

We sat with the kind man, who's name I didn't remember and was too embarrassed to ask. Until it was time to go to sleep, we talked about our families and which camps we were in. He told Mania that she was very lucky to have survived with her mother and all of her sisters. He had lost his entire family, including his wife and child. The next morning, before we left for our shopping spree, the man gave us a piece of fresh bread and butter and reminded us that we could come back and stay another night if we needed to.

By late afternoon, our sacks were full. The German women were only too anxious to sell their belongings. The sun had long gone down, and we knew that it was time to quit and go home. Only, we had to decide if we wanted to travel all night or stay over and leave in the morning.

"Let's go back to your friend's house and stay the night," Mania said. When I agreed, she added, "I still have money. We could stuff in more things in the morning."

We had made so many turns throughout the day, we couldn't find our way back to the man's place. We had no choice but travel at night. As long as we were going to be traveling all night anyway, we decided to knock on more doors, until we filled our sacks to capacity.

The sky was gray by the time we reached the train station. My sack was getting heavier by the second, and my stomach was growling. Yet, I was excited, for we had filled both sacks.

Before we entered the train carrying the bulging sacks, Mania had bought two bowls of soup from a vendor, and this time, I gratefully accepted.

Again, the train was full, and it was beginning to rain. The roof would be too slippery and dangerous if we dosed off. We had decided to stand inside the train rather than risk our lives on a wet roof or get our merchandise wet.

A Russian Soldier saw us standing at the door and motioned to us with his index finger to come inside. He said something to two lower ranking soldiers, and they immediately stood up and walked towards the next passenger car. As soon as we stepped inside the car, the soldier pulled me down next to him and told Mania to sit on the seat across from me. His superior officer was sitting in the next isle to our left, his arm around a girl's shoulder. The soldier next to me was a perfect gentleman until it turned dark. He began by inching his arm around my shoulder and said, "I like Polish girls."

I immediately stood up and told him that I don't like him touching me. I don't know where my courage had come from. I believe it was when he said that he liked Polish girls. I suddenly remembered a time long ago, when outside my home, I felt no different from my Polish friends. I also remembered that the last six years I was in hell for being a Jew and, therefore, had no right to live. Hearing the soldier calling me a Polish girl, I felt like a snake that walks away from it's old skin and is reborn. When I told the Russian soldier who was trying to molest me that a gentleman does not touch a lady, I was not the frightened Jewish girl speaking, but the Polish Catholic girl speaking.

"Please, sit. I want to be like a Polish gentleman, so if you say no touch, I'll be good" he said humbly.

I looked across the isle and saw the girl who a minute ago was sitting next to the officer, and now, she was beneath his body, and I became frightened, but I quickly reminded myself that I was Polish and in my country. The soldier that was sitting next to me kept his hands to himself only several minutes at a time. Each time I had to pry one hand from my shoulder and the other from my thigh, I struggled to keep his face and vodka breath away from me.

"I like Polish girls, and I want to marry you. You will teach me to be a Polish gentleman," he said.

When I didn't answer, for I was in shock, he said, "Do you want to marry me?"

I knew that it was going to be a long night, and I didn't want to end up like the girl in the next isle. I pushed his hand away from my body and looked at him with a scowl.

"Yes, I will marry you under the condition that you do not touch me until we are married."

"Why can't I touch you? You said you would marry me."

"You told me that you would like to be like a Polish gentleman, and a Polish gentleman does not touch the girl until after the wedding," I said.

"When will we get married?" he asked, as his hand began to wander to my legs.

"We may never get married if you continue to touch me."

"I can't help myself. You're very pretty Polish girl."

"Go to sleep now, and in the morning, when we stop in Ludz, I will take you to my home. You will meet my mother, and she will make our wedding. After we are married, my mother and I will help you to become a Polish gentleman," I said and looked at Mania, hoping she wouldn't laugh or say it out loud that I did not live in Ludz and did not have a mother. Mania understood and closed her eyes.

"I want to sleep, but I want to hold you in my arms while I sleep."

"No, that's not proper," I said.

He fell asleep for about two hours, and I, too, dozed off, clutching my sack of clothes to my body. When he woke up, his hands began to wander all over again, and it seemed as if the night would never end. Every few minutes for the next four hours, I kept reminding him that if he wanted to be a Polish gentlemen, he had to keep his hands off me.

"My mother would never approve of such behavior," I said, lifting his large hand off my leg and placing it back in his own lap. He lit a cigarette and began to smoke. Suddenly, he began pushing his cigarette to my mouth.

"Here, smoke," he said.

"No, thank you. I don't smoke," I said, turning my face from his hand with the cigarette.

"Why don't you smoke?" he asked.

"Because ladies don't smoke," I said.

"Why not?"

Just as I opened my mouth to answer him, he pushed the cigarette in my mouth, and I began to choke. He dropped the lit cigarette on floor and pulled out a bottle of vodka from under his seat and pushed the bottle to my mouth. I suddenly remembered Theresienstadt and the Russian soldier in the park, and I kept my mouth tightly closed. Even if he broke every tooth in my mouth, I told myself, the vodka would never reach my throat. The vodka was spilling all over me, but not a drop touched my mouth. I began to cough from the smell of the vodka, and his superior said something to him in Russian, and he replaced the cork on the bottle and put it out of sight. I had stopped coughing, and he said that he would never do it to me again.

"You promised to marry me, so now you have to," he said and waited for an answer.

"Of course, I'll marry you. We'll soon be in Ludz, and my mama will make our wedding and invite everybody. I have a very large family in Ludz. I have sisters and a brother and many aunts and uncles and cousins."

While I was telling him about my large family, I had wished it were true. As the train neared Ludz, I stood up and told Mania to stay close to me. When the train came to a full stop, the soldier, who's marriage proposal I accepted, stood up and turned to his superior officer and saluted.

"I'm going to Ludz to get married. I'm going to be a Polish gentleman," he said proudly.

The officer returned an indifferent salute and returned his attention to the girl who looked as if she had been fighting a war all night.

The soldier stood at the door close to me while I tried to figure a way out.

When I felt his hand on my shoulder, I knew that, in order to outsmart him, I had to think fast or pay the consequences.

As the door opened, my betrothed rushed in front of me. I was grateful that he hadn't yet learned to be a Polish gentlemen. He turned his head towards me.

"Which way to your mama?"

I strained my neck to the left and saw a train across the railroad tracks marked, 'Kelce.' Kelce was one station from Radom. I pointed to the right.

"This way," I shouted.

He jumped off the train, being sure that I was following him, and began walking to the right, amidst hundreds of people crowding the train station. I picked up my sack and jumped off the train and urged Mania to hurry. In the confusion, Mania began running to the right in the direction of the soldier.

"Mania, follow me!" I screamed, pulling her sack to the left where we got lost in the large crowd. Mania was beginning to slow down, dragging her sack behind. I was frantic. If the soldier turned around, he would see me. I ran after Mania and picked up one end of her sack and urged her to run. I was afraid to turn my head for fear the soldier was chasing after me. Just when I was beginning to think the train marked 'Kelce,' was a mirage, it suddenly appeared in front of me. I tossed my sack inside and pulled myself up. I took Mania's sack from her, then pulled her inside the train. Huffing and puffing, I thanked God that I got away and that there was enough standing room inside. I stood at the window and saw the soldier looking in every direction, and for a moment, I saw him looking in the direction of our train, and I allowed myself to breathe easier when the train began to move. If only my mama could have seen how well I handled myself. She would've been very proud of me. She would tell everybody how smart her little Jentala was. It would have felt really good to hear Mama say that I was smart, I mused.

In Kelce we changed trains one last time to get to Radom.

It felt good to come home to the aroma of soup cooking on top of the iron oven.

Mrs. Marmelsztain was very pleased with our purchases, and Bela was on her bunk reading a book. Her approval of me was a bright smile.

Mrs. Marmelsztain served us a bowl of hot potato soup and bread.

Exhausted, Mania and I went to sleep, and we didn't wake up until the next morning. I never told Bela about the Russian soldier. I wanted us to get out of Poland before the Endeks would kill us.

Abramek came over, and we went to the movies, for walks in the park, and to have our pictures taken. The photographer posed us together with our faces close to each other. It never occurred to me that Abramek and I would ever be more than friends.

The handful of survivors that had returned to Radom after the camps saw each other almost daily. The day before Mania and I went on our second shopping trip, we were invited to Esterka and Jakob Chlebowski's wedding. Every survivor in Radom was invited. It was all word of mouth. The wedding was held in the couple's very small one room apartment.

I wrote a poem for the bride, and part of it read, "I'm giving you these pansies so you'd never feel the loss of your mother." The poem rhymed in the Polish language.

Hours before the wedding, I was running around looking for pansies. I didn't have the money to buy them, and I couldn't find a friendly garden where I could pick them. I ended up running to an empty field and picked some wild flowers. I had changed the words from pansies to flowers, which still rhymed. I recited the poem right after the ceremony and was pleased that the bouquet of wild flowers added color to the table. It was the first time in six years since I'd seen a table set with a white tablecloth, and it was the first time in six years that I had tasted cake. It felt strange, yet wonderful and hopeful. It was a promise for a future and a better place if only we had the money to get out of Poland.

Mania and I left Radom the next afternoon. We were prepared to travel all night and get a fresh start in the morning. This time we didn't even consider going inside the train. We climbed directly up onto the roof. There were other survivors on the roof, mostly men, and we felt safe. We were even able to doze off. Each time we changed trains, we climbed up on the roof and held onto each other to keep from sliding off. The next morning, we arrived at the Wroclawa train station and had an early start. By late afternoon we had filled both sacks and walked to the train station. The sky was clear, and we climbed up on the roof. We arrived, home tired and hungry, but glad to be home so quickly. Again, Mrs. Marmelsztain was pleased with our purchases, but it would take several more trips before we had enough money to get out of Poland, she told us.

After a day of rest, we started out again. We were aiming for the same arrangement as on the last trip. Everything went as planned except that we had wandered away too far, and by dusk, our sack were only half full. We were hungry and tired and had no idea where we would sleep. In desperation, we stopped people in the street we recognized as survivors. Most people were rushing to catch a train, but one man offered his apartment. When he saw us hesitate, he said, "Don't worry. I won't take advantage of you. The landlady lives in the same apartment."

We were both very tired and accepted his offer. It was exactly as the man promised. It was a large room with two single beds one on each side of the only window. A simple wooden dining room table stood in the middle of the room. A light bulb, skirted with a glass lampshade, hung from the ceiling.

The landlady was a humble middle-aged German. She gave us each a basin with warm water for bathing and a towel.

The tables had turned since only a few months ago, I mused. A few months ago, the same woman could have decided our fate. If we were still healthy enough, she had the power to enslave us, beat us, and starve us. Nobody would care if she killed us. Now, her head was bowed as she returned with two large slices of bread and two tall glasses of milk. She walked out and told our host that we were dressed.

He stepped inside and said, "I didn't introduce myself. My name is David. You can have the bed on the left, and don't worry. Nobody will bother you. He sat at the table with us while we ate our bread and milk. "You know that it's dangerous for two young girls to travel alone so far from home," he said with genuine concern.

We told him our predicament, and he told us that he too was doing the same thing for the same reason.

"I'll let you get ready to for bed," he said and walked out.

I was just about to dose off when I heard him tiptoe through the door and soundlessly went to his bed.

I woke up to bright sun and looked into the eyes of a young man with bright red hair and freckles. "Your skin is pure alabaster. Now that you opened your beautiful cat eyes, I'm in love," he smiled.

I pulled the sheet over my shoulders and asked him to please step away from our bed. He stepped away only two feet, but his smiling eyes didn't leave my face. "I apologize for staring, but I can't keep eyes off you," he said softly.

I was now angry for being called cat eyes. I remembered when I was a child and the neighborhood kids and some adults teased me, "Cat eyes, cat eyes, can you see in the dark?" I would often run home crying. Now, I wondered if he was making fun of me, and I became angry. "Who are you? And what are you doing here?" I asked annoyed.

He introduced himself, but I have forgotten his name. "I live in Ludz and come here on business, and I stay here when I come."

"Where is David?" I asked.

"David went home to Ludz. He told me to tell you that you can stay here as long as you like."

"Would you mind leaving so my friend and I could get dressed?"

He apologized and left the room. He returned ten minutes later with bread and milk. "I have to go and do some business, but I would like to you see again. I'll wait for you here at four o'clock, and we'll go back together," he said possessively.

"We may have to stay another night. It takes time to knock on doors and ask women if they want to sell their clothes," I said.

"You don't have to knock on doors. The women bring their belongings and sell them on the market place. I'll see you later at the apartment," he said again.

I was so naïve I didn't know why he wanted to see me again. Although I enjoyed the attention, I didn't trust the red headed man who called me cat eyes. If Bela were here, she would know what to do. By the time we left the apartment, I had forgotten about the redheaded man. We were to busy trying to find the market place. We stopped a survivor on the street, and he directed us.

The marketplace was swarming with survivors looking to buy merchandise from German women standing next to piles of used clothes spread out on blankets. Mania and I were standing amidst shouting German women trying to sell their clothes. Each was trying to survive; each was trying to get out of Poland.

I strained my neck to get a better look at the clothes. I now had the experience and knew what Mrs. Marmelsztain would like to sell on the market place in Radom. I flinched when I felt fingers touching the back of my neck. I turned around and looked into brown eyes and a face full of freckles. Before I had a chance to pull away, he kissed me on my cheek. "I love you and want to marry you," he whispered in my ear.

How times have changed. I was thinking of Fraida and Joel. They were in love all their lives before they were married. At the age of eighteen, when Fraida announced that she and Joel wanted to get married, my tata was against it. "He isn't good enough for you," he pleaded. I couldn't help wondering what my tata would have said to me about the red headed man, who only knew me a few minutes while watching me sleep and whispered in my ear that he wanted to marry me. I wondered what it would be like to have a man a few years older than myself. To be taken care of and not having to worry about anything. I was tired, and I told myself to put the man from my mind and concentrate on filling our sacks. It was six o'clock by the time we returned to the apartment. The landlady met us at the door and told us that the man with the red hair waited until ten minutes ago. "He was very upset that we hadn't come back, but he had to catch the train," she said.

I was glad that he was gone, and yet I wondered how my life would have turned out and what Bela would've said, had I come home with him. Though we were tired and needed to stretch out and go to sleep, I remembered before we left on our trip that Mrs. Marmelsztain told me that we would have to make several more trips before we would have enough money for a smuggler. We thanked the landlady and picked up our sacks to leave for the train station.

"It's too late for the train. You will have to stay another night," she said. It didn't take too much persuasion, for I would have been too tired to carry my sack to the train station. We woke up early and filled our sacks to capacity and went to the train station. We didn't bother checking out the inside of the train. We climbed up on the roof and were home in the evening. We ate Mrs. Marmelsztain's soup and went to sleep.

The next late afternoon, we put the empty sacks under our arms and climbed the roof again. We arrived in Wrocwawa early the next morning. We went straight to the marketplace, and in the afternoon, we knocked on doors. We lost track of time. By the time our sacks were full, it was too late to catch the train home. We had no choice but to go to David's place. David welcomed us in and again gave us bread and milk. He told us that he wasn't going to sleep here tonight, and I failed to ask him if anyone else would be sleeping in his bed. Though it would have been great to have a bed all to myself, I was grateful to David for his hospitality, for I had no money of my own to pay for a place to sleep.

We bathed and went to our bed. It had been a warm night. Although I was very tired, the thought of sleeping against Mania's warm back didn't sound restful, and I went to sleep at the footboard where only our feet were touching. Just before I was beginning to dose off. Everything that transpired all day played in my mind as if it weren't real. Only three months ago, these German women had the power to rule over thousands of Jews, beat us with whips, and threaten our lives. Now, they were standing in the marketplace selling us their clothes, for they too were anxious to get away from the Russians.

I was awakened from a deep sleep by strange sounds and movements in our bed. I opened my eyes to bright moonlight and saw a man lying on the edge of our bed close to Mania, his hands on her breasts. I saw in the moonlight that it wasn't David. Unlike David, this man was bald and overweight. Although Mania was several years older than I was, I felt responsible for her. I knew absolutely nothing about sex. I once overheard a conversation between my mama and her friend, talking about another friend. "As soon as he puts his body next to her, she gets pregnant." I was afraid that if Mania would get pregnant, Mrs. Marmesztain would blame me for not protecting her daughter, and she wouldn't allow Mania to go on buying trips, and we wouldn't be able to get out of Poland. Frightened and angry, I jumped out of bed.

"What are you doing here on our bed, touching my friend?" I demanded.

"I'm not doing anything. Go back to sleep," the man said as Mania lay spellbound beneath the man's hands.

I could see in the moonlight that she had a smile on her face, and it bothered me that she would allow a total stranger to touch her and keep his body so close to her, especially when she didn't know his name or see his face clearly. I reached for my dress next to my bed and slipped it over my head. I stepped into my Theresienschtadt shoes and looked around for a stick to hit the man with, but it was too dark. I remembered what my tata would say when he found out that anti- Semites attacked old bearded Jews, "I'll kill the bastard anti-Semite with my bare hands!" I stood in front of the man's round doughy face.

"I demand that you leave my friend alone and go to your own bed!" I shouted.

"I'll go to my bed if your friend will tell me to go to my bed! At this moment, I don't see her protesting. Do you, little girl?" He snarled and pushed his bulk closer to Mania.

I took off my shoe and aimed it at the man. "Mania!" I shouted. "We are leaving right now!

The man stood up, "Alright, you can go back to bed. I'm going to my bed," he said hoarsely and sauntered to his bed. Though I didn't trust the man, by the way he was looking towards Mania as if sending her secret unspoken messages, I was exhausted and couldn't very well be standing at the window all night. I went back to sleep and dreamed that I was asleep next to Mama, and Bela was sleeping at the footboard, kicking me. I opened my eyes and saw the man in bed next to Mania, lifting her nightgown, and he was about to drape her with his body. Again, I slipped into my dress and stepped into my shoes. "Get up and get dressed, Mania. We are leaving right now!" I shouted.

Mania didn't move or attempt to push him off her.

"It's still dark outside. Where will you go at this hour? It's too dangerous for two girls alone," the man said, easing himself off Mania.

I stood at the open window, too embarrassed to turn my head. "I don't know where we'll go, but we can't stay here. It's more dangerous than it is outside!" I shouted at the black sky.

"I don't understand," the man said. "Even in the dark I can see that she is older than you are. She should be looking after you," he said and walked briskly to his bed while I was swinging one of my shoes by the shoelaces.

"Normally, it wouldn't be my business to care what she does, but I promised her Mama that I wouldn't let anything happen to her, and I always keep my promises," I said firmly.

This time the man didn't wink at Mania. He said good night and turned towards the wall.

Though Mania was fast asleep, I stayed awake, my shoes on the floor next to me, but I didn't take off my dress. I lay quietly, making sure the man didn't leave his bed, until it would be safe for us to leave the house. When daylight finally broke through the clouds, the sun had remained hidden and threatened rain. I was worried that being on the roof when it rained, our merchandise would be ruined. I saw the man in the next bed lift his head and looked towards our bed. He slipped his pants and shirt on and tiptoed from the room. I woke Mania and told her it was time to go.

We never talked about what had happened the night before.

The landlady knocked on our door and placed a loaf of bread and two glasses of hot milk on the table. We thanked the woman, but she said that the man who just left asked her to give it to us. We ate hungrily and saved the rest of the bread in our sacks for later. By midmorning, the sun was playing hide and seek with the clouds, but it didn't rain all day. By three o'clock in the afternoon, our sacks were so heavy we could barely carry them to the train station. As always, the train was full, but even if it hadn't been full, I wouldn't take another chance in getting trapped inside with Russian soldiers. I was glad that the sun was still strong, and there was no sign of rain.

Mania and I began climbing, holding onto the ladder with one hand and pulling our sacks with the other.

Three Jewish men, survivors from Poland, were already on the roof and saw us struggling. The men rushed over and pulled up our sacks. Once our hands were free, we climbed up quickly. As the man handed our sacks back to us, Mania tripped and was pulling me along with her. One man grabbed me around my waist, and another man steadied Mania, but we never lost our grip on the sacks. It would have been devastating had my sack fallen off the roof. The thought of not being able to get out of Poland was unacceptable to me. These used purchases were the difference between escaping from Poland and living in fear. We sat down only minutes before the train began to move and placed our sacks under our heads. The sky had turned gray, and I didn't know what we would do if it began to rain. I was very tired from lack of sleep and worrying about rain. I closed my eyes and drifted off to the sound of the train's tapacka, tapacka, tapacka…. The men asked us many of the usual questions, "Where we were from? Which camps we were in?" Drowsily, I answered most of the questions directed towards me, and sleep had to be postponed.

I recognized one of the men from Theresienstadt. I remembered that all of his teeth were bonded with silver, but I didn't tell him. I was too tired to begin a conversation. It was going to be a long night until morning, but the men were friendly.

As the train was moving, my eyes were closing. I heard Mania and the men talk about the camps and where they would like to live once we got out of Poland.

Since I didn't think it was polite to mumble when asked a question, I sat up with my sack against my back.

The man sitting close to Mania reached in his pocket and showed us a woman's gold wedding band he had purchased today, and Mania asked to see it. Mania looked at the ring. She tried it on, but it was too small.

"You try it on, Jadzia," Mania said.

"No, thank you," I said.

As Mania was handing the ring back to the man, the man with the silver teeth asked to see it. He held the ring in his hand and looked at it admiringly. Suddenly, he took my hand in his and held it in a tight grip. He slipped the ring on my finger and said, "All of you are my witnesses." He began chanting words in Hebrew, words I didn't understand, and when he was finished, he said, "You are now my wife." He tried to kiss me, but I turned my face from him, and he kissed my hair. Laughing, I removed the ring from my finger and placed it in the owners hand. "Now, we are not married," I said facetiously.

"But we certainly are," he said, and everyone stopped laughing. "Those words I said to you in front of all the witnesses made it as legal as if a Rabbi had married us in a Synagogue, but if you want a real wedding, you can have that too."

"Please, stop frightening me. I don't want to marry you. I don't know you. I don't even know your name. Why are you trying to frighten me? If this is supposed to be some kind of joke, it's not very funny. So, I'm telling you in front of all the witnesses that I'm not married to you!" I shouted.

"In that case, you'll have to find a Rabbi and get a divorce. It's going to be difficult to find a Rabbi, so you might as well stay married to me," he said casually.

I looked to Mania for guidance, but she smiled, and I felt completely alone and didn't know if I should laugh and consider the situation a joke or take this man seriously.

Turning my head towards the wind, I said, "Mania's mother told us that there aren't too many men that survived, but there are lots of girls looking for husbands. You could have chosen someone older, smarter, and prettier. Why did you choose me?"

The man with the silver teeth moved closer to me and gripped my hand again.

"I saw you in Theresienschtdt. After the Russians liberated us, I saw you many times walking in the garden. I knew then that I wanted to marry you, but you and your sister disappeared, and I lost track of you. Now that I found you, I know that it was meant to be, and that's why I quickly put the ring on your finger and made you my wife. I didn't want to lose you again. So now, unless you get a divorce, we are married."

I was very tired and realized that there was nothing I could say or do to change his mind.

It was turning dark and chilly. I was only wearing a summer dress, and I felt drops of rain on my face. It began to rain hard, and my teeth were chattering from the cold. I huddled close to Mania, but it didn't help. I couldn't stop shaking. My new husband pulled a sheet from his sack and draped it over us. The roof had become very slippery. The slightest wrong move would send us flying, as if on an icy slope. I didn't protest when he lifted the sheet and moved close to me. The warmth of his body calmed my teeth, and I had stopped shaking. The man with the ring moved close to Mania and pulled the sheet over our heads. It was a heavy sheet, and it slowed down the drenching. With two people on each side of me, I felt warm and protected and fell asleep.

I woke up when the train came to a full stop. I removed the sheet from my face and felt the warmth of the sun and saw the steam rising from the rooftop.

We had three more stops, first Lodz, then Kelce, and then Radom. I tried to sit up, but my husband had me locked in his arms. I lifted his arms off me, and he opened his eyes.

"Good morning, my wife," he smiled, revealing a mouthful of silver.

I had put yesterday's marriage from my mind and looked forward to be home.

The fiasco with the ring had again surfaced.

"I'm not your wife," I said, but he only smiled.

The train began to move again, and two Russian soldiers appeared on the roof.

"What do you have in your briefcase?" one soldier bellowed at the third man sitting next to his belongings, while the other soldier was keeping an eye on me, and I was immediately frightened. I remembered the last train-ride with a Russian soldier and looked in every direction except his.

The first soldier picked up the briefcase, opened it, and saw that it was filled with bars of soap.

"You have vodka?" he shouted.

"No," the man said.

The soldier closed the briefcase, tucked it under his arm, and left.

I allowed myself to breathe when I saw the other soldier follow him off the roof.

"This whole trip was for nothing!" the man who lost his soap shouted, banging his fists on the wet roof.

Ten minutes before the stop over in Lodz, one of the soldiers returned and pointed a finger at me. When I dared to look at the tall burly man standing over me, I was thinking of a giant with large hands. "You are coming with me!" he roared.

"No, I will not go with you!" I shouted, holding the sheet close to me the way a child holds a security blanket.

He bent down and grabbed my arm and pulled me to my feet. "If you don't come willingly, I'll throw you off the roof!" he bellowed.

My husband's silver teeth shined in the sunlight as he smiled and said, "Leave her alone. She's my wife."

"I don't care. She's mine. I could take her alive, or with one push, she goes flying off the roof, and nobody will have her."

"Look, you can come with us to Lodz, and I'll give you all the girls you want."

"No, I want this one. She's young and pretty, a pretty little Polish girl," he vaunted as if he had won a prize.

As my husband inched closer, the soldier inched closer to the edge, and I felt as if I was a rag doll dangling in the soldier's hand. I visualized myself flying off the roof and could see Bela crying in front of my broken body.

"I'll make you a deal," my husband said. "Let's sit down and talk."

"Talk now!" the soldier shouted in the wind.

"Alright, listen. I told you that we live in Ludz, and I know plenty of girls that would be happy to be with you. And why not, you are a very handsome soldier and our liberator! We will all sit down in my house and drink vodka, and I'll show you the beautiful girls. If you don't like them, you can have her and plenty of vodka."

The train had stopped in Ludz, and the soldier shouted, "Okay, but no tricks." Though he removed his arm from my waist, he was only a whisper away. I was thinking of Aunt Hanna's 'Man with the Black Hand' and shuddered. As my heart had begun to beat again, I became lightheaded and almost fell of the roof, and the soldier pulled me back and held onto my wrist until we climbed off the roof. It was a short walk to my husband's apartment, but the soldier never loosened his grip on me. He held onto my wrist while he sat at the kitchen table in front of a full liter of vodka. He began gulping the vodka the way a thirsty man would drink water. The bottle was almost empty, yet he hadn't loosened his grip on my wrist. The other two men placed more vodka bottles in front of him, until he had forgotten why he was holding onto my wrist, and my husband pried his hand open.

My hand felt numb, and my wrist was purple. I massaged my hand and wrist, then picked up my sack, and backed out of the kitchen. I found myself standing in the dark hallway, looking to find my way out and onto the street. I heard no sounds coming from the other apartments. The only loud voice was the soldier's, and I didn't know where to look for Mania. Did she catch the train home, or was she hiding in someone's apartment? I couldn't call her name for fear the soldier would hear me. I was startled when I felt someone touch my shoulder. My eyes had adjusted to the darkness, and when I turned around, a woman was standing in front of me. She touched her index finger to her lips, warning me to be quiet. She took my hand and guided me to a small room with a window facing the street. A single bed pushed against the white wall took up the entire room. The bed had a mattress, a pillow, and a blanket. A dusty light bulb on a white wire dangled from the ceiling. I knew that if I would put my head on the pillow, I would be able to sleep forever.

"Stay here until it's safe," the woman said. At a quick glance I could see that she would be Bela's age. She had thick curly, raven hair and round brown eyes and an oval face. She was wearing a short sleeve dress, and the number from Auschwitz was clearly visible. She was not pretty, but it was easy to see the willingness to lend a helping hand, and her kind, caring words gave her an angelic glow. She told me her name, but with so much on my mind, I had soon forgotten it. I was suddenly very frightened. What if the soldier would never get drunk? What if he would hurt the men who helped me? What if he finds me?

"Where is Mania?" I asked the woman.

"She's in the next room talking to Motek. He's one of the men you traveled with, and the other man, Szmulek, is my husband."

"I feel really bad for your husband. The Russian soldiers robbed him of his briefcase full of soap. He was very upset," I told her.

"You must be tired. Why don't you get some rest until the soldier leaves?" she said, closing the door behind her, and I didn't have a chance to thank her. I was hungry and tired, but I stood at the window, hoping to see the Russian soldier leave so that Mania and I could go back to the train station and leave the nightmare behind us. I would ask Mania not to tell anyone about what had happened. I didn't want to worry Bela. I only hoped that with these two sacks, Mrs. Marmelstain would have enough money to get us out of Poland. I'm not sure how long I was standing at the window before I saw my husband holding on to the soldier's arm and guiding him away from the building. Several times, my husband kept him from falling off the sidewalk. I left the room and went looking for Mania to tell her that we could leave now. It seemed to me that survivors from the camps had occupied the entire building, and I felt comfortable knocking on any door. I didn't have to knock on anyone's door. Szmulek's wife met me in the hallway again and guided me to Motek's room, a replica of the room I was in. Motek and Mania were sitting on his bed his arm around her shoulders. Mania seemed uninterested when I told her that the soldier was gone. "Why don't we go to the train station? We could be home in about two hours," I said, feeling lightheaded and sat down on the bed next to Mania.

The woman must have seen my face turn white and took my hand. "Come in the kitchen. I cooked a pot of soup this morning. You can eat, rest an hour or two, then go home," she said, her voice kind and caring.

I hadn't eaten since the bread yesterday morning and was grateful for the offer, but I wanted to go home before my husband would come back, or worse, the soldier.

"The soup sounds really good, but we need to go home," I said.

"You missed the train to Kelce. The next train won't leave until three o'clock," Motek said.

Mania and I ate the soup and bread hungrily and thanked the woman for her hospitality, and I went back to the little room, removed my shoes, and climbed on top of the bed with my clothes on. An hour later, I opened my eyes, and my husband was standing in front of my bed. Before I had a chance to stand up, he flattened his body on top of me, locking his lips on mine. I expected my first kiss to be romantic, the way I often watched Fraida and Joel locked in each other's arms. In my daydreams, the man kissing me was close to my own age, maybe a year or two older than I. Most of all, he would be my friend first. I would crave for his lips to touch mine. We would hold hands and walk in the park, not in Poland, but maybe Palestine or America. I had no idea what the word 'love' meant, other than loving and longing for my family. Though I was grateful to him for saving me from the Russian Soldier, that man was not what my dreams were about. I pushed at his chest until he loosened the suction on my lips and stood up. He was still standing very close to me, as if ready for another round of the same. Bewildered, I stood up, and being only five feet tall, I was able to twist and turn around him and leave the room dragging my sack behind me. I found my way to the kitchen, for it was the safest place to be, and I sat down at the table. He followed me in and sat down next to me and pushed his chair close enough for our thighs to touch. He rounded his arm around my chair and slowly inched up to my shoulders. The kitchen was very small, only enough room for a small round table and four chairs.

"What happened with the soldier?" I asked, still in shock from the unexpected kiss and stumbled on each word.

"It's alright. Don't worry. I took him to a place where he'll have a good time. He won't come back again," he said squeezing my shoulder.

"Thank you. I appreciate what you did for me, " I said and picked up my sack.

"What's the rush? Let's talk and get acquainted," he said, his hand kneading my shoulder. I slowly backed away with my chair towards the door until he had to loosen his grip on me.

"I have to go home, or my sister will worry," I said.

"The train to Kelce won't leave for another two hours. Let me show you around Lodz. I promise I won't touch you, but we have to make some arrangement so we can start our marriage," he said casually, as if he had made up his mind that we were truly married. I knew now that it would be useless to try and convince him that we were not married.

"You will have to talk to my sister about it," was all I said, and I agreed to go for a walk with him. I didn't protest when he held my hand. I felt secure. I didn't know his age, but I could tell that he was not a boy like Abramek. I guessed him to be at least ten years older than I was. We walked two blocks, and he stopped in front of an apartment house and knocked on a door. A man and woman let us in. After hugs and kisses from the woman and back slapping with the man, he introduced me as his wife.

"My name is Jadzia Sztraiman, and he's joking. We aren't married. We met only yesterday on the train, and we spent the night on the roof. I'm here with my girlfriend," I said quickly, to let them know that he and I didn't spend the night together alone. His friends looked puzzled, but nobody asked questions. We stayed only twenty minutes while he told his friends about the adventure with the Russian soldiers and made no mention about the quick wedding with the ring, and I was glad. I had decided that if he wanted to tell them about the ring, let it be later, when I'm gone. On the way back to his home, I said, "My name is Jadzia, and I would prefer it if you called me by my name, not wife."

"Alright, my name is, Herszel. After I'll sell the merchandise, it will take two or three days, and I'll come to Radom. After I talk to your sister, we will have a proper wedding," he said, as if I had no say in the matter.

All I wanted was to go home and find out if we had enough money to get out of Poland. The thought of going on another buying trip was very stressful. Herszel and Motek walked with us to the train station and didn't leave until our train to Kelce left.

"I'll see you in two days," he said, as the train was beginning to move.

It was dusk when we arrived home with the bulging sack on my shoulder. Bela was on her bunk bed reading a book by candlelight. I climbed up on the ladder to Bela's bed.

"We bought a lot of things. I'm sure Mrs. Malmelsztain will have enough money for the smuggler," I whispered happily so as not to be overheard.

Bela looked at me as if she had a secret, but she didn't want me to worry. "We'll see," was all she had said.

Mrs. Marmelsztain had just finished cooking potato soup and told Mania and me to sit down and eat. Though I wasn't too hungry, for four hours ago I had eaten a bowl of soup in Ludz, I ate Mrs. Marmelsztain's soup. I was conditioned to be hungry when there was food available, and tomorrow we might not get any food. I could switch my mind off and not feel hunger, if food was unavailable. It was as simple as turning off a light switch. I wanted to be rested if we had to go on another trip, but I hoped that we could get out of Poland before Herszel would come looking for me, though I didn't think he would. I was sure that after Mania and I left, he had a good laugh with his friends about the ring and forgot all about me. Again, I didn't tell Bela about the danger I was in on this trip or about Herszel and the ring. I had risked my life too many times so Bela and I would have enough money to get away from Poland, and I wasn't about to give up now. I was still in bed the next morning when Abramek came to see me and wanted to know if I'd like to see a movie with him.

"It's a musicale," he said excitedly.

Bela had left to visit her friends. Mrs. Marmelsztain had gone to the market place to sell the merchandise, and Mania was returning from the outhouse.

"Did your mama leave you money for us to go on a trip today?" I asked her.

"No!" she shouted. "I wouldn't go anyway today. I'm too tired. I'm not even sure if I want to go on another trip. I'm surprised that you are ready to go again after the last one?" she said, standing next to my bed.

"It looks like I'm free today," I told Abramek.

"I'll be back in one hour, so be ready," he said happily.

After eating a piece of bread that Mrs. Marmelsztain left on the table for us, I bathed and put on my only light blue, cotton skirt that Bela had made for me. We didn't have enough of the blue material for a dress, only a skirt. We didn't have the money for a zipper or elastic, so Bela and I sewed together pieces of the leftover blue material and made suspenders to hold up the skirt. In Wroclawa, a woman gave me a white cotton blouse, and I had another clean outfit. With the shoes from Theresianschtadt, I looked like a poor orphan, which I was, wearing ill-fitting clothes. All that mattered to me was that the clothes were clean, and Abramek didn't seem to be embarrassed being seen with me.

In the theater, Abramek held my hand the entire time. It was a wonderful war movie, and as we were leaving the theater, everyone sang the song the girl had sung to her beloved soldier. "Be brave and strong! For the Russian soil fight bravely! But don't forget the one you love, and come back to me whole!"

Though it was the end of August, it was a warm day. We walked in the park on carpets of large yellow leaves amidst lush shrubs and trees. We sat down on a bench, and Abramek took my hand in his and looked at me with sad brown eyes as if a great weight was sitting on his shoulders.

"I will soon be leaving Poland," he said, looking down at a leaf the breeze lifted off the ground.

"I'm hoping that Mrs. Marmelsztain has enough money from our trip so that Bela and I could get out, too," I said.

Abramek tightened his hand on mine. "I wish I could marry you and take you with me, but I live with my aunt, and she thinks that I'm too young. I can't disobey her. She's all I have left," he said sadly.

How could I have told him about what had happened to me on almost every trip and that I didn't need another marriage proposal? It never occurred to me to think of Abramek as more than a good friend, yet I couldn't fathom the thought of never seeing him again. Though the war was over, we were like two abandoned little birds trying to survive.

"When are you leaving?" I asked, trying not to show the loneliness I felt.

"As soon as we can arrange it," he muttered.

I felt a pain in the pit of my stomach. I wasn't sure what that meant? Maybe because everyday some survivor was leaving Radom, and Bela and I couldn't seem to find a way to get out, no matter how many trips I made. I was anxious to go home and find out if we had enough money to get out of Poland. When I walked in the room lined with bunk beds and saw the empty sacks, I was hopeful, and it must have shown on my face.

Mrs. Marmelsztain put a bowl of soup in front of me and said, "You have to go again. We don't have enough money for a smuggler."

The thought of going on another buying trip and climbing up on the roof was very stressful, but what choice did I have if I wanted us to get out of Poland?

Mania agreed to make one last trip, and we left that night to get an early start in the morning. We filled our sacks and spent another night on the roof. After two sleepless nights, we returned with two full sacks.

"I'm not making another trip," Mania announced, and her mother hugged her and said that she didn't have too.

Bela cornered me. "Do you know a man named Harszel?" she asked. "He claims to be your husband," she said, an angry tone in her voice.

I was so tired and had forgotten all about the man claiming to be my husband.

I had no choice but to tell her the story about the ring, leaving out the incidence with the Russian soldier.

"What did you tell him?" I asked.

"I told him to leave and never come back," she said with a scowl.

Abramek, with my friend Sala and her boyfriend, came to see me the next midmorning. We went to the photographer and took pictures together, but Abramek wanted more pictures with only the two of us. He always had the photographers make doubles so that I, too, would have pictures to remember us by. At the photographer's, Sala whispered in my ear that she and her sister were leaving in a day or so. Nobody spoke of leaving in the open. I couldn't understand why the authorities wouldn't let us leave, when they hated seeing the few survivors returning from the camps. All they had to do was open the borders and let us go. Abramek and I had spent the entire day together. We walked in the park and held hands, yet it felt as if he had already left. The next day I was told that Abramek and his aunt had left.

Now that Mania didn't want to go on any more trips, Mrs. Marmelsztain didn't feel obligated to us. She claimed that she had spent all the earned money on food for us and didn't have enough money for the smuggler. When she cooked the soup, she invited us to eat with her family, but it felt like charity.

Mrs. Marmelstain's son had returned from Russia and became very ill with malaria. A week later, he recovered, and the Marmelsztain family made plans to leave, but not with Bela and I. Two weeks later, they said good-bye and left us alone with all the empty beds. All the life threatening sacrifices were only for a piece of bread and a bowl of soup. Bela and I were on our own again. Each morning was colder than the previous day. We had no warm clothes or money for food or heat in the large room.

At dusk, Bela was still out visiting her few remaining friends. We had no electricity, and the room was cold. I undressed in the dark and remembered how much I missed my mama, and since I was alone in the room and wouldn't upset anyone, I allowed myself to cry until I heard Bela coming home. I turned around and pretended to be asleep. I didn't want her to be concerned about me.

In the morning, Bela said, "I want to talk to you."

I had planned on staying in bed all day, for there was no reason for getting up. "What do you want to talk about?" I asked.

"Do you remember Josek? He said he saw you several times."

"Yes, I remember him. He's the ugly boy with yellow teeth. Every time I turn my head, he's always staring at me. What about him?" I asked, wondering why she would bring up a boy's name I hardly knew and couldn't stand. Then, I wondered if he was another casualty to the anti-Semites, and I felt bad for having unkind thoughts about him.

"He's got some money and is offering to smuggle us out of Poland, but you would have to marry him first," Bela said, avoiding my eyes.

I was glad that he was alive. Then, I wondered if Bela was joking about the marriage part. The thought of marrying a man who always had a mouth full of saliva was repulsive to me, and I couldn't imagine my sister suggesting such sacrifice.

It was bad enough to almost getting raped by Russian soldiers or getting thrown off the train, but to spend the rest of my life with someone whose face I couldn't look at wouldn't be fair to Josek or to me. It would have been the same as selling myself at the market place.

"No, Bela. I can't stand him. He's repulsive," I said scrunching up my face.

When I saw the disappointment in Bela's green eyes, I buried my head in the pillow and soundlessly cried myself back to sleep. The next two days, we barely survived on Mrs. Marmelstain's few left over potatoes. On the third morning, I told Bela that I would marry Josek.

"He will have to smuggle us out of Poland before we are married," I said.

Bela left our room and told me to stay put until her return. After she left to deliver the message, I felt like a lamb going to the slaughter.

Bela returned an hour later and told me to get dressed and be ready to leave.

"Will I have to marry him before we leave the country?"

"No, you won't have to marry him at all. He's gone."

I couldn't stop my tears from showering my face. "I let you down," I said sobbing.

"It's alright. We are leaving here. Get ready. We'll be picked up in fifteen minutes."

"What do you mean? How?"

"A few minutes ago, a man stopped me on the street coming home and said he was a soldier from Palestine. He will pick us up and take us away from here to a kibbutz."

"We are going to Palestine?" I asked, not sure if I should be glad or disappointed.

But at that point, I didn't care where we were going, as long as it was far away from Poland.

"No, not right away," Bela said excitedly. "For a little while, we'll be in a kibbutz in Poland, with a group of boys and girls, and when we are ready, we'll get out of Poland to Palestine," she said proudly.

Chapter Thirty-Four: Leaving Radom and Beginning a New Journey

It was a chilly morning, and I put on both of my dresses for the journey. Bela and I were ready and waited outside when the pickup truck stopped in front of the building. A man jumped out from behind the steering wheel.

"My name is Benjamin Feldman. I'm a soldier and I live in Palestine. I'm here to recruit survivors for our homeland," he said.

Benjamin was a tall handsome young man, and I guessed him to be in his late twenties. Blond tendrils covered blue eyes. As he helped us on to the bed of the pickup and asked us to sit on the blanket that was spread out, a dimpled smile escaped his lips. He didn't have the wary look of a survivor. Benjamin was self-assured and knew what his mission was.

Bela and I held on to each other as the wind attempted to lift us off the blanket. I didn't know how far we were from Radom or where we were going. We stopped once on a quiet street, and Benjamin gave us a large piece of bread and butter, and he cut a slice from the round loaf for himself. He sat next to us on the edge of the pick-up bed, our feet dangling, and he talked about a Jewish homeland.

"We will build our land with our bare hands, and we will walk with our heads up high. Nobody will ever call us, 'dirty Jew,'" he said proudly.

Bela looked at him, tears stinging her eyes, and I remembered when we were children, she longed to go to Palestine, live on a kibbutz, and help build a homeland. I remembered my dream, too. In 1936, when Uncle Jacob and his wife Sala visited us from America, he looked rich and struggle-free. Aunt Sala was dressed in fine clothes. Everyday, she wore a different dress and new shoes and a very beautiful wristwatch. Uncle Jacob promised Mama that he was going to bring his entire family to the land of milk and honey. I wanted to have the opportunity to have a real home with my family. I was certain that Uncle Jacob, being rich, would send me to school, maybe even college? After all, his entire family vanished. Bela and I were the only survivors. He wouldn't want me to go through life with a fourth grade education. As I listened to Benjamin describing kibbutz life and Jewish farmers, I felt warm all over. The thought of living in a country we could call our own, where nobody would call us a dirty Jew or threaten our lives, was beyond anything we prayed for. But America, Uncle Jakob, Aunt Sohpy, and Uncle Charley were never far from my mind. I craved to be cared for and protected by older family members, the way an infant needed to feel it's mother's arms. I craved to be a child. I needed open arms to hold me and kiss my forehead and tell me that the man with the black hand would never touch me again.

After we finished eating, Benjamin climbed up on the pickup bed and lifted a large can from under a blanket. He filled the gas tank through a funnel and placed the empty can back on the pickup, next to several full cans fastened to the truck with ropes. He covered the cans with a blanket and told us to hold on to the sides of the truck.

It was dark when we arrived at a two-story house. Benjamin knocked on the door three times. A short teenage boy, a rifle swinging from his shoulder, cautiously unlocked the door and let us inside a dim entrance. A tiny light bulb hung from the ceiling on a short black cord. He had a warm smile for Benjamin. "Shalom Benjamin. Go upstairs. Our house is warm," the boy said, then locked the heavy door and remained at his post.

A door at the top of the stairs opened, and a man and woman greeted us warmly.

"My name is David. I'm the Madrit," he said. Since he looked older than the rest of the boys and girls, I understood that 'Madrit' meant that he was the elder. The mature woman stood next to the Madrit, smiling, and said, "My name is Sonia."

Bela spoke for both of us, "My name is Bela Sztraiman, and this is my sister, Jadzia."

Everyone stepped aside, giving us space to step inside. Sonia gave us a tour of the house and assigned us a room with six other girls. The room was lined with single and double beds and clean sheets, but all the beds were occupied, and we were given blankets and pillows to be spread out on the floor in a corner close to the door. I didn't mind at all, as long as I belonged. The entire house consisted only of the essentials. The main room had two large rectangular, weathered, splintered, wooden tables and benches. The laundry room was combined with the bathroom. Laundry was soaking in a large wooden balia atop a wooden stool. It was the same type my mama used to wash our clothes and bathe us in. A wooden stopper kept the water from leaking out. A large bar of soap set on the washboard. To my delight, there was a bathtub on four legs and a cold-water faucet. The bathroom was also the kitchen. Across from the bathtub, stood a wood burning stove. Large pots of water were heating on a roaring fire. "Feel free to get to know the other boys and girls," Sonia said and left us to browse.

Bela and I were hungry and very tired. We spread out our blankets and were about to go to sleep. Suddenly, voices echoed in song with Israeli lyrics. Hands reached out for us to join in dance. Bela remembered the Israeli dances from Shomer chatzair, the organization she belonged to before the war, and joined right in. As always, I emulated her every step. With arms on each other's shoulders, we danced in circles, and everybody sang the Hebrew songs, though nobody understood the meaning of the words.

Later in the evening, we were given a thick slice of bread with tea.

For the first time since my family was taken away from me, I had elders to do all the worrying for me. I didn't have to worry about the next meal, and I felt protected by the boy with a rifle on the bottom of the stairs. Everyone had chores to do. The boys and men took turns standing guard and helped with heavy lifting. The girls cleaned the house and helped with the cooking and laundry.

My job was laundry, and the men had to lower the stool underneath the balia, for I was unable to reach the washboard.

Sonia was a Lithuanian Jew and spoke mostly Yiddish. She did all the food shopping, but her Polish was flawed. She didn't want to be identified as a Jew and asked me to come along. Before we left the safety of the house, she dictated a list of food items to me. At the marketplace, I did all the talking, and nobody suspected that we were Jewish. I enjoyed going with Sonia. It reminded me of the times when I tagged along with Mama. Everything I did, every corner I turned, I was looking for Mama. At night when the house was quiet and everyone was asleep, I buried my face in the pillow and soaked it with my tears. Every Friday evening, the town's Jewish population visited our kibbutz for the Shabbat celebration, and all day, we were busy preparing our meager refreshments.

The kibbutz put on a stage show with skits, song, and poetry. Each week, I wrote and memorized one or two poems, and I was also included in the skits. Every Friday after the Shabbat candles were lit, I recited my poems in front of the audience, a group of about twenty to thirty people. Some of my poems were very sad, often a cry for Mama, and others were hope for freedom and a Jewish Homeland. My sad poems always brought tears to the guests' eyes. Since I was the most visible on stage, Sonia wanted me to have a new dress. Of course, it wouldn't be completely new. Someone taller and larger all around wore it many times before she gave it away. The large navy blue dress was in good condition. The dressmaker and her husband were survivors and lived in town. Every Friday night, they were our guests. The dressmaker looked at me with sad brown eyes and promised to make me a dress that would look as good as new.

"You will have to come by trolley-car to my house for several fittings," she said, running a motherly palm lovingly down my hair.

"I'm not afraid of riding in the trolley-car. I'll just pretend to be a Polish Catholic. All I have to do is cross myself when I see a priest or a nun, and I have to act like I'm not afraid," I said reassuringly.

A smile escaped the dressmaker's thin, lined face, but her brown eyes were as sad as the blackest clouds. My appointments with the dressmaker were always in late afternoon, after my chores.

Winter had begun early in November. Hail mixed with snow was biting into me each time I went for a fitting. I should have been use to the cold by now. All the time during the war, I never had more than a thin dress to wear, even in blizzards. Now, I had a paper-thin coat Mrs. Marmelsztain left on my bunk before she and her children left Poland. The gray spring coat was left over from the shopping trips Mania and I went on. The coat was a very small size, and Mrs. Marmelsztain couldn't find a customer for it, and it didn't fit any of her children. The coat didn't keep me warm, but it was better than no coat at all. The trolley stopped only one block from the dressmaker, but I had to walk three blocks from and to the kibbutz. I didn't mind. I was grateful to get a new dress.

The dressmaker and her husband had a son. I guessed him to be about twenty years old. They all lived in a small one-room apartment. All I could see by a dimly naphtha lamp was a very old scratched wooden table and chairs. Three single beds lined the walls. Each time I arrived, she had a hot cup of tea with sugar and lemon on her table for me. She held up a sheet for me to change for the fitting and told the men not to peek.

The dressmaker must have sensed how much I needed my mama and doted over me as if she was my surrogate. For my third and last fitting, I finished my chores earlier, and it was still light outside when I arrived at the dressmaker. When I put on my finished dress, she was pleased at the perfect fit.

"Isn't Jadzia a beautiful girl?" She said looking at her son, and I felt my face burning when I saw the tall man with curly black hair grinning at me. "You wait here. I have a few finishing touches on the dress. Then, you can go home," she said.

I had no idea what the finishing touches were, as she held up the sheet for privacy. Obediently, I slipped off my new dress and slipped into the old. She kept me another hour, fussing with the dress, a stitch here, a tug there, then ironing, and all the while telling her son, in Yiddish, how talented I was. I felt my face burning the entire time.

"You should come with me next Friday night and see how beautiful Jadzia recites the poetry she herself writes. I cry my eyes out every time. Sonia takes her to the Goyim shopping," she said, as her son sat by the window pretending to watch the falling snow, but I could see his subtle glances when he didn't think I was looking. When he didn't respond to his mother's statement, she said, "Do you know why Sonia takes her shopping? Because she looks and talks Polish like a Shiksa." While ironing a sleeve, she said, "Jadzia, do you speak Yiddish?"

"I understand most of it?" I said apologetically.

"Didn't your family talk to you in Yiddish?"

"Yes, but without thinking about it, I answered in Polish because it was easier."

"I understand. Our Szulimek does the same thing with us," she said, looking lovingly at her smiling husband, and the eyes of both parents turned to their son, and my heart was breaking with envy. I had never missed my parents more than at that moment.

Though it was dark by the time I left the dressmaker's house, the streetlights bathed freshly fallen snow in golden sparks. With my new dress folded over my forearm, I was the only passenger in the trolley car. I was apprehensive, but I quickly remembered the time when I was a child and began to think like a Catholic. All of my fears dissipated. I straightened my back and lifted my chin, and for the entire trolley car ride, I was a Polish Catholic.

Three blocks from the kibbutz, I stepped off the trolley car into two feet of soft snow. I wrapped my thin coat tightly around my chest and stepped onto the sidewalk where the snow had hardened, and I began walking briskly. The street was soundless. The packed snow made crunching sounds with each step I took. It was eerie, yet the gold sparkles from streetlights on pure white snow in the still of the night felt holy. Though my toes and fingers had never thawed since the camps, and they ached, I slowed my pace to a stroll until I heard another pair of footsteps. I looked around and saw a Russian soldier crossing the street and speeding towards me. I began walking faster and heard his footsteps closing in on me. I began to run, and he began to chase me. My nightly nightmares since the liberation had become reality. I was running from the Gestapo, and his whip and dog with enormous teeth, and my legs were barely moving. Just as the whip was about to burn into my back, and the dog's teeth closed in on my legs, I woke up with my heart beating so fast that I could barely catch my breath. I forced myself to run and tripped on the ice, but I didn't fall. The soldier was less than five feet from me when I saw our boy with the rifle. He ran out and pulled me inside, locked the door, and told me to go upstairs and alert the Madrit. That night, four boys with rifles stood guard on the stairs, and the Madrit gave an order that nobody was to leave the kibbutz after dark alone, not even the boys.

Chapter Thirty-Five: Bela Was Leaving Our Kibbutz

At the end of November, a man, I guessed to be in his thirties, arrived to our kibbutz and had a lengthy conversation with Bela. I didn't question her, and she didn't volunteer. Two days later, he returned, and again I saw him speaking animatedly with Bela. When he left, Bela told me that the man was a Madrit from another kibbutz named Shomer Chatzair.

"Jadzia, he asked me to come and live in his kibbutz. He said that he wants to send me on a seminar to study to become a teacher. When I'm ready, I'll be teaching children in Israel. That's what our country will be named, Israel!" she voiced excitedly.

"Isn't Shomer Chatzair the organization you belonged to before the war?"

"Yes, and that's where I would like to be."

"If that's what you want, we'll go," I said.

"No, Jadzia. He wants only me. You will stay here. The boys and girls in this kibbutz are your brothers and sisters now," she said, her face flushed.

I felt my throat tightening ,and the lump getting bigger with each painful breath. I forced a smile. "When do you have to go?" I asked, choking back the tears.

"I'll be here for the Shabbat celebration and leave Sunday morning," she said, her eyes had a far away look as if she had already left.

"So soon? This is already Thursday?"

"I have to. Don't be afraid, Jadzia. I told the Madrit, and he understands."

But I didn't understand. I wanted to say, Bela, we only have each other now. Why do you want to separate? I didn't say anything for fear I'd begin to cry and make her feel guilty. I knew all along how badly she needed to be away from me, away from her stupid little sister who had given her so much grief. After all, she was only a teenager herself and was forced to be burdened with me in five concentration camps and even after the liberation. We were free now, and she shouldn't have to worry about me. She deserved to be happy, and I should be happy for her. I told myself.

"You're right, Bela. All the boys and girls and the Madrit are now my family. We'll go to Palestine and build a homeland, and we'll call it 'Israel,'" I said, and I could see Bela's shoulders drop and her face relaxed.

I sat down at the table and wrote a poem about building a homeland brick by brick for every Jew to have a place, and I recited the poem Friday evening at our Shabbat celebration.

Our kibbutz boys were not as forgiving. Bela had to be punished for leaving the kibbutz. It was tradition, and everyone knew about the punishment except Bela and I.

The night before Bela's departure, the house was quiet, and everyone went to sleep.

I couldn't fall asleep. I was worried that once Bela and I separated, we might never find each other again.

Three weeks ago, Bela was given a bed, but it was too narrow for both of us, and I didn't mind sleeping on the floor. I heard footsteps coming toward our room. Quietly, so as not to wake Bela, I stood up and saw that the entire kibbutz was tiptoeing towards our room. In my bare feet, I walked over to the door, and a boy put one hand over my mouth, and with the other hand, he encircled my waist and hauled me out of the room. I squirmed, trying to get him to loosen his grip on me, but he held on tight.

"If you promise to keep quiet, I'll tell you about our tradition, and you can watch," he whispered.

I relaxed in his grip, and we tiptoed back to our room, but he never loosened his hold on me. I watched helplessly as one boy uncovered Bela's feet, and another eased a rolled up page from a note pad between her big toe. A third boy lit a match to the rolled up page. As the paper began to burn, I fought to get out of the boy's grip, and Bela woke up screaming.

The boys extinguished the flame with a pitcher of water, and everyone except Bela and I laughed. Bela was angry, but only for a moment. She knew it was tradition.

I was awake all night, hoping Bela would change her mind and decide to stay, or she would ask me to come with her. When I saw her leave in the morning, I remained on the blanket and pretended to be asleep. I watched my sister tiptoe from our room and hoped that she would find happiness. She deserved to be happy. She was smart and funny, and she had a good heart. I remembered how she took care of Tusia and her friends in Blyzin who were stricken with typhus, and she took care of me when I had typhus. I knew that she would be a wonderful teacher. The children would love her.

A week after Bela left our kibbytz, she came for a visit and told me that she was learning a lot and looked forward to teaching the children in Israel.

I told her not to worry about me. "You were right. Everyone here is my family," I said.

I could see in her eyes that she was relieved. Bela came to visit when she could, and I was always happy to see her, but I didn't cling to her as I had in the past. I continued with my chores and entertained our guests with poetry and skits, but I felt as alone as an abandoned bird in a nest, and I knew that I would have to learn to fly. I made friends with Bronia. Bronia was one year older than I was. She was very pretty with blond curly hair and blue eyes. Her mama lived in town and visited often. On one of her visits, Bronia's mama strolled in with a young man and introduced him to Bronia. They fell in love, and he came to visit every day.

A new girl, close to my age, arrived with her mama. Lola was a pretty girl. She had dark hair and a fair complexion. We became good friends, but she spent most of her time with her mama.

The boys in the kibbutz were very nice, but after all of the previous marriage proposals, I kept my distance.

Other girls were in pairs with friends or sisters. I was well liked, but I was still alone, sleeping in a corner on top of a blanket, and I didn't mind. I knew that I had to accept the fact that I was alone, and I was beginning to dream of going back to school and getting an education.

A week before our departure from Poland, several people joined our kibbutz. Bela came to visit that week, and I told her that we were leaving in a few days.

"Do you know when you are leaving Poland? I don't know where you will be or how to find you?" I asked.

"No, I don't know when I would be leaving, but don't worry. I'll find you," she said, and we never said goodbye or hugged. The minute Bela left our kibbutz for the last time, I felt as if half of my heart went with her. I knew that the other half was left in my chest and could never be whole until my sister and I reunited. Having her with me, I still felt that I was a family member. Now, except for complements on my poetry from the guests and glances from the boys in the kibbutz, I felt as if I didn't matter, and most of the time, I felt invisible.

Chapter Thirty-Six: Leaving Poland

One day before our departure from Poland, a man arrived at our kibbutz, and the Madrit lined us up military fashion. "This is Gidon. He is a 'chaial,' a soldier from Israel. Gidon will be traveling with us to make sure that we cross the border safely."

Gidon, I guessed to be in his mid twenties, was of medium height, had light brown hair, and a warm smile. Though he was a young man his demeanor made me feel secure.

After our evening meal of potato soup and a slice of bread, Gidon called a meeting to order. "I want you to listen carefully," he began. "Tomorrow, early in the morning, we are all leaving Poland," he said, but he failed to tell us where we were going. The way everyone always talked about going to Israel, I was sure that that was where we were going, and I felt bad to be arriving in the land of Bela's dream before her. But now, I knew that I would find her, for I was sure that she too would soon be in Israel because that's where she always wanted to be.

Gidon sat at the head of the long rectangular table, where everyone was in his full view. He handed each of us a passport and asked us to memorize the name, in case we were asked.

"You are not to speak Polish or Russian at the border. You can speak any other language, make up words, anything but Polish, and you must give up everything written in Polish. We are leaving Poland as Greek citizens. If we are searched at the border and the patrol finds anything, the smallest word written in Polish, we will all be put in prison, and we would never leave Poland," he said. Gidon's eyes rested on everyone separately and asked, "Do you have anything that would identify you as being a Polish citizen or with the Polish language?"

I told him that I had a book of poems, and he asked me to give it to him.

Reluctantly, I handed him my scribbling, and he put it in his pocket. After he finished questioning everyone, he reached in his pocket and began to read my poems. When he finished the last page, he stood up and sat down next to me.

"You are very talented, Jadzia, and I will take good care of your poetry. Your poetry will be translated into Hebrew for our people to enjoy," he said, running a hand over my hair.

We were awakened at dawn and told to get dressed and be ready, but to be very quiet. "We don't want to alert the neighbors," the Madrit said.

By the time we were ready to leave, all of the town's Jews, including the dressmaker, her husband, and their son fell in line with us. We left the house that had been my sanctuary for, at least, four months. With our backpacks in place, we walked to the train station where a passenger train waited for us to enter a vacant car. I remembered the crowded trains that Mania and I went on shopping sprees to Wroclawa, and I was thinking that this was luxury.

A middle-aged man, not from our kibbutz, was sitting alone. He saw that I was alone and looking for a place to sit. He moved to the seat next to the window and asked me to sit with him. He told me that he was a doctor in Poland before the war and was sent to Auschwitz in 1941.

"My wife and two children perished in the Ghetto. My firstborn daughter would now be your age. She, too, was a pretty child. I don't even have a picture of her. My son didn't live to have a Bar mitzvah," he said, turning his head towards the window and dabbed at his eyes with a handkerchief. He was a kind and caring man, and I confided in him that I worried about my sister. He reassured me that we would find each other.

"Your sister sounds like a very smart young lady and a patriot for Israel. The war is over, and you both survived, so you'll find her." The way he said it, with a positive tone in his voice, sounded like a promise. When my eyes were closing, he gently guided my head on his shoulder, and I dozed off. When I next opened my eyes, I saw a man from the town's Jews sitting on the floor on blankets close to a girl his own age. While they were whispering and laughing and touching each other, he held his gaze on me. He had bright red hair and a full freckled face. I guessed him to be in his early twenties. I was feeling very uncomfortable and to avoid his steady stare, I kept my eyes closed.

We vacated the train during the night. I had no idea where we where. We walked and stumbled many miles on icy hills holding on to each other, or tree stumps. It was still dark when we marched into a structure with torn down barbed wires. Inside, the wooden house was lined with bunk beds, and everyone lined up for the latrine.

I welcomed the warm bed, even if it was only for two hours sleep. At dawn, we walked to the railroad station and again occupied an entire passenger car and traveled until the train stopped for the night. Again, I had no idea where we were. We left the train at dawn and began walking knee deep in snow and icy hills.

At noon on January the third 1946, Gidon brought the group to a halt. "We are coming close to the border, so remember what I told you. You do not understand a single Polish word. I will be your translator," he whispered.

"These hills have ears," he added.

After another mile of climbing slippery hills, the border patrol came into focus. Gidon lifted his hand, motioning us to stop. While he showed his passport to a patrol officer, a Polish and Russian soldier stood in front of us, asking for our passports?

We didn't respond, for we weren't supposed to understand Polish.

Gidon mumbled something in Hebrew mixed with Yiddish, giving us a signal, and we all held out our Greek passports. All at once, we became animated and began speaking with each other in a mixture of languages, and none of us knew what we were talking about. We could have won an award for best acting. After the border gate lifted and we began crossing the border, I overheard a Polish border patrol saying, "The Greeks have the craziest language I ever heard." Their laughs echoed in the icy hills we still had to climb. Exhausted, we rested on the snow-banks.

Though we had passed the border I didn't believe that we had reached freedom. All that snow and ice didn't resemble the Israel as it was described to me. I visualized Israel where the sun always shined and where fields of orange trees, grapes, and figs were in abundance. I became very anxious to get away from the border for fear the patrol would become wise to us. I turned to the Madrit, "This doesn't look like Israel. How many more borders do we need to cross before we reach Israel? " I asked.

The Madrit smiled, "We aren't going to Israel yet. We are in Munchen, Germany, on the American side, but we will soon go to Israel," he said proudly.

I was happy to be away from Poland and on the American side, but I now worried that I may never find my sister.

We continued climbing icy hills until we reached civilization. After five or more blocks of walking on sidewalks, we were marched inside a museum of art. We were guided to a room on the far right. The walls were lined with bunk beds. In the center of the room stood a large rectangular table filled with slices of white soft bread, and everyone ate hungrily.

Chapter Thirty-Seven: We Have Crossed the Border to Freedom

Standing at the cul-de-sac's entrance, my mind far in the past, memories were pouring in with heart breaking emotions. As my eyes were fixed on Fraida's white lace curtains, I suddenly remembered Bela's words in Willischtal, "If by some miracle we should survive, we will be placed in a museum for everyone to look at us." I was now thinking that we should have been placed in a museum for people to look at the remnants that returned from hell. "Oh Bela, my wonderful sister, I wish we were reminiscing together. How I loved and respected you. Not a day goes by that I don't miss you," I whispered to the waving curtains.

I was startled when Carla Stevenson touched my shoulder, "It's time to catch the train to Warsaw. We have a plane to catch," she said softly.

"Thank you, Carla. I was just standing here, remembering a time long ago. I have a hard time believing that I actually survived such atrocity. If I should write a book about my life, I wonder if anyone would believe me."

"I would believe," Carla said, taking my hand, and together, we walked back to the Hotel Europa to collect our backpacks.

As we passed Janina's house on the way to the hotel, I was thinking that, much as I was glad to see my three school friends, it was a grim reminder that being Jewish in Poland was still a sin. I was grateful for my American passport. Being an American citizen is the most precious gift, and I shall never forget and never take for granted the chance for freedom.

"Thank you, Carla. You're good friend," I said, as I turned away from my roots for the last time.

As I boarded the plane, I returned the attendant's smile. "I'm going home," I said with pride. She didn't know how precious the word home was to me, but I will always cherish the privilege.

Again, I watched as the plane lifted with ease and was soon above the clouds. Again, I invited all my relatives to follow me home. "So, you'll know where I live," I mused. My mind went back to January 3, 1946 and to Munchen, Germany, when we arrived at the museum.

We didn't come to look at old paintings. It was our first step to freedom. It was our temporary sanctuary. I put my little backpack down on a bunk-bed by the door and sat down, hoping to see my sister arriving with her group. I didn't see the red headed man sitting next to me until I was startled when he touched my shoulder. I turned my head towards him for only a moment. I didn't want to lose sight of the open door.

He took my hand in his. "Jadzia, I couldn't keep my eyes off you throughout our journey. You are a beautiful girl and lady. I'm asking you to marry me and leave the libbutz. I will take good care of you and make you very happy. All you have to do is say yes, and we'll leave right now. I have many friends in Munchen. We'll have a place to live, and later we'll decide where we would make our home."

I withdrew my hand from his grip and stood up. I moved closer to the door, and my eyes hung on the entrance. He stood next to me, making promises, and tried to persuade me to leave with him. I became annoyed and said, "Please, why don't you ask the girl you romanced on the train? I'm not leaving the kibbutz for you. I don't know you. I don't even know your name, and because of the way you behaved with that girl on the train and then just walked away from her, I don't want to know it. I'm going to Israel," I said and sat down on the edge of the bunk, hoping to see my sister come through the door.

The red headed man sat down next me, trying again to persuade me.

"The girl on the train didn't mean anything to me, but I respect you," he said, reaching for my hand.

I turned my back towards him and my eyes towards the door. "Please leave, I don't want to miss my sister in case she comes looking for me."

He stood up, his broad shoulders hunched, and left the room.

Lola sat down on the edge of the bunk next to me. "Don't worry, Jadzia. Your sister will find you. Why don't we take a walk? There are so many people outside."

"Thank you, Lola, but I want to stay here in case she shows up."

While Lola tried to give me solace, a tall thin man wandered in. He had black straight hair, combed back, and dark complexion. The cuffs of beige slacks were tucked inside black boots. He placed himself close to the door and stood against the wall, a lit cigarette between his fingers. I suddenly remembered who he was and exclaimed, "Look, Lola this man is from Radom! I know him from the Blyzin concentration camp!"

"How do you know him? He is even older then your sister," Lola argued.

"He was an electrician. In Blyzin, that meant he could roam the camp. He bribed the Ukrainian to look the other way, while he bought bread at the barbed wires from the Polish people and then sold it to the girls in our barracks that still had some valuables. Of course, my sister and I didn't have the money or valuables to buy a piece of bread," I said, remembering how we starved.

"Do you know his name? Why don't you ask him if he is who you think he is," Lola said, curiosity written allover her face.

"I'm too embarrassed. If he is who I think he is, he had a nickname, but I don't remember it. I knew his girlfriend, Hanna. Hanna first dated Jacob, this man's younger brother.

"How did you know?"

"We were in AFL together. It was no secret. Jacob once came to see her. When we were transferred to Blizyn, Hanna started seeing this man, Jacob's older brother.

Lola was getting confused with the two brothers. Was Hanna dating both brothers at the same time?" she asked.

"This man," I said, pointing with my head without looking at him, had been shipped to Blizyn from Radom early on. When we were transferred from AFL to Blizyn, his younger brother, Jacob remained in Radom. Hanna must have fallen in love with the older brother in Blyzin because he was bringing her food, and he was always on her bunk. My bunk was at the far end, and I had to pass Hanna's bunk to get to mine. I closed my eyes each time I passed them, for I was so embarrassed."

Again, Lola was confused. "Why were you embarrassed?"

"Because...on Sundays, he was always on her bunk, and they were in each other's arms," I said, feeling my face becoming hot from the memory.

"So, why is he standing here alone? Where is his girlfriend?" Lola asked.

"I don't know. After Blyzin, we were in different camps."

"Maybe she dropped him when the war was over and took up with his younger brother, Jacob, again?" Lola laughed.

"Max! That's his name. I'm certain!" I said louder than I meant to.

Max heard me and began strolling towards us.

"He's coming over," Lola whispered, and I wished I hadn't spoken so loud. Max stopped in front of me. "Who are you? Are you from Radom?"

"Yes," I said feeling embarrassed. "My name is Jadzia Sztraiman. I was in the same barracks with your girlfriend, Hanna, in AFL and in Blyzin."

"She died of tuberculosis in one of the camps," he said, puffing on his cigarette. Then, he smothered the glow with his thumb and index finger and put it in his shirt pocket.

"I'm so sorry. She was such a pretty girl. She had an older sister. Did she survive?" I asked. Nobody was surprised to hear that people didn't survive. It was more surprising that someone did survive.

"Yes, Gucia survived," he added and continued staring at me as if I reminded him of someone. "I wish I knew you, but I don't," he said, adding one short dry cough. As I began to walk away, I turned back and said, "I'm Bela-Boy's sister," hoping that he knew Bela.

Nobody knew me, but many people knew Bela. If I said that I was Bela-Boy's sister, people would most often say, "I know Bela-Boy," and sometimes through her, I too was remembered.

"No, I don't know your sister," Max said.

I glanced up at him and saw that he would have been closer to Fraida's age.

"Maybe you knew my oldest sister. Her name was Fraida. She was married to Joel Altman?"

When I mentioned Fraida, he turned his attention back to me.

"I knew a girl named Fraida. She was very pretty. Did she like to dance?"

"Before the war, she and Joel went dancing a lot," I said hopeful.

"Was she taller than you, and do you look like her?"

"Yes," I said, grateful to have found someone that knew a member of my family.

"I knew your sister, Fraida. What did your tata do?"

"My tata was Jeremy Sztraiman. He was a baker," I said excitedly.

"Was your tata a short man, not much taller than you are?" He smiled facetiously, and I wondered why I cared that he knew me or my family. I suddenly felt as if I was a lost child, far away from home, waiting for someone to claim me.

"Yes," I said, looking down at my fingers as if trying to count them.

"Now I know who you are," Max said, bending his head to look at my face.

"Your tata and I were good friends. I installed the electricity when you moved from the Penc House to the cul-de-sac in Old Town."

I was preoccupied to have found someone that knew my family and failed to realize that Lola had walked away to stand next to her mother, and both looked in my direction as if making sure I wouldn't disappear.

Max lit the same cigarette he had smothered a minute ago. "Did you know that Joel survived?"

"Joel...my brother-in-law? He's alive?" My heart pounded with happiness.

"Where is he, and did you see my sister, Fraida?" I asked without taking a breath. Please, God, let him say yes.

"No, I didn't see her."

I felt all the blood draining from my head to my toes, and I sat down on the bunk for balance.

"Joel lives in Stuttgart. It's possible that you sister is with him. Would you like to see him? I could take you to him and bring you back."

"Do you think that you could bring me back before we leave for Israel? We are leaving in a day or two."

"I could bring you back right after you see your brother-in-law."

"Oh. thank you. I'm very grateful. When can we go?"

"Right now."

I ran to Lola and told her everything in less than two minutes.

"Be careful, Jadzia. You don't know this man," her mother cautioned.

"But I do know him. I mean, I don't know him personally, but he just told me that he was my tata's friend, and he knew my entire family."

"Talk to the Madrit," Lola advised me.

I didn't have to approach the Madrit, for he was already talking to Max, and I was sure that he would give me permission. But when I saw the anger in the Madrit's face, I knew that I would have to convince him to let me go, and I would reassure him that Max would bring me back right after seeing Joel and hopefully Fraida. I would bring Fraida to the kibbutz in the museum and introduce her to everybody, and then, I'd go to Israel and find Bela and tell her that Fraida was alive.

The Madrit's shouts could be heard on every street in Munchen. "You can't take her away from here! She's an innocent child! You should be ashamed of yourself!" the Madrit bellowed.

I was sure that any moment Max would leave, and I would never know if my oldest sister survived.

"Please," I begged the Madrit. "All I'm asking for is your permission to leave for only one day to go to Stuttgart and find my brother-in-law and find out if my sister is alive?"

"Jadzia, I don't trust this man. He's lying. He doesn't know your family."

"But he does know my family. He told me where I lived in Radom."

"Alright," he said to Max. "If you knew her family so well, what was her Tata's name?"

"Jeremy," Max said, inhaling his cigarette and blowing smoke.

"What was his last name?"

Max was unable to answer, then said, "Nobody bothered with last names.

He was known as Jeremy the Baker."

"You see, Jadzia. You see. He didn't know your family at all. I can't let you leave with him. He can't be trusted," the Madrit said. Meanwhile, the entire kibbutz had formed a circle with Max being boxed in between two men. One threatened him with a stick. The other, a man in his mid twenties, was holding up his precious violin, ready to sacrifice it on Max's head. I stepped inside the circle.

"Please," I cried, "I'll be back tonight or in the morning. I have to go to Stuttgart and see my brother-in-law. I have to find out if my sister's alive?" I cried and pleaded on deaf ears.

I saw that any moment Max was going to be clabbered on the head with a stick and violin. I left the circle, picked up my backpack, and ran back inside the circle with my backpack on my back. I grabbed Max's large hand, pulling him out of harms way and out the door. We were being chased by all of the kibbutz's boys, but we ran faster. Max guided me through side streets, and we hid in a building behind a door until dusk. We left the building and began walking at a normal pace. I had no idea where he was guiding me, but I trusted him and followed like an obedient child. After a long brisk walk, Max was out of breath, and we stopped in the middle of the street in front of a large old well. The well was secured with about three feet high bricks. I leaned against the well with my backpack on my back. Max sat down on top of the well and lit a cigarette. I had no idea where Stuttgart was. Was Stuttgart a street in Munchen? Was it a walking distance or a bus ride? While he was exhaling thick gray smoke I said, "Are we going to Stuttgart, now?"

"It's too late now. The trains are not going anywhere now," he said between puffs.

I now knew that Stuttgart was a different City. "So where are you taking me now?" I asked meekly, being grateful for his kindness.

"I'm sharing a room with a friend in a German woman's apartment. It's not too far from here. You will stay tonight."

I suddenly felt lost. What would happen to me if Max left me standing next to the well and walked away? On my darkest days, I always had Bela and other people around me. Now, I only had Max, and he was a total stranger, someone I saw in Blyzin, and he told me that he was friends with my tata and promised to take me to my brother-in-law. I tried hard to mask my fears, but I had to know.

"When will you take me to Stuttgart?" I ask, trying to keep desperation from revealing itself in my voice.

"Do you want to marry me?" Max asked casually, as if asking me if I was hungry or was tired from the long trip. I could have answered yes to both questions.

After so many marriage proposals in the last months since the liberation, it seemed natural to me now. Though this time, I was taken by surprise. It had never occurred me that Max would be interested in me. He seemed so worldly, and I was only a teenager with a fourth grade education. In all the years of the war and the seven months after the war, it was the first time I had found myself alone. What if I declined his proposal, and he would walk away from me and left me stranded in the middle of the street? My mind raced as if my decision to give Max an answer had been a matter of life and death. "Yes," I found my saying.

Without another word, Max walked, and I followed. Being about seven inches taller than I was, he could just as well have been a giant. Max's long stride doubled mine, and I found myself jogging behind him. The fear of getting lost after dark, in the middle of Munchen among Germans, was too frightening. I had to trust him. After almost getting clabbered by the boys in the kibbutz because of me, I had to believe that he would take care of me. My mind was racing a mile a minute, until I found myself following him up three flights of stairs. Max unlocked a door to an apartment, and I followed him into a dim room. A light bulb, skirted with a glass shade, hung from the ceiling on a black wire. A window separated two full-sized beds, one against each wall. A brown wooden nightstand stood next to each bed. A small sofa stood at the foot of the bed on the left side. A chest of drawers stood next to the door. A large rectangular table with four chairs stood between the two beds.

I hadn't had much sleep since we left the Kibbutz in Poland, and I was tempted to sit down on the sofa, but I was afraid that if I did, I would fall asleep sitting down. I put my backpack on the sofa and asked Max where I would sleep. He told me that I could sleep in the bed on the left side of the wall.

"My roommate sleeps in this bed," he said pointing to the bed on the right side. "But he's out of town for a few days."

I didn't ask where he would sleep. Since he had made a point of telling me that his roommate was out of town, I was certain he would sleep in his roommate's bed,

"Would it be possible for me to bathe?" I asked as he was leaving the room.

Within minutes, the apartment owner entered the room carrying a basin filled withwarm water, a piece of soap, and a towel. A tall slim young teenager followed her in. "My name is Baierlib, and this is my daughter, Inga," she said. Frau Baierlib was a middle-aged, non-descriptive, medium height woman. Her salt and paper hair hung straight, close to her ears. Her face was heavily wrinkled with loose skin under her chin and neck. She looked old enough to be Inga' s grandmother. As most Germans after the war, Frau Baierlib was very polite. Before she left the room, she said, "If you need anything, please ask?" Inga lingered, though her mother ordered her to give me privacy. At thirteen, Inga was about five feet, seven inches tall. She had a pretty oval face, dark blond hair, and the largest and bluest eyes I had ever seen. She looked lonely and eager to interact with another teenager, though I was four years older than she was. She hadn't made a move to leave my room, until her mother called to her several times. After I finished bathing, I put on my only white, cotton nightgown that I had salvaged from the days of my travels when I was buying clothes from German women. After many months of sleeping on the kibbutz' floor, sitting in trains, and climbing hills, the bed felt as if I had been gliding on a heavenly a magic carpet. Exhausted, I fell asleep as soon as I closed my eyes. I was dreaming that Bela and I went to Stuttgart, and we found Fraida. We were very sleepy from the long trip, and I curled up between my two sisters in our tata' s small white bed. Suddenly, I felt as if I was buried beneath their arms and legs and couldn't breathe. Gasping for air, my eyes flew open to the ceiling light, and I saw Max in my bed pressing his body against me and was lifting my white cotton nightgown. I wanted to push his hand away and get out of his bed and sleep on the little sofa, but I couldn't move. I wanted to tell him not to touch me, to please leave the bed, but my throat had collapsed, and I was unable to utter a single word. I felt as if I were a ghostly being looking down at my body, unable to connect. Max's muffled voice sounded as if it had come from a tunnel, "Tomorrow morning you will be my wife."

Only seconds later, without warning, I felt his body on top of mine, his knees separating my legs. Piercing pain, such as I had never known possible, had begun. I felt as if my body was being shredded into a million pieces. A guttural scream, "Mama, where are you! Help me!" echoed from the hollow of my throat. The pain lasted only minutes until he rolled off me, but it felt as if it would never end. I'm not sure if I had lost consciousness, but when I woke up to a sunny day, my cotton nightgown was wet up to my waist. I hadn't wet my bed since I was a very young child, and I was frightened. I

317

was glad that I was alone in bed and in the room. My bath water from the night before was still in my room. I took off my nightgown and washed it. The sheet was wet, and I washed it too. I put on the dress I wore the day before and left the room to empty the basin, and I filled it with cold water. I rinsed the nightgown and sheet and hung them to dry on chairs. I filled the basin again and washed my body. I now knew that I had to marry Max. Nobody would want a girl that wasn't a virgin. I dressed quickly in my new dress the kibbutz had remodeled for me. I put on the shoes from Theresienstadt and was ready to go to Stuttgart, but Max wasn't home.

Frau Baierlib was in the little kitchen sitting next to a little round table.

"Good morning, Frau Max," she said.

I wondered why she addressed me as Mrs. Max?

"My name is Jadzia," I said.

"Did you see Max?" I asked her.

"No, I just came out my room," she said.

I returned to my room and waited. One hour later, Max sauntered in to tell me that there was bread and butter in the dresser drawer.

"Are we going to Stuttgart now?" I asked feeling anxious.

"I'm busy today. I'll take you tomorrow," he said.

I felt myself becoming smaller than I had already been, and before I had said another word, he had left the apartment. I stood in the middle of the room, not knowing what to do next. I stretched out on the little sofa and closed my eyes, but I couldn't sleep I wanted to see Joel. It was the reason why I left the security of the kibbutz. I put on my thin coat and went back to the kibbutz, hoping to find Bela. I retraced my steps and found my way to the museum. Lola and her mother were the only two people in the room. I showered them with questions. Lola told me that the entire kibbutz had left early this morning.

"No, I didn't see Bela," she said avoiding eye contact.

I told her that Max was taking me to Stuttgart tomorrow, but Lola"s silence spoke volume, and I didn't have to ask. It was easy to see that my friend was angry with me for leaving, and I knew that it was because of me the kibbutz had left abruptly. They didn't want to lose any more people. With my shoulders hunched up to my ears, I walked back to the apartment where Max was waiting for me, and I told him where I had been.

"You are still a virgin. If you have changed your mind about marrying me, it's still time. Otherwise, it will be over tonight," he said grinning.

I didn't believe him. It wasn't possible to have remained a virgin after so much pain. I remembered Mrs. Marmelsztain telling Mania before we went on our buying trips, "Don't let a boy touch you. You'll lose your virginity," I was sure that Max was lying when he said that I was still a virgin. He lied yesterday about taking me to Stuttgart today. Now, he said tomorrow. But he wasn't lying about my still being a virgin, and he proved it to me that night. I had endured the same amount of agony as the night before, until he broke though, and now I hoped that he would marry me. A girl without her virginity had no value. When I woke up the next morning, I sighed with relief that my nightgown and sheet were dry.

Max's roommate, I'll call him, 'Stubby,' had returned. He was a short man with sparse hair. Max proudly showed his roommate the sheet with the drop of blood, proof that he had a virgin and introduced me as his wife, and Stubby smiled and said that I was pretty. I wished Max, instead of Stubby, had told me that I was pretty. I needed to hear it from the man promising to marry me.

The next few days I was clinging to Max, but he pushed me away except in bed.

Max was always out, and I was alone in the one room doing the laundry for Max and Stubby. Stubby brought food for me to cook, though I had never cooked before. I was able to cook soup for the two men, and somehow, it was edible. Just as I was beginning to feel alone, Max took me to a restaurant and treated me to a meatless dinner of potato dumplings with gravy. I had forgotten how to use a fork and knife and watched closely, emulating his hands. While cutting and stabbing the large potato dumpling, the size of a matzo ball, he told me that he had survived with three brothers and a sister. Since he had not as yet taken me to see my brother-in-law, and I didn't know where Bela was, and I didn't know if my brother had survived, I was anxious to meet his family.

"Most of my family lives in Feldafing, near Munchen. My oldest brother lives in Stutgart with his girlfriend, and they will soon be married," he said

"When will you take me to Stuttgart?" I asked again, trying not to sound ungrateful.

"As soon as I find the time," was his answer. The tone in his voice was letting me know that he was becoming impatient with me.

On the fifth day he said, "We are going to take the train to visit my family." As we walked towards the train station, Max held my hand.

"Are you taking me to Stuttgart?" I asked excitedly, hoping that he was going to visit his oldest brother in Stuttgart.

"No, I have some business in Feldafing, and we can visit my family at the same time," he said.

I was glad that he was taking me to visit his family, but I hoped he would take me to Stuttgart instead. The waiting had become unbearable. I turned my head and blinked away the tears that were about to roll down my cheeks.

A Russian soldier stopped us at the train station and asked Max, "Is she your daughter?"

"Yes," Max said.

The soldier reached out his hand for my arm. "I take her, and she'll be my wife," he said. Deja vu, I thought. Although I was less frightened than when I was in Poland on the roof of the train, my heart was pounding.

Max offered him a cigarette. "She's too young to marry," he smiled and quickly pulled me inside the passenger car.

"Isn't this the American side?" I asked, frightened that the Russians had invaded Munchen.

Max laughed, "This is the American side."

"So why are Russian soldiers here?"

"I don't know. It must be politics," he said, but I prayed we would get out of Europe before we were left in Germany to be finished off.

Feldafing was a small village once occupied by rich Germans. Now, the entire village had been taken over by displaced Jewish survivors. Main Street was busy with survivors strolling and standing around in large groups. Yiddish was the main language spoken in the village, but I also heard Polish, German, Hungarian, Czechoslovakian, Greek, Romanian, and other languages. They were speaking loud and with the help of their hands. I looked at each face, hoping to see Bela in the crowd. I did see some familiar faces from the camps, but not my sister's.

Housing in Feldafing was scarce, and it wasn't unusual for several people to share a room even if they were couples.

Max's sister and her husband were married in court and were soon to have the wedding ceremony by a Rabbi. His middle brother, too, was married in court. He and his wife would be third in line to be married by a Rabbi. The two couples shared a large room in Feldafing.

Max didn't knock on the door. He turned the knob and walked in, and I followed behind.

Hanna's older sister, Gucia, was sitting at the rectangular wooden table, and Max greeted her warmly. I gathered that she was visiting the family. "Look who is taking my sister's place?" were the first words leaving Gucia's lips, and nobody said anything in my behalf, including Max. Gucia's eyes pierced at me like daggers throughout the day, and her acerbic remarks continued, chipping away at the little bit of self-esteem I had left. I wanted to tell her that it wasn't my fault her sister had died in the camp and that I wished she were alive and well. Seeing that Max's family hadn't stop Gucia from letting me know that I didn't belong, I knew that everyone in the room would have preferred that Hanna had been sitting at the table across from her sister instead of me. The worst part of it was that Max insisted on staying the night, and I had to share a single bed with Gucia. I cried silently all night. The next morning, Max and I returned to Munchen.

Stubby was smiling when he saw me. "Sit down," he said, pointing to a chair.

Obediently, I sat down on a chair next to the table. Stubby knelt beside me and took off my shoes from Theresienstadt and slipped a new pair of brown shoes on my feet and tied the laces.

"Now stand up, and let's see if they fit?" he said proudly. The shoes fit perfectly, and I thanked him for being thoughtful. "Max and I are partners, and it's not right that you should walk around with torn shoes," Stubby said, and I wished that it had been Max buying me the new shoes.

I had never learned how to cook, except potato soup. Everyday, I invited Stubby to eat with us until I learned how to cook chicken soup, and Stubby never failed to tell me that it was the best he'd ever eaten.

I was so grateful to Stubby for the new shoes and gracious complements that I couldn't do enough for him. Each time I washed sheets and Max's underwear, I also included Stubby's sheets and underwear.

There hadn't been a day when he didn't let me know that Max was very lucky to have me, and I was grateful for the kind words.

One day, Stubby sat at the table with us eating chicken soup, and he said, "I have been seeing a girl from Radom and would like her to move in with me, but she refuses." He looked at me with pleading brown eyes, "Jadzia, I would be grateful if you went to see her and put in a good word for me." I was grateful to be able to do something for the man who bought me my first pair of shoes and went to see his girlfriend and persuaded her to come home with me. My reward was to see the delight in Stubby's eyes. The first few days were wonderful. I had a girlfriend. I'll call her, Edka. Edka was short about five feet, the same height as I was. Though Edka was obese, she had a pretty round face, blue eyes, and dark-blond hair. I couldn't have been happier. We went to the museum together, looking for newcomers, and bought chocolate on the black market to surprise Max and Stubby.

In the beginning of February, Max left our room and didn't return until the next late afternoon. He claimed to have business in Feldafing, and many nights after, he didn't come home. Each trip was longer than the next. As time past, he was away more days and nights than he was at home. He had been away so often that I was afraid that one day he would leave me like an infant at a stranger's doorstep. As I watched Stubby showering Edka with love and affection, I began feeling unworthy of being loved. Something must be wrong with me for Max to always be going to Feldafing. He said it was business, but his partner was always with Edka. I looked at my reflection in the wardrobe mirror and saw sad eyes and a lifeless face. If I was married, I wouldn't feel so worthless, I pondered. Every chance I had, I asked Max when we would get married. His answer was always the same, "We have to wait for my older brothers and my sister to be married."

"But they are already married in court. Why can't we do the same?"

"I don't have the time now," was his final answer.

At the end of February, Max returned from Feldafing and gave me a piece of paper with a name and address from America. "I found David Borenstein in Feldafing, and he gave me your Aunt Sophy's address."

"How did he have my Aunt Sophy's address when I didn't know it?" I asked bewildered.

"It turns out that David's uncle is married to your aunt, and he has been corresponding with his uncle for a while," Max said.

I remembered Mama often talking to her sisters about their sister Sophy, and about the time when Sophy went to America, leaving her oldest son, Lopek, with our family because there had been something wrong with his eyes. America wouldn't allow him to enter the country until his eyes improved.

Max urged me to write a letter to my aunt. "When your aunt sends you a letter and tells you that she wants you to come to America, we'll take the letter to immigration and get a visa. Tell her that you are married and that your name is Borenkraut," he said.

Though I knew why Max was now anxious for me to use his last name, I pushed my ego aside. I needed to be married to have a reason for not being a virgin. I immediately wrote a letter in Polish, for I didn't know how to write Yiddish or English.

While I waited for a letter from my Aunt Sophy, Max was anxious for us to be married, but I was underage. Helen, Max's sister, offered to be my guardian, and Max and I were married in the German court.

As the Judge handed me our marriage certificate, Helen said, "You will be fourth in line to be married by the Rabbi."

I liked Helen. She was fair and friendlier than Max's two older brothers were, or their wives. As soon as we left the courthouse with the certificate in my hand, I felt the shame I was feeling the last two months had been peeled away from me. Now, when Max would go to Feldafing and stay over night or two nights claiming that it was business I didn't mind, even though each trip took longer than the last. Though Max had never confided in me about his business, being left alone with Stubby and Edka, the situation had slowly become torture. I was being blamed for Max being away on business in Feldafing and not sharing the profit with them. They never failed to belittle my every step. Every night, I silently cried myself to sleep. I had nobody to confide in, and Frau Baierlib only cared about the food I would give them, and Inga only wanted to talk about what it was like being married, and I truly had no clue. In the camps, the thought of boys and dating had never occurred to me. The few months since the war had ended, I had never known what it was like to have a real date, be kissed by a boy, feel puppy love, or fall in love. I only felt a hunger to connect with another human being.

In the spring of 1945, after the liberation from the camps, survivors resembled a swarm of birds in spring searching to mate and make nests. Most of us were orphans and alone without a single living relative. The need for beginning a new life and become a family member had been fervent. By 1946, many babies in carriages were seen wheeled by young mothers in displaced persons' camps. Myself being a married woman and not experiencing affection from my husband, I was as inexperienced in love and marriage as Inga was. In my heart I knew that there had to be more to being married than what I was experiencing with Max. I remembered my mama and my tata always kissing and hugging. The way I was being treated by Max and our roommates with each passing day, I was feeling less worthy of the slightest kindness. Though before I had met Max, I was often told that I was pretty, I now felt unattractive.

Five weeks went by, and I still hadn't seen Joel and had never found out if my sister was alive, though I knew in my heart that she wasn't. Everyday, I went to the museum hoping to find Bela.

Max had been away three days, and again I had been left alone with Stubby and Edka. The daily needling by the two people I helped bring together had chipped away at   the little self-esteem I had left. In the beginning of March at around five o'clock in the afternoon, Max had returned from

Feldafing. He handed me a letter from Brooklyn, New York. The letter stated:

Dear children,

I am very happy to know that you survived. I would like you to come to America as soon as possible.

Love,

Your Aunt Sophy

It was too late to take the letter to emigration, and Max said that we would go first thing in the morning. In the morning as we were leaving the apartment to go emigration, a girl claiming to be related to my Aunt Sophy by marriage stopped us at the door. She seemed very friendly, and Max invited her in and showed her our letter. She read the letter and while she was telling Max how very happy she was for us and wished us good luck, she held the letter in her hand until Max and Stubby walked out to take care of business, and the girl followed the men.

"I'll be back soon, and we'll go to emigration," Max said at the open door.

After everyone left, I looked for the letter to put it in a safe place, but the lette had disappeared. I was sure that Max had the letter in his pocket and waited impatiently for his return. He returned two hours later. "Take the letter, and let's go," he said.

"You and Uncle Ben's niece were holding the letter. I thought you put it in your pocket," I said.

"I left the letter on the dresser," he shouted.

I was certain that it had to be the visitor who walked away with my letter. But why would she want my letter? It was addressed to me. I suddenly remembered that my aunt didn't have my name on it. The letter began with 'Dear children.'

Max was angry with me for being careless. I fought back the tears and wrote another letter to my aunt, telling her what had happened to the first letter and asked her to please send me another letter.

By the time the second letter arrived, the law had changedm, and we had to have a visa from a relative, guaranteeing us a livelihood. I later found out that the girl with the friendly smile had stolen my letter and immigrated with her husband to America; however, I did receive a visa from my uncle Jacob, but we had to wait our turn.

Chapter Thirty-Eight: Time For a Change

Max had been more in Feldafing than in Munchen, and I had been left with Stubby and Edka. With each passing day, my ego had become more deflated until I realized that unless I left, I would shrivel up and die.

It was a beautiful spring day, and Max had been gone four days. I walked to the museum and lifted my face to the cloudless sky, and I knew that I had to make a decision to change my life.

When I returned late afternoon, Stubby and Edka sat on their bed, reminding me of two woodpeckers pecking away at my already broken heart. I picked up my backpack and packed up the meager articles of clothing with which I arrived.

I wished Stubby hadn't thrown away my old shoes. I would have gladly given him back the new shoes he had put on my feet two days after Max brought me to his apartment. I hung the backpack on my back, and without uttering a single word to the two people that had made my life a living hell, I walked out. I only stopped in the kitchen to say goodbye to Frau Baierlieb and Inga. Mother and daughter were sad to see me go, for they knew that Edka wasn't generous, and they would miss the food I had shared with them. I promised Inga that I would come to see her.

I walked to the train station and stepped inside the car marked Feldafing. I was glad that there had been no charge for the train ride, for I had no money with which to pay.

Fledafing was less than an hour's ride from Munchen, and it was dusk when I reached the apartment that housed Max's family. I wished that I didn't have to knock on their door, but I didn't know where else to go. I would have preferred to go to Stuttgart, but I didn't know where Joel lived. I now knew that I only had myself, and if I were going to survive, I would have to become independent. I was also certain that I was never going back to Munchen.

Max was shocked to see me, as if the unwanted child he had left at the doorstep with strangers found its way back to him. His family and their spouses were sitting in a circle on straight chairs as if having a meeting, and their unfriendly eyes were on me.

"What are you doing here?" Max grunted.

"I want to stay with you," I muttered.

"You have to go back. I have to take care of business here," he ordered.

The Feldafing village stood on unpaved hills, and the long walk from the station tired me out, and I sat down.

Max's sister-in-law leaned into her chair, only slightly raising her head. In a soft voice, as if counting every word, she said, "We have no place for you to sleep here."

I felt all eyes on me. Nobody, not even Max, uttered a single word in disagreement. Humiliated, I picked up my backpack and left the room. It was black as ink outside, and I had no idea where to go, but I continued walking. I knew that the trains had stopped running for the night, but even if they did run, I had no place to go. I had made up my mind never to go back to Munchen and take the abuse from Stubby and Edka. I had decided to sleep on the bench at the station, and in the morning I would go to Stutgard and ask around until I found Joel. I would divorce Max and tell emigration that I was a minor. They would send me to America, and Uncle Jacob would send me to school.

"If I get an education, I'll be able to take care of myself," I cried to dark skies. Now that I had made my plan, I stopped crying and walked towards the station. I heard footsteps following me, and I began to walk faster. I was sure that someone would be at the station to protect me.

"Don't walk so fast. I can't keep up with you," I recognized Max's voice. On one hand, I was relieved that the footsteps were Max's. On the other hand, I had good plans and didn't want to change them.

"Come on. Let's find a place to sleep, but tomorrow you are going back to Munchen," he said, leaving no room for arguments.

I didn't answer him, but I knew that he could not talk me into going back.

We knocked on several doors, and nobody, including Bela's good friends from the camps, had room for us to stay the night. After an exhausting search, we found a dark basement made into living quarters. The basement had several rooms, and we found one unoccupied room with a bed. I was so tired. I can't remember if I took off my clothes before I fell asleep. In the morning, Max ordered me again to go back to Munchen, but I had told him that I was staying in the basement with or without him, and he never asked me again. The basement had a stove with an oven, and the women living there with husbands and babies graciously taught me how to cook simple meals, and I even baked a cake. Several days later, Max found a tiny apartment converted from a storage room.

The bedroom was only large enough to hold a single bed, nothing else.

The front room had only enough space for a very small square table, two chairs, and a one-burner wood burning iron stove with pipes pushing through the ceiling. The once white walls were streaked with blood from smashed bedbugs, but the bedroom had a window.

Max brought a can of white paint, and I painted over the bloody walls. Within a few days, the walls didn't look any different than before I had painted them.

Although I woke up every morning with bites allover my body, I still preferred the bedbugs to Stubby and Edka. Everyday, I cooked meals for Max, but he almost always came home after I was asleep, and I gave the food to a hungry German woman.

I had quickly learned that Max would say "no" to everything I had suggested.or asked for. I knew then that if I waited for his permission or his decisions about my necessities or well being, I would still be wearing the shoes from Theresienstadt and stay in the bedbug riddled apartment waiting for him to come home and never accomplish anything.

There was too much I needed to learn in a very short time, but first, I needed to go to Stuttgart. In my mind I knew that my sister did not survive the war. Had she survived, she would know that I was alive and would have found me. My heart wanted her to be alive so much that I visualized myself opening the door in Joel's apartment and being embraced by my beautiful sister.

A week after we had settled into the apartment, Max still didn't have the time to take me to Stuttgart. I boarded the train alone. At the station in Stuttgart, I recognized survivors by their Auschwitz numbers and asked if they knew Joel Altman, and a man told me which bus to take that would drop me off at the survivor section.

As in Feldafing, survivors were standing in the street and at the windows. Almost every survivor living on that street in Stuttgart was from Radom, and everyone knew Joel and pointed me in the right direction.

My heart pounded as I stood at Joel's door. The longer I stood in the dimly lit hallway, the more hopeful I became that my sister and her children were behind the door.

My mind had traveled a million miles. What if Fraida went to Pani Franciszkowa for help during the liquidation of the Ghetto? What if Franka, Fraida's friend, took them in and hid them? She could have taken her to another town on Polish papers until the war was over? Fraida surely didn't look Jewish, five-year old Abraham had blond hair and blue eyes, and so did three-year old Eva. In another town where nobody knew them, they could have walked freely on every street, and nobody would question them. She could have saved them if she wanted to. What if, what if, what if…. When I finally got up enough nerve to knock on the door, a tall girl with blond hair and blue eyes greeted me. Just as I was beginning to turn back, thinking that I had the wrong address, Joel turned the bend and was standing in front of me. He reached out his arms for an embrace, "Pociecho!" He remembered my nickname, Joy. "You haven't grown at all," he bantered, but I felt my legs buckling, and I sat down on his couch. Joel whispered something to the girl, and she left. He didn't wait for me to ask about the girl in his apartment. "The girl you just saw here is the cleaning store owner's daughter. She was here to deliver my laundry," he said, and I wanted to believe him. I knew how much he loved my sister and couldn't believe that he would replace her so quickly. I didn't expect him to be alone the rest of his life. After all, he was still young, but not with a German girl. It made no sense to ask if my sister was with him. I only needed to know why he had survived without my sister and his two children, and I asked for an explanation.

Joel sat down next to me on the couch. "The night of the liquidation of the Ghetto, the lights went on, and the cul-de-sac was as bright as day. Within minutes, gunshots were heard, and the SS shouted for us to leave our homes and line up. We all lined up, and the selection began," he said, wiping his eyes with the back of his hand and continued. "People with work permits were told to stand on one side, everyone else on the other side. I had a work permit, but I was standing next to Fraida and the children and wanted to go with them. Fraida pushed me away, and I ended up on the side with the working group. I never saw my wife and children again," he said and stood up and went to another room. He returned a few minutes later with several pictures of Fraida and Abraham. The war had already been on when Eva was born, and there were no picturesof her. "You can keep these if you like," he said. I wondered how he was able to save the pictures, but I didn't think of asking. I was more interested in knowing why he didn't want to keep the pictures of his family. He had kept the pictures hidden from the Germans throughout the entire war. The pictures of Fraida and Abraham were too precious to me, and I didn't question him as to why he had been so eager to part with them, for fear that he would change his mind. I told him that Max and I were married in court, and I would invite him to our wedding when the Jewish ceremony would take place.

"It will be sometime in December," I said, but I didn't feel the brotherly closeness I once felt towards him when I was a child. I couldn't confide in him about my lonely life, not after seeing the German girl in his apartment. I stayed overnight and cried myself to sleep, only to wake up trembling from a nightmare. I dreamed that the pretty blond girl was dressed in SS uniform holding a whip. She aimed the long snake-like whip at Fraida. I woke up, as she was about to burn the whip across Fraida's back. My entire body was drenched in perspiration. Joel had breakfast on the table for me with fresh bread and butter, but I couldn't eat. Last night's nightmare stayed with me, and I couldn't get the blond girl out of my mind. Though the girl wasn't in the apartment, the way her feet were grounded to the floor when she opened the door, it looked to me as if she had been very familiar with Joel and his apartment. As much as I tried to believe Joel, I couldn't get the nightmare out of my mind.

Before I returned to Feldafing, I took a walk hoping to find a familiar face. Again, people were standing in the middle of the street and at windows and open doors. I passed an open door and heard a familiar voice say, "Come in, Jadzia." I turned and followed the voice. I looked inside an open door apartment and saw Ida, Renia, and Lusia at a rectangular table sitting next to two young men, and Mrs. Rojal was serving chicken noodle soup. I was invited to join them at the table, and Mrs. Rojal served me a bowl of the chicken soup. I was happy to see them, and they were glad to see me. I told them about Bela, and Mrs. Rojal assured me that Bela would find me. Leaving the Rojal family, I was reminded of how alone I was.

Although the return train to Feldafing was full, I found a seat. My eyes rested on a sleeping woman sitting directly across from me. The woman's face and the way she was sleeping, suddenly looked very familiar. I recognized the SS woman named Anna from Willischtahl. The once light blond hair, styled in a curly coiffure, was now drab and straight. I remembered her standing against a wall in the ammunition factory, holding a whip in one hand, and the next minute, her eyes were closed, and she was sliding slowly down onto the floor, her head dangling as it was now on the train's wooden seat.

I tapped her shoulder. "Anna, it is you," I said, letting her know that I didn't make a mistake. Startled, she lifted her head and opened her sleepy blue eyes. I knew that she recognized me. Although I wouldn't harm her, I wanted her to be afraid of me as I had been of her.

"You were SS in Willischtahl," I said calmly.

She became flustered. "That was such long time ago," she muttered.

"No, not such a long time ago, only a year ago," I said. "But don't worry, you were not as bad as the other SS," I said.

Several young men overheard the conversation and stood up, ready to take action.

"You want me to take her to Feldafing and teach her a lesson?" one man asked in Polish, while the others were ready to grab her.

"No," I said. "She wasn't so bad. She was too sleepy to hurt anybody," I told them, and they all sat down again.

As soon as the train had stopped, Anna stood up and fled.

When I returned to Feldafing, I was thinking about school and began making plans. It never occurred to me that Max would react with so much anger.

"You are not a child!" he shouted. "You don't need to go to school! You need to stay home the way other wives do!"

After his outburst, I realized that if I didn't take my life in my own hands and ignore him, I would live the rest of my life with a fourth grade education.

I left the bedbug bitten apartment and searched for schools. I found the schoolhouse and walked into each room, looking for the right subject to begin with. The instructor in one of the classes was a Concentration Camp survivor from Poland. He was a short man in his forties with a kind face and dignified demeanor. He told us that before the war, he had been a professor in Poland. When he saw how eager I was to learn, he offered for a small fee to give me private lessons and bring me up to high school level.

Since Max was rarely home during the day and didn't come home until very late at night, I studied until late into the night. My brain had suddenly awakened and like a sponge soaked up whatever that generous man taught me. I was gratefully for the opportunity and never felt more alive, until Max came home one afternoon while I was sitting at the little table studying with my professor. He demanded supper.

"Why isn't supper on the table for me? What is it with this school and learning day and night? You are acting like a child!" he shouted and stormed out.

I had never been more humiliated in my entire life. As always when I was verbally attacked, I would become speechless. The professor saw that I was shaking and holding back the tears. He smiled. "A man's heart is through his stomach," he said. But the professor didn't know how many suppers I had thrown away or given away due to Max's constant absence and lack of refrigeration.

Max came home angry that night. "If you have to go to school, why don't you take a sewing class, so when we go to America, you could work in a factory, instead of wasting time learning childish things?"

To keep the peace I took a sewing class the 'Ort' had offered, but I didn't give up the professor. Deep in my heart, I knew that I wanted more than to work in a factory.

Max joined a soccer team in Feldafing. Now between playing cards with his friends and soccer, he was only home late at night. Most nights I was already asleep when he came home.

My neighbors didn't know that I was married, for they never saw me with Max. I studied day and night, not because I had to, but because I loved to learn.

My friend Marsha had finished a short course in nursing and worked at the Medical Center in Feldafing. When she wasn't busy, she would read novels. I had never allowed myself such a luxury. Whatever I would read needed to be educational.

It was Sunday in the end of September. Max had a soccer game and would be angry if I wasn't there to cheer him on. I tried to avoid giving him reasons for bringing up my studies. Besides, he had become quite proficient at bouncing the ball on his head and often won the game for his team, and I enjoyed seeing him happy. I rushed to take my bath so that I wouldn't be late.

I was standing over the basin, my body was covered with soap, and there was a knock on the door.

"Who is it?" I called out impatiently.

"Open the door, little sister!" Bela bellowed.

I became flustered and danced around the basin, spilling soapy water all over the floor, mumbling, "Bela...Bela...Bela..."

"What's the matter? Don't you want to see me?" she quipped again.

I began turning the knob, but my hands were too slippery. After several minutes of playing musical chairs around the basin, I found the towel and placed it on the knob and opened the door.

Bela stepped inside the tiny front room, and without muttering a single word, she bent me over the basin and washed my back. I wiped quickly, and with only the towel covering my body, I wrapped my arms around my sister, and we stayed that way several minutes until Max's youngest brother, Jack, who had directed Bela to me, knocked on the door to remind me that we mustn't miss Max's game.

"Give us five minutes," I said, trembling with happiness. I put on a new

331

royal blue dress made over from a larger size. I had bought the dress from a German woman and dressmaker; a survivor from Latvia had completely redesigned the dress, adding a narrow white collar and white trimmings at the sleeves and a little pocket with white trimming on the left side below the collar.

"That's a very pretty dress. Let me try it on," Bela said.

I quickly took off the dress and handed it to her.

"I like it," she said.

"Then, why don't you wear it?" I told her, and quickly I put on the dress the kibbutz had made for me.

I thanked Jack for bringing my sister to me, and the three of us went to the game.

Max's team had won that day, and Max was in a good mood.

I never told Bela the truth about my life with Max. What would be the point, if I left Max, I would become a burden to her allover again. I told her that I was very happy and was glad that she came in time to be at my wedding.

"Moniek died in Buchenwald," Bela said, looking at me with the saddest heart and breaking green eyes and immediately changed the subject, though my heart, too, was breaking. Moniek was the kindest man, and I knew for certain that he would have made my sister very happy.

I didn't want to ask her about Moniek. I had the feeling that he didn't survive the camps. Had he survived, he would have found Bela. I remembered how devoted he was to her in Blizyn, and I knew that it would hurt her to talk about him.

I immediately wrote to Uncle Jacob and Aunt Sophy to let them know that my sister Bela was with me, and Uncle Jacob began sending us care packages.

Bela had found some friends in F eldafing and was spending most of her time with them. Although I was a married woman, Bela still thought of me as her little sister, and I gave her space. Knowing that she was close by was enough for me. I had a lot of studying to do.

December 12, 1946 was Max's and my turn to be married. The ceremony took place in Munchen at the photographer's studio. The studio had been used for small   weddings, but the cooking and preparations had to be done by us.

The night before our wedding, Max stayed at his brother's house.

The morning of my wedding day, Bela and I overslept, and Max's older brother, Sam, banged on our door. He was angry with us for not being in

Munchen preparing the food for the wedding.

Embarrassed for lack of responsibility, we dressed quickly and took the train to Munchen.

Now that Bela was with me, I didn't feel alone. We had thirty guests. Almost all of the guests were Max's family and their friends. Joel came from Stuttgart with a woman as his guest, and I was glad that he didn't bring the German girl.

After the ceremony, Max wandered away, talking to everyone and completely ignoring his bride.

Bela pulled me into the bathroom, and without saying a single word, we cried on each other's shoulders. Later that evening, Bela went back to Feldafing, and Max and I spent our wedding night on the floor at his sister's apartment in Munchen, where she and her husband now lived in a one-room apartment. I never did find out why we didn't go back to Feldafing where we at least had a bed, but I didn't question his motives.

The next day, Max and I went back to Feldafing, and nothing had changed; although, he had acted a little warmer towards me since Bela had arrived. A week after my wedding, Bela met Zvi Altus.

"I want you to meet him, " she said, her green eyes glistened with excitement.

The next day, Bela and I walked to the displaced person's office in Feldafing where Zvi worked. He sat at a desk and gave off an authoritative air, and I was impressed. Zvi was a very handsome man. He was of medium height. He had blond curly hair and blue eyes. Even his eyelashes were blond. He was polite and smiled easily. After the introductions, we went home to the bedbug infested two little rooms.

"I'm in love with him," Bela said suddenly, as we sat down at the little table.

I was very happy for my sister. I knew how sad she was to have lost Moniek. I hugged her and wished her happiness.

"Zvi wants to go to Israel, and I'm going with him," she said.

"I was hoping that you would come to America with me and Max. I don't want to lose you again, " I pleaded, but Bela's mind was made up to go to Israel.

"At least, get married before you leave so I could be at your wedding," I cajoled.

"No, Zvi and I will be married in Israel," she said proudly, and I could tell by the tone in her voice that there was no room for discussion.

333

In spring 1947, on the day when Bela and Zvi were leaving, I gave her all of my clothes. The clothes I was wearing were all I had now. I had a coat made over from a man's coat. I offered it to her, but she said, "It's hot in Israel. I won't need a coat."

Bela stood proudly next to Zvi as I chased after the pickup truck filled with young pioneers. I ran until the truck and my sister was out of sight. I knelt in the mud in the middle of the road and cried hysterically.

To keep from missing my sister, I devoted my time to studying. I had learned so much from the professor that he ran out of things to teach me and told me that I was now ready to learn any profession that would make me happy.

I begged him to continue teaching me, and he did, until his quota came up, and he left to go to America.

I never again saw the man who gave me my first push in the right direction. I never knew his name, only his title which was 'Professor.'

I was so busy studying and taking classes at the sewing school that I often forgot to eat and became very thin.

In the sewing school, I was sitting at the sewing machine with my back close to the belly of the metal heater, trying to sew a perfect corner. I tried over and over, but the corner came out uneven. I asked the instructor for guidance, but she lost patience with me and refused to show me one more time how make the boring corner. I fainted, and my forehead fell hard onto the sewing machine. I was taken to the hospital and stayed several days for observation, but Max was too busy to visit me.

I lay in bed watching, with envy, visitors coming and going several times a day. I realized that I only had myself, and if I didn't learn the profession that I would like, I would end up working in a factory for the rest of my life, only to please Max. By the time I left the hospital, I knew that I wanted to be a nurse. Against Max's wishes, I quit the sewing class and began taking classes towards nursing.

Every day since I began studying nursing, Max shouted at me for quitting the sewing class that would have given us a wage in America. His shouting and insults hurt my feelings and made me cry almost every night. I loved nursing and continued my studies with the same gusto as when I studied with the professor.

I studied with the help of Doctor Zepken, who everyday at the Queen Elizabeth Hospital gave me private lessons for a small fee, and I sometimes bought meat for him at the camp's black market. Rumors were that all the people who had left Germany, thinking that they were going to Israel, were taken prisoners and sent to Cyprus. I hadn't heard from Bela, and there wasn't a day when I didn't think about her. I tried to think good thoughts and told myself that even if she was in Cyprus, she was fine, and the English would soon open the gates to the promised land, and Bela would be among the first Holocaust survivors to enter the country of her lifelong dream.

To keep from worrying about Bela, I buried my mind in books and soaked up everything I could learn about medicine.

Each day, more survivors were leaving Feldafing for different destinations. Some went to America, Australia, Canada, and Israel. Only very few that went to Israel were able to sneak through the English watchful eye.

As much as I wanted to finish my studies, I craved to go to America and feel my family's embrace. I pictured Aunt Sophy resembling my mama and her arms around me would feel just like my mama's arms.

With Max's friends leaving every day, it had become difficult for me to find someone who would translate my aunt's Yiddish letters. Aunt Sophy didn't remember Polish, and I didn't write or read Yiddish. I didn't even speak it well. I understood the language, but I was too embarrassed to speak it because I was unable to carry on a conversation.

By the end of 1947, I studied part time at the Queen Elizabeth Hospital, and the rest of the time, I worked at the Outpatient Medical Center assisting Doctor Zepken in minor surgery and internal medicine. I became acquainted with a patient from Latvia. I had told him of my problem, and he offered to teach me to read and write and even speak Yiddish for a small fee. I was delighted. I felt as if a door to my American family had opened. Once I learned the Yiddish alphabet, within two weeks, I was writing letters to my Aunt Sophy and Uncle Jacob, and I was reading letters they wrote to me.

Aunt Sophy was sending me packages containing her daughter's and daughter-in-law's clothes. In January 1948, I received my cousin Fay's beautiful blue coat with a lavish gray imitation fur collar. I bought a gray felt hat from a German woman, and on Saturday afternoon, I strolled outside in the muddy Feldafing village, and all heads turned to look at me in my new coat and hat. I never felt more elegant.

In the spring of 1948, I had accumulated a very nice wardrobe and gave it all, including the beautiful coat, to a couple leaving for Israel. I included a letter to my sister, her name in large letters on the envelope, and taped it to the package.

Although I hadn't heard from Bela since she left with Zvi on the pickup

335

truck, I trusted the couple when they promised to find my sister and give her my clothes.

Chapter Thirty-Nine

In May 1948, I was working at the Medical Center when loud noises and Hebrew songs filtered in from the street. I followed all of our patients into the street and joined fellow survivors in dance and song to the news of Israel's independence.

I became caught up in the excitement, and as I cheered with the rest of Feldafing, I prayed that Bela and Zvi had made it safely to the Promised Land.

After two hours of dancing and singing the Hebrew songs that I had learned in the kibbutz, the crowd was beginning to thin out.

Knowing that no matter how sick our patients would be, I was certain that the Medical Center would be deserted. I didn't expect Max to be home before midnight, and I decided to go home and catch up with my studies.

It had rained the night before, and there was no escaping the mud in F eldafing.

My thoughts were with Bela. I prayed that she had been free to enter the Promised Land.

As I walked with hooded eyes avoiding the mud-puddles, I heard a man shouting, "Pociecho!" The last time I heard my nickname was in Stuttgart when I saw Joel. I squinted up into the bright sun and found myself standing face to face with Shama Malach.

"Shama! Thank God you're alive! Is my brother, Sonny, with you?"

Shama lifted me up in the air, the way he did when I was a young child and twirled me around as if I was a rag doll.

"Put me down! I'm not a child any more!" I shouted.

"You could have fooled me. You haven't grown at all since I last saw you," he laughed.

"The Germans didn't believe in feeding me too much. They were afraid I might grow too tall," I said.

Shama laughed again. I remembered his handsome face, sharp brown eyes, and brown curly hair. He seemed to have grown a foot since I last saw him. I also remembered the day when he and Sonny disappeared. How his father and mine ran all over town looking for them. Reluctantly, he set me down, and my feet sank into the mud.

I strained my neck to look up at him, "Are you going to tell me what has happened to my brother?"

He gently touched my face, and I was sure that he was going to give me bad news.

"Sonny is fine. He's living in Italy. I just came from there," he said reassuringly and removed a pencil and a piece of paper from his pocket and wrote down my brother's address. Shama's handsome face suddenly contorted and became ashen.

"Pociecho," he said in barely audible voice. "Can you tell me what happen to my family?"

I remembered his family well. His mother, Haja, was a tall pretty woman with wavy black hair and brown eyes. His father was a shoe repairman. Joel Malch was a tall thin man. He was always sitting on a little stool, nails tightly held together between his lips. I liked standing next to him and watch as he was bent over an old shoe, taking nails from his mouth and hammering one nail at a time into a new sole. Shama's younger brother, Mendel, and sister, Idesa, clung to their parents, even in the Ghetto. I was certain that the entire family went together to Triblinka.

"Shama, during the liquidation of the Ghetto, I was behind barbed wires in AFL," I said. I didn't have the heart to tell him that his family went to Triblinka together with my family. I was sure that he already knew but reached out to me for a glimmer of hope.

"Thank you, Shama, for telling me about Sonny. Will you be staying in Feldafing?"

"No, Pociecho, I'm leaving town now," he said and again lifted me up in the air and kissed the top of my head. He never said where he was going, and I never saw Shama again. Such were the times we were living in. People were coming and going, and nobody thought of asking, "Will I see you again?"

I ran home and wrote a long letter to Soony. I told him about Bela and that I was corresponding with Uncle Jacob and Aunt Sophy.

The next morning, I ran down the stairs and waited for the mailman to come around the bend. I handed him the letter addressed to Sonny in Barletta Barry, Italy.

As I began walking away in the direction of the Medical Center, the mailman shouted, "Wait. I have a letter for you!"

I completely forgot the Medical Center and the long patient line as I recognized Bela's handwriting on the envelope postmarked in Israel. I sat down on the outside steps leading to my apartment. My hands were shaking as I ripped open the envelope, being extra careful not to destroy the return address. My heart pounded as I read about my sister's ordeal at the Cyprus Camp, and I lifted my face to the cloudy sky and thanked God for keeping Bela safe.

She had enclosed a small wedding picture of herself and Zvi. I couldn't stop my tears from streaming down onto the letter. How I wished that I could have stood next to my only surviving sister on her special day as she did for me. I sat timelessly looking at the little wedding picture. Bela looked beautiful in a white dress and vale, a bouquet of flowers in her hands.

Zvi was wearing a jacket and tie. His blond curly hair neatly brushed back. He stood in back of Bela, his arms tightly around her waist. A dimpled smile graced his handsome face.

"It was taking too long before we were allowed to enter Israel, so we were married at Cyprus," she wrote.

I immediately wrote her a letter and told her about Sonny and that I hoped for our turn to immigrate would come soon. Bela and I never lost touch.

As more people were leaving the displaced persons' camp in Feldafing, an apartment in the same building had become available. We left the bedbugs and moved to the second floor, to a one-room apartment with a very small sink and faucet. I could now wash my face with running water instead of having to fetch buckets of water. We even had a toilet in the hallway. I corresponded with Bela and Sonny and the entire time while I was in Germany. In each letter, Sonny wanted to know what had happened to our family? And each time I wrote that he would know everything when we would see each other in America. I was unable to tell him in a letter how our parents were murdered.

The summer of 1948, I had found out that I was pregnant. Though I was petrified of having to be responsible for a helpless little person, I was happy that we were going to be a family again.

Having a bad case of morning sickness, I never stopped my studies, and I continued working at the Medical Center.

As it often happened, Max hadn't been home all night. I had stopped questioning his whereabouts, for I knew that he would be angry and bring up my studies.

It was a sunny day, and I was standing outside waiting for the mailman before going to work. A large German shepherd dog, with a thick rope around his neck, jumped on top of me with his front feet, smudging my white, cotton, starched uniform and began licking my face.

Max stumbled behind him, a long rope wrapped around his hand, trying to catch up with the dog. "He likes you," Max laughed, tugging at the rope.

Since I grew up with animals, I wasn't afraid of the dog. I was only startled. "What's his name?" I asked Max.

"His name is Rex. He's a smart dog. I'll keep him," he said.

While I was untying the rope from the dog's neck, I asked Max, "Would you like breakfast? I could fry some eggs for you."

"No, I have business to take care of," he said and left.

As I ran up the stairs to wash my face and change uniforms before leaving for the Medical Center, I was certain that Rex would follow Max. Instead, he followed me to our tiny room, only large enough to hold a small round wicker table, two wicker chairs, and a single bed with a thin mattress. It was the smallest room in the building. All the other apartments had stoves and plumbing inside.

I was glad to get away from the bedbugs, and the tiny room with the toilet in the hallway had been a large improvement. It was not large enough to include a German shepherd who stormed in behind me, causing me to trip and knock over a chair.

I soaked bread in a bowl of water, and he ate hungrily. On my return from work, I bought meat and bones for Rex, which became a daily routine.

As the days went by, I had become very fond of Rex, and he of me. We kept each other company. The problem was that he knew the time when I was coming home from the hospital or the outpatient clinic. He always found me and jumped on me with muddy feet, and I was constantly washing uniforms.

Max and I moved, again, several blocks away to a larger one-room apartment on the second floor. The new apartment had two beds close together, a small rectangular, wooden table, two chairs, a wood burning stove, and a sink with running water. I had become so used to Max's absence that I never expected any help from him.

Except for a floor lamp, we didn't have to bring the furniture, only our clothes and household essentials. I took the day off from work and made several walking trips to transfer our belongings. The apartment was sufficient as a temporary place to live. It had enough space for us to move around. Even Rex seemed to be content stretched out on the floor near a little brown love seat.

The outpatient clinic where I had worked the last weeks of my pregnancy had been very busy. Patients waited in a long line to be vaccinated before leaving for a new homeland. Others waited to be treated for ailments left over from the camps. We had two other nurses, both German, and everyone was busy.

We only had five glass syringes and needles, and most of them were ill fitted and too large for vaccines. The old sterilizer was continually boiling the few outdated instruments. After boiling the syringes and needles, we soaked them in alcohol. It took too long to clear the alcohol and push out the air from the syringe, and sick patients waited in a long line to be treated.

April 5, 1949 was an especially busy day. In the morning, I was treating a man's foot with advanced gangrene, and in the afternoon, I assisted Doctor Zepken in removing a large cyst from a man's armpit. I was standing on a footstool holding up the man's arm with one hand and dripping ether on his covered mouth with the other hand.

We were finished with the surgery at three o'clock. As I stepped off the stool, I felt a sharp pain in my lower back. I thought nothing of it. I was sure that my back was stiff from standing on the footstool assisting Doctor Zepken. By four o'clock my abdomen harmonized with my back, and each contraction was stronger than the previous one. I wasn't timing the contractions. We still had a clinic full with sick patients, and I didn't have the heart to leave. As I bent over a patient to check her blood pressure, Doctor Zepken said, "I'm not pleased with your flushed face. It's time to go to the hospital."

"No," I said tenaciously, "I am fine." I continued working until six o'clock, though the contractions had become stronger and more frequent.

Again, Doctor Zepken cajoled, offering to take me to the hospital in the ambulance that had been stationed at the Medical Center's door. All my nightmares seemed a reality when I saw myself sitting in the ambulance with a German driver and a German doctor.

"It is raining really hard. If you should fall, you could hurt yourself and your baby," he pleaded. When I refused to go in the ambulance, he said, "Please, I would like to help with your delivery. Tell the hospital staff to call me."

I promised that I would, but I was too frightened to have a German deliver my baby. The death of thousands of Jewish babies by the hands of Germans were too deeply embedded in my mind.

Doctor Laitner was Jewish and was Chief of Staff at the Queen Elizabeth Hospital. He was the only one I trusted to deliver my baby.

I walked in the rain holding onto my abdomen for fear I would drop my baby in the mud.

Though lightening and thunder followed me home, it didn't stop Rex from meeting me. His muddy feet took possession of my shoulders and his tongue of my face as rainwater gushed from his pelt.

I stopped at the black market's meat booth and picked up the usual package of meat and bones for Rex.

As I ran home, I prayed for two things. My first prayer was that I wouldn't drop my baby, and my second was that Max would be at home waiting to take me to the hospital. My first prayer was answered, but not the second. The house was quiet, the same as I left it in the morning. I gave the dog his meat, which he finished in two minutes, but he continued chewing the large meaty bone. He lay on his stomach next to me, the bone between his legs, never taking his eyes off me. I was certain that the dog knew that something was wrong. Like a good soldier, he didn't move from my side.

I had no way of contacting Max. He could have been anywhere, out of town on a farm where I found him only a month ago. It was Sunday early morning, and Max hadn't been home several days. Max's partner lived on the first floor of our villa with his wife and two-year old twins. He knocked on my door.

"Max is staying on a cattle farm. I'm going there now. Come along, and we'll surprise him. I'm sure he would be happy to see his pregnant wife," he said, avoiding my eyes.

It was nine o'clock in the morning when we arrived at the farm. I was only about five feet from the farmhouse when I saw Max coming out of the darkened house, followed closely by a tall German girl. He was startled to see me, and he quickly told me that the girl worked on the farm, and I believed him.

Now, I hoped that he would be playing cards with his friends, for Rex had followed him to that house many times before. In desperation I cupped the dog's face in my hands and said, "Rex, go find Max." The dog licked my face and turned towards the door. He pushed the door handle down with his mouth, opened the door, and ran down the stairs.

I now knew how he was able to meet me every day after work. I stood by the window and watched as the dog ran ignoring the storm. I knew it was a long shot that the dog would find Max, and I was preparing to deliver the baby by myself

When the last contraction subsided, I put a blanket on the floor and two towels and scissors to cut the umbilical cord on top of the blanket.

I was in too much pain to light a fire in the stove. As I sat and waited for the next contraction, I remembered that I didn't have string to tie the umbilical. As I began searching for string, a contraction so strong enveloped my entire lower body, and I had a sudden urge to run, but in my mind, I knew that I had to find a piece of string.

I was wearing laced boots, a gift from my neighbor. She wore them during her pregnancy. "You are on your feet all day, and the shoes will help your ankles from swelling," she said, and she was right.

I untied my boots and kicked them off with my underpants. I pulled the lace from a boot and scrubbed it with soap and water and dunked it in a bowl-full of alcohol. On my hands and knees, I place the bowl with the shoelace on the blanket, and I sat down and waited for my baby to begin pushing through. Just as I was certain that Max was out of town, Rex pushed through the door with Max following behind.

"I have a car waiting outside with the motor running," he said.

My shoes in my hand, I ran barefoot down the stairs, Rex and Max chasing behind me. Rex pushed past me and jumped into the back seat.

At seven o'clock, I was given an enema.

The hospital rooms had no showers or bathroom. The only toilet was in the hallway where all the other expectant fathers were standing against the walls to hear their baby cry for the first time.

Max followed me as I ran to the bathroom.

"Does it hurt?" he asked several times during my run.

Before I closed the bathroom door, I bellowed, "Men should be giving birth!"

I was frightened when I entered the delivery room and saw a tall German nurse standing next to Doctor Laitner urging me to get on the table.

Doctor Laitner was a tall handsome man with kind eyes and a soft soothing voice.

I told myself that he wouldn't let the German nurse hurt my baby.

The contractions were now constant. As the doctor lowered his face towards mine urging me to push, I grabbed two fistfuls of his lab coat and screamed in his ear. "I want you to give me ether, now!"

Being the Chef of Staff, Doctor Laitner saw me at the hospital as a student nurse and when he visited the outpatient clinic where I continued to work. He also knew that from the beginning I worked under the wings of Doctor Zepken and that I would be aware that ether was now the anesthetic in Germany for childbirth.

"Nobody in Feldafing has been given ether or any other anesthetic for childbirth," Doctor Lightner explained.

"I don't care if you never gave it to anyone else, you will give it to me now!" I bellowed again.

Doctor Laitner was tired of my pulling at his clothes and screaming in his ear and said, "Alright push two more times, and I'll give you ether." He kept his promise.

With the last push, I drifted off and dreamed that the German nurse held a large frightening instrument and drilled into my guts leaving me hollow, and I felt paralyzed, unable to fight back.

I was in a bed when I opened my eyes. The room was dark, and the pain was gone. I touched my stomach, feeling for my baby, but my stomach was flat. Just as I began to panic, I heard a baby cry, and I climbed out of my bed, blood dripping between my legs and onto the floor as I followed the crying baby's sound.

When I reached the nursery ,I knew instantly that the crying baby wasn't mine.

"You have a beautiful daughter, but you must go back to bed," the friendly petite nurse with light brown hair and brown eyes said.

My daughter was sleeping peacefully. When I kissed her pink cheek, she opened her beautiful light-brown eyes, and I could have sworn that she smiled up at me. I wanted to pick her up and cradle her in my arms, but I suddenly felt lightheaded, and the nurse helped me to my room and back to bed.

Doctor Laitner came to see me the next morning and said, "From now on, everyone gets ether, and by the way, your daughter is the prettiest baby in the hospital. What will you name her?"

"Mindala, after my mother, and Laia, after Max's mother," I said proudly.

When eight days later I returned from the hospital with my daughter, Rex was gone. Max said that the room wasn't large enough for the dog.

"I gave the dog back to the original owner," he said.

I missed the only devoted friend I had, but I now had my baby. I called her, Mama shaina, beautiful mama.

Max went into a partnership in a little candy store with his brother, Sam, in Munchen and was home every night now.

He had become more caring since Mindala was born. He even made up a song for her. "Mindala, oh Mindala, my beautiful, sweet Mindala."

I was sure that he had changed since he was now a father with responsibilities, and for a while, he did change.

I went back to work in the outpatient clinic with my daughter in the baby carriage outside the sliding door where I could see her. I worked until it was our turn to immigrate to the United States.

At the end of July 1949, we had to leave Feldafing and stay at a German military barrack, named Funk Kaserne, in Munchen.

I refused to believe that I would be allowed to see my family in America. With my luck, I would be standing at the end of the line and hear a voice announce, "Sorry, no more space for you," I mused.

On the evening of September 12, 1949, I was still skeptical when we were asked to report early in the morning to an airstrip and be ready to fly to America. Because we had a five months old baby, we were privileged to leave Germany by an American military airplane instead of by ship.

Not until I would see the faces of my Aunt Sophy and Uncle Jacob, whom I was certain I resembled, would I feel secure enough to believe that we were truly on American soil. Now in 1985, forty-four years later, I'm sitting in a large airplane. Though I was in a coach seat, I'm being treated with dignity and respect and thanking God for allowing me the privilege to go home to Los Angeles, California, my country, my USA. As the attendant served me a plastic glass of orange juice, I smiled up at her from my seat.

"I'm going home" I mused, fingering my American passport as my eyes filled with tears and my heart with pride.

The plane landed in Los Angeles, and I thanked Carla for patiently traveling with me and allowing me space to endure my past. I knew that it had not been an easy task for her, but she had pointed out to me that she would not have had the opportunity to learn as much as she did had I not been with her, for she only spoke English.

When I saw my son's smiling face waiting anxiously at the airport, I ran into his welcoming arms and was grateful to God and America for the opportunity to have a child that was born on American soil. I prayed that my children and their children would never have to endure what I had endured.

As I unlocked the door to my own home in Marina Del Rey, where I now lived happily alone. I put my travel bag in the laundry room and stretched out on the couch in my den. My mind couldn't rest. It was filled with the memories of leaving Germany and my life thereafter.

In September 1949, my five month old daughter and I were being helped inside the American Military Plane. Families with babies and older people lined wooden benches inside the American airplane.

Though the air was stifling, I felt luckier than the people traveling many days by ship. The first two hours in the army airplane were fine until the turbulence began. A man sitting on the floor leaned against the wall and began vomiting. Many others including myself did the same. There were no wastebaskets or paper bags. Soon, the floor was lined with vomit and a most unpleasant stench.

I held Mindala in my arms trying to nurse her, but she refused. I touched my lips to her forehead and immediately panicked. All of the medical training and the many hours of Doctor Zepkens lessons were forgotten. My baby was sick, and we were in midair, and with every tumbling move, I felt as if I was losing my stomach.

I was grateful when Max stretched out in a dry spot on the floor next to us. It left me enough room on the bench for our baby. I now had a chance to rest my arms and to change her diaper, but I was happy when we landed.

The fresh air as we stepped off the plane, though chilly and cloudy, felt heavenly. As we were marched inside a gray room decorated with large, wooden, rectangular tables and benches, I believed I heard someone say that we were in Ireland. I was terrified that America had decided not to accept us, and we would be forced to remain in Ireland, of which I had never heard, or worse, we would be sent back to Germany or Poland. My mind was in turmoil of the constant fear of not reaching America. I longed to fall into the arms of my Aunt Sophy and Uncle Jacob. After all, they were my mother's brother and sister. Though I had never laid eyes on Aunt Sophy, I was sure that I would recognize her. I knew nothing about my Uncle Charley. He never wrote to me while I lived in Germany, and I didn't know his address. I knew that my family would be kind and treat me as if I was their own daughter, for I needed parents. But if we were sent back or forced to stay in Ireland, I would never know them, and they would never know how much I would appreciate their love and warm outstretched arms.

Large platters of red meat were set in front of us. I was beginning to feel sick at the sight of the bloody meat. I wrapped the baby in her blanket and turned toward the door.

"You can't take a baby outside in the cold. She'll catch a cold," Max scolded.

I could see that he was notably afraid that the cool air would make the baby sick. I tried to explain to him that cool air would make her feel better, that she wouldn't catch a cold from cool air, but to no avail. I sat at the table, trying not to look at the meat, and I was grateful for the cool air when we were marched back to board the plane.

Until we landed in New York, where the sun was shining bright, I didn't want to get my hopes up. I wouldn't be able to endure the disappointment.

Many American families waited at the landing strip. I strained my neck towards the crowd, hoping to get a glimpse of Uncle Jacob. I was certain that I would recognize him. Though I was only about seven years old, I remembered the tall rich American who came to Fraida's wedding in 1936. He had no hair on top of his head and a face resembling the moon. His green eyes mirrored everyone in my family including my tata's eyes; though, my tata's eyes were shaped like almonds and Mama's were round like uncle Jacob's.

Names were being called, and with outstretched arms, Americans collected their refugee relatives. We were among five unclaimed couples with babies in our arms. People from a Jewish organization drove us to a street lined with railroad tracks. I paid no attention as to where we were. I only knew that we were in New York. My only concern was my baby. She still felt hot and was not interested in nursing, and since I hadn't had anything to eat or drink for about twenty hours, my breasts didn't have enough to feed a newborn, much less a five months old child.

We sat on wooden benches in the hot sun and waited for our American relatives. Each time I saw someone approach, I was hoping it was my aunt or uncle. One by one, everybody had left, but nobody had come to claim us. Even when Bela had left me at the kibbutz, I didn't feel as abandoned. She had a job to do, and I wasn't a child anymore.

The kibbutz elders had been as protective of me, as if they were my family, and deep in my heart, I knew that my sister and I would find each other again, and we did find each other again. Now, as we were sitting outside close to railroad tracks with a feverish baby in my arms, I felt lost. Max didn't mind letting me know that my family didn't care about us and didn't want us. Though it hurt to hear it, I too was beginning to wonder if he wasn't right. Even though I told him that there hadn't been enough time to notify my family of our arrival, I wasn't sure if I believed it myself. As I was defending my relatives to Max, I also knew that the Jewish organization, Haias, would have notified them of our arrival. Why, then, didn't they come to take us to their home? My mind was tortured. A small part of me was listening to Max's raving and ranting about my uncaring relatives, but the other part wanted desperately to believe that there was an explanation. After all, they had lost four sisters and most of their nieces and nephews. Bela, Sonny, and I were the only survivors.

"No," I mused into Mindala's ears. "Why would Uncle Jacob send us visas if he didn't want us? He will come." So, I rocked my baby in my arms and gave my relatives the benefit of the doubt.

Throughout the day, volunteers from the Haias stayed with us, making sure that all the arrivals were being picked up. I had approached each one and told them in my newly learned Yiddish from my patient, the Latvian that my baby had a fever. Everyone sympathized, but it wasn't until late afternoon when a woman from the Haias arrived in a yellow taxi and asked us to get in the car.

I now worried that we were being sent back to Germany, but I had been more concerned about my child and didn't care where we would be sent to, as long as she would get my baby medical help. The taxi stopped at a sidewalk in front of a building.

The sign said 'Haias.' My eyes hadn't left Mindala's face, and I failed to notice the size of the building or the color. We followed the woman up a flight of stairs and were led to a room with two small beds and two straight wooden chairs.

"You can stay here until your relatives come for you," she said in Yiddish. Before the woman left the room, I told her again that my daughter was running a temperature and needed to be seen by a doctor. The woman nodded and left.

I knew I should have been happy. After all, it was what I was waiting for my entire life, to be in America, a free country, where a Jew could walk down the street unafraid that a Polish boy would throw rocks and shout, "Jew to Palestine!" I wouldn't have to pretend to be Catholic anymore. I should be jumping with joy! So, why did I feel as if I was lost, and nobody was looking for me?

Max left the room, and I put the baby at my breast, and she began suckling hungrily. He returned thirty minutes later. "Take the baby. We were going to find your Aunt Sophy."

A taxi was waiting for us in front of the building. The driver smiled and spoke Yiddish with Max, who sat in the front seat next to the driver and reminisced the years in the Camps. I realized that they knew each other from the Camps, but my mind was only on finding my relatives and getting my baby's temperature down; though, she didn't feel quite as hot as she did an hour ago. The driver looked in the rearview mirror and said in Polish, "You are very pretty."

I didn't feel pretty. I never thought that I was pretty. I certainly never heard it from Max. From lack of not knowing what to say, I mumbled in

Polish, "Jewish women are not considered pretty."

"What are you talking about," the driver said shocked. "Bess Myerson is Jewish, and she is our newest Miss America!"

I had no idea what he was talking about. I didn't know what a Miss America was, and I didn't answer him. I just busied myself with my baby.

The taxi stopped at a curb in front of a brick apartment house. The sidewalk was lined with women and baby carriages.

"I'll wait outside," Max said and turned to talk to the driver. From writing letters to my aunt, I remembered the address and apartment number in Brooklyn by heart. With Mindala in my arms, I ran up the third floor and knocked on my aunt's door. First, I knocked lightly, then harder. Nobody answered the door. Frustrated, I knocked loud enough for the next door neighbor to open her door and ask me what I wanted.

With my broken English, I said, "Is Mrs. Borenstein home?"

The woman looked at me with recognition and began speaking Yiddish.

"You must be Sophy's niece? You resemble her."

"Yes, Aunt Sophy, is my mama's sister. I arrived this morning," I said, hugging Mindala to my chest.

"She was expecting you, but she didn't know when you were arriving. They are not home. They went to see their new grandchild," the neighbor said, looking at me with pity in her eyes that mirrored my pain.

"Thank you, " I said, making use of the little English I had learned in Germany and ran down the stairs where the women were standing next to waist high baby carriages.

The baby carriage I had in Germany for Mindala was knee high. I wondered what people would say when the little wicker carriage would arrive in a few weeks. It looked like a carriage for a doll in comparison. I stood for a moment, observing the carefree women, chatting and admiring each other's children, while Max was anxious to know if I found my aunt. When I said that she wasn't home and tried to tell him that she didn't know when we were arriving, he became angry, and I felt as if I had done something wrong again.

"Let's go back to the Haias. Come on and get in the cab," he said, pointing to the open door.

Just as I began walking towards the cab, my eyes caught a glimpse of a woman on the sidewalk. I recognized Fraida's face from a picture my aunt had sent me. Timidly, I walked over to her and placed myself in front of her. I remembered that on the back of the picture was written Fay.

"Is your name Fay?" I asked in English.

"Yes," she said, a puzzled look on her face.

"My name is Jadzia. I am your cousin."

"Yetta!" she shouted.

"No," I corrected her, "Jadzia." I wanted to make sure that she knew who I was, for I didn't know who Yetta was.

"Yetta!" she voiced again and tightened her arms around me. I didn't correct her again. With my child bouncing on my shoulder, I ran to Max and breathlessly told him that I found my cousin.

"My aunt Sophy's daughter is standing on the sidewalk. Why don't we talk to her? She's very happy to see us," I said.

"We are going back to the Haias," he said, and I could see anger in his eyes and in the tone of his voice. Before I stepped inside of the cab's back seat, with Mindala's little arms around my neck, I ran back over to Fay and told her where we were staying.

The driver stopped the cab at the curb in front of the Haias. Max dug his hand in his pocket and dug out a handful of dollar-bills and asked the driver to take what he needed, but the man refused to take his money.

"You have a pretty little wife and child. You'll need every penny."

While Max lit a cigarette and was standing at the curb talking to the driver, I climbed the stairs to our room, slipped out of my shoes, and curled up on the little bed next to my baby, and I dozed off. I was awakened to the sound of voices. I opened my eyes and saw two older men standing two feet from our bed with Max grinning behind them.

From the picture Aunt Sophy had sent to me, I recognized her husband. He was of medium height, completely bald, dark complexion, brown eyes, and a thick nose. I stood up and wrapped my arms around him and said with a question in my voice, "Uncle Ben?"

"Yes," he said, returning the greeting with a warm embrace. The other man, standing next to Uncle Ben, was short, about five feet, five inches in height and moderately overweight. I remembered that in Radom, an overweight man represented wealth. The man standing next to Uncle Ben had a friendly, full square face, a very fair complexion, and green eyes. He, too, was completely bald. He was wearing a gray suit, white shirt, gray vest, and a bow tie. He was the personification of a rich American. He was the exact image in my mind of how an American doctor would look. I picked up Mindala and handed her to the doctor and waited for him to examine her. When his demeanor lacked professionalism, I began to question the American method of treating patients. It was not the technique I had been accustomed to in the last three years.

He held my baby in his arms and smiled affectionately as Mindala tried to take of his glasses that were pinching his short nose.

"She has a fever," I said worriedly, hoping that a stethoscope would manifest itself in his hands, and he would begin to examine my child, but the man smiled and kissed Mindala's face.

Just as I opened my mouth again to ask the doctor if he was going to examine my child, the door opened and a tall thin man holding a black bag stepped inside to the already crowded room. The man seemed younger than Uncle Ben and the other man. I believed him to be in his early thirties. He had thick brown wavy hair, brown eyes, a straight thin nose, and a pallid complexion. He was wearing a brown suit, white shirt, no vest, and a long, thin, striped tie. He was the opposite of what I expected an American doctor to look like.

"Who is the patient?" the doctor asked.

The man holding my baby placed her gently on the bed. Mindala reached her little arms out to me, and I kissed her face and whispered, "It's all right Mama shaina" (pretty mama.) I always called her that. It just came natural, and she didn't cry.

The doctor opened his black bag, retrieved a stethoscope, and listened to Mindala's chest. He palpated her abdomen and looked inside her throat.

"You have a beautiful daughter," he said in Yiddish. When he saw the worry in my eyes he added, "She's all right. The mild fever is from the travel. It will go away after a day or two."

I suddenly realized that the man I had mistaken for a doctor was my Uncle Jacob. How could I have forgotten the uncle who came to Poland the summer of 1936? My mind suddenly traveled back in time, and I remembered with a child's eye, the vibrant tall man with a straw hat who pointed his moving camera at almost every Jew in Radom.

Before he left my tearful Mama, he promised her again, as he did when she was only twelve years old, "I will send visas one at a time until you will all be in America."

Tears welled up in my eyes as I wrapped my arms around the brother my mama worshipped. Uncle Jacob placed some cash in the doctor's hand and thanked him.

"Let's go. Your Aunt Sophy is waiting for you," Uncle Ben said as he turned towards the door. I looked at Max still standing close to the door and was happy to see a smile on his face. I hoped that America would heal us and let that smile become permanent.

The apartment we had left in Feldafing wasn't much larger than Uncle Jakob's car. I had never seen such a beautiful automobile, shiny white exterior and soft leather interior. I couldn't believe that any one person would have that much money to own such a luxurious car. I was in awe at the smooth, soundless ride to Aunt Sophy's apartment.

My heart pounded as I climbed the stairs for the second time today. When the door opened, Uncle Jacob's wife, Sadie, whom I remembered well from the visit to Poland in 1936, immediately took my daughter from my arms.

I remembered the red curly hair. She was still wearing the tiny watch I had admired with a child's eyes. Aunt Sophy's small, one bedroom apartment seemed large. I had never lived in a place with a separate living room. I immediately recognized Aunt Sophy, not only from the picture she had sent to me in Feldafing, but the resemblance to my mama, Uncle Jakob, and myself was easy to see. The only difference was that my mama was tall and slim with a thin chiseled face and high cheekbones and large green eyes. Aunt Sophy was short, only five feet tall. She had a large bosom, and like uncle Jacob, she was moderately overweight. She had a pretty, full, square face and the same green eyes, though smaller than Mama's were. My arms were aching to embrace her. When she unfolded her arms and invited me in, I never wanted to let her go. I must have held on to her too long because she took my hand and guided me to the table in the living room and told me to sit down in front of a deep dish filled with peaches in heavy syrup topped with sour cream.

To please her I would have done anything she would ask of me, so desperate was I for family, but the sweet peaches in the heavy syrup of which I had never tasted before were as offensive as the cod liver oil Mama forced us to drink. I told Aunt Sophy that I was still queasy from the travel, which was not a lie, and asked if I could take a bath.

She guided me to the bathroom, not out in the hallway, but inside her apartment. The bathroom had been equipped with a sink and two faucets, for hot and cold water, a toilet, and a bathtub. Before she left me to myself, she turned on the faucets and showed me which was the hot water and which was cold.

"Be careful with the hot water. I don't want you to bum yourself," she said lovingly.

Greedily, I luxuriated in the hot bath water with a bar of Ivory soap all over my body and hair.

When the water turned cold, I stepped out of the tub and wrapped the soft towel around my body. Then, I pulled out the stopper and watched the soapy water going down the drain. As I rinsed the bathtub with clear water, I felt as if I had finally shed Poland and Germany, and I was ready to begin a new life in a free country where I could say it out loud, "I am Jewish and proud of it." We stayed until dusk, and Uncle Jacob asked if we were ready to return to the Haias. "Jack," Aunt Sophy said, "I have a sofa in the living room that opens into a bed. They can stay here for as long as they need to."

I now knew that Uncle Jacob was called Jack, and I tried to memorize his name. There was a lot I needed to memorize. But the thought of staying at my aunt's house reminded me of the many times I stayed over at my Aunt Hanna's house, or Aunt Hudesa's, or Aunt Pearl's. I felt a knot twisting in my stomach when I realized that I would never see them again.

Though I wasn't a child anymore, I would have loved to stay with my aunt forever. Max wanted to go back to the Hias, but he agreed to stay a few days.

During our stay, my aunt bought a little stroller for Mindala, and Aunt Sadie changed Mindala's name to Marian, but I only called her Mama Shaina. My cousin Fay gave me her small sized dresses that she hadn't been able to wear anymore, but she insisted on calling me Yetta, which I hated. She told me that Yetta was the appropriate name, and since I had no idea about American names, I didn't protest. I loved staying with my Aunt Sophy and Uncle Ben. They loved my baby and played with her. I especially loved it when Uncle Jack came to visit. Although Aunt Sophy and Uncle Jack didn't have the same faces and their personalities were not the same as my parents', I felt as though my parents had returned to give me the love I so badly needed.

A week later, Max told me to pack up our things.

"We are going back to the Haias. If we stay here, the agency won't help us with an apartment," he declared.

I tried to tell him that we didn't need the agency, that my uncle would help us find a place to live, but he was beginning to raise his voice. Though I hated to leave my aunt's protective walls, I didn't want her to witness Max's anger, and I obediently put our few possessions in the suitcase. Marian in my arms, I followed him downstairs to where his friend the taxi driver was waiting with open doors.

While staying at the Hias, Max's friend, the cab driver, told Max that since the war was over, it had become almost impossible to get any kind of apartment in New York. "The soldiers returned from fighting the war and need places to live."

Sunday, early afternoon, Uncle Jack came to visit us at the Haias and drove us in his car to Aunt Sophy's home. There, we met his son Harry and Harry's wife, Ida, and their two teenage daughters. Aunt Sophy had four children and grandchildren, and all were there to meet their green cousin.

A long rectangular table was set with a white tablecloth, and we all sat down to a delicious feast, roast beef and brown potatoes and cheesecake for desert. She even had jars of baby food for Marian.

Everyone wanted to hold Marian, and she loved all the attention. In the evening, he returned us to the Haias. Just as I was beginning to think that the Haias would become our home
for a long time, Uncle Jack arrived a week later and told me to pack up our things and meet him downstairs. With the clothes Fay gave me and the baby clothes handed down from the cousin's babies, I now had more to pack. I followed Max and Uncle Jack down the stairs, holding Marian in my arms and the old suitcase I came with. I didn't know where we were going, and I thought that he was bringing us to stay in his house until he found us an apartment.

Uncle Jack looked in the rearview mirror and said, "We are going to look at an apartment."

"Do you think it's possible to get an apartment with a bathroom and a bathtub inside the apartment?" I asked, expecting a negative answer. After all, Aunt Sophy lived in America since before I was born. I couldn't expect to have an apartment as nice as hers.

But Uncle Jack said, "I'll do my best."

Like an obedient child I sat in the luxurious car in the back seat, not knowing and not caring where he was taking us. As long as he was with us, I felt secure. He turned to a street called Linden Boulevard and parked his car in front of a wide sidewalk and a large gray building number 322. My baby in my right arm and the old suitcase in my left arm, I followed Max and Uncle Jack up five flights of marbleized stairs. Each flight was dimly lit by a light bulb hanging on a thick wire from the ceiling.

We stopped in front of an apartment on the right, and Uncle Jack unlocked the door with a key. I was tempted to ask him, to whom that apartment belonged? But I was too embarrassed. He pulled at a string hanging from the ceiling, and a bright, round, crystal lighting fixture revealed white walls and a wood floor in a long corridor. On the right was a large kitchen, twice the size of Aunt Sophy's kitchen. A faded, checked, linoleum covered the floor.

A new gray formica table and four matching upholstered plastic chairs set against the far wall. There was a bread-box on the table with a loaf of bread inside.

The doors to white cupboards were open, revealing new aluminum pots and pans and white china. The top shelves were filled with bags of sugar, flower, baby food, and a box of corn flakes. The drawers were lined with stainless steel silverware. A clean gas stove with an oven stood next to the sink in front of a window.

I was thinking how easy and wonderful it would be to cook on the four burners and bake in such wonderful oven. I was sure that if I had a stove and oven, Aunt Sophy would teach me to cook and bake. And the cleanup would be so easy in the large sink with hot and cold running water. Uncle Jack opened the door to an old but clean white refrigerator filled with milk, cheese, butter, apples, cold cuts, and sour cream. The freezer, too, was filled with meats.

On the left, across from the kitchen, was a large living room with a shiny wood floor and two bare windows.

Along with my sewing machine, my school-books, and the little wicker baby carriage we had shipped from Germany, were two white embroidered curtains that would fit the two windows perfectly. I made a mental note that I would offer the beautiful curtains to Uncle Jack as soon as the crate would arrive. I was certain that the curtains would be a perfect fit for the two long narrow windows. I was elated as I remembered the curtains, for I would have something to offer him for his kindness.

"So what do you think of this living room?" Uncle Jack asked smiling proudly.

I took in the new red black and gray checked couch, a matching club chair, and a mahogany coffee table.

"It's beautiful, Uncle," I said, and I was thinking that his living room was larger than the apartment I lived in with my family in Radom.

Uncle Jack pointed out that the couch opened to a bed, and I figured that he was letting me know where Max and I would sleep.

Still holding my baby and the suitcase, Uncle Jack opened double French doors leading to a large bedroom furnished with everything new. A double mahogany bed, a new mattress covered with a white sheet and two pillows with pillowcases, and a chest of drawers.

I was beginning to get very tired. Both my arms felt like lead. I would have loved to throw the suitcase on the floor and stretch out on that wonderful bed and cuddle up next to my child who was as patient as an angel. But I saw that my uncle wasn't finished showing me his luxurious apartment.

I wondered where he and Aunt Sadie were living now. That apartment had been furnished with all the particulars, but it didn't look occupied. Maybe, they just rented it and didn't have the time to move in, and I didn't think it would be polite to ask.

My thoughts were interrupted when Uncle Jack urged me to follow him through a small corridor and to a second bedroom furnished with a used but sturdy brown, wooden baby crib and a new mattress covered with a white sheet and a baby blanket.

I was tempted to put Marian into the crib, but that would not be polite. After all, he didn't tell me to put my baby in the crib. The crib could have been there for his grandchildren of whom I had yet to meet. He had told me that he had two granddaughters, but he didn't tell me their ages. Next to the crib was a double size bed with a new mattress covered with a new sheet, two pillows, and a quilt.

Uncle Jack took Marian from my tired arms and gently placed her in the crib. I put the suitcase on the floor and changed her diaper. She immediately fell asleep. I picked up the suitcase and began to leave the room.

"Put the suitcase down and follow me," Uncle Jack said, and I gladly did as he asked.

I followed him to a bathroom that had everything Aunt Sophy's bathroom had. This bathroom also had a shower over the bathtub. I was overwhelmed by the luxury. In Radom, only the very rich would be privileged to live in such home. I followed him into the living room where he sat down on the couch with the clean smell of newness.

"Sit down," he said, a happy smile graced his handsome face. When I did, he asked, "how do you like it?"

"It's a beautiful apartment. When are you moving in?" I finally asked.

"I have my own house. This is yours. It cost me three hundred dollars under the table to get it for you," he said proudly.

His generosity rendered me speechless. Three hundred dollars, plus the money he had spent on all the new furniture, utensils, and supplies. It sounded like a fortune. At that moment, the man sitting on the couch he had paid for had been the closest to a loving parent I could hope for. I was so grateful for his generosity that I wrapped my arms around my uncle's neck and never wanted to let him go. So very needy was I for my parents.

When I loosened my grip on him, I was embarrassed for being so demonstrative. How could I have told him of my longing for a warm parental embrace. I hadn't felt anyone's arms around me since the last time I saw Mama on August 1942. I stood up and shuffled to my daughter's room, folding my arms over the crib and looked at the sleeping child as my tears dripped down on her new colorful little quilt. I didn't want my uncle to see my red eyes and stepped into the luxurious bathroom and washed my face with the fresh bar of ivory soap and wiped with the soft new towel. Without uttering a word, I sat down next to my uncle, unable to find the right words of thanks. I kissed his face and told him that I would never forget his kindness.

He stood up. "Sadie is waiting for me at home. I'll come back tomorrow," he said, as I stood up hoping for an embrace. Uncle Jack looked me straight in the eye, green on green, and said, "You look just like my mother, your grandmother. You are as pretty as she was. May her soul rest in peace." When he realized that I didn't understand his last sentence, which he said it in English. He repeated in Yiddish, "to your long life." It's not a word for word translation, but the gist is the same.

I kissed my uncle's face, this time gently, because I had never been more flattered and had not felt more loved for such a very long time.

Two days later, Uncle Jack returned with a man holding a large suitcase. "This is my brother, your Uncle Charley," he said. Though I remembered my mama referring to her brother Charley as the selfish one, I only saw one more family member for me to love.

Uncle Charley was shorter and thinner than his brother Jack was, but it was easy to see the resemblance. Before I had a chance to properly greet Uncle Charley, Uncle Jack guided him to Marian's room. I realized then that the double bed in the second bedroom was furnished for Uncle Charley. I didn't mind. In fact, it felt good to have and elder family member in the same apartment.

Uncle Jack found a job for Max working in a factory, making bow ties. It was piecework, and he had to make a lot of bow ties in order to pay the bills.

Several times a week, Uncle Jack came to visit with his wife Sadie, his son Harry, and Harry's wife Ida, and their two beautiful daughters. Myrna was eight years old. She loved playing with Marian. Francis, at sixteen years old, was wearing makeup. I had never seen a girl her age wearing face or eye makeup before. In 1936 on her wedding day, Fraida didn't own a lipstick and painted her lips with a red paper used for school projects. I watched Mama moisten the piece of red paper in a drop of water and rubbed the color on Fraida' s lips, then used her finger to spread it.

In 1946, when I lived in Munich with Max, I had bought a lipstick on the black market, and with my tiny mirror, I carefully applied it on my thin lips. The lipstick stayed on my lips long enough until I stepped through the threshold of our room. Max made me feel as if I had committed a crime and ordered me to wipe it off.

When I saw Frances for the first time wearing face makeup, eyeliner, mascara, and bright lipstick, I couldn't stop looking at her and wondered why she would mask her beautiful face. After seeing her several times, I was happy to be living in a country with so much freedom.

Myrna had the sweetest smile, and both girls adored my daughter, taking turns holding her. I looked forward to the visits, and Uncle Jack always brought a strawberry short cake, and I made coffee in the percolator he had bought for me.

After my Aunt Sophy had spent several afternoons in my apartment teaching me to cook and bake, I always had fresh baked cheesecake or apple cake. The more my uncle praised me for my baked goods, the harder I tried to please him.

I had friendly neighbors on Linden Boulevard and appreciated having my English pronunciations corrected.

It was hard living on Max's salary and with the weekly allowance he gave me for food, I had learned to manage well, and I even bought clothing for us all. I tried hard not be portrayed as the poor refugee. Being very thin, I would buy a skirt for two dollars and a blouse for two dollars, and my daughter and I always looked well dressed. When my sewing machine arrived along with the little wicker baby carriage and the embroidered curtains, just as I thought, the curtains fit my living room windows perfectly. I made use of my sewing machine by buying a piece of material on sale, and with the help of my next door Italian neighbor, Marry, I made some simple clothes for myself and later for my daughter.

I had befriended my ground floor neighbors, Bea and Lou. They had a daughter three month younger than Marian. Though Bea thought of me as a refugee, we nevertheless became lifelong friends. Strolling with our babies back and forth on the sidewalk or sitting on chairs next to our babies, Bea spoke to me in Yiddish.

After living in America one month, I said, "Be let spik Enlish."

From that day on, we only spoke English, and I was quickly becoming Americanized. Six months later, I asked Bea to walk with our strollers to the Kings County Hospital.

"I would like to apply for a job," I said.

Bea waited outside with the children while I was directed to the personnel office. Sitting behind a small dark desk was a large woman with blond hair and very small blue eyes. She pointed to a brown wooden chair in front of her desk, and I sat down. Looking at the smiling woman, my head was suddenly throbbing. She reminded me of the smiling Germans when I lived in Feldafing.

I also remembered that only a short time ago, the same Germans could have killed me for no reason at all. I had become conditioned not to turn my back towards a German, especially when he or she smiled. But this was America, and I had nothing to be afraid of. The woman gave me an application to fill out, and I did surprisingly well, except for one question of which I left unanswered. The question was 'Race?' I didn't know what the word 'race' meant. I placed my diplomas in front of the woman. Most were translated into English. Among my papers was a letter from Doctor Zepken, explaining my excellent nursing skills and that I had worked under him, assisting in surgery.

I sat in front of the woman as she read every inch of my papers. On intervals, she lifted her face looking impressed and smiled. Her tiny eyes were only blue slits. When she finished reading my diploma, the hospital's and Doctor Zepkin's recommendations, she put my papers neatly in front of her and covered them with doughy hands.

"Our pay is twice a month. Which shift would you like to work?" she asked while reading my application. Before I had a chance to respond, she said, "You missed a question," and she showed me the application with the question where it said "Race."

"I'm sorry, but I don't understand the question," I said timidly.

"Which church do you go to?" she asked, still smiling.

"I'm Jewish. I don't go to church," I said proudly, feeling secure that I was living in America, the land of the free, where everyone is equal, and I don't have to be afraid to say, "I am Jewish!"

Suddenly, the woman stood up, her hands pressed carelessly on my papers, her doughy face had become red as two plump beets.

"You're Jewish, not German!" she bellowed.

My heart began to pound. I felt as if it would fallout of my chest.

"Does that make a difference?" I asked, stumbling with every word.

She gathered my crumbled papers and handed them back to me. "Oh no, no, but why don't you apply at the Jewish hospital?" she growled in the same tone as when the Gestapo raised the whip.

Another woman a few feet away stood up from her desk and shouted, "What's going on?"

"Oh nothing," doughy face, shouted back. "She never worked in a hospital!"

I looked at the lying woman's tiny piercing eyes and suddenly saw every Kapo, every Nazi, and Hitler and his mustache. Suddenly, the papers I worked so hard for had become a threat to my baby and me. I felt that if I held them in my hand much longer, I would have been attacked by the Blizin German shepherds. I quickly tore them into tiny pieces and threw them in the woman's angry face as if it were confetti.

"I will never work for you again," I shouted and ran out of the building as if I was being chased.

When Bea saw me approach, she must have seen the ghosts from my past. She turned her stroller around, and I mine, and we walked back in silence. She had never asked me what had transpired at the personnel's office or if I was going to be working or not. From that day on, all my fears had returned, and I believed that a Jew wasn't safe in any country. Since that day, I never volunteered to reveal my religious background. If anyone asked me my nationality because my accent had been prominent, I always said, "Polish," which was not a lie, but I could have said that I was a Polish Jew.

The Yiddish that I had learned to read and write and speak in Feldafing, I had forgotten, as if I had never learned it. At home when Max spoke Yiddish to me, I automatically answered him in English. I understood the Yiddish words, but was unable to carry a conversation. It had been the same when I was a child. Being a Jew meant that I would go to hell and that I did not deserve the quality of life a Polish child was entitled to. When my family asked me a question in Yiddish, I answered in Polish, and nobody, including myself, realized that I seldom uttered a word or two in Yiddish.

In the Camps we all spoke Polish, and German when necessary. After many years of waiting, hoping and praying, I was privileged to live in America where I could hold my head up high and be proud of my heritage. Now, even in America, ignorance prevailed, and my privileges were not the same as if I had not been a Jew. In the street walking with Bea pushing my child in the stroller, I had the feeling as if I was being followed and constantly turned my head looking back. One day Bea stopped walking and touched my arm.

"Why do you keep turning your head as if you were looking for someone? You are doing it all the time," she said and waited for an answer.

I couldn't tell her the truth and said, "Thank you for correcting me." The truth was that I was unable to reveal to my new friend the fears that lived in the very core of my being, like an old wound that heals over and keeps coming back because the infection had never been completely excised. I tried to be aware of my movements. I didn't want my neighbors to think that a crazy refugee was living on the fifth floor.

The summer of 1950, my brother Sonny arrived from Italy. I don't know how he ended up in Italy, for his story was changing from day to day, but it had been the happiest day of my life. I wrote a welcoming poem in the Polish language for him, letting him know how happy I was that he had survived. But from the very first day of his arrival, I could see that he was not the same person I saw for the last time in 1940.

The brother I knew had foresight when he was only eighteen years old. He knew that it would be impossible to survive under the German rules. That was why he begged our parents to leave and go to the Russian border. And when our parents did not take his advise, he escaped with Shama, his friend and neighbor, to save his own life, and now the guilt won't let him live a normal life.

Since Uncle Charley had the bed in Marian's room, Sonny had to sleep on the couch, which also opened into a comfortable bed.

I wrote a letter to Bela letting her know that our brother was with me. Bela wrote back to say how happy she was, but her mind had been occupied with worries of constant threats of war in Israel. Her husband was in the reserve and could be taken away from her at any moment, and she was expecting her second child.

After four weeks of sleeping on the couch, Sonny gave me an ultimatum, "It's me or Uncle Charley. If Uncle Charley continues to live here, I'm leaving," he said. I was torn between my uncle and my brother. After many years of not knowing if Sonny had survived the war, I finally got him back. The thought of losing him again had been unthinkable. I had become accustomed to having Uncle Charley with us, but my brother had to come first, and I had to tell my uncle to find another place to live, and he understood my predicament.

After Uncle Charley moved out, Sonny announced that he was married in Italy to an Italian girl, and his wife was expecting a child any day.

"As soon as I get a good job, I'll send for her,'" he said, and I was happy for him. But my brother wasn't reunited with his family until his daughter, Linda, was ten years old.

361

I had given up on ever working at my profession, and on September 7, 1951, I gave birth to a boy at the Jewish Hospital. At the time when doughy face at Kings County Hospital snarled at me and told me to get a job at the Jewish Hospital, I didn't know that there was such a place called the 'Jewish Hospital' We named our son Israel, after Max's father, and Jeremy, after my father. The names were immediately Americanized to Ira Jay. Soon after Ira Jay was born, I came down with a throat infection and a hundred and three temperature.

Max had to work, and Sonny was deathly afraid of catching my illness. He moved out, leaving me to take care of two small children. I prayed I wouldn't infect them, and my prayers were answered. After I recovered, my brother returned for visits, then moved back to my apartment. It seemed that every two months, he moved out and moved back. I tolerated his whims because I knew that he had not been the brother I knew and loved.

After three months of colic and constant crying, Ira Jay's wrinkled face and body had filled out, and he became a beautiful boy, with curly blond hair and blue eyes which later turned green.

Now, Bela and I had two children each. Bela had two sons, Eli and Yerry, and I had a daughter and a son. My friend Bea gave birth to another girl, and the family moved to a new home.

When Ira Jay was one year old and Marian three and a half, much to Max's disapproval, I enrolled at Erasmus High School in Brooklyn, NY. Every night after dinner, when the children were in bed and Max asleep at the television my Uncle Jack had co-signed for us, I walked to school. Classes were from seven to ten in the evening. I graduated in June 1954, and Max came to my graduation.

Max's sister Helen, with her husband and children, emigrated from Germany to Pasadena, California, and in each letter to Max, Helen described the sunshine and opportunities.

In July 1954, Max left New York to establish himself in Pasadena and make a home for us. Two weeks later, he telephoned and told me to sell everything in the apartment and come to California. My heart was breaking. I didn't want to leave my aunt and uncle and all my cousins, but I had no choice. If my husband felt that he had a better opportunity in Pasadena, I had no right to keep him back.

When I told Sonny that we were moving to California, he decided to join us and left New York a week later to stay with Max. As per Max's order, by the middle of August, I had sold everything except my Electrolux vacuum cleaner, my sewing machine, and our clothes. Since Max told me that he had an apartment ready for us with everything in it, there was no need to pay for shipping our things from New York.

After I sold everything, I gave up my apartment. The children and I stayed one week with my Aunt Sophy and departed for Pasadena, California. With Ira Jay in my right arm and Marian's hand in my left hand, we stood at the airport, surrounded by an entourage of family members. After being an orphan for such a long time, I had found an aunt and two uncles and cousins whom I loved and clung to. Now, I was leaving them and wasn't sure when I would see them again. I hadn't felt so much pain since the lights went on during the night in the Radom Ghetto in August 1942, and my entire family had vanished. I know that this is not a good comparison. The family I was now leaving behind was safe in America. As the time was nearing to board the plane, I remembered Mama's tears stinging her beautiful green eyes when she said, "I don't think I will ever see you again."

The children and I stepped inside the airplane with a bag of pastries Aunt Sophy had baked for us, and I was unable to hold back the tears. I wasn't certain which family I was weeping for, but I was thinking of my mama, my tata, Fraida, and her two beautiful children, and Edzia. I suddenly missed Bela and wished that she had been sitting next to me. We went through such horror together, and it was not right for us to be apart. Israel seemed so far away, and I wasn't sure if I would ever see her again. I wept long after we were airborne.

There was no food being served on the plane, and the children began to eat Aunt Sophy's pastries. I was beginning to get queasy, for I hadn't eaten since breakfast the day before, and I ate a piece of Aunt Sophy's Danish from the brown bag. There were no disposable bags in front of our seats, and Marian and I ran to the bathroom vomiting more than we had eaten. After my last run to the bathroom, I was unable to catch my breath.

The flight attendant saw me gasping for air and covered my mouth with an oxygen mask.

Ira Jay, who was one month away from being three years old, sat in his seat like a little man, a perfect gentleman. After several hours of flying, he stood up to go to the bathroom and collided with Marian on her way back from the bathroom and was covered with vomit from head to toe. I watched helplessly as the flight attendant desperately tried to clean the vomit from my son's golden curls and his white shirt, bow tie, and gray vest.

When the plane finally landed in Los Angeles, Ira Jay stood at the plane's bottom stairs and looked around. "So... this is Califoornia...and where is my Daddy?" he said, just as Max appeared with Joe, Helen's husband.

Chapter Forty

It was dark when Joe parked his car on Fair Oaks Avenue, in Pasadena. "This is my house," he said proudly.

Since Max wrote to me that he had a fully equipped apartment for us, I was certain that that was just a quick stop to see Helen. With my daughter's hand in mine and my son asleep on my shoulder, I followed Max through the back entrance to a room connected to the main house. I wondered why Max was bringing in our luggage, and why were we going around the back, but I didn't ask I was too tired. I was guided to a back entrance, to a room off of the main house. A dim light revealed three single beds, a small metal table, four plastic chairs, a very small stove, an old sink, and an old refrigerator.

Helen greeted me and offered a cup of tea. I explained to her about the airsickness and asked if we could shower. The bathroom had enough room for a toilet, a sink, and a very small stall shower. I put Ira Jay under the shower and washed the smelly vomit from his hair and body. After I put him to bed, my clothes were wet, and Marian and I showered, and both children fell immediately asleep. My hair was dripping wet, and I too would have gladly gone to sleep, but I was anxious to see my brother.

"Is Sonny here?" I asked no one in particular, wondering if he went back to New York. Sonny appeared through the door of the main house, and I was unable to stop myself from hugging him. He was the only relative I now had, and I never wanted to let him out from my sight.

Though our new home in Pasadena wasn't at all that Max had described in his letters and on the telephone, I hadn't forgotten to be humble and that nothing stays the same forever. The next morning, I paid Helen for the first month's rent with the money I got from selling the furniture in New York, and her oldest daughter, Lilly, walked with me to the super market. I loved Lilly. In Feldafing, until April 5, 1949 when my own daughter was born, I babysat her and spent all my free time from work studying with Lilly. I knew that she wouldn't remember me. She was, after all, only three years old when we parted in Germany. Yet, when she saw me in the morning, she hugged me and called me Tante Jadzia and wrapped her arms around me.

Sonny told me that he had a job doing alterations at a tailor store. He paid Helen rent for sleeping on the couch in the main house. I would've preferred that he stayed in our room, for I was afraid that if I lost sight of him, he would disappear.

After two days of rest, I was anxious to get a job. Max worked as a roofer, and from what he told me of his earnings, I knew that we would never be able to get a place of our own, but I also knew that I could not work at my profession. The mere thought of the experience at the Kings County Hospital brought back an avalanche of nightmares.

Joe and Helen were selling clothes on time, door to door, to Negroes.

In my entire life, I had known one Negro. He was the Superintendent in the building on Linden Boulevard in Brooklyn. James was a kind and caring person. When he saw the number from Auschwitz tattooed on my forearm, he came up to our apartment with a lemon and tried desperately, though in vain, to rub out the number. When I needed to take my children to the doctor on a rainy day, it was James, the Super, driving us there.

So when I learned that Joe and Helen were selling to Negroes, I told Max that I wouldn't mind doing the same thing, but Max didn't think that I would be capable of buying at the jobbers in Los Angeles and selling door to door on time.

"You don't know anything about buying and selling. Why don't you get a job in a sewing factory?" he said.

I was anxious to please him and scanned the newspaper and underlined a want ad for seamstresses in a garment factory. Helen was kind enough to offer to keep my children while I went for the interview.

"Joe is now out knocking on doors, and most of our customers are coming to our house. So, as long as I'm staying home with my children, yours can stay too. After you get a job, you can sign them up in a child care facility," she said, and I was grateful to her and called the factory, and the manager told me to come now.

Joe gave me directions, and I took a bus, hoping to get the job so we could move into a normal apartment. Maybe then, Sonny would be happier and wouldn't threaten to go back to New York. He hated not having his own room. After waiting a long time for a bus, I was dropped off six blocks from the factory. I didn't want to keep the manager waiting, so I ran the entire six blocks. I was out of breath when I arrived. I knew that if I were going to work, I would have to learn to drive. I stood on the steps to catch my breath before entering the factory.

The large room was lined with rows of about twenty sewing machines. Only about ten were occupied with young Spanish girls. The manager approached me as I walked through the door. I gave him my name and told him that I knew how to sew and would work hard if I got the job.

"Did you ever sew on a sewing machine?" he asked,

"Oh yes, I have a sewing machine at home," I said feeling more secure. He pointed to a sewing machine and told me to sit down. He saw me looking for the foot paddle and said, "No, this one doesn't have a foot paddle," and showed me the speed control that was located at my right knee. He placed a piece of cloth under the presser foot. "Now, make a straight seam," he said.

How hard could it be? I mused. I did have a Singer sewing machine. I had made some of my own clothes. Only, I didn't know that electric sewing machines had been invented. I pressed my knee against the speed control, and the machine took on a life of it's own.

"Stop!" The manager shouted. "You almost took my hand off!" he shouted again when I stopped. When he saw how frightened I was his voice softened. "Look, young lady, come back when the boss is here, his heart is stronger than mine," he said, and I saw that all of his blood had drained from his face. The nurse in me wanted to stay, take his pulse, and make sure he was all right before I left, but I could see that he was anxious for me to be gone.

Again, I waited a long time for a bus home, but this time I felt useless. I couldn't face Helen or Joe or Max, especially Max. Helen saw the sadness in my face after I told her what had happened, and she opened her closet, and Joe loaded my arm with about thirty garments he had been unable to sell. Though I had no idea what people were wearing in California, I recognized that these garments had been taking up space in her closet since she and Joe first started the business.

"Now remember," Joe said and gave me a list of streets. "This is my territory, and these are my customers. You are never to enter these streets." he said with a scowl. He gave me another list of several streets. "These are the only streets you can go on, " he said and wrote down his charges for each garment. He gave me the bill and said, "This is what you owe me. For you to make a profit, you need to ask for double and for down payments. Many customers won't pay, and the paying customers will have to pay more so that you could come out even," he said and told me how much of a down payment I needed to ask for each garment.

I began walking with the load on my arm, looking for the first assigned street. By the time I reached the first mile and was no where near the streets I was allowed to enter, my arm felt as if it would break in have. But when I knocked on the first door and was invited in by eager and smiling faces and was receiving more hugs than I had since the last time I saw my Mama, I knew I could do the job.

That late afternoon I returned home with sore but empty arms. When I showed the down payments and the ledgers to Helen, she couldn't believe her own eyes, and the next day, Joe loaded me up with another armload of his garments, and again, I returned empty handed and with the down payments.

After several days of the same, I was able to pay back Joe for his garments, and Max decided that it was time for me to go to Los Angeles and buy my own garments and sell them. After several weeks, I developed a substantial clientele within my own territory, and before I entered a new street, I asked Joe his permission. I would never cross them.

After two months, Joe saw how I well I was doing and was worried that I may be cutting in on his territory and asked us to move.

We moved into an apartment, and for the first week, we slept on the floor, and I made a closet from the wooden crate my sewing machine and the vacuum cleaner had arrived in. Sonny didn't want to live at Helen and Joe's without us, and he didn't like sleeping on the floor. Though I begged and cajoled, promising that we would get beds in a few days, I couldn't persuade him to stay, and he returned to New York. I knew that sleeping on the floor for a few days was only an excuse because I could tell even before we moved that my brother was ready to leave California. I, too, missed New York and my family. Many nights I cried myself to sleep, but I had to give us a chance. It didn't take long before we had beds and a table and four chairs.

Max bought an old Plymouth for two hundred dollars so that he could be at work on time.

Since my job was to knock on doors and ride the bus to Los Angeles on buying trips, I enrolled Marian in child care, and she didn't mind at all. She made friends easily.

The hard part was leaving Ira Jay, now three years old, in the nursery school. On his first day, he stood at the fence and sobbed. It broke my heart to walk away. I felt like a deserter. I almost turned back to pick him up in my arms and take him home, but I knew that I had to be strong if I was to be helpful to Max.

We moved two more times before Max asked his oldest brother, Herman, to return the twelve hundred dollars he borrowed from us. It was all the money Max had earned in the little candy store in Germany, which Herman had borrowed from us only two months after we arrived in New York. He had started a textile business in Pittston, Pennsylvania, where he lived and kept our money the entire time without paying us interest. When Herman's check for twelve hundred dollars arrived, we put a down payment on an eighty-five hundred dollar house in Altadena. After we moved into our new home, it was a long walk to the bus station and child-care. Now that we had moved away from Pasadena, a long distance from Joe's territory, I could knock on as many doors as I pleased.

Our three-bedroom house was devoid of furniture, and I knew that I had to work longer hours and go to Los Angeles on buying trips more often. The rainy season had started, and I was running out of clothes to sell. Monday, early morning, Max dropped the children off to child-care, and I left on the bus to Los Angeles. The days were now shorter, and it was dark when the bus dropped me off on Fair Oaks Ave. As soon as I stepped off the bus, it began to rain. I took off my coat and covered the garments. It was a two-mile walk. By the time I arrived home on West Medocino, in Altadena, I was soaked, but thanks to my coat, I was able to salvage the merchandise. I knew that if we were to stay in business, I would have go to Los Angeles on buying trips, but I couldn't risk getting caught in the rain again and take a chance ruining the garments. When I told Max that I was going to learn to drive, he became furious.

"You are acting like a child! You want to show why you need a car? The bus isn't fancy enough for your? First, you want to go to school. Then, you want to be nurse! Now, you want to drive. Everything you do is to show them," he bellowed.

I cried all night. I cried that I worked so hard and turned over to him every penny of my earnings, and he made feel worthless. I cried for being born a Jew, and because of it, I threw away the profession I loved so much. I only had myself now. I knew that I could never expect Max to be proud of me and appreciate my hard work. I hoped that someday my children would know how much I love them and wanted to set a good example.

When I woke up early the next day, my eyes were swollen. I washed my face and got the children ready for school. It was raining that day, and Max drove them to school.

When the empty house was quiet, I opened up the yellow pages and called a driving school. On the third lesson, I drove with the driving teacher to Los Angeles and filled his car with garments. After I got my driver's license, Max bought me a used Oldsmobile for two hundred dollars. Though the car kept stalling and often wouldn't start, I felt a sense of freedom I never thought possible. I worked hard remodeling some of the clothes I bought. I sewed little pearls on black dresses, giving them a more elegant look, which made the dress more valuable. In my spare time I bought paint and painted the entire house. We had a big yard and a rusted manual lawnmower, but I was happy to plant a garden. I bought a used stove for five dollars and a washing machine.

Though Max was earning a salary as a roofer and I was giving him the money I collected everyday, we still didn't have living room furniture.

One day after dinner, Max looked over the ledgers and said, "I'm going to start collecting money on the accounts." There was no need for Max to go to my customers at night to collect money. Most of my customers were housewives or women with children on welfare. They lived on small budgets and could only afford to buy on time. They paid small amounts every week on the accounts. There were some that took advantage. They bought with a very small down payment, and when it came to make the payments, they never had the money, and I went to the next customer that did make the payment. Such was the nature of the business, but Max decided that I didn't do a good enough job.

"I could make more money by selling suits to men, than you can selling dresses," he said, and I didn't want to stop him from wanting the business to grow. Each night Max left after diner and came home late at night. When I asked how he was doing, he became angry and made me feel guilty for asking. Now that I had the car, I was buying more men's suits for Max to sell. He began staying out later and later and often until two in the morning, claiming that he was waiting for the customers to come home.

When I told him that I worried when he was out so late, he became angry and said, "I'm working hard, and you are stopping me from trying to better our lives."

When I would ask him if he was collecting money on the suits, he became angry. "I work hard day and night and am dead tired, and you are doing nothing all day!" he bellowed, but he never answered my question. I wanted to ask him what he had done with the money I gave him everyday from knocking on doors. I wanted to ask him if he ever wondered how I managed to have dinner on the table every night, a clean house, and the lawn mowed with an old rusty manual mower. I wanted to ask him to come home one day early and peek through the keyhole and watch me rub my aching arms and feet, for I didn't use my car going door to door. Instead, I was feeling guilty for doubting him. I wanted to make him happy and began to think that it was time I started looking for a job with a regular paycheck. I began looking in the want ads in the Sunday newspaper.

A medical agency advertised for nurses. I underlined the ad, and Monday morning, after I dropped the children at school, I went directly to the agency. I now knew that not all Americans were Jew haters, but I decided not to tell the agency that I was Jewish, unless I was asked. I filled out the application, and this time, the question was not race or religion. The question was nationality, and I put down Polish.

During the interview, I told Betty, a tall middle-aged woman with dark blond hair and a pleasant smile, that I had three years of nursing training in Germany, but my papers were destroyed. She didn't ask how my papers were destroyed, and I didn't volunteer. I was wearing a long sleeve dress to cover the Auschwitz Number on my forearm. She did, however, ask me if Yetty was a Polish name. I told her that my real name was Jadzia, but nobody could spell or pronounce it.

"My cousin in New York began calling me Yetty. I don't like the name, but I'm stuck with it," I said, and we both laughed. The phone rang just as I was unlocking my door. I picked up the receiver on the third ring.

"Is this Yetty Borenkrout?" I recognized Betty's voice, and I said "yes," hoping that I didn't sound too anxious.

"Tomorrow at ten o'clock, you have an interview with the Director of Nurses at Las Encicas Sanitarium," she said and gave me directions on how to get there.

After dinner when the children were in their beds, Max lit a cigarette and was about to leave the house when I said, "Tomorrow at ten o'clock, I have an interview for a nursing job at a Sanitarium."

Max laughed so hard he began choking on the smoke. "You're a nurse? Do you really believe that you would get hired as a nurse?" He was still laughing and coughing as the door closed behind him.

I went to my room and cried. It suddenly occurred to me that the man I was married to for nine years and had two children with had never taken an interest in me at all. He had no idea what I was doing during the almost four years we were married and living together in Germany. I also remembered that he was seldom home then, as he was now. I really didn't care to prove to him that I was indeed a professional.

The thought of divorce entered my mind many times during our marriage, but it would have been a shameful thing to do in 1955, especially among the survivors. Max pretended to be a loving husband whenever we had a special occasion to get-together with the people from Radom. If I divorced him, I was certain that I would end up being portrayed as the villain, especially by his brothers. Helen was the only one that knew her brother Max well.

I wasn't completely unhappy. My children were my joy. They were most important to me, and I wanted to be able to give them the things I never had. I tiptoed to my daughter's room and picked up her clothes from the floor and kissed her beautiful face.

"You are my bubbly girl," I mused. She stirred and turned on her side. Ira Jay's clothes hung neatly in his closet. "My cuddly little man," I whispered, as I kissed his silky curls.

The Director of Nurses was pleased with my medical terminology and medical knowledge, and I was hired as a Graduate Nurse. My salary was to be two hundred dollars a month. I asked for the morning shift, and I was given the seven to three shifts.

I didn't have enough money to buy my uniform at a regular store, so I went directly to the downtown Los Angeles wholesale stores and bought an inexpensive white uniform, a white nurses cap, white stockings, and white nurse's shoes. The shoes were very uncomfortable, but I had never been happier. It was as though my life was now beginning.

Childcare didn't open until seven thirty, which meant that Max would have to take the children to school, and he agreed, for he didn't think I would last a day on the job. I very seldom looked at myself in the mirror, except to brush my hair. Monday morning, I looked at myself in the full-length mirror hanging on the closet door and smiled.

"This is who you are, Jadzia Sztraiman, and nobody will ever again take it away from you," I mused and prayed that my car wouldn't disappoint me on my first day, and it didn't.

Orientation took up the entire first day. I was taken under the wings of Mary Warren, a middle-aged nurse. I was thinking of my Aunt Hudesa, when Mary told me that most of the older nurses worked and lived on the premises.

La Encinas Sanitarium had taken up an entire block. The main building housed geriatrics, the terminally ill, patients with debilitating diseases that needed long term care, and comatose patients. Smaller buildings housed alcoholics, drug addicts, and psychiatric. All of the patients received care of the highest standards. The sanitarium was staffed with high quality professionals. The private rooms were larger than the finest hotel rooms, and the food was gourmet. The grounds were landscaped with trees and flowers of every variety. There was a tennis court and much more. I was the youngest nurse and was referred to as the little Polish girl. The director of nurses and the supervisor recognized my professional skills, and a month later, my paycheck was ten dollars more. I liked the nurses and the patients. Everyone was treated with respect.

With my first paycheck, I opened a joint savings account.

Every night when the house was quiet I prepared lunches for Max and the children, and in the morning before I left the house, I fixed breakfast for Max and the children. On the way home, I picked up the children from school, and dinner was on the table when Max came home from work. I always worked weekends, and Max stayed home with the children until my return from work. On my days off, I bought merchandise in Los Angeles, and customers now came to my house to buy clothes.

Max continued to stay out late. He was selling suits and collecting money, and he gave me twenty dollars a week for groceries, but according to Max, we still couldn't afford to buy furniture. Twice a month when I signed over my paycheck to him, he never failed to tell me that the money I'm earning doesn't help.

"It all goes to income tax," he would say.

I knew it wasn't true, because he wasn't earning very much working as a roofer. On rainy days, he didn't work at all, but I insisted that we put some money in a savings account. By May 1956, we had a little over twelve hundred dollars in the savings account.

I never had enough money to fill up the tank and always asked for a dollar's worth of gas. My old car didn't have a gas gage, and as long as I put in a dollar's worth, I knew that I would have three or four days worth of fuel.

Saturday, June, 1956 was a hot afternoon. I came home from work, and Max was anxious to leave the house. He gave me five dollars and said, "Take the children to movies," and he left before I had a chance ask him where he was going in such a hurry.

I changed from my uniform and was anxious to spend time with my children. I was two blocks from my house, and the car stopped dead.

A woman passed by and pushed me with her car to the gas station on Fair Oaks Avenue.

Two attendants lifted the hood and told me that I was out of gas and attempted to pour gasoline into the carburetor. I had the five dollars Max gave me earlier and felt rich.

"Why don't you fill it up, and then we'll see what will happen," I said, but he didn't hear or didn't want to hear me.

My children were sitting in the back seat, and one attendant asked me to move over, and he sat down at the wheel next to me. I didn't want to crowd him and stepped out of the car. Suddenly, the carburetor ignited, and the breeze blew the flames in my direction and engulfed my hair.

Suddenly, people were all around m,e covering my face with a black ointment, and all I could think of were my children.

"Please, please, my children are in the car. Please, get them out quickly!" I begged. When I was told that my children were all right and out of the car, I was frightened that they would get lost, and I pleaded again, "Please call my sister-in-law." After I cried out the telephone number, I heard sirens. I must've passed out because the next thing I felt was unbearable pain. I was only able to open my left eye and saw that I was on a table surrounded by doctors and nurses scraping the black ointment from my face, and they were angry with the Good Samaritan for piling it on me.

"My children," I managed to utter and was assured that they were safe. I was bandaged and given an injection. The next time I opened my left eye again, I was at home in my bed.

In a drugged daze, I saw Max and Joe sitting three feet from my bed discussing a lawsuit. "Where are the children?" I muttered.

"They are in my house," Joe said and continued the conversation on how to get rich off my burns, as if I was invisible.

When I woke up the next morning, my head was clear, but the right side of my face felt as if it was on fire, and I was alone in the house. I needed to relieve myself and rolled away the covers and saw that I was wearing a hospital gown. When I stood up to go to the bathroom, the entire house was rolling with me. I held on to the walls and somehow managed to reach the bathroom and stumble back to bed. My throat felt as if I had swallowed hot coal, but I was afraid to take a chance and go to the kitchen for a drink of water.

Some hours later when I didn't think I could bare the pain much longer, Max came home with a doctor. The doctor lifted the bandages, only to take a quick look, and replaced them. He gave me an injection and said, "She has second and third degree burns to the right side of her face, forehead, and shoulder. She has to be hospitalized." I heard the sirens, and when next I opened my eyes, the bandages were replaced with light gauze.

I could see from both eyes and was told that I was at the Alta Vista Hospital. The doctor came to see me every day for two weeks and released me.

I came home with visible scars on my right cheekbone, the right side of my forehead, and shoulder. The right eyebrow and eyelash were singed, but

I thanked God that my right eye was undamaged.

Max had engaged a lawyer named Brody, the same lawyer who later died in a car accident with Jane Mansfield.

Two months after the accident, Sonny arrived. When he saw the scars on my face, he was ready to go back to New York the next day. I needed someone's arms around me, someone to reassure me that the scars will disappear, and I will soon feel stronger. I needed someone to cry with me, and I was happy to see my brother, though I wished it had been Bela. I remembered that Sonny liked pigeons, and I convinced Max that my brother would be a big help with the children if he stayed. Max put a cage in the back yard with five white doves, the same as Sonny had at home in Poland when he was a young boy. Three months later, Sonny let the doves fly away, and he went back to New York.

After Sonny went back to New York, Max stayed out until all hours of the night, claiming that he was trying to collect money for the suits he sold. One day Max didn't come home all night, and in the morning, I had a call from jail. I was informed that my husband was arrested for gambling. I called the judge and told him that my husband was innocent.

"Your Honor," I said. "My husband is not a gambler. He was in that house trying to collect money owed us for garments we sell on time door to door." I gave the judge our company name, General Merchandise. "Please, Your Honor, my husband is a good, hard working man. He works two jobs to support his family, and he would never do anything that was against the law," I said pleadingly. The judge was very understanding and promised me that he would not keep Max in jail.

"Your husband should be home soon," the Judge said.

I was drained after replacing the receiver. I wanted to believe that Max had not been gambling with the customers. I wanted to believe that all those nights he stayed out until two in the morning, he was, indeed, waiting for the customers to come home. If I didn't believe him, I wouldn't have been able to convince the judge. But something was eating at me, and I needed a shoulder to cry on. I felt so alone. I wished Mama would suddenly appear and hold me tight in her arms and tell me that everything was going to be alright. My head was throbbing, but I didn't take my prescription pills. I wanted to be able to think clearly. I tried to think back to the time when Max began staying out late. I remembered with pride that after I worked six month at Las-Encinas, we had saved over twelve hundred dollars. I had my first Saturday off, and we went to a furniture auction and bought three inexpensive, but new, bedroom sets and a pink sofa for the den, that opened to a double bed. The children's bedroom sets were beige. The headboards had sliding compartments for books, and the dressers had good sized drawers. The master bedroom set was pink, and it had a vanity with a round mirror. It was very feminine, and I loved it.

I remembered that approximately three months before I had the accident, Max began staying out late, often until two in the morning. One morning, I woke up at five o'clock to get ready for work and realized that Max had not come home. He always complained about how tired he was, and I was thinking that he might have fallen asleep at the customer's house while waiting for the man to come home, but I needed him to take the children to school, and with each minute that passed, I was beginning to think the worst.

I fixed breakfast for the children and Max, hoping he would walk through the door. At six o'clock, I called the police. A squad car arrived within minutes. I told the two officers that my husband didn't come home last night.

Just as one officer began asking me questions, Max walked in and told the officers that he was in Los Angeles visiting friends and lost track of time.

I was late for work and never questioned him about the incident. I somehow knew that I would never know the truth. The next few weeks he was coming home from work at the roofing job and only left for an hour or two after dinner, and the ledgers did show some deductions. It didn't take long before he began staying out later and later.

The children and I hardly ever saw him except at dinner time, which only took him a few minutes to eat, and he was gone. After working eight hours five days a week at Las Encinas and the other two days I was buying and selling clothes and taking care of two children, a large house, and a yard, I had no energy left for arguments. I was happy that Max didn't complain about my working and that my paycheck was putting us on a higher bracket. Now, I wondered if it was possible that he was gambling with his customers.

My mind was running a million miles a minute with memories of Max's card playing in Feldafing.

I would never believe that Max would gamble with the money we saved to buy furniture.

Was everything a lie when he told me how hard he worked so our children's needs would be met? But Joe never stayed out late at night to collect money. He was always home with his family. I had to know. It was Sunday, and the children were still asleep. I opened the top drawer in our bedroom where we kept our bankbook and felt my legs turn to rubber when I saw a balance of five dollars. My hands began trembling, and I reached for the bottle of tranquilizers, but I never opened it.

"I have to keep my head clear," I whispered to no one in particular. I opened another drawer where we kept the ledgers and saw that all the ledgers where untouched. He hadn't sold or collected any money since I had the accident. He never took the ledgers with him when he left the house at night. The checkbook, too, was totally withdrawn. We were penniless. We were living on my disability check. Chances were that he gambled away his paycheck. I stretched out on the couch in the den until I heard his car. I tried to be calm and sat down at the kitchen table, away from the children's bedrooms. I knew how loud Max could get when he was angry, especially when he was feeling guilty, and I didn't want to frighten the children. He soundlessly unlocked the living room door and tiptoed towards our bedroom. As he passed the kitchen, he was startled to see me sitting at the table. He had a fixed smile on his face, instead of his usual scowl.

"I waited for a customer that owed me a lot of money, but he didn't come home all night," he said, reaching for a cigarette.

"What are you doing up so early?" he asked smiling, and I realized that he didn't know that I had cajoled the judge into letting him go free. I didn't care to take the credit for his freedom. I wasn't interested in small talk and more lies. I placed the open bankbook in front of him, showing the five-dollar balance.

"I needed money to buy merchandise. Do you think that I bought all the suits for nothing?" he said, raising his voice. I told him that the children were asleep and showed him the checkbook and the ledgers. I wanted to scream and cry and ask him why he cared so little about us, but I did neither.

"You gambled away every dime, and last night, you ended up in jail."

"How did you know that I was in jail?"

"I had a phone call from the police department. I couldn't believe that you would be guilty of gambling, and I convinced the judge to let you go," I said.

His tears began flowing from his eyes. "I was gambling with the customers and lost all of our money. I promise I will never do it again," he said, puffing on his cigarette and filling the kitchen with clouds of smoke.

I ignored his tears and promises. "I want a divorce," I said with a tone in my voice unfamiliar to him.

I heard the children waking up and turned on the griddle. I made the little dollar size pancakes, and we all ate breakfast as if nothing was wrong.

Max slept most of the day, and I went about doing my chores. The entire day was spent as if we were a normal family.

Monday morning after the children went to school and Max to work, I called Brody and asked him to file for a divorce. Brody was very upset and told me that it wouldn't look good for my case. At that point, I didn't care about the case. After I told him about the gambling and the arrest he changed his mind.

"A jury wouldn't look kindly at gambling, " he said and agreed to file for divorce.

Max was ordered by the court to move out of our house, and I didn't want to know where he lived. While staying indoors, my scars blended in with my light complexion. I knew that it would take a long time before most of the scars would fade. It didn't look as if the dollar size scar on my right cheekbone and the entire right side of my forehead would completely disappear. I experimented with makeup and felt confidant that I could function in a workplace. I was beginning to feel better and slept without drugs, and I began to make plans on going to back to work, if not at Las Encinas, then at a hospital close to home. My only concern was that working in a hospital would be difficult. I wouldn't have anyone to take the children to school. Nevertheless, I was beginning to look for work in the Sunday newspaper. In the meantime, I was collecting disability, which helped pay the bills.

Several times a week, Max came to see the children. Marian was now in first grade and was busy with her friends and didn't seem to notice her father's absence, or at least, she never asked why her daddy wasn't sleeping at home. When Max did come to visit the children, he spent more time begging me to take him back, and the plea was always the same.

"I will change, and I promise to be good to you."

But I had made up my mind, and no pleading would change that. I was free and feeling good about myself, and no one was going to break my spirit ever again. I had been abused long enough, and enough was enough.

Six weeks after Max moved out, Ira Jay had a temperature and was in bed. Max came to visit him with a toy in his hand, and I heard him plead with the child.

"Ira Jay, tell Mommy to take me back. I'll be good from now on," he said pleadingly.

Ira Jay, cried, "Mommy please...take Daddy back. He'll be good from now on. Please, Mommy," he pleaded. His little chin quivered and his arms were tightly around his father's neck. I felt helpless. How could I be so selfish to refuse my child his father? Though, during the six weeks since he had moved out, Max was spending more time with our children than ever before, the whimpering, flushed face, clinging to his dad, was breaking my heart. I felt as if I was the villain, and I assured my son that his daddy could come home. Max did stay home more, and I was thinking that he had changed. I went back to the routine of being a mother and wife, and I did not need the pills. Except for a twinge from a wrong movement, my shoulder was healing. I told Max that I would like to go back to work.

"We can't be without living room furniture forever," I said.

"I will call Brody and ask him," he promised. At that moment, Brody called to tell us to get ready for a deposition, which was to take place within a few days. I was standing next to Max, sharing the telephone receiver and said, "Mr. Brody, I'm feeling better, and I would like to go back to work?"

"Under no circumstances can she go back to work, Max!" he said with irritation in his voice. "The insurance company is watching her every move. If she goes back to work, we will lose the case. It's up to you, Max. Make up your mind. Do you want to win or not?"

I knew how badly Max wanted to have his own business, and I said, "I won't go to work until the case is over."

It was worth the sacrifice to see a smile on Max's face, for he seldom smiled. I walked away from the telephone and heard Max say, "Okay, Mr. Brody, I understand." He stayed on the phone another two minutes before he said, "Thank you."

After all the pain Max caused me, I trusted him and didn't ask what the conversation was about. The next morning was raining. Max left the house and returned an hour later with Katie.

During the six weeks while Max had moved out, I had let Katie go. I was feeling stronger, and though Brody said that he would pay her to do the housework, I didn't want to pretend to be sick for the insurance. It was true that since my face was burned, my nightmares from the war had returned, and I must have injured my shoulder, for it was throbbing almost all the time, but I could still take care of my own children and keep the house clean.

"Brody said that you shouldn't have let Katie go, and he wants her back," Max said.

Though Katie was a very pleasant, middle-aged woman, I felt that, not only couldn't I go back to work, I have also been fired from taking care of my home and my children. I felt as if I had been punished for getting my face burned.

Max took me aside, away from Katie's ears, "Since you can't be seen doing any kind of work, Brody will pay me back what ver I will pay Katie to take care of the children and the house," he said.

"I know that Brody will pay you back, but I can take care of my own children. I'm feeling fine, and doing nothing will make me sick," I protested.

"You are not allowed to go out to the front or back yard to rake the leaves, hang out the wash, or do any work around the house. Brody is convinced that the insurance company has you under surveillance with cameras. They may even be looking through the windows with binoculars to see if you are doing housework," Max said.

I was suddenly feeling as if I had been stripped of my entire life.

Two days later Brody arrived and told me that he was taking me to be evaluated by a psychiatrist. "We are claiming that the accident had brought back all the memories of your past experiences," he said, and I felt as if the little self esteem I had gained during the six weeks when Max had moved out had been ripped away from me.

After the evaluation, Brody had found a different psychiatrist, and I was to see him twice a week. After two sessions with the new psychiatrist, Poland and the Germans had come alive in my mind. I had developed severe headaches and right shoulder pain. The internist put my arm in a sling. Due to lack of movement, I had developed a frozen shoulder, and I was now in constant pain. I had sleepless nights, and with help of the generous internist, I never ran out of tranquilizers, painkillers, or sleeping pills. I could barely walk, and the nightmares from the war heightened, and I was waking up in pools of perspiration.

The insurance company wanted to settle, but Brody was sure that having a jury trial would win us millions.

Day after day, I stayed home and vegetated because Brody and Max wanted millions.

Except for a trip to the doctor or psychiatrist, I barely saw the sunlight. My eyes were constantly swollen from crying. I couldn't stop the tears from flowing. I cried for Mama, my father, and my sisters. I even cried for Aunt Hudesa and Aunt Hanna. I couldn't tell Aunt Sophy about my problems because she had a bad heart. My head was always on a pillow, and even the sleeping pills didn't work.

After three years of feeling brainless, my scars were fading, and I had the first jury trial. At the end of his summation, Brody addressed the jury, "Ladies and gentleman, if you should decide against my client, I will not be mad at you."

After a short deliberation, the jury returned, "Not guilty for negligence."

Brody told Max that he would file for a second trial. The second trial was the same as the first.

Brody sat down at our kitchen table and spoke to Max as if I wasn't in the room.

"The only way we can win this case is for her to be admitted in a mental institution. We will claim that the accident brought out the nightmares of the war," he said, and Max didn't protest, and I was too drugged to defend myself. All I now wanted was to die. As in Auschwitz when I was brutally beaten by the capo and signed up for the hospital, which was the same as the crematorium, that was how I felt right now. I have had enough. The little food that I had forced myself to eat before, I had stopped eating all together. My head was hurting more than ever, and my internist prescribed more pills. Day after day, I walked from room to room or lay on my bed, moaning and crying, and I remained awake at night, praying for the sleeping pill to take affect. When I did fall asleep, the nightmares woke me, and I stayed awake the rest of the night.

Max called the internist at all hours of the night. He, too, must have thought that he would get rich on my pain. He would come to my house and give me an injection and sit at the kitchen table with Max, waiting for the injection to take affect. Often, it took two injections until I would succumb. Many times after such nights, I was unable to get out of bed the next morning. One morning after such a visit, I didn't wake up at all. I heard as if from a distance, people screaming and tugging at me, slapping my face, and I heard my children cry, but I was unable to move, as if paralyzed.

When I next opened my eyes, I was told that I was at the Huntington Hospital. I looked around and recognized the stomach pumping equipment. My hands were strapped to the table, and a nurse sat in the corner, knitting and watching my every move. I felt like a criminal. I wanted to tell her that I didn't do it intentionally, but words didn't come. My throat felt as if a smoldering fire was burning my vocal cords. I lost consciousness, and the next time I opened my eyes, I was in a large room.

The door opened, and Doctor Lince, my psychiatrist, a tall man with kindly eyes, stepped inside. He informed me that I was in a sanitarium because I tried to commit suicide. I explained to him that it was unintentional, but I didn't think he believed me.

The first four days, I lay in my bed in the large room, looking at the ceiling, and I worried about my children. I hoped Max didn't stay out all night and leave them alone in the house.

Doctor Robert Jay Lince, M.D. was my only daily visitor. My head felt now clear, and I slept without drugs. On his fifth visit, Doctor Lince sat down next to my bed. He placed a thick black hardcover book in my lap. The title of the book was "Emotional Problems of Living." The authors were O. Spurgeon English, M. D. and Gerald H. J. Pearson, MD. Doctor Lince told me that he had used the book when he was a student. "Read this book, and if you like it, you can keep it," he said, a soft smile on his handsome face.

With, the fact that someone had enough confidence in me to entrust me to tackle a book written for student psychiatrists, my self-esteem received a little boost. It was the first day in three years that I began healing. I read the book from cover to cover. I still have the book, and I will never part with it. I was given no drugs, and all I did was rest, exercise my arm, and read. My head stopped hurting, and with each new day, I was feeling like my old self again, but I missed my children.

Thanks to Doctor Lince, who believed in me, I left the Sanitarium two weeks later, knowing that nobody would ever again succeed in trying to take away my mind and destroy my will to live. My spirit was strong, and I never had more confidence in myself than I did on that Saturday morning when Max's younger brother, Jack, who two years ago had come from Detroit to live in Atadena with his wife and two children, picked me up from the sanitarium.

It was September and a glorious Saturday early afternoon. I didn't remember the sky ever being as blue and the sun as bright. Having the children in my arms was the best therapy.

It didn't occur to me to ask where Max was. I found my purse with twenty dollars in a hidden compartment. I took the children on the bus to the movies and for pizza. Later, we went to the supermarket and bought enough food to last a week.

Max wasn't home when we arrived in the late afternoon, and I didn't let it bother me. I changed the linen on the children's beds and helped them with their bath. The house had been neglected during the two weeks while I was gone. I put away the groceries and began to load the washing machine and clean the house.

When Max came home later in the evening, the children were already asleep. He didn't ask me any questions, and I didn't ask him why he didn't pick me up from the sanitarium or where he was. I wasn't interested in any more lies. Usually, I would've made sure that dinner was waiting for him, no matter how late he would come home, but not this time. It was Saturday, and he wasn't coming home from work. I continued cleaning the house and changed the linen in our bed, and I took a shower and went to sleep.

Max followed me to bed, and I wished he had taken a shower, for he reeked of nicotine. I turned my back to him, and he said, "Brody had stopped paying for Katie, and I had to let her go."

"We don't need Katie. The children are in school all day," I said, without turning to face him. I went to sleep and slept soundly.

Monday morning after breakfast, I packed lunches for the children and Max. When the house was quiet, I looked through the want ads and made an appointment for a job interview at Don Carlos Convalescent Hospital on Fair Oaks Avenue. It was a long walk from my house, but I enjoyed every moment. After the interview, the owner asked me if I could begin the next day. I asked for the morning shift, and she agreed. My salary was slightly higher than what it was at Las Encinas.

I was given the tour by one of the nurses, and I liked what I saw. Don Carlos was a small, clean, respectable Convalescent Hospital. The patients were well taken care of. I couldn't compare Don Carlos to Las Encinas. Don Carlos was much smaller, and all the patients were geriatrics, with the many disabilities and diseases due to aging. But the owner and staff were friendly, and I could walk to work, and I was promised every other weekend off.

Monday evening Max was home from work on time, and dinner was on the table. At eight o'clock, after the children were asleep, I sat down on the sofa in front of the TV next to Max.

"I'm going to work in the morning," I said in a casual tone of voice.

Max lit a cigarette and inhaled deeply. "You can't go to work. You don't have a car. It will take you two hours to get to Las Encinas by bus," he said, being certain that I would tell him that he was right.

"I don't need a car. I'll be working at Don Carlos on Fair Oaks."

Max's face turned red with anger, and he began to cough the usual dry cough. "Brody said that since you were in the sanitarium, we have a good chance to win the case, but if you go to work, we'll lose the case, and we won't get a dime!" he bantered and waited for me to sink my head between my shoulders and mutter, as I had done so for the last three years, "I'll wait a little longer." I saw the surprised look in his eyes when he saw me stand up and walk out of the den. I went to my bedroom to get my shoes and uniform ready and went to sleep. I don't know what Max was thinking. As I lay in bed waiting for sleep to come, I felt reborn with a sense of pride in myself I hadn't felt since before I left the kibbutz on January 3, 1946.

During the two weeks at the sanitarium, I had time to think back to all the years of my marriage to Max, and I realized that Max had never cared about me as a person, or as a woman. In the twelve years of our marriage, he never paid me a compliment. I had become so accustomed to feeling undesirable that I never thought much about my looks, even if men did turn their heads for a second look.

We very seldom went anywhere for an evening out. When we were invited to weddings or Bar mitzvahs of Max's survivor friends from Radom or relatives, Max would put on his blue suit and bow tie. He would stand in front of the mirror and say, "Look at the handsome husband you have." On those occasions Max danced with me and lifted me off the dance floor to the rhythm of a Polka, and I was the envy of every woman.

Always, a woman would follow me to the powder room and say, "What a wonderful husband you have." I nodded and was thinking, if she only looked though the keyhole of my home she would be shocked.

Other days, my only concern was to look nice, but pretty never entered my mind. If a man or woman paid me a complement, I didn't believe that he or she meant it, and my answer would always be the same, "Oh, sure." When Doctor Lince once said, "Don't worry about your scars. They will fade, and you will be just as pretty as before," I turned my face away from him and muttered, "I was never pretty," and he couldn't convince me otherwise. The only thing I was sure of was being capable of learning anything I set my mind to, especially in regards to my profession.

Now, as I lay in my bed, I'm beginning to get drowsy without sleeping medications or pain killers, and I made a promise to myself. As of tomorrow, I would never let anybody take that new feeling of self-confidence away from me.

It was still dark at 6:15 in the morning. The house was quiet. Everyone was asleep. Three breakfasts and three brown bags were on the table. I tiptoed to my children's rooms and kissed each sleeping face. I put my shoes on in the kitchen and left my house to begin a new job.

I liked the nurses and the patients. I fell into the routine, as if I had been there all my life. At the end of the day, the owner told me that she was very pleased with me. "You're good nurse and very caring," she said, and I thanked her for telling me.

I was home at 3:30, the same time my children were home from school. I enjoyed every precious moment with them. At every bend, or when they sat at the dining room table doing their homework, I would kiss and hug them. I couldn't get enough of them.

Two weeks after I went back to work, Brody called and told Max that he settled the case for ten thousand dollars and told us to pick up the check. Just as I didn't mind signing my check over to Max twice a month, I also signed the check for the ten thousand dollars and handed it to him. The money didn't matter to me, for all I wanted was to keep the peace.

From the twenty dollars a week he gave me for groceries, I managed to put away a dollar or two and buy clothes for us all. I even managed to buy material and made drapes for the den to keep out the hot afternoon sun.

Max was now staying home more at night, and on my days off, I began, again, going to Los Angeles to buy armfuls of ladies clothes and selling from my house. I still had enough time to have dinner on the table when Max came home from work.

Within three month after I went back to work, we filled the entire house with green carpets, for that was the latest style, a green couch, matching chairs, a walnut coffee table with matching end tables, and two large ceramic lamps that looked like wood. We bought lively chenille bedspreads for the children's rooms and a colorful bedspread for our room. Suddenly, our house wasn't just a house. It was a very nice home.

The raining season began, and it was difficult to shop for groceries and walk home two miles, pushing a shopping cart with paper-bags of food. I needed a car, and Max bought me an old Pontiac for two hundred dollar. The car's interior had been reupholstered in Mexico with blue and white heavy plastic. The car had no dents, and it started fine in the morning. I had no problem going to work and back. The engine had enough time to cool down.

Though Max had been staying home more after work, he still didn't go anywhere with us. It was always the children and I. We named our capricious car 'Nelly Bell.' When I forgot about the car's problem and stopped at the store to buy candies before going to the movies, usually three sugar daddies that lasted us through the entire movie, the car wouldn't start. We pushed Nelly Bell and talked to it as if it were a person. "Come on, Nelly Bell, or we'll miss the beginning. Please, Nelly Bell," we begged and pushed until Nelly Bell began gurgling, and the children clapped their hands. We thanked Nelly Bell for being good to us. Other times, if we were lucky, there would be a man in the parking lot, and he would push us until Nelly Bell began to cough and start. On the way back from the movies, Nelly Bell had enough time to rest, and the car took us home.

Once in a while, Max came to the movies with us and for pizza, which was a treat for the children.

My children were my life. I enjoyed every moment with them. Since I never had a childhood myself, I enjoyed doing everything my children did, including rolling on the grass, the hula hoop, and getting on the floor pretending to be a horse. The children would get on my back and ride me. We made so much noise laughing that Max, who had fallen sleeping at the TV, would wake up and scold us for disturbing his rest.

I was, again, health chairman in the PT A, helping with Polio vaccines and arranging dental care for the school children. I never missed a single game or practice with Ira Jay's Little League. Rain or shine, I sat on the bleachers, a first aid kit next to me. Though I didn't understand the game too well, I shouted with the other parents, "Run, Ira, run!"

At night when the children were in bed and Max asleep at the TV, against his wishes, I resumed classes at Pasadena City College to my continue education.

In 1959, Max got a job working for Ma-Gorden's Deli in Los Angeles on Fairfax Avenue and commuted every day. On his days off, he continued going to Los Angeles, looking to buy a liquor store. A year later, he still hadn't found one.

Chapter Forty-One: Family Reunion

In May 1960, Bela wrote that she was coming in June for a visit to New York.

My cousin Lucian, Aunt Hudesa's only surviving son, was arriving from France with his wife Silvia and their daughter Evelyn.

Max agreed to let the children and I go to New York.

In June 1960, Marian was eleven years old, and Ira Jay was eight and a half years old.

When school let out for the summer, Max bought three tickets for three nights and four days on the Greyhound bus to Brooklyn, New York. He gave me a meager allowance for our stay in Brooklyn.

The children and I occupied the bench in the back of the bus. At night, the children curled up on each side of the bench. I sat on the floor, my back against the bench, creating a buffer during a sharp turn. Most of the nights, I stayed awake with a large notepad, writing the story of my life by the road lights. All the while, I was watching over my sleeping children, the way birds protect their young. The food at the bus stops was too expensive, and I needed to stay within my very small budget. I made sure the children had enough to eat and drink; however, I wasn't very hungry or thirsty, and it didn't occur to me to buy a regular meal for myself, and I existed on a piece of Danish pastry.

Uncle Jack picked us up at the bus stop and told me that we were the first to arrive. He dropped us off at Aunt Sophy's house. Aunt Sophy still lived in the small one-and-a-half bedroom apartment in Uncle Jack's building in Brighton Beach, Brooklyn, NY.

My legs felt like rubber, and I knew that if I didn't lie down quickly, I was going to pass out. Aunt Sophy had a heart condition, and I didn't want to get her blood pressure up. I had to get out of sight for a few minutes. I kissed and hugged my aunt and Uncle Ben and disappeared into the bathroom and sat down on the toilet just before I lost consciousness. I must've left the bathroom door unlocked because I felt someone touching my shoulder. I looked up and saw my cousin Fay asking me what was wrong. I whispered, "Don't say anything to your mother. I don't want to worry her." I told her that I was alright and would be right out. Holding onto the sink, I raised myself off the toilet and washed my face with cold water. I felt unsteady, but I managed to stumble into the small bedroom and stretch out on top of the daybed. As I lay motionless, perspiration flooded my face. I closed my eyes, hoping for the feeling to pass. Through my muddled mind, I realized that I was suffering from dehydration. I became frightened by the feeling of helplessness and was grateful when I saw Fay entering the room. I asked her for something to drink. She quickly returned with a glass of orange juice. She helped me to sit up and drink the juice. My head cleared, but my clothes felt damp. I took a quick cool shower and changed clothes. Aunt Sophy had made cheese blintzes with blueberries, only she called them huckleberries. I didn't realize how hungry I was until I started eating the blintzes.

After the children went to sleep on the pullout sofa in the living room, my aunt and I sat at the kitchen table and shared a cup of tea. She told me how proud she was of me that I was a nurse. It took me by surprise because I was a nurse when I arrived to New York from Germany, and in my letters to her, I had told her that I was going to nursing school, but nobody asked me anything when I lived five years in New York. It didn't matter to me. I only wanted to hold onto my aunt whom I loved as if she were my mother. I didn't tell her about my life with Max, and when she told me that she had a heart problem and high blood pressure, I didn't tell her that I knew. From the first day when I left New York to go to California, I telephoned my aunt once a week, and she had kept me informed about her health problem, and each time, I was feeling more helpless than the time before. I always called her from a pay phone on the way back from the supermarket when I had some change left over. Now, sitting in front of her and seeing her swollen feet and ankles, I had a sick feeling in my gut that that would be the last time I would see this woman I often called Mama. I wanted to spend as much time with her as possible and decided to stay the entire summer. I knew that we couldn't stay in her house, for it would be too stressful for her, especially with all the other guests soon to arrive. I was going to find a place to stay, but it would have to be near my precious aunt. The next day, Sonny came to see us and invited us to stay with him in the Bronx. There, I met his wife Lucy and daughter Linda who had arrived a few months earlier from Italy. Lucy was a short pretty woman. She had black hair and brown eyes and was very friendly. Linda was ten years old with black curly hair and beautiful big green eyes. It was easy to see that she was my brother's daughter. As much as I would've loved to spend more time than the two nights with my brother and his family, I had to look for a place near my aunt. I walked on every street and looked at 'for rent' signs in Brighten Beach, but every place I looked at was unaffordable. On the third day, I found a low rent, one-room basement apartment in Brighten Beach. The room had a stove, a sink with running hot and cold water, a toilet, and a shower. The best part was that it was within walking distance to my aunt's house, and I was able to visit her every day.

Finally, after praying for the day when I would see my sister again, her ship from Israel arrived. I would've liked to go with Uncle Jack to pick her up, but he was also picking up Lucian and his wife and daughter, and Uncle Jack's wife Sadie had first priority to go along. There wouldn't be enough space in his car for me. Like an expectant father, I was pacing back and forth on the sidewalk in front of my aunt's house. I ran into a little clothing store a block away from my aunt's house and bought a very nice summer dress for Bela. I wanted to give her something, and at that moment, I wished I hadn't signed over my checks to Max. I wished I had enough money to take her places and buy her everything her heart desired. The money Max gave me was dwindling, and I wondered how I could stretch it to last me long enough until we would go home. No matter, all I now wanted was to see my sister.

After thirteen years of being apart, seeing my sister step out of Uncle Jack's car, I felt my heart pushing through the ribcage, breaking through the skin, and taking off to intertwine with the heart that was loved unconditionally. Our arms were so tight around each other's necks that we could barely breathe. I never wanted to let her go. I was afraid that if I moved one inch away from her, she would again disappear. We didn't separate until Uncle Jack touched our shoulders and said, "Sophy's waiting. Let's go upstairs."

I met my cousin Lucian, his wife Sylvia, and their daughter Evelyn for the first time. Each kissed me on each side of my cheeks. "The French way," I mused. After the last five years living in Altadena with Max, I felt as if I'd at last come home. Aunt Sophy's long rectangular table was decorated with a white tablecloth, a bouquet of roses in the center, and an abundance of her many specialties. But mostly, the elaborate table was graced with my family, whom I needed for support, the way a young tree needs a brace for fortification.

After the feast, Bela told me that she was invited to stay with Lucian and his family at a hotel in Manhattan. "They will take me with them to see New York," she said excitedly.

I would've loved it if Bela wouldn't mind staying with the children and me in the little one-room basement apartment. We had so much we needed to tell each other and so little time. She was only staying two weeks, and it was her first trip to the US. I couldn't expect her to be with me every moment and stay with us in the tiny basement with two twin beds. I was glad to be able to spend whatever little time she could spare.

After a week in New York, Bela stayed one night with us, but she wasn't comfortable. In the morning she said, "Call Max and ask him to send you bus ticket money for me, and I'll come back with you to California for a week."

The thought of having my sister all to myself for a week prompted me to find the nearest payphone. It was ten a.m. in Brooklyn and seven in Pasadena. I knew that Max would still be at home. He answered on the second ring. When he heard my voice, he said, "Are going to see your Uncle Jack today?"

"I don't know," I said, and before I could get the words out to ask him for the ticket money, he said, "When you see your uncle, ask him to lend me ten thousand dollars. With ten thousand dollars, I could have my own business."

"I'll ask him," I said, "but I need to ask you to send me money for a bus ticket for Bela. She would like to spend a week with us in California."

Max's answer was immediate, "I can't afford it."

I should have been immune to hearing these words. God only knows I heard them enough times, but this time I was too embarrassed to face my sister and tell her what Max had said. When I did tell her, I couldn't look into her beautiful eyes. I saw the disappointment in Bela's eyes, but the disappointment and embarrassment I felt opened my eyes to the realization that I had to continue my education until that time when I would divorce Max and support myself. I knew that Max would not support me.

I didn't want to have to lie to Max, and the next time I saw my Uncle Jack, I said, "Max would like to borrow ten thousand dollars from you to go in business."

My uncle's answer was, "your husband is not a business man and it would be a waste of money."

After Bela left to spend time in Paris with Lucian and his family before going back to Israel, I felt an emptiness that was impossible to put into words. During my remaining stay in Brooklyn, my aunt was in bed most of the time. I had spent all day and every day at her bedside. I gave her bed-baths, for she was too weak to stand in the shower. My children, too, clung to her. I hated to leave her, but the children had to go back to school.

Two weeks before we left to go home, my aunt felt better, and she had left her bed. We went walking on the boardwalk in Brighton Beach, and I was happy to see that the swelling in her feet and ankles was minimal.

I was surprised and grateful when Max sent us plane tickets and insisted we cash in the bus tickets and come home by air.

After the children went back to school, I went to work at the Alta Vista Hospital on Fair Oaks Avenue, the same hospital I had stayed two weeks after I was burned at the gas station. I enjoyed working at Alta Vista. The work was more challenging than the convalescent hospitals.

Chapter Forty-Two: Moving to Los Angeles

In the spring of 1961, Max decided to sell the house in Altadena and move to an apartment on Ogden Street in Los Angeles. He used the money from the sale of the house and borrowed the rest from a friend and bought a liquor store in South Central with a partner named Izzy..

I went to work at West Side Hospital, and my paychecks went to paying back the loan. After working a year and a half at Westside, the loan was paid in full, and I went to work at Mount Sinai Hospital for a better wage.

A year later, the landlord was turning the building we lived in into a nursing home, and we had to move. I pleaded with Max to put a small down payment on a house.

"The loan on the liquor store is paid off. I'll continue to work, and we could easily pay off a mortgage," I said.

He became angry and bellowed, "We don't need a house. We can't afford a house!"

We moved to a two-bedroom apartment on Harper Avenue in Hollywood. Three days before we moved, I came home from work very ill with the Asiatic flu. On the day we moved, I was still very ill with a high fever. Max came home with people frequently visiting the liquor store. I felt hands pulling and tugging at me, as if I was part of the furniture being transferred to our new apartment. I lay for days in bed in our new apartment, getting weaker and feeling invisible. I was alone all day, and at night, Max brought a woman from the liquor store neighborhood with him. I could smell food cooking, but nobody came close to my bed to ask me if I needed something, and I could barely get out of bed to use the bathroom. After the fever had dropped, I was too weak to go into the kitchen and find something to eat, and I began to panic. I had the feeling that if I didn't do something, I'd die. As luck had it, the telephone was next to my bed. I called my friends Fern and Gene. Gene had been a milkman for the Altadena Dairy.

When he knocked on my door in Altadena for the first time, I said, "No, thank you." I didn't like the obligation of having to pay weekly bills with my twenty dollars a week budget, and I told him that I prefer to buy my milk in the supermarket. Gene wouldn't give up. He once caught Max at home and talked him into having me buy milk from him. When Gene delivered my first milk, he told me that he lived in El Monty and that his wife was Italian and from New York. I needed a friend and was anxious to meet his wife. Fern and I talked on the phone several weeks until we met. After we met, we became best friends for life. Now hearing Gene's cheerful voice, I immediately felt safe.

"Gene, I'm dying," I said in barely audible voice.

"What's wrong? Are you sick?"

"I had the Asiatic Flue, but I'm better. I am alone in the new apartment, and I don't remember when I had anything to eat or drink, and I'm too weak to get out of bed."

"Don't worry. Fern and I will be right over," he said and hung up.

I must have dozed off, and I didn't know how or who let them into the apartment. When I opened my eyes, I looked up at two angels named McHugh. Fern's beautiful exotic face contorted.

"How long have you been sick?" she asked, unable to hide the anger.

"I don't know," I muttered.

Gene, the other angel, was a tall husky Irish man with dark blond hair and blue eyes and a heart of pure mush. He helped me to sit up, while Fern lifted my pillows and placed them behind my back. Gene placed a tray with a thick steak, a baked potato, and peas from a restaurant on my lap. He went to the kitchen and returned with a large glass of milk.

"We won't leave your sight until you finish every bite," he said, as both my friends sat on my bed until I finished the entire dinner. I suddenly felt well, and with the help of my two angels, I was able to get out of my bed and stay out. I could honestly say that these two angels saved my life.

There were many times when I wanted to leave Max, but it was never the right time. He was always promising to change; though, he never did. That last illness was as if I was hit in the head with a sledgehammer to knock some sense into me. I also knew that if I were going leave Max, I would have to be prepared not to count on anything from him. A week after my illness, I went back to work and continued night school. I had to continue with my education if I was ever to leave Max. I couldn't possibly work in hospitals until retirement. It was becoming harder to wake up at five a.m. and only once in while have a weekend off.

In1965, Max told me to quit working. "You don't have to work now," he said, sounding sincere, as if he actually cared about me, and he added, "On Izzy's days off, you can help me out in the store."

Again, I was the dutiful, obedient wife and gave Mount Sinai a two weeks notice.

On Izzy's days off, Max slept late. I set the alarm clock for five a.m. and left the apartment in the dark, being careful not to wake the family, and drove to Watts. It was still dark when I unlocked the store while men waited at the door to get their bottle of wine. I was frightened to be in the area where many of the shoppers were alcoholics, but I was anxious to please my husband, and I stood behind the counter and sold liquor.

When Max arrived at noon, I went home to be ready to do my chores. If there were many customers in the store, I stayed to help him out until the children would be home from school and in time to have dinner on the table when Max came home.

On August 11, 1965, the Watts riot broke out. The liquor store was ransacked, and Max was out of business. The riot lasted only five days, but it took several months to repair the damage. To pay the bills, I went to work on twelve-hour, private-duty shifts. When Max went back in business and had enough help, I decided that the only way I could have a normal life would be to work in a doctor's office. I enrolled in the Los Angeles College to become a Certified Medical Assistant. I worked part time in Beverly Hills for a German doctor, Tea Girth, MD. Doctor Girth was a cardiologist, but he specialized in treating obesity. The job paid for my tuition, and this time my paycheck went directly to the school.

On April 6, 1967, one day after my daughter's eighteenth birthday, I graduated from Medical Assisting School. I immediately went to work for Doctor Blackmun and enjoyed the normal nine to five hours. Most of Doctor Blackmun's patients didn't know what a Jew looked like, but the doctor's daughter was married to a Jew.

When I forgot to wear a long sleeve uniform, the patients questioned my Auschwitz number.

"Is this your boyfriends telephone number?" some would ask. Others wanted to know if it was my social-security number, and I answered "yes" to all of the questions.

One afternoon Doctor Blackmun asked me if I would like him to surgically remove the number from my forearm? My answer was an immediate "Yes, thank you." After the last patient left the office, Doctor Blackmun removed my number. Although the scar will remain for as long as I live, the constant reminder is gone. If today anyone should ask me what my number was, I remember it better in the German language, A-15791. I enjoyed my new job, but Max continued to complain about my working and going to school at night, but he didn't mind taking my paycheck. I often wondered how long I could go on before my brain would shatter from overload with misery.

In June 1967, Marian graduated from high school. She became rebellious and wanted to go to San Francisco. We consulted a psychologist, and we were advised to let her go. Four months later, she returned with a broken heart, and Max ordered me to leave my job and take her to Israel and leave her in a kibbutz. After a month in my sister's house, Zvi drove us to Kibbutz Kfar Blum. Marian loved living on the kibbutz, and on September 1968, Max, Ira Jay, and I went to Marian and Josef's wedding.

After we returned from our daughter's wedding, Max's behavior had changed.

"You don't have to go back to work. I'll try to be a good husband to you," he said, and I wanted to believe him. I was tired of his constant complaints about my working and about giving all my paychecks for taxes. Maybe this time he will change, I thought.

The next two weeks he never raised his voice to me, and I was beginning to think that he was really changing. On the third week, Max came home and said, "Izzy is sick again." I knew that Izzy had emphysema, and from time to time, he became ill, but his wife always worked with him or in his place.

"What about Sima? She always goes to work in his place," I said.

"Izzy is too sick, and Sima can't do it alone. They want me to buy them out. We have fifteen thousand dollars in our savings. It would be the right amount for me to have the store free and clear. I'll hire help, and you wouldn't have to work," he said and waited for an answer.

Without a second thought I said, "Yes." He'd been so nice to me and wanted to better our lives. How could I refuse to let him take out the money from the savings account?

One week after the store was his and there was no money that I knew of in the bank, Max had reverted to the same demanding, complaining, uncaring self.

I woke up in the morning, and it was October 6. I looked at my reflection in the bedroom mirror.

"Today is my birthday," I said to the mirror.

Suddenly, I saw that year after year had passed by, and I couldn't remember a single good day in my life. I was feeling as if my wings were clipped. If not for my beautiful children, I was certain that I would have nothing to live for. I needed to do something to make me feel better. I got dressed and went to the May Company on Faifax Avenue. Whenever I felt my self-esteem dwindling, I would go to a department store and try on hats. As I was trying on a light brown felt hat, I saw a beautiful, beige, imitation fur coat on sail and tried it on. I looked at myself in the mirror and felt beautiful. I never wanted anything as much as I wanted that coat. But from the twenty dollars a week Max gave me for food, it would take me a year to pay for the coat. When Max came home that evening, I told him about the coat and asked him to buy it for me.

"I can't afford it. I have insurance to pay and merchandise to buy, and all you can think of is a coat!" he shouted.

"I could go back to work if you need money," I said.

"No! You need to help me in the store!"

"But I have been helping you, and you have men working for you. If you need me to go in more often and help you, I'll go," I said.

He became angry and turned on the TV and fell asleep.

Two weeks later, he came home from the store and said, "I don't feel good," but he ate his dinner. After dinner he said, "Tomorrow is my day off, but I forgot to leave the keys for my sales clerk to open the store."

"Don't worry," I said, feeling bad that he wasn't feeling well. "We'll wait until Ira Jay gets home. I want to be sure that he eats his dinner. Then, I'll go with you to the store, and you can give the sales clerk the key."

Ira Jay came home a few minutes later. While he was eating, I filled him in on the details. Then, I told Max that we could go now.

"You'll drive," Max said.

"Alright, I'll drive," I said and went to the kitchen to take with me a paper bag with garbage to throw in the bin a few feet from my 1964 Chevrolet Impala.

Max stood unmoving at the door. I handed the garbage bag to him, and he reluctantly took it from me while I opened the door and locked it from the outside.

As soon as I finished locking the door, he tried to give the garbage bag back to me.

"Come on, you're already holding it. You can carry it down the few steps," I chuckled, trying to put some humor into the pathetic seen, but Max didn't see the humor and shouted all the way to Watts.

"You don't give a damn about me! I'm sick, and you make me carry heavy garbage bags!" The shouting and accusations went on until we arrived at the store and back. When we returned home, Max went to sleep, and I went to the bathroom and vomited for half an hour. I was still nauseous and took a paper bag with me and kept it next to my bed. Max heard me retching and never asked me what was wrong. It was ironic. He had come home and said that he was sick, and I was burning up all night with fever. Max woke up in the morning and left the house looking healthy.

I later found out that he was visiting with friends. When he returned late afternoon, I was still in bed, but he didn't ask me what was wrong with me. He was still angry for letting him carry the garbage bag.

All week, I was taking aspiring and looking in the newspaper for a job. Now that Marian was married and Ira was seventeen, I was certain that if I found a good steady job, I would be able support my son and myself. We wouldn't live in luxury, but I knew that I could pay the bills.

Everyday when Max came home from work, I had dinner ready for him, and after he ate, I washed the dishes and went back to bed, and he never asked me how I felt. He was still angry.

Thursday was the first day when my temperature was normal without the aspirin. Friday morning, I was hungry and ate a full breakfast with eggs and English muffin and a glass of warm milk. I was feeling stronger and answered several ads, but none sounded suitable. At 3:30, I called my school and was given a telephone number to call for a job interview. When I called Doctor Roberts, on Santa Monica Boulevard in Hollywood, he said, "Come right over."

"I'm getting over the flu and would like to stay home one more day. Could I see you Monday morning?"

"My nurse is leaving in an hour. You have to come now, or I'll get someone else," he said.

I was dressed and out of the house in ten minutes.

The office was a corner house located on Santa Monica Boulevard and Heliotrope. A few feet from the parking lot was a nursery, laden with concrete blocks, lumber, garden tools, and pottery and plants of every kind. I later found out that the landlord owned the nursery and the office building.

Doctor Roberts was a short man, about twenty pounds overweight, bald, blue eyes, and a handsome face. Instead of a lab coat, he wore a hospital gown. If he hadn't been sitting behind his simple light wood desk, I would have thought that he was a patient. He had many certificates on the walls in his office and pictures of newborn babies. The certificates indicated that he was a general practitioner and surgeon. When he saw me looking at the pictures, he proudly said, "I delivered all of them." He told me that he had two offices. "The office on Gateway Boulevard in West Los Angeles is used for personal injury. There, we do x-rays and treatments. This office is used for my general practice," he said. He already knew my qualifications through my school and only asked me a few personal questions and handed me the key to the office.

"You're on your own. My nurse quit this afternoon. You will have to unlock the office at nine a.m. Monday morning. I have to be at my Gateway office in the morning, but I'll be here at noon," he said and failed to tell me what I was suppose to do before he arrived.

On my way home from the interview, I went shopping and bought enough food to last a week. I cooked dinner, and we all ate, and Max still wasn't speaking to me.

Monday morning, Max left the house one-hour before my alarm clock went off. I was at the office at nine o'clock and strolled from room to room looking for something to do. As I stepped inside one of two treatment rooms, I felt as if I were back in Germany, working in Feldafing at the Medical Center. Doctor Roberts still used glass syringes and reusable metal needles and sterilized them in an old sterilizer and soaked the instruments in alcohol. Except for white sheets on the treatment tables, outdated medicine cabinets, an old scale, and stethoscopes hanging from the scale, there was very little that resembled a medical office.

At 9:30, a middle-aged female, looking like a bronze goddess, strolled in.

"Good morning. You'll have to forgive me. This is my first day, and I don't know your name." I said humbly.

My anxiety quickly faded when she lifted her graceful head and smiled.

"My name is Evelyn Hearn. I come here once a week for my blood pressure check and an injection," she said, her smile never left her chiseled face.

I found her chart and saw that she was getting B12 injections. "Would you mind if I did that for you? Doctor Roberts won't be in until noontime."

"I don't mind at all," she said with her southern drawl.

After I completed the vitals, she lowered her underpants for her injection.

When I saw the purple patches on her buttocks, I asked her to come back next week for the injection.

I soon found out that Doctor Roberts didn't believe in appointments. It was first come first serve. More patients strolled in, until the waiting room was full. I didn't see which patient came in first. I opened the door and said, "Next." Like soldiers, each knew who was first, and soon I didn't feel as if it had been my first day. After seeing a few more purple patches on patient's buttocks, I asked everyone to come back next week for his or her injection.

When Doctor Roberts walked in through the back door, he slipped on a clean patient gown, tied the two strings together in back of his neck, and sat down in his office behind his desk.

I ushered in the patients that were waiting for him to refill prescriptions, and when the last patient had left the office, I asked him for the telephone number of the pharmaceutical company where he was buying his supplies.

He tilted his head to one side looking downwards. His chin was dug in his neck, and his eyes squinted as if disturbed by the sun's glare.

"What do you need?" he asked, as if uninterested in the answer.

"We need disposable syringes and needles. Every patient that came in today had a purple buttocks."

"I don't like using disposable syringes. I have used glass syringes for thirty years, and you are here three hours and have turned my office upside down!" he shouted.

Something told me that Doctor Roberts didn't like change, and I knew that I had to make changes or look for another job.

"You can use the glass, and I'll use the plastic," I said, looking into blue angry eyes. "And I also need the telephone number of the lab you send the blood samples to. I have to order supplies to do phlebotomies. All the supplies are free. They are glad to give them to you. They want your business," I said calmly and was thinking that this wasn't going to work, and I was abut to hand him over the office keys.

He must've read my thoughts for he handed me the telephone book and said, "Order what you need."

By Tuesday, I had all the supplies I ordered, and the patients thanked me for the almost painless injections. At the end of the day, I showed Doctor Roberts the lab supplies and asked him if he would like to order blood tests on his patients.

"Do you know how to use all this?" he asked.

"Yes, and more," I challenged. "While we are on the subject, do you have an EKG machine?"

Again, I saw his head tilting to the left, and his eyes squinted to where I could only see a tiny part of blue.

"I don't know how to interpret EKGs," he admitted. "I have an old Sanborn at the Gateway office. If it works and you want to use it, we would send the tracings to a friend of mine for interpretations," he added.

I respected my new boss for putting his ego aside and admitting to me that he didn't know how to interpret EKGs. I was thinking of asking Doctor

Girth to teach me EKG interpretations. If we were going to do complete physicals, we couldn't send dozens of EKGs for interpretation to his friend, not for very long anyway. As I remembered, Doctor Girth was seldom in his office during regular daytime hours. He often came in after his staff had left, and he stayed in his office most of the night. I was planning to call Doctor Girth, but I first needed to see if the machine he'd bring me still worked.

After I cleaned up the old Sanborn, it printed out a pretty good tracing. By the end of the week, Doctor Roberts' office was beginning to look and feel like a Medical Office.

Chapter Forty-Three: A New Beginning

One week after I began working for Doctor Roberts was Election Day. The liquor store was closed, and Max was still asleep when I left the apartment. He was at home watching television when I returned from work. He lifted his head and was surprised to see me in uniform. As always, his eyes glistened when I started a new job. He knew that twice a month my paychecks would be in his hands with my signature. And to make sure I wouldn't feel too good about myself, he never missed telling me that I didn't have to work because my paycheck goes to pay the taxes.

For the first time in two weeks, he stood up and looked directly at me. He put his arms around me and tried to kiss me. I turned my head quick enough and pulled away from him. He reached in his pocket and took out two twenty-dollar bills.

"Why don't you go and buy yourself that coat you wanted?" he said lovingly, as if the last two weeks or the entire twenty-two years of our marriage had been bliss.

I remembered my birthday, how I humbled myself, asking him to buy me an imitation fur coat I saw at the May Company. "I can't afford it!" he snarled. I knew, then, that I would never ask him for anything again. I also had a flashback with the garbage bag and how totally alone I felt.

"Thank you, but I don't need your money or your coat," I said.

"In that case, we have to make an end of it," he shouted.

"You damn right we have to make an end of it," I countered and backed away from him and went to the bedroom to change clothes and start diner. After I said those words, I felt as if the clouds had rolled away, not just from the sky, but from my entire being. Layers and layers of hopelessness pealed away, and I felt as light as a feather.

Countless times during my marriage to Max, I thought of myself as if I were an accordion. Each time I lifted myself up, I was being squeezed back into place. Now, I felt the kind of freedom that I never thought possible.

With Doctor Roberts' mood swings, I wasn't sure what my future would bring, but even that didn't worry me. I was a qualified medical professional and would have no problem finding work.

We had one attorney between us. Though I was the one who hired the attorney and paid him three hundred dollars, Max got to him first. It was agreed that when Max would sell the store, I would get half, and he was to pay forty dollars a month for childcare. After the divorce, I was left penniless. If I didn't have the job, I wouldn't have the rent money to pay for our apartment, but I didn't care, and I never felt better about myself and more self assured in my profession.

The divorce to Max was final in 1969, and Max remarried immediately.

Though I joined parents without partners and went out on dates, I put my heart and soul into my work. Titus and Sons Pharmaceuticals introduced me to the Diagnostic Unimeter machine. Doctor Roberts called a carpenter, and I soon had a practical lab with a worktable built for my height. We bought the reagents from Titus and Sons, and I now had a full laboratory where I was able to do all the chemistries myself. I was only sending out a very few specimens to an outside lab.

Doctor Girth was only too happy to teach me EKG interpretations. "It will give me a chance to brush up on what I forgot," he said lightheartedly. Every night, I sat at Doctor Girth's office and learned. Because I loved the subject, I was able to learn it quickly. He gave me my first book, and I used it as a reference for many years to come.

After I learned the basics, Doctor Roberts paid for a home study course. Since the checks had his name on them, the credits were given to Doctor Roberts, and I didn't care, for I only wanted the knowledge. The name of the course was called 'Difficult Electrocardiographic Diagnosis,' at the Department of Postgraduate Medical Education, University of Kansas, School of Medicine, Kansas City, Kansas. Once a week, I received a study course with a graded paper from the previous week. When Doctor Roberts saw the perfect scores on the test results, he told me that he trusted me with diagnosing our patients. It was at the same time when Doctor Roberts' friend and colleague informed him that he was too busy to diagnose our patients.

I was now qualified to place an entire diagnoses on the doctor's desk, but in order to be worthy of the profession, I had to be one step ahead. There was always something new to learn, and I loved learning it.

Letters were sent to physician's offices, stating that an x-ray technician had to be licensed. I had learned x-rays in medical assisting school, but now I would have to go back to school and get a license. Since I didn't have to go to Doctor Girth's office, I went to night school. I didn't want just a limited license. I would only be allowed to do chests, sculls, and extremities. I wanted to be a Certified X-ray Technologist, a CRT. If I would have to go to work in a hospital, I wanted to be qualified in every field.

My well-meaning friends persuaded me to start going out and date. I was forty years old and anxious to find out what a good marriage was all about. I made friends with other single women and went to singles dances.

In June 1969, Ira Jay graduated from high school, and I pointed the moving camera and proudly filmed him from every angle; though, I must admit that I'm a very poor photographer.

On June 18, 1969, I became a grandmother. My daughter gave birth to a son in Israel. I was so excited to be a grandma that when I went to a dance at a Jewish Temple that evening, I gushed to every man I danced with, "I'm a grandma, I'm a grandma!"

That same evening, I met Jerry. We went out for coffee and talked, and I shared the excitement of my newborn grandson. Jerry was forty-two-years old and a bachelor. He was about five feet, seven inches tall and slightly overweight. He had light brown eyes and was completely bald. Dark red hair crowned an obvious toupee. The freckles on his full round face made him look younger than his age. After two weeks of dating, I found that he had all the qualifications I was looking for. Jerry told me that he was an importer of toys and novelties. I went to his warehouse and saw many toys and novelties. He took me out to nice restaurants and always opened the door for me. I was certain that I had found the man of my dreams, my soul mate. We laughed at the slightest things, and he never failed to complement me. For the first time in my life, I felt pretty, loved, and admired. Six months later, when he asked me to marry him, I said "yes."

Jerry had five thousand dollars saved up, and we put a down payment on a house with a small one-bedroom guesthouse for my son. I couldn't ask for anything more.

With the money I had saved, we furnished the house.

It was Jerry's first marriage, and he wanted a formal wedding.

Marian telephoned and said she would like to come back home with her family. Marian, her husband Josef ,and my grandson Aylon arrived in January. Although I was happy to have my daughter home, we were planning a wedding, and we, all except Jerry, lived in my two-bedroom apartment. There was chaos until we found an apartment for my daughter and her family.

Jerry and I were married on Valentine's Day 1970, with a sit-down dinner, red tablecloth, and white napkins.

Jerry rented a tuxedo, and I bought a beautiful long silver dress at Lomans' for twenty-five dollars, and a dressmaker made a short veil for me to match my dress.

As I slowly walked on the red carpet towards the man I loved, I, too, felt as if I was married for the first time and never felt more beautiful.

Soon after we were married, I found out that Jerry had lied to me. He wasn't much of an importer. I was paying all the bills, including the mortgage and everything else. Even that wouldn't have been so bad, but his attitude toward me had changed, and I realized that I had made another mistake. Still, it was better than being married to Max. I decided not to rush into another divorce before giving us a chance. As time went on, we had good days and bad. I told myself that as long as the good still outweighed the bad it was worth it. I knew that Jerry had been a bachelor and never had to consider another person. I kept telling myself to give him time.

In the spring of 1975, I received a letter from Bela. Though it was a very warm day, a shiver went through my spine as I read the first two lines. "Jadzia, I had cancer of the colon. Don't get upset; I had an operation, and I'm feeling fine, and the doctor gave me a clean bill of health. I only have a tiny scar," she wrote, and I thanked God that she was operated on in time. The thought of losing my sister was unacceptable. I knew that she didn't have to have a colostomy. I knew how my sister prided herself on her athletic figure and flat belly. I remembered my last visit to Israel. It was a hot summer day, and Bela knew how badly I burned in direct sun, and she put up a tent for me on the beach. After I was shaded, she swam out as far as the eye could see, wearing a little bikini, in the Haifa Sea. When she swam back, she picked up a racket and immediately had a group of young men willing to paddle the ball back and forth, and she was always the winner. Bela could swim faster and farther than any young man could.

At the age of fifty, she was thin, beautiful, and athletic.

"Jadzia, I'm coming to visit you," she wrote. I held her letter to my chest and looked for someone with whom I could share my happiness. I couldn't wait for Jerry to come home so I could tell him the wonderful news. I ran outside to my back yard where I had planted many fruit trees and vegetables and read the letter again and again.

In July, 1975, I took my vacation time from work and was jumping with joy when I saw my sister coming through the gate at the El Al Terminal. She looked pale and thin, but she brought with her a letter from her doctor stating that she was clear from cancer.

I knew that Bela was an early riser, and I didn't want to lose a single moment away from her. I made an American breakfast of pancakes and natural maple syrup. My throat constricted, and my stomach went into knots as I looked up from the griddle and saw Bela breaking open an ampoule and swallow the clear liquid. I must have turned pale, for she quickly reassured me that the doctor gave it to her only as a preventative measure.

Had she been a patient, not my beloved sister, I would be suspicious and would know the name of the medication and the reason she was taking it. But this was the sister I loved so much, and I would gladly give her any part of my body if she needed it, and I desperately wanted to believe that she was all right. The letter from the doctor was written in English, and it said that he found no cancer cells in the surrounding tissues. I wanted so much for it to be true, and I believed every word.

After two day's rest, we went on trips to see the country in Jerry's van. When we returned, Bela told me that the medication made her feel tired. I advised her to take it at bedtime. She did so and was much more alert during the day. She said that she needed clothes. I took her to Lomans and bought her many outfits. She said that she needed a coat. Since it was July, we were unable to find the right winter coat.

Bela turned fifty, and I invited more than forty people. I proudly introduced her to all my friends. She took part in the celebration and made her specialty, German potato salad. We had a large banner that read, "Shalom Bela." It was a very festive occasion.

After the party, we went to Las Vegas and had a wonderful time. I dreaded the day when she had to leave. If only I could have found a way to keep her with me forever, but I knew it would be impossible, for her family was in Israel. With each waking day, I found myself trying to hold on to her a little longer. Though I told myself that I should believe what the letter from her doctor said, I had an ache in my heart and feeling of loss. Whether it was a gut feeling or my professional mind's eye, I didn't want to know. I told myself to enjoy my sister, that she was going to be all right. Still, each time I saw her break open an ampoule and swallow the liquid, my heart ached for my sister.

Jerry often told me that my sister and I were like Siamese twins. "Even when you are not together, you are together," and I knew he was right. When we hugged and kissed goodbye at the airport, I was already looking forward to her next visit, but my hopes and dreams for years of happy days and frequent reunions were shattered with the next latter from my sister. In November of 1975, Bela wrote, "When I returned home, I went to see the doctor for a follow up examination. The examination was very strenuous, and I wasn't told anything about my condition. The doctor sent me to another hospital for injections. The injections are making me lose my hair."

I put the letter down and couldn't stop the flood of tears. I was suddenly remembering the camp in Villischtal when the machine Bela worked with broke down.

The SS woman was to shave her hair as punishment, which was going to be the third time since the war broke out. I was about to knock on the SS woman's door and beg her to shave my hair instead, but the girls pulled me away from the door. I now had the same feeling. I would gladly shave my hair if it meant that my sister could keep her hair. But this time I wasn't crying for her hair, I was crying for the loss I felt when I drove her to airport. I wiped my burning eyes and continued reading. "I couldn't decide if I should let them give me the injections and lose my hair or do nothing and take my chances and maybe get better without the injections. Though I have been feeling ill, I didn't want to know what was wrong with me. The entire time while I was in turmoil, my husband didn't think that there was anything wrong with me. I asked him to go and see my doctor to find out what was wrong with me so he might understand me better and be a little more caring. He didn't understand that I didn't want to know the truth. When he returned from the doctor's office he said, 'The cancer is now in your liver. Only a miracle can help you.'"

I must've been holding my breath the entire time while reading the last few sentences, for I began to choke. I was startled by the sound of my own exhalation, for it sounded as if it was coming from a cave. I ran to the bathroom and rinsed my face with cold water. While blinded by my tears, I continue reading my sister's painful letter.

"My children are suffering. I love them very much. I'm sure that they know it. I have a wonderful little grandson. He's my heart. I don't want to leave him, but....Tell Ira Jay that I will never forget him. He was to me like a son."

Ira Jay and Bela had become very close when she was here for a visit, and I was now grateful for her pleasant memories. I was thinking how lucky I am to have such devoted children. I wiped my swollen eyes and continued reading Bela's agonizing letter.

"Jadzia, I know now, though a little late, that you always truly loved me. Please, I need you to be strong for me. You are the only person that will know what to do when the time will come. I don't want to die in the hospital. I want you to come here and take care of me at home. I will let you know when the time comes."

I needed my children. I needed their arms around me. Marian and Josef had gone back to Israel. When their son was three years old, Marian divorced her husband, and she came home with Aylon. Again, I found her an apartment, but she wasn't happy, and three years later she took the child and went to live in Portland, Oregon.

Ira Jay now lived in his own house, and I didn't want to tell him such news on the telephone. Even if I didn't tell him everything, he would know by the sound of my voice that something was wrong.

Jerry was sympathetic, but it would have been impossible for anyone to understand my pain, not even Sonny. He didn't know us the way Bela and I knew each other, and I felt completely alone. My sister needed me, and I couldn't be with her now. She would need me to take care of her on her last days. I telephoned Bela, and we both cried. I reassured her that I wasn't giving up.

"I'll do everything in my power to keep you alive," I said and meant every word.

As if he knew that I needed him, the door opened, and Ira Jay was at my side. Both my children loved Bela very much, but Ira Jay was at a young age becoming an entrepreneur and was in a good financial position. He saw how distraught I was and took time out from his busy schedule and immediately made reservations for himself and Janis, his girlfriend at that time, and went to visit his aunt in Israel. He stayed two weeks and spent the entire time with his beloved aunt. He took her with him to Tel Aviv and put her up in a hotel in a room next to his to divert her from thinking about her disease.

When he returned, he gave me hope. "Don't worry, Mom. Aunt Bela's a fighter. She looks great."

Though I knew that my sister didn't have a chance, I prayed for a miracle and held onto that hope. I couldn't let my sister die. She had finally taken her first step to visit me, and I wanted more. We were now mature women, and the three years difference didn't matter now. We could understand each other and be friends. I couldn't lose her. I lost too much, and we only had each other. I began reading everything on the subject. There was an article in a supermarket magazine that the Sloan Kettering Institute was experimenting with platinum for treating cancer. I wrote a letter to the Sloan Kettering Institute, Oncology Department describing my sister's condition. I asked if they could give me hope even if it was experimental. I enclosed a copy of the letter from Bela's doctor describing her condition. A week later I received a letter telling me that there was no cure for my sister's condition, experimental or otherwise.

I couldn't sleep. I read the letter over and over, hoping to find one word that would give me hope. I was standing at the supermarket checkout line. My thoughts were only with my sister. I saw an article on the front page of the Enquirer. "Duke University Medical Center found a cure for cancer derived from mushrooms." I bought the magazine and wrote a letter to the university, quoting the article in the magazine, and described my sister's condition. Again, I sent them a copy from Bela's doctor. I told them that if necessary, I'd bring my sister from Israel and would do anything that was asked of me, as long as they could give me a glimmer of hope.

A week later, I received a letter stating, "Unfortunately, the report in the Enquirer was quoted out of context."

I was grasping at straws. I read every book in the heath-food store and every magazine. All I was thinking about was liver cancer and how to cure it.

A patient told me about a friend of his who had been cured of bone cancer by Doctor Harry Hoxsey in Mexico. My patient telephoned his friend and gave me the doctor's address in Tijuana, Mexico. In February 1976, I told Doctor Roberts that I needed the next day off. I woke up at dawn to a storm. I drove, not caring that the windshield wipers could barely keep up with the falling rain. After crossing the border to Tijuana, I had no problem finding Doctor Hoxsey's clinic. The clinic was a little shabby storefront in a drab area, yet there wasn't an empty seat in the waiting room. While waiting to see the doctor, I talked to patients in the waiting room and heard nothing but praises for this miracle doctor. I was beginning to gain hope. I bought Doctor Hoxsey's book titled "You Don't Have to Die."

After reading several articles about patients that had been cured of carcinomas by Doctor Hoxsey, I felt as if I had come to the right place and ignored the gray chipped walls and old sagging couches. When it was my turn to see the doctor, I already knew a little about his treatment. I explained to Doctor Hoxsey that my sister lived in Israel and told him that I could bring her to him if he thought that it would be better.

His answer was, "It's not necessary."

He sold me two quart bottles of pink liquid with directions and several bottles of special vitamins, also with directions. I returned home in plenty of time to translate the directions into Polish. Then, I wrapped the large carton and took it to the post-office and mailed it first class airmail. I was convinced that the medicine and vitamins would cure my sister. When I returned from the post office, I telephoned Bela and told her to expect the cure.

"I sent it air mail so you should get it in a few days. Please, Bela, I beg you to take the medicine and the vitamins. I saw patients in that doctor's office with cancer in every part of their bodies, and they were completely cured. So, start taking it as soon as the package arrives."

Bela, too, sounded hopeful and promised that she would take the medicine as directed. I slept through the night for the first time since I found out about my sister's disease. I telephoned Bela often, and she told me that she was taking the medicine and was feeling stronger.

April 22, 1976, I received a telephone call from Zvi. "You must come as soon as possible," he urged.

I became hysterical. "Bela told me that she was feeling better and that the medicine was helping," I cried.

"Jadzia, please come as soon as you can," he repeated and hung up.

I made plane reservations for the twenty-fourth and found my passport, but it was expired. Jerry drove me to the photographer and passport agency. I received a temporary passport that would expire July 1976. I was so distraught that I paid no attention as to what I was putting into my suitcase. I remembered that when Bela was visiting me, I had bought a half of a pumpernickel raisin bread, about two pounds, at the Diamond Bakery. She liked it a lot and ate it every day.

Sunday afternoon, I went to the Diamond bakery and bought the biggest pumpernickel raisin bread the bakery had. I wrapped the round, heavy bread in a paper bag. It weighed about five pounds, and I packed it in my suitcase. After I had everything in order, I telephoned Sonny to tell him about our sister.

"It hurts me to hear it," was all he said. Knowing his mental state, I didn't expect much.

Monday morning April 24th, I left my job and my home, not knowing when I would return. I had a window seat and was glad that nobody sat next to me. My head was turned towards the window, and I dabbed at my eyes and nose. The thought of losing my sister would be the same as loosing my identity. I was always known as Bela's sister. I pressed my forehead against the little window, steaming up the glass.

"It was always only you and I, Bela. You have to live. We are as one. Without you, I'll only be half and never stop looking for the other half," I mumble to the glass.

It was a hot and humid day when I arrived in Israel. Zvi picked me up at the airport in Tel Aviv. He complained about the humidity. When I questioned him about Bela, all he said was, "It's not good. I'm glad you're here."

It was a long drive to Haifa. I sat silently and prayed that Zvi was wrong. The medicine must have worked. Bela said so each time I called. As I stepped out of Zvi's car in front of the building, I looked up and saw my sister standing on her balcony in the living room waving to me. I ran up the three flights of stairs as if I was being chased. I was shocked to see my beautiful sister, who always prided herself on her vitality and whose body never aged. Now, her beautiful thick blond hair was drab and wispy. Her swollen abdomen seemed to weigh her down. As she put her thin, frail arms around my neck, I felt my heart crumble. We stayed entwined in each other's arms until she was tired and wanted to go to bed.

Bela and Zvi's bedroom consisted of twin Danish-style beds pushed together, a dresser, and two nightstands on each side. Only one framed eight by ten picture hung on the apposite wall of Bala's bed facing her.

The picture was of me in uniform in my office sitting at my desk. I had EKG tracings wrapped around my neck, ready to be mounted and read. At the time the picture was taken, we had a college student working for us part time in the front office. She majored in photography and needed black and white pictures, and each time I turned around, she was snapping pictures of me. When Bela visited me, she must have taken that picture with her. I never knew before that Bela was sentimental.

I sat down at the edge of Bela's bed, trying unsuccessfully to hide the tears.

"The medicine didn't work?" I asked, feeling a lump in my throat as big as my fist.

"I didn't take it," she said.

"Why not? It could've saved your life," I said, remembering how happy I was to have found the miracle cure.

"I was afraid the doctor would be angry and wouldn't want to treat me," she said, her voice only a whisper.

I went into the kitchen and saw the entire carton untouched. I became hysterical. I put my hands to my face and was unable to stop sobbing. I stayed in the kitchen until I was able to control my emotions. I washed my face at the kitchen sink with cold water and opened my suitcase that was standing on the kitchen floor. I removed the bread and cut an end piece, buttered it, put it on a little plate, and took it into the bedroom. It felt good to see a smile on Bela's face as she took her first bite and finished the entire piece of bread.

Bela asked Zvi to sleep in the second bedroom. She wanted me next to her.

Every morning, Bela stayed out of her bedroom only long enough to take her shower. She sat on a chair until I finished changing her linen. She perspired profusely, and her bed linen had to be changed often.

One week after my arrival, Bela went to her bed after I helped her with her shower and never stepped foot on the floor again. As much as I begged and cajoled, telling her that she needed to move her legs, she refused to leave her bed.

"I was sure that you would bring me something to get me out of my misery," she complained.

I couldn't believe what I was hearing. "You know I couldn't do that. Do you want me to go to jail?" I counted.

For the next two months, I slept on the bed next to my sister and took care of her every need. She was amazed that in the middle of the night when she opened her eyes, I lifted my head and asked her if she needed something.

"Don't you ever sleep?" she asked.

Eli, Bela's oldest son, spent every lunch hour at his mother's bedside and cried while Bela talked and prepared him for the time when she would no longer be with him.

Eli's one year old son, Tom, clung to his grandmother and repeated her name over and over, as if the child was trying to memorize her name. "Bela, Bela, Bela, Bela...."he would say.

Bela's youngest son, Yery, was in his early twenties. Each time he came to see his mother, he cried as Bela talked to him and tried to prepare him for the loss he would soon be feeling. He didn't come as often. He loved his mother very much, but as I looked into his eyes, I could see that it was too painful for him to see his once vibrant mother in such a debilitated state.

The lunch hour that Eli spent with his mother, I went out to an empty field with dry brush and tall dry bushes. I was always alone in the field and stood behind a thick bush where nobody could see me and had a loud and angry argument with God.

"Isn't it enough that I lost my entire family? Why do you have to take from me the only person I have left and love so much? She has a one year old grandson whom she loves, and Tom loves her. Now, she will never see him grow into a young man, and he's not old enough to remember her. What kind of God are you? If you were a good, loving God, you wouldn't take my sister from me! Do you hear me, God? Don't take my sister away from me!" I cried.

Everyday for six weeks I cried and begged God to create a miracle. It was agony to watch the changes from day to day, to see my beautiful sister, once a powerful athlete, a devoted mother and grandmother, deteriorate in front of my eyes.

The last ten days before my sister went into a hepatic coma, I had different arguments with God. I couldn't watch my beautiful sister slowly become emaciated. I begged God to take her. "I know that you have a time for all of us. My sister suffered enough!" I screamed. "Can't you make an exception and give her peace?" I cried, until I began to hiccup. I stayed a few minutes longer until I stopped hiccupping. I didn't want Bela to see my red swollen eyes and always stopped in the bathroom and washed my face before entering her bedroom.

Living in America, I couldn't possibly know how much stress my sister had endured living in Israel with the constant threat of war. First, her husband went to the army and fought for his new homeland, himself a survivor of the Holocaust. Later, Bela's two sons, Eli and Yery, fought for the precious parcel of land so that every Jew in the world could keep his or her head up high. My sister never knew what the next moment would bring. She could never relax her mind. As long as there was still breath left in her lungs, her heart always skipped a beat when one of her sons were in the army, reserve, or even coming home late from a date.

The last two weeks of her tortured life, I sat on my bed next to Bela. I'll never forget the fear in her eyes. "I'm so…afraid…Jadzia.…" she cried.

I kissed her damp forehead reassuringly. "I'm here, Bela. I'll protect you," I cried silently.

The week when Bela went into a hepatic coma, Eli and Yery had been sleeping at their parent's house. Gunfire was heard through the open window almost every day. I wasn't sure if it was real or maneuvers. Though Bela was now in a deep coma, her body jerked with each explosion.

June 22nd, 1976, I woke up next to my sister at two o'clock in the morning, and heard her exhale her last breath. I gently woke up Zvi and told him.

When Dvora, Eli's wife, arrived in the morning, she told me that Tom woke up at two o'clock in the morning and stood up in his crib.

I began to believe in the soul when my little sister Edzia knocked the fever out of me with a broom when I had typhus fever in the Blyzin concentration.

Rest in peace my beloved sister. I will never forget you. When you left, you took half of my heart with you.

I believe in you, my family. You traveled with me and guided me to Poland and back. You helped me to remember, and I'll never forget you. You are my angels, my guiding lights.

Chapter Forty-Four: Never Again

After twelve years of an unhappy marriage to Jerry, I filed for divorce and have been content living alone.

Soon after my divorce to Jerry, I went to court with an attorney and changed my name from Yetty, back to Jadzia. Only, I have changed the spelling to Yaja, the American way.

I worked for Doctor Roberts twenty-two years until he retired. I too, am now retired.

I have two devoted children and three fantastic grandsons. My daughter was blessed with one son, Aylon, and my son with two sons, Michael Drake and Brian Harris. I am blessed with them all.

I now live in a little house in a peaceful neighborhood, and I planted many fruit trees. Each tree I named after a departed relative. It gives me comfort when I wake up each morning and open the sliding door to my back yard. I say, "Good morning, Mama. Good morning, Tata, Good morning, Fraida. Good morning, Edzia. Good morning, Bela." I say "good morning" to each of the other departed relatives, though not loud enough for my neighbors to hear me. I don't want them to think that I am strange. I miss all of my departed relatives, for I lost them when we were all much too young, but most of all I miss Bela. We had been together in hell and back, and I wish she were with me now.

While I'm patiently waiting to be in the arms of my departed souls, I take pleasure in my children and grandchildren, and I communicate with Bela's children and her grandchildren, by email. They, too, have turned out to be extraordinary, and I love them very much.